The General Theory
of Labor-Managed
Market Economies

The General Theory
of Labor-Managed
Market Economies

JAROSLAV VANEK

Cornell University Press

ITHACA AND LONDON

First published 1970

Standard Book Number 8014-0557-2
Library of Congress Catalog Card Number 78-106355

PRINTED IN THE UNITED STATES OF AMERICA
BY THE SCIENCE PRESS, INC.
BOUND BY VAIL-BALLOU PRESS, INC.

To My Old Country

Preface

This study is the result of research begun in 1961. In that year I received a grant from the Guggenheim Foundation, and in 1967 I was the beneficiary of a Ford Foundation Faculty Research Fellowship; to both organizations I express my sincere gratitude.

My interest in the theory of a system based on management by labor was stimulated by extensive discussion and correspondence with my brother Jan, of the International Labor Organization, who has devoted many years to the study of Workers' Councils in Yugoslavia. Even if I must concede that we have disagreed on just about everything, my greatest debt and my deepest gratitude belong to him.

The original manuscript of the study contained, in addition to the four parts included in this book, a fifth part, more speculative and philosophical. A revised version of the latter, intended for the general reader, will be published separately, also by Cornell University Press, under the title *The Participatory Economy*.

J. V.

Ithaca, New York
March 1970

Contents

Contents

PART IV: ECONOMIC POLICY AND PLANNING

Figures

Tables

The General Theory
of Labor-Managed
Market Economies

1. An Overview

1.1: *Scope and Purpose of the Study*

In approaching this study we are taking upon ourselves a rather formidable task. We want to construct a comprehensive theory of a new economic system which hitherto has not been studied in a comprehensive manner. As always when one deals with a subject of this kind, a careful statement of key definitions and a proper organization of the material are imperative: to provide them is the principal purpose of this chapter. Following a general outline and definition of our subject in the rest of this section, we will speak briefly of the coverage and function of each of the four principal parts of the study.

The economic system that concerns us is defined by five basic characteristics and one derived behavioral principle; by and large, these will remain with us throughout the study. The first characteristic is that of *labor management* of firms. The term "labor"—to be differentiated from "workers"—is used here to include everyone working in the enterprise. The process of management is one based on democratic majority rule, with each member of the enterprise given equal voice. The management activity itself consists of a combination of direct decision-making in major matters, and indirect decision-making in other instances through elected representatives, including the director of the enterprise.

The second characteristic is *income sharing* by all members of the enterprise. By "income" we understand here the value of sales minus all costs, including material costs, capital costs, and tax liabilities of any kind. The sharing is to be equitable—in the case of a homogeneous labor force, based on equal incomes for everyone—and its precise forms will be the subject of specific assumptions made in the various later parts of the study.

The third characteristic of the system is its full *decentralization* of decision-making and full reliance on the *market mechanism*. More

1

specifically, all buyers and all sellers—that is, firms, households, the government, and so on—act *freely* and to *their best advantage* in all markets at prices equalizing supply and demand. This is not to say that necessarily any prices equalizing supply and demand—or income distribution implied by them—would be desirable. Indeed, the authorities or the society may prefer certain prices over others, but to attain what is considered optimal, they must respect the market forces just indicated. Thus, for example, the government can impose an indirect tax to increase the price and stem the production of a product, but it cannot order any single firm to reduce output, or sell it at a prescribed price.

The fourth characteristic—related to the first two—is that the members of an enterprise enjoy collectively the *usufruct* of the assets of the enterprise but not full ownership, in the sense that they can neither destroy the assets nor sell them and distribute the proceeds as income. In a "pure" theoretical model this condition can most easily be approximated by the postulate that all assets—physical as well as financial—are rented by the enterprise on a current basis; we will make such an assumption in some parts of the study. It should also be made explicit that the right of use (usufruct) is exclusively related to an employee's current participation in the enterprise, and is not transferable or negotiable.

The fifth and last universal characteristic of the system is *freedom of employment*. Each and every member of the national labor force is perfectly free to choose and/or change employment according to his best interest, while each firm is free to hire or not to hire a new employee. On the other hand, the right of enterprises to dismiss a member may be limited by law or by the workers' collective itself; but this will be the subject of more specific assumptions later in the study.

The one key operating principle—derived from or implied in the first two of the five characteristics just stated—is that of *maximization of income per laborer*. This principle, which is quite different from maximization of profit, is the natural and rational concern of all participants in an enterprise. Everyone engaged in a collective endeavor is naturally interested in receiving—subject to some democratically agreed-upon rules of income-sharing—maximum remuneration for his efforts. And this desire then becomes the motivational basis of the decision-making of the enterprise. More specifically, given factor and product market conditions, the managers of a firm take such decisions as will maximize the net income per employee. Of course, there can and generally will be other motives—but none should be in a fundamental and lasting conflict with the one just stated.

We cannot overemphasize the fact that maximization of income per laborer is a natural operating principle in a labor-managed and income-sharing system. Note for example that an instruction to those actually making the day-to-day management decisions to maximize aggregate net income, or to maximize profit (reckoned at some preassigned wage rate), would be bound to lead to conflict between such managers on the one hand and the entire working population on the other. For example, net income might be increased by 10 per cent through doubling of employment—but this would reduce the income of all those originally employed by some 45 per cent, a result which clearly would be opposed by the original employees of the enterprise. And thus, for reasons such as those just given, the fundamental operating principle consistent with our definition of the system is maximization of net income per laborer.

It may also be useful to point out, even at this stage of the argument, that there is a principle perfectly equivalent to the principle of maximization of income per laborer, which is much more concrete and operational, and thus easier to understand. That principle is that the firm should increase its labor employment whenever the net contribution to total income by the last man employed is more than the income per laborer currently earned, and reduce its employment whenever the opposite relation prevails between current income per laborer and the incremental income. That both of these alternative actions must lead to maximization of income per laborer should be obvious because in either case the last man either employed or released from work, while earning the same as everybody else, generates net income a portion of which can be added to the income of all those in the enterprise.[1]

Especially when we consider the operating principle in its more concrete version just given, a difficulty comes to light which calls for a little further elaboration and qualification. If the income-per-laborer maximizing action calls for expansion of employment, all is well. But what if a reduction in employment is called for in order to maximize income per laborer of those remaining in the enterprise? Especially if there is

---

[1] Of course, the implication here is that only one type of labor is used in the productive process. But the principle can easily be generalized for other more realistic situations; e.g., see Chapter 11. It is also implied that the divisions with respect to employment of capital and raw materials are consistent with income maximization.

no alternative employment for those who are asked to leave the enterprise, this might lead to a conflict among members of the labor force. The full resolution of this problem does not belong to this introductory chapter; it will be discussed, and alternative assumptions will be made concerning it, later in the study. Not to leave the reader entirely in suspense, however, two observations are in order. First, if the equilibrium behavior of the firm calls for a reduction in the labor force, in any real context such a reduction would only rarely be more than a few percentage points per annum; whereas natural attrition through retirement or other voluntary cessation of work may run to 10 per cent per annum and often considerably higher. Thus a frictionless reduction in employment would be possible in most situations. The second observation is that, contrary to what we might expect by common sense, reductions in employment in the labor-managed firms would generally coincide with periods when business conditions for the industry as a whole were very good, and when there would be a strong impetus for the entry of new firms; the released employees would then form natural nuclei for the formation of the new firms. We will return to this "bee-swarm effect" (note that it is perfectly analogous to the phenomenon in nature of swarming bees) and explain it more thoroughly in Parts I and III. Here let it only be noted that, as with bees, the exit of workers and the formation of new firms could be entirely voluntary, since everyone, whether leaving or remaining, would be bound to attain a higher income. On the other hand, if the desire to leave the firm were lacking, this still could be seen as a maximizing objective.

Hereafter, when we speak about the economic system defined by the above five general characteristics and one operating principle, we will avoid using a term incorporating the entire definition, and use a more convenient, even if less accurate expression. Most of the time we will choose the simplest one and refer to the system, or economy, or firms of which the economy is composed as "labor-managed." In some instances, we will use other expressions—but their exact significance will always be clear from the context.

Before moving on with our discussion, a little more ought to be said on the philosophy of the first and most important characteristic, that of labor management. It is interesting to note that the almost universally accepted principle is that the right to manage—or more broadly, to control—an economic enterprise derives from the ownership of the capital assets used by the enterprise. This principle is equally applicable in western capitalism where the owners are private individuals; in Soviet-type socialist countries where the owner is society, or more operationally the state; and even in many traditional producer cooperatives where control has been linked to shares of joint ownership of the participants. The principle of labor management is entirely different, not having anything to do with ownership of productive assets. Rather, it postulates that in a productive activity where a group of men cooperate in a joint effort, the right to control and manage that effort rests with all members of the group.

It is important to note that the principle of labor management is in conflict with the principle of control and management by capital—i.e., by the owners of capital—but not with the principles of private or social ownership of productive assets. Capital assets still can be owned by individuals or anybody else outside the enterprise, but the owners cannot decide on the complex of human activities which constitute the production. The owners can only expect an adequate compensation for the use of their assets, established through market forces or in any other manner. The owners—be it society or otherwise—also may require adequate guarantees or insurance against spoilage or any other loss of value of their property.

Given the principle of labor management, the second basic property of the labor-managed economies—that is, income sharing—can in fact also be thought of as a derived characteristic. Indeed, it is only natural and rational that a group of men vested with the right of, and actually exercising, self-management should share the net return of their joint activity.

Conceived of as a fundamental principle of organization of human production, labor management thus appears as a principle founded on *integral, active human involvement.* As such it is in sharp contrast with management and control by the owners of capital, who need not be and most often are not humanly and actively involved. The moral, psychological, and social implications of these facts are far-reaching. Perhaps the most important is that we have in labor management a precondition for a truly egalitarian and classless society. Moreover, the status and dignity of human work and activity is increased and thus a more natural balance is attained with the "status of ownership." Finally, in an active involvement in labor management resides a way—perhaps the only way—out of the alienation of the workingman in modern industrial society.

Now a word about the purpose—or, in a slightly different context, the inspiration—of a study of the economic system as defined. When begun several years ago, this work was intended to deal specifically with the economy of Yugoslavia, which by and large has adopted a labor-managed system. The Yugoslav economy is thus the principal inspiration of our study. And one of its purposes is to make it better possible for economists and other social scientists, whether Yugoslav or other, to understand the properties, functioning, and efficiency of the Yugoslav economy.

That we have not remained in the narrower context of the Yugoslav economy is primarily because other attempts are being considered or actually made today in the world, by both socialist and nonsocialist countries, in the direction of labor management. Profit sharing, industrial democracy, codetermination, or labor participation in national planning are all well-known and by now extensively applied procedures in western countries, some of them even in the United States; at the same time they are elements of the labor-managed system. On the other hand, many if not most socialist countries are attempting to improve their socioeconomic condition by moving in the direction of decentralization and the market mechanism. For them the present study can serve as a blueprint for perhaps the only viable form of the system they seek. And last but certainly not least, there are the uncommitted countries, uncommitted both with respect to a political bloc and with respect to an economic regime, who may need a comprehensive study of the labor-managed system, if for no other reason than to be able to make a rational choice among several alternatives.

Another important inspiration for the present work is of an altogether different kind. The social encyclicals of Pope John XXIII, so well received in many parts of the world, speak quite explicitly about the desirability of workers' participation in profit and management. But the encyclicals also enunciate such broader principles as the superiority of the human element in socioeconomic matters, the principle of subsidiarity, and the preferability of cooperation and harmony to conflict.[2] All of these may be viewed as an integral part or a natural consequence of labor management as we have defined it. In this context, the present study can be understood as an economist's verification of the efficacy of a system reflecting certain principles advocated by the Catholic Church on moral grounds.

---

[2] The reader is referred here especially to the Encyclical letter *Mater et Magistra*, and in particular to its paragraphs 23, 53, 75–77, 82, 84, 91, 117.

Another reason why we have chosen not to make our study exclusively that of Yugoslavia is that some other more specific attributes of the Yugoslav system, political or economic, besides those contained in our five defining characteristics, might have been mistaken for essentials of the labor-managed system. For example, and perhaps most important, the labor-managed economic system is consistent not only with a one-party political system but also with a multiparty political democracy. Either form of state, of course, must have written into its constitution articles on producers' democracy (embodying something like our five defining characteristics) in very much the same way as many countries over the past two hundred years have written articles on political democracy.

The labor-managed system need not even be socialist: the productive assets whose usufruct the workers enjoy might be procured and leased by banks or savings associations. Of course, there will be a great advantage if such functions are assumed by the society as a whole, represented by a democratic government. Similarly, the labor-managed system need not even involve economic planning. The fact that it will function even if left entirely alone is actually one of its greatest strengths—although, as we will show later, forecasting and some kind of indicative planning is highly desirable because it enhances considerably the efficiency of the system. Actually, the gains attributable to planning are far more significant in a labor-managed economy than in a capitalist economy; but the fact remains that planning should not be introduced as one of the definitions in the system.

As a further step in our introductory exposition, a few general observations on methodology are called for. We restrict ourselves here only to general observations because the specific method of each of the five subsequent parts will be indicated in the following sections. As should be apparent from the foregoing, we derive the five basic premises of the system which we are about to study mostly from real experience. We do the same regarding some other more specific premises later on in the study. Beyond that stage, however, our analytical procedure is mostly deductive. More specifically, most of the time we deduce from our premises defining the labor-managed system a number of properties of the system, such as its efficiency, ability to adjust to changes in various economic conditions, the nature of market equilibria prevailing within it, and others. It is not our purpose here to verify rigorously the conclusions of this study against any real situations. For one thing, such a verification would go well beyond the possible scope of the present volume; for another, it will be attempted, together with outright empirical induction, in subsequent volumes to appear under the same auspices,[3] and bearing primarily on the economy of Yugoslavia.

Turning now to more technical questions, we realize that plain prose intelligible by everyone would be the ideal analytical tool and means of communication with the reader. Unfortunately, this is not possible because a large number of derivations and deductions would be extremely cumbersome or even impossible without some measure of exact mathematical—or far more often geometrical—analysis. Realizing, however, that such analytical tools are beyond the reach of a large number of potential readers, we try to do two things: (1) we endeavor to restrict the use of technical analysis to a minimum and the use of technical tools to the simplest ones consistent with a rigorous exposition or derivation; (2) having gone through the four parts of the study, we summarize our main findings in simple and nontechnical terms in Chapter 19. Even with the summary chapter, however, it remains an unavoidable fact that at least some acquaintance with formal economic analysis will be an important asset to the reader. An altogether popular treatment of the subject at hand must wait for another volume.

1.2: *Scope of Parts I and II*

When we deal with a highly complex problem or situation involving a large number of variables and factors it is often desirable—sometimes it is the only possible approach—temporarily to isolate some variables or factors and treat them as constants; the functional interdependence and the mechanics of the rest of the system then can be analyzed more easily. Once the partial results are obtained one can usually return, with far greater ease, to the problem in all its dimensions. The basic philosophy behind Parts I and II is of that kind.

While recognizing that the labor-managed system comprises a virtually infinite number of dimensions, especially in the sphere of the human, in Parts I and II we "dehumanize" it in the extreme by developing an economic theory of a system in which there is only one type of labor, or labor force, perfectly homogeneous and of perfectly uniform and invariant quality. It is true that such assumptions often are encountered within the theory of a capitalist system, but within such a system they are far more realistic in view of the fact that labor is called on only to produce—and not to participate in management or profits.

[3] Cornell University Program on Comparative Economic Development.

This initial simplification is expedient not only because it allows us to analyze more clearly other, often complex, aspects of the labor-managed system, but also for another reason. Having assimilated qualitatively the labor force to what it is in a capitalist system, we are in a position to develop a perfect analogue of the capitalist general economic theory, in all of its stages, using the same categories and analytical tools; the only basic changes in our assumptions, compared with the capitalist model, are those implicit in the five defining characteristics given in the preceding section.

Not only is it far easier to tread what is at least partially familiar ground, but this procedure permits us at various stages of the analysis to compare the efficiency and mechanics of analogous situations under labor management on the one hand and under market capitalism on the other. For example we can compare—*ceteris paribus*—the pricing of monopolies in the two systems, or the welfare effects (i.e., gains from trade) of international exchange. In situations where perfect competition and some other ideal conditions are fulfilled, moreover, the comparisons imply comparisons against an optimum absolute standard (Pareto-optimality, as it is called among economists), because, as is well known, under such conditions the capitalist system grinds out an optimal national product.

Of course these comparisons are made with the all-important proviso that labor is one and the same under the two systems, a condition which is clearly untrue in any real situation. Thus the conclusions drawn cannot be considered as final. They can, however, be used as a point of departure in further analyses where the identity-assumption is relaxed.

As we have pointed out already, beyond the five defining characteristics and beyond the specific assumption just discussed regarding the nature of the labor force, the categories, analytical tools, and concepts used in Parts I and II resemble very much or are directly taken from the conventional capitalist analysis. Thus we will speak about the short and the long run, free and restricted entry, factor and product markets defined by supply and demand schedules and the like.

The general outline of Parts I and II also is traditional. While in Part I we cover what usually is called the micro-theory, in Part II we develop the macro-theory or what is sometimes referred to as the theory of national income determination; of course, these theories now are descriptive of the labor-managed system. The development of micro-theory proceeds along the familiar path from the theory of the firm to the theory of industry and price determination, under perfectly competitive, oligopolistic, and monopolistic conditions, and finally to the theory of general equilibrium; within the latter, questions both of positive analysis and of social efficiency—or welfare economics—are answered.

In Part II we are concerned with the determination of aggregative variables such as total national product, the general price level, the rate of interest, the level of labor employment, the national average income per laborer, and others. The nature of the equilibria within which these aggregate magnitudes are determined is another important—and in the case of a labor-managed system, most interesting—subject to which we turn in Part II. Following the methodology of modern macroeconomic theory, the analysis is one in general equilibrium where each of the major aggregative variables, such as real national product, employment of labor, money, securities (i.e., credit), and conceivably foreign exchange is related to an individual market and where prices and quantity solutions are determined simultaneously for all markets of the system. A special section—interesting not only from the point of view of macroeconomic theory, but also from the point of view of individual firms' behavior—is devoted to the theory of investment in the labor-managed system.

Throughout Parts I and II we develop what should be called "pure theory" in the strictest sense; in other words, we exclude entirely from consideration questions of economic policy. In a few situations where a policy parameter must be introduced for reasons of consistency, it is treated as a constant. The reason for doing this is not only the analytical simplification of the *ceteris paribus* type outlined at the beginning of this section, but also our desire to separate clearly the natural and autonomous forces inherent in the labor-managed system from the effects of economic policy.

However, the analysis presented in Parts I and II constitutes a *conditio sine qua non* of a consistent and systematic study of economic policy and plan implementation. But such an analysis can be carried out only later, in Part IV, after some of the key simplifying assumptions of Parts I and II have been relaxed in Part III.

Perhaps a few words of warning, and at the same time of apology, are due the reader before he approaches Parts I and II. He may find the analysis overly extensive, out of proportion with its importance and relevance for labor-managed systems; he may feel that the treatment of the system's "special dimensions" or of planning and economic policy should have been given comparatively greater space. If we used exclusively the criterion of comparative importance for our subject, such objections could not be entirely refuted. The absolute and comparative extent of the first two parts of the study can be justified, however, or at least explained, by the fact that, as we have already indicated, we retread here ground previously covered—or fill in boxes previously established—by the theory of western-type economies. And not to cover some of the analytical categories, not to fill some of the boxes, cannot be justified if what we seek is a comprehensive theory of the labor-managed system.

The parallel with the conventional capitalist theory brings to mind another possible objection to the analysis of Parts I and II. In the context of the theory of the firm, students especially of the modern large corporation have questioned the real applicability of the principle of profit maximization.[4] The criticism certainly is not without foundation. But in that case, could not analogous objections be made regarding the income-per-laborer maximizing principle postulated to govern the labor-managed firm? While it would be hard to argue that under no conditions could the basic motivating principle of the labor-managed firm be violated in any real instance, it can safely be claimed that the possibility is far less likely than nonadherence to profit maximization in a capitalist corporation. Without going here into the detail of the argument, let it only be noted that the pursuance of motives in conflict with profit maximization in a capitalist firm most often stem from the separation between those who control the corporation and those who earn the profits; whereas no analogous separation exists in the labor-managed enterprise.

1.3: *Scope of Part III*

In one significant sense Part III is central to the entire study. In it we deal with what we may term the "specifics" of the labor-managed system. In other words, we take up in Part III all the numerous aspects and problems which do not have their analogue in other economic systems—in particular, in the capitalist market economy. Thus, Part III is the very opposite of Parts I and II, in which we develop a theory as analogous as possible in its general approach to the conventional theory of the capitalist economy. The utility of Part III for

[4] Professor Galbraith in his *New Industrial State* is perhaps the most vociferous proponent, and certainly the most noted author belonging to the group.

the whole of the study should be obvious: not only does it contain the analysis of many important aspects of the labor-managed system, but it also makes it possible for the reader to keep separate what is specific to the system.

One important category—but by no means the only one—falling under the heading of "specifics" is that containing all the dimensions of the labor-force variable which were eliminated, as a simplifying and streamlining device, from analysis in Parts I and II. For one thing, it must be recognized that there is not one type of labor, but a large number of types and qualities of labor. The question then must be asked as to how the analysis of the equilibrium behavior of the labor-managed firm (as presented in Parts I and II) should be modified, and how its conclusions will be affected, if more than one type of labor is introduced. The related problem which immediately arises is that of distribution—or sharing—of the jointly produced income among laborers of diverse skills and qualifications.

An even more important problem specific to the labor-managed system is that not even the services supplied by an individual laborer can be considered to be a constant. Quality and intensity of labor can vary, and in a system where income is linked immediately and directly to the performance of labor, labor's quality hardly can be treated as an exogenous variable. A closely related and somewhat more concrete problem is that of plant and firm atomization for the purpose of capturing the optimum return from the natural system of incentives inherent in labor management and income sharing.

Still another new dimension—this one deriving more from labor management than from income sharing—is the far greater ability of autonomous producers' groups to take out their income from the enterprise not in the form of monetary or other physical returns but rather in the form of intangibles—such as longer vacations or a substitution of a conveyor belt for a wheelbarrow even in situations where a "capitalist" maximization "on the margin" would not warrant such change.

In Section 1.1 we have alluded to a possible limitation of the basic behavioral principle of maximization of income per laborer in cases where reductions in the number of workers would be called for. A full treatment of this question also belongs to Part III. Among other things, we will be able to substantiate what we have previously referred to as the bee-swarm effect.

The "pure theory" as presented in Parts I and II contains, as one of its parts, the phenomenon of entry and exit of firms so important for the efficient functioning of a competitive market. In the context of that analysis, however, only a very rudimentary behavioral rule—or signaling device—for entry was envisaged, based on the comparison of potential and actual incomes of a given labor group. Such a rule certainly does not offer an adequate description of the actual process of entering or leaving the industry by labor-managed firms. Clearly, the role played by the entrepreneur in the capitalist system must be taken over in the labor-managed system by someone else—and this raises a whole score of specific problems whose treatment also belongs to Part III.

If we add the postulate that the labor-managed economy is a socialist one—as is most likely[5]—some other "new dimensions" emerge. One is the impact on national productivity of sharing most advanced technologies if the latter are embodied in the nature and quality of socially owned (tangible or intangible) capital assets. After all, it is only the usufruct of such assets that individual firms enjoy—and it is fully in the interest of the true owner, society, to procure the most technologically advanced assets (including patents) for the maximum number of firms.

While different from Parts I and II in one respect, Part III contains an important similarity in another. It is entirely devoid of considerations of planning and economic policy. At the same time, however, as much as Parts I and II, it constitutes a necessary precondition and background for a study of economic policies in Part IV.

The special position of Part III in this study can also be seen in another way. We recall that in Parts I and II labor management and income sharing were translated into the sole behavioral principle of maximization of income per laborer. It can then be argued that in such a simplified world not much labor management is going on in actuality, because the decision-making of the working collective has been used up, so to speak, on a single and immutable instruction to the director of the enterprise. By contrast, the special dimensions analyzed in Part III without exception involve or are based on other specific decision-making activity by the working collective.

Thus, for example, the distribution of jointly produced income among members of the collective possessing different skills must be subject to a management decision by the collective. Similarly, discretionary labor management must play a central role in the attainment of optimum efficiency, or work intensity, by the enterprise. Moreover, as a part of the labor-management process, dozens of other types of decisions will have to be taken, bearing on expansions or contractions

[5] This question belongs to and will be taken up in Part IV.

of activity, adoption of new products, labor-force training, collective consumption, community action, and many other administrative measures.

This multiplicity of decision-making may make the reader ask whether in fact the labor-managed firm does not have a multiplicity of objectives, some of which might be in conflict with the basic maximizing principle that underlies the analysis in Parts I and II. The question is a highly pertinent one, and its complete exploration goes a long way in providing a full understanding of the essence of labor management. A fuller treatment is presented in Part III, based on some underlying pieces of analysis produced in Parts I and II. Here let it only be noted that such a conflict generally will not occur. For one thing, many of the alternative objectives are related to the distribution or allocation of income, and not to income generation, to which pertains the maximizing principle. For another, in many real situations it appears that the income-maximizing principle leaves the decision-makers with one degree of freedom, which they can employ in pursuing another objective such as maximization of employment in the community. Another consideration is that in many instances where a conflict between the fundamental behavioral principle and other objectives of the labor-managed firm would seem to arise, this is merely a result of too narrow a definition of income.

1.4: *Scope and Role of Part IV*

In our examination of the labor-managed economy in the first three parts of this study we assume, explicitly or implicitly, that either there is no government at all or a government that is perfectly neutral and inactive with respect to the economic system. While there is nothing fundamentally inherent in the labor-managed economic system that would require the existence of and deliberate economic action on the part of the government, in any real situation the public authorities will play an important role. In fact, three major roles or spheres of influence can be distinguished, and they are reflected in the organization of Part IV.

The first sphere, in a sense the most general, involves the questions of implantation and implementation of the labor-managed system, and of the actual form of ownership and the mode of generating capital assets. We have noted already that the socialist formula, even if probably the most natural and most efficient, is not imperative, and other approaches are conceivable. This and a number of related problems are set forth in the first chapter of Part IV. The second sphere or category of government action is more concrete and specific, and involves the whole spectrum of activities usually referred to as economic policymaking, or just economic policy. Using the theoretical analysis of the first three parts of the study as the underlying formal structure, we develop in the subsequent two chapters (Chapters 16 and 17) the two major subdivisions of economic policy as customarily distinguished—that is, microeconomic policy and macroeconomic policy.

In the sphere of microeconomic policy two approaches offer themselves, and we have explored both. On the one hand, we have drawn on the analysis, experience, and conclusions of the foregoing three parts regarding the potential inefficiencies of the system, and study the corresponding ways of coping with such inefficiencies. On the other hand, we simply consider the major standard forms of policy action, such as income taxes, sales taxes, capital taxes and others, and study the effects such policies should have, given the underlying structure, on the behavior of firms or industries.

Under the heading of macroeconomic policy, we study in Chapter 17 the effects of short-run stabilization policies such as monetary policy and budgetary or credit policy on the major aggregate variables such as national product, employment, interest rates, and the price level. We also consider the stability of the macroeconomic solution of the labor-managed system, design certain policy actions that guarantee that stability, and point out some errors and misconceptions which have appeared in the literature dealing with the subject. We consider certain basic combinations of policy instruments leading to specific targets to be attained by the labor-managed economy and, finally, offer a general assessment of the power and desirability of macroeconomic policies in a labor-managed economy and contrast the situation with that encountered in the capitalist Keynesian environment.

The third, last, and perhaps most important category involving action by the public authorities in a labor-managed situation is that of long-range economic planning. Again, as we have pointed out already, planning activity is not the *sine qua non* of the labor-managed economy, but it is most desirable for a healthy and efficient functioning of that economy. The first task of the concluding chapter of Part IV is thus to show why and to what extent planning is desirable, and at the same time to indicate what type of planning activity best fits the situation.

Once this is done, the remainder of the analysis falls naturally into two parts. The first concerns the problem of steering the economy in order to avoid frictional maladjustments imputable to time-lags, imperfect information, or differences between social and individual valuations. The second, primarily relevant for the developing countries, concerns the problem of national savings and accumulation of capital assets in excess of what would be forthcoming without government action. The problem contains an institutional and a more strictly economic, quantitative facet, the former belonging to Chapter 15; thus what remains for Chapter 18 is the second facet. Foremost under that heading is to show the growth potential of a labor-managed economy on various assumptions regarding the capacity to accumulate. Because the formal treatment of the subject is not too different from conventional growth analysis, and because the necessary theoretical foundations have already been worked out (by the author in cooperation with Trent J. Bertrand), the analysis of potential growth has been developed only briefly, relying on the previously obtained results.[6]

[6]T. J. Bertrand and J. Vanek, "Growth with Technological Change, Variable Returns to Scale, and a General Saving Function," *Rivista Internazionale di Scienze Economiche e Commerciali*, XVI, No. 8, 1969.

PART I
MICROECONOMIC
THEORY

2. Equilibrium of a Competitive Firm

2.1: *Preliminary Considerations*

In the preceding chapter we have explained what we mean by and given the rationale for the "pure theory" of a labor-managed market system. Our task in this chapter is to enter into the substance of that theory. Following the traditional organization of microeconomics, we shall begin with an analysis of the equilibrium of a competitive firm. In many respects, and especially when we speak about short-run equilibria, we retread ground previously covered by Ward.[1]

The firm is characterized (defined) by its technology, relating certain inputs to the maximum attainable level of output, by the motivation governing its business decisions, and by a set of environmental characteristics. Four productive factors—representing four categories of factors—enter the production function. In addition to capital and labor, we shall also consider two factors, representative of intermediate inputs, one continuously substitutable for other inputs and the other entering the production process in a fixed proportion to the level of output. All factors are perfectly homogeneous and divisible, and to the extent that they are not consumed in the production process, they are compensated for services rendered.

As we have stressed in the preceding chapter, the basic principle of its operation differentiates the labor-managed firm significantly from a capitalist firm. Instead of attempting to maximize profit, the labor-managed firm operates under the principle of maximization of net income per laborer.[2]

The factor and product markets constitute the operationally relevant economic environment of the firm. Since our concern is with a competitive firm, it is postulated that all markets in which the firm operates

[1] B. Ward, "The Firm in Illyria: Market Syndicalism," *American Economic Review*, 48 (September 1958), 566–589.

[2] By "net income" we understand what in a capitalist firm would be the sum of the wage-bill and profit.

are competitive. Specifically, the firm hires its capital at a constant cost per unit; it purchases intermediate goods and sells its own products at constant prices. As for labor, as indicated above, it receives compensation by sharing in total net income; moreover, it is assumed that at the going (or offered) income-share the firm can hire any number of laborers consistent with its equilibrium operation. The case where certain employment levels would be impossible because of labor-supply limitations certainly is a possibility in the real world, but this will be considered below in the context of industry and/or general equilibrium adjustment.

The analysis presented in this chapter is organized along the same lines as the conventional theory of a firm. In the next two sections we will discuss the short-run equilibrium of the firm and in the subsequent section the long-run equilibrium. As usual, the distinction between the two types of equilibria hinges on whether the capital stock (plant and equipment) is permitted to adjust to market forces. A reconciliation between the present analysis and conventional cost analysis is attempted in the concluding section.

In the main part of the text I shall attempt to make the exposition as clear and nontechnical as possible, limiting the use of mathematics to the minimum and using diagrams only when a more rigorous formulation is necessary. However, the principal findings of the main text are rigorously derived in a mathematical appendix.

2.2: *The Equilibrium in the Short Run: A Simple Case*

The specific questions to be explored in this and the subsequent sections are (1) How much will a labor-managed firm produce? and (2) What amounts of variable inputs will it use in the short run, given the various technological, behavioral, and market characteristics explained in the preceding section? Because the material to be covered is of prime importance for all of the present study, and because we want to introduce several new concepts and analytical tools, I propose to proceed slowly, dealing first with a simple situation in the present section, and considering a more general one in the next.

Besides answering our two key questions, an additional purpose of this section is to familiarize the reader with two alternative analytical approaches to the solutions sought. This duality will prove useful not only in giving two ways of looking at the same problem but also, and perhaps principally, in handling problems of comparative statics or of economic policy. As will be seen through the subsequent chapters, one set is more suitable for one type of problems, while the other set is better for other problems.

The simplification underlying the analysis of the present section consists in the fact that there is only one variable factor used by the labor-managed firm, namely labor, the only other factor being capital, fixed in supply in the short run. This allows us to write a simple production function

$$X = X(L) \tag{1}$$

where X and L are physical output and labor input respectively. The function is assumed to be subject to diminishing (marginal) returns everywhere or at least beyond a certain level of employment.

Because we are concerned here with a competitive situation, the two relevant prices, that of capital, p_K, and that of the product, p_X, can both be taken as given constants from the point of view of our labor-managed firm. Similarly, the capital stock used by the firm is a constant, K_0. With these observations and notations, the decision-making problem facing the labor-managed firm is to maximize the net income per laborer, Y, given by the expression

$$Y = (p_X X - p_K K_0)/L \tag{2}$$

In terms of a diagram, as shown in Figure 2.2.1, this implies the maximization of the vertical distance between the average value product of labor (AVP_L)—that is, the first term on the right-hand side of relation (2)—and the cost of capital per laborer, $(p_K K_0/L)$—that is, the second term on the right-hand side of that relation. The maximum is reached for employment L_0 where Y attains the level indicated by point A (or

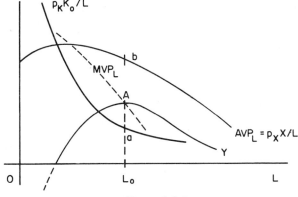

Figure 2.2.1

that indicated by the distance *ab*). A very important fact is that at its maximum the income per laborer Y must also equal the marginal value product of labor. This completes our simple derivation using the first approach.

The second approach differs in that it deals with total, rather than average and marginal, variables; it is illustrated by Figure 2.2.2. In

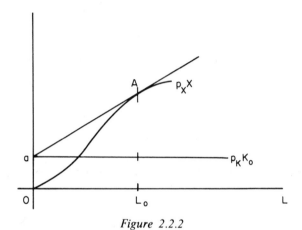

Figure 2.2.2

that diagram the total value product of labor $p_X X$, diminished by the fixed cost of capital $p_K K_0$, measures the *total* net income of labor corresponding to various levels of employment. The net income *per laborer* is now measured by the slope of a line connecting point a and a particular point of the total value product curve. It is immediately apparent that that slope is maximized when it also is equal to the slope of the total product line, at point A, that is, when the line passing through a and the contour are tangential (with, of course, by secondary conditions, the curved contour touching the straight line from below). Because as is well known the slope of the total value product line equals the marginal value product of labor, it immediately becomes apparent that in equilibrium the income per laborer of the labor-managed firm must equal the marginal value product of labor.

2.3: *The Equilibrium in the Short Run: A General Case*

We now turn to the more general case of short-run equilibrium of the labor-managed firm, involving in addition to labor also other variable inputs. It is this more general case whose characteristics were outlined in the introductory section.

Recalling that in the short run the capital stock is fixed at the level K_0, the relevant production function, relating variable inputs of labor L, the substitutable material M, and the nonsubstitutable material N to the level of output X, is now expressed by the two relations

$$X = X(L,M) \qquad (1)$$

$$N = nX \qquad (2)$$

where n is a constant input-coefficient reflecting how much of the material N is needed per unit of product X. The function $X(L,M)$ is continuous and subject—at least beyond a certain level of employment—to the law of diminishing returns for both inputs.

As we have pointed out previously, the market prices of the product, p_X, of capital, p_K, and of the two materials, p_M and p_N respectively, are fixed. These four prices together with relations (1) and (2) are sufficient data for a manager whose mandate is to maximize net income per employee. Let us now describe in detail the procedure through which the desired solution can be obtained.

The net income per employee (per laborer), Y, is the excess of the value of sales over capital and material costs divided by the number of employees, that is,

$$Y = (1/L)(X[p_X - p_Nn] - Mp_M - K_0p_K) \qquad (3)$$

Recalling that all prices and K_0 are constants and that X is given by relation (1), it becomes apparent that the net income per employee depends on total employment L and on the input of the substitutable factor M. Of course, it must be postulated that the necessary inputs of the nonsubstitutable factor N are always forthcoming.

Suppose for the moment that the level of employment is given. Then the only problem confronting the management of the firm is to select the appropriate level of input M which will make net income (and net income per laborer) as high as possible. The rule to be used here is the same as that used by a capitalist firm: use so much of M—to be referred to hereafter as M^*—as will equalize the price of M and the *marginal value product-added* of M. The "value product-added" is to be understood as the value of product of M, added by M over and above the value of the nonsubstitutable factor N. The value product-added is obtained from the marginal physical product of M by multiplying the latter magnitude by $(p_X - np_N)$. As in the context of capitalist production decision-making, the simple logic of this rule is that if the marginal value product-added is different from the price of M, it is always possible to increase the net income of the enterprise by an appropriate change in the employment of that factor.

For a prescribed level of employment L we have thus derived the income maximizing employment of M, M^*. More precisely it is possible to think of M^* as a definite function of L, that is,

$$M^* = M^*(L) \qquad (4)$$

In relation (3) defining the net income per laborer it is now possible to postulate that M always assumes the maximizing value M^*, thus yielding a special "optimum" variable Y^*. Its property is that it depends only on the level of employment L, the level of use of M being at all times adjusted to the prevailing L through the maximizing procedure just described, and leading to relation (4).

We are now ready to proceed to the final and most important step in deriving the short-run equilibrium of the labor-managed firm. The optimum variable income per laborer now can be written as

$$Y^* = (X^*/L)(p_X - np_N) - (M^*p_M + K_0p_K)/L \qquad (5)$$

where X^* is used to indicate dependence of X on L only, M (in relation (1)) itself always assuming the value M^* corresponding to L.

In the first term on the right-hand side of relation (5) we recognize the average physical product of labor multiplied by the price of the product diminished by the cost of the nonsubstitutable factor per unit of output. It is what we shall call, perhaps not quite conventionally, the average value product-added of labor, using for it the abbreviation $AVPA_L^*$, the asterisk again indicating that the employment of M is always optimum in the sense explained above. The $AVPA_L^*$ is illustrated in Figure 2.2.1. Because it is nothing but an average productivity valued at a constant price, the contour resembles the conventional average productivity curve. Note that beyond a certain point it is declining for increasing levels of employment: this is the consequence of the fact that one of the variable and substitutable factors—namely, capital—is fixed.

The other term on the right-hand side of relation 5—by which the first term is to be diminished to obtain Y^*—is the (constant) capital cost plus the (variable) cost of material M per laborer, the latter input always being employed at the optimum level M^*. The value of that term normally will be declining from an extremely high value for low levels of employment to low levels for high employment. The second term is not explicitly illustrated in the diagram; however, because the net income per employee, Y^*, is shown in Figure 2.2.1, the value of the second term can be identified for any level of employment as the vertical distance between $AVPA_L^*$ and Y^*.

From the over-all shapes of the contours reflecting the two terms on the right-hand side of relation (5) just explained, it is evident that at first, for very low L, the net income per laborer must be negative, then with increasing L become positive, reaching a maximum and then declining. That pattern is illustrated by the line Y^*, the maximum being reached at point A, for the "equilibrium" level of employment L_o.

Now the manager wanting to maximize the net income per employee could, using all the data laid out at the outset of this section, go exactly through the procedure outlined above, find point A, and the corresponding (maximum) income L_oA, and hire the optimal number of laborers L_o. But he could also follow a more straightforward procedure, quite similar to that followed (or which should be followed) by his capitalist counterpart—namely, to employ the number of laborers for which the average income Y^* equals the marginal value product-added of labor. The latter variable is the marginal physical product of labor valued at the product price corrected for the cost of the non-substitutable factor. At each level of employment L, however, the input of M for which the marginal physical product of labor is reckoned is the optimally adjusted M^*.

Now consider a level of employment such as L_1 in the diagram. As is indicated by the segments L_1c and L_1b, an additional laborer hired at the level of employment L_1 will add to the net income of the enterprise more than the going income per laborer $Y^* = L_1c$. If that additional laborer is hired, the excess of his value product over the previous paycheck of each laborer (i.e., the amount represented by the segment cb) can now be distributed to all employees of the enterprise, and thereby, with the additional laborer, everybody's income can be increased. This is why the Y^* contour in Figure 2.3.1 must have a positive slope—i.e., income per laborer must be growing with increasing employment—as long as it finds itself below the contour $MVPA_L^*$, and, conversely, Y^* must be declining whenever it finds itself above the marginal value product line. It will decline in this range since additional laborers add to the income of the enterprise less than what they are paid, and the resulting loss must be distributed over the entire working collective. And thus maximum Y^* is found at point A where the income per laborer is equal to the marginal value product-added of labor.

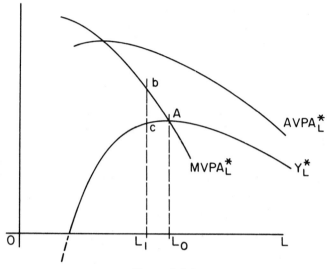

Figure 2.3.1

To sum up the task of the manager of our hypothetical labor-managed firm, let us say that with all the data he is given, in the short run he must follow two basic rules: first, he must at all times hire as much of material M as to make its net marginal addition to income equal to its price; second, he must invite as many workers to participate in the enterprise as to make everybody's income equal to the net product of the last man joining the collective. This leads to the establishment of the equilibrium levels of employment of labor and the use of the substitutable material, and finally, through relations (1) and (2), to the equilibrium level of output and employment of the nonsubstitutable factor.

At first sight these conclusions appear to make the short-run equilibrium of the labor-managed firm resemble that of a capitalist firm: factor earnings of substitutable and variable factors are to be equal to the marginal value products of those factors. But in reality the resemblance of the two equilibria is only partial, at the most, and when it comes to the adjustment of the two alternative types of equilibria to changing market conditions, or other autonomous disturbances, the differences become much more significant. While such proofs and propositions in comparative statics will concern us in several subsequent chapters, let us concentrate here on a comparison of the equilibrium solutions.

Suppose that all the specifications of the labor-managed firm given at the outset of this section—i.e., the production function and the four constant product and factor prices—pertain equally to a capitalist firm. Clearly, the capitalist situation is underspecified because we do not have a (competitive) wage rate at which the firm hires its labor. Call such a wage rate p_L and consider various levels of that rate. If p_L equals the equilibrium (maximum) level of income per laborer in the labor-managed firm Y^*, then of course the equilibria in the two alternative firms will be exactly identical: employment of all inputs and the levels of output will be the same. A new variable, that is profit, in the capitalist firm will be zero. This follows from the fact that the wage rate in the capitalist firm is equal to the income per worker in the labor-managed firm, and the latter, by definition, is exactly the difference between selling revenue per laborer and nonlabor cost per laborer.

If profit is positive, a situation that may be termed as normal for a capitalist firm, the wage rate, of course, in the capitalist firm must be less than Y^*, and so must be, as is well known, that firm's marginal product of labor. Consequently, recalling that in the short run the capital input is fixed, the capitalist firm will hire more laborers and produce more output than its labor-managed equivalent. Conversely, if the capitalist firm operates with a loss (covering fully only its variable costs), it will produce less than its labor-managed counterpart and hire fewer laborers. An implication of these results deserving mention is the fact that the capitalist firm will operate with a lower capital-labor ratio than the corresponding labor-managed firm if it makes a positive profit. If the capitalist firm operates without (with a negative) profit, it will be using an identical (a higher) capital-labor ratio.

2.4: *The Competitive Equilibrium in the Long Run*

Our purpose in this section is to derive the long-run equilibrium of a labor-managed firm and set forth some of its main properties. As usual, by "long-run" equilibrium we understand a situation wherein all factors of production are variable, and consequently the process of maximization will involve the adjustment of all inputs to an optimal equilibrium level. Unlike the situation examined in Section 2, capital thus becomes a variable, and the production function as stated in Section 2 must now be altered. Specifically, it is replaced by

$$X = X(K,L,M) \qquad (1)$$

with the relation of proportionality between X and N remaining unchanged. All other postulates, including the principle of maximization of income per laborer (Y) and the constancy of all product and factor prices, also remain unchanged.

For reasons that will become clearer as we proceed with our analysis of the decentralized labor-managed economy, we will consider separately two alternative forms of the production function expressed in relation (1).[3] The first form is most clearly described as the production function which generates for a fully competitive capitalist firm a U-shaped long-run average cost curve. In other words, it is a production function which yields at low levels of output increasing and at high levels of output diminishing incremental outputs to successive inputs of small constant bundles of all factors, the bundles having any arbitrary composition.

The second form of our production function is one involving constant returns to scale, or what is customarily referred to as linear homogeneity. As is more descriptively expressed by the first term, the production function is one wherein multiplication of all inputs by a given factor multiplies output by that same factor. We shall explore the implications of that special function for the long-run equilibrium of the labor-managed firm for a number of reasons, of which three deserve mention here: (1) if it is postulated that *all* productive factors are truly variable, then it is rather difficult to argue that the *physical* relationship between inputs and outputs ought to be anything but one of constant returns to scale; (2) the linear homogeneous production function has played a prominent role in the theory of both competitive industry and competitive general equilibrium; and (3) there is empirical evidence that by and large, beyond a certain minimum level of output, constant returns are effectively present in many industries.

But let us now return to the first form, that is, the "conventional" increasing-decreasing-returns production function, with all inputs variable. Actually, very little in the way of formal analysis, beyond what has been done in section 2 of this chapter, is necessary to derive a full long-run equilibrium. As before, the problem is to maximize the income per laborer employed in the firm: the difference here is that the management now has another input, K, to adjust to its optimum level.

We shall begin our analysis by pointing out that the two short-run rules, that is

$$MVPA_M = p_M \tag{2}$$

[3] Actually this procedure is not uncommon in the context of conventional theory of the firm.

and

$$MVPA_L = (1/L)(X[p_X - p_N n] - Mp_M - Kp_K) \qquad (3)$$

must hold in the long run as well. This follows from the fact that the two rules were established for any level of capital input K_0, and hence also for the long-run optimal level of K, whatever this latter may be.

To determine the one additional equilibrium level, that is the long-run equilibrium employment of capital, an additional rule is needed. This rule is most easily established by analogy with the rule regarding input M (see relation (2) above). Indeed, while M and K may be entirely different inputs in physical terms, they are identical in respect to the manner in which they enter our "optimum" analysis: both have a fixed price, both are variable inputs and both are continuously substitutable factors in the production function. And consequently, the long-run rule regarding employment of capital is analogous to relation (2), that is

$$MVPA_K = p_K \qquad (4)$$

This rule together with the other two short-run rules is sufficient for the first form of the production function to determine the long-run equilibrium of the labor-managed firm. In other words, given relations (1) through (4) (relation (1) assuming our first specific form), the levels of input of all the substitutable factors and the corresponding level of output can be uniquely determined; and of course, the input of N is obtained from the level of output through the proportionality factor n.

While relation (4) embodies the essence of the analysis of this section, it is desirable to elaborate somewhat on this finding. First, it ought to be noted that the result could have been obtained from the analysis of long-run average and marginal product schedules, similar to that developed in section 3 for the short-run equilibrium. The only basic difference would have been that with variable capital, for each level of labor input (along the horizontal axis), not only the input M but also capital would have to be optimally adjusted to factor and product market conditions.

Perhaps of greater analytical interest—considering the first form of the production function—is the position of the long-run equilibrium on that function. Contrary to a capitalist firm, the firm studied here can experience a long-run equilibrium only at a rather limited set of points on its production function. To substantiate this proposition, let it first be noted that in our labor-managed firm (recall the definition of

Y) the entire value of the product is distributed among the factors of production. Moreover, in a long-run equilibrium, each substitutable factor earns its marginal value product-added. But it is well known from the conventional theory of the firm that these two conditions cannot prevail simultaneously on the production function of the first form —or of the first kind—considered here (that is, on the increasing-decreasing returns function) except at the points for which (with constant factor prices) the long-run average cost curve of a capitalist firm is at its minimum point.

All such points on the production function constitute the *locus of maximum physical efficiency*, in the sense that for a prescribed set of factor-input coefficients the maximum average products (of either factor) are attained on that locus. The long-run equilibrium of the labor-managed firm must be on that locus. For a simple production function of the first form involving only labor and capital inputs as shown in Figure 2.4.1, such a locus is illustrated by the contour *EE*. In fact the contour is a projection of points traced on the (three-dimensional) production function (recall that the function looks something like a mountain with steeper and steeper slopes at first and gradually diminishing slopes thereafter, for comparatively high inputs of capital and labor) by the points of tangency between the function and rays through the origin. Thus an alternative way of looking at the locus of maximum

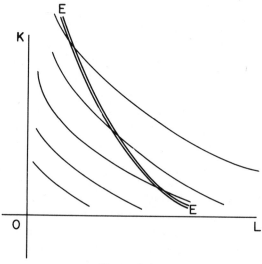

Figure 2.4.1

physical efficiency is to say that it is a line of demarcation on the production function (of the first form) between the region of increasing
and the region of decreasing returns—that is, the locus of (instanta-
neous) constant returns to scale. From our definition of the first form
of the production function it follows that the locus (such as EE in Figure 2.4.1) must have only one point for each set of factor-proportions.

With all that has been said thus far it is comparatively easy to study
the long-run equilibrium of the labor-managed firm whose technology is subject to constant returns to scale. As is well known,
with such functions marginal-product pricing of all substitutable factors of production exactly exhausts the product (-added) at all points of
the production function, and thus the entire production function becomes a (degenerate case of a) locus of maximum physical efficiency,
and the long-run equilibrium of the labor-managed firm can arise
anywhere on the function, that is, for any set of factor proportions
and at any level of output.

An alternative way to view this situation is to observe that a fully
competitive capitalist firm operating under conditions of constant returns to scale must have a horizontal long-run average (and marginal)
cost curve: the minimum of the cost curve now is the entire cost curve.
But because the labor-managed equivalent of the capitalist firm can operate only at points where the capitalist would be at minimum cost, the
labor-managed firm can operate in the long run anywhere. Indeed, all
scales of operation correspond to the minimum cost.

To analyze more precisely the long-run equilibrium with constant
returns to scale, let us consider—as we did before—marginal-product
and net-income functions for labor. These are shown in Figure 2.4.2.
In the long run these two functions coincide, and assume the form of a
horizontal line, as shown by the line passing through e. That this must
be so is best seen by considering the short-run situation corresponding
to a constant level of capital stock K_0 and illustrated by the short-run
net-income function (Y^*) and the marginal value product-added function ($MVPA_l^*$).

From our discussion in section 2 we know that when the net income
per laborer Y^* is at a maximum at the level corresponding to point e,
it is also equal to labor's marginal value product-added; moreover
(by definition of $MVPA_l^*$), the marginal value product-added of input
M is equal to p_M. But for the production function of our "second
form" (i.e., the constant-returns-to-scale functions), we know that if all

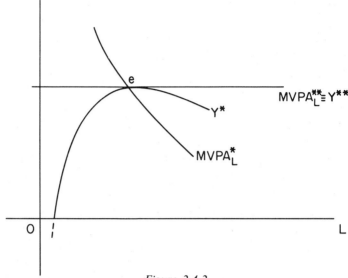

Figure 2.4.2

substitutable productive factors earn the value of their marginal products (-added) then the total value of the product (-added) is exactly exhausted. This implies—because at point e two factors (L and M) earn
their respective marginal value products-added and because we know
that (by definition of Y^*) the value of the product is exhausted by
factor-payments—that K (at level K_0) is also paid its marginal value
product-added when the solution is at e. And thus (with all three relations (2), (3), and (4) satisfied) e corresponds not only to a short-run
equilibrium of the labor-managed firm but also to a long-run
equilibrium.

Now suppose that all inputs—K, L, M, and N—are doubled or
tripled. This means that we will move in Figure 2.4.2 two or three
times further to the right from point e; but as is well known for a case
of constant returns to scale, all the marginal products will remain unchanged, and thus, with unchanged factor and product prices, all substitutable factors still will be earning the same marginal value products-
added as at point e. And consequently, the new point e, two or three
times further to the right from and at the same vertical level as e, will
again represent both a short-run equilibrium, corresponding to a capital stock two or three times K_0, and a long-run equilibrium.

We thus conclude that for our production function of the second
form all short-run equilibria are also long-run equilibria, and vice

versa. The only difference between the two is that while the short-run equilibrium is always determinate, corresponding to a given K_0, the long-run equilibrium is indeterminate. In other words, our manager whose mandate is to maximize income per laborer will know exactly how many laborers (and other factors) to employ in the short run (that is, with a given plant and equipment), but in the long run the scale of his firm's operation will remain indeterminate, all scales being equally desirable. However, from the optimal Y^{**} and the prescribed factor prices our manager will be able to select the "optimal" long-run factor-input mix (i.e., factor-proportions).[4]

Before concluding the discussion of the long-run equilibrium of the labor-managed firm, three important observations remain to be made. First, for firms using the technology of the first kind it will be observed that both the labor-managed and capitalist models will have exactly the same level of operation provided that the capitalist firm does not make any profits, that is, provided that the equilibrium Y is equal to the capitalist wage rate. As we have pointed out previously, in this situation both firms will be at the locus of maximum physical efficiency. If the capitalist (but otherwise identical) firm makes some profits and p_L—the capitalist wage rate—is less than Y, the capitalist firm will operate at a scale higher than the locus of maximum physical efficiency (to the right and above EE in Figure 2.4.1) while the labor-managed firm will remain at it and use a higher capital-labor ratio than its capitalist equivalent. This is an immediate consequence of the fact that the capitalist firm making positive profits and having a U-shaped long-run average cost curve will operate to the right of the minimum cost point.

The second important point again pertains primarily to a situation with a production function of the first kind. The fact that the labor-managed firm will always be at the locus of maximum physical efficiency ought not to be interpreted as a property which would make the labor-managed alternative necessarily more desirable. Indeed, when it comes to the question of optimal resource allocation, it is the maximum economic efficiency—involving both technical and value considerations —rather than maximum physical efficiency that becomes the relevant criterion. Much more will be said about these matters when we discuss the industry and general-equilibrium solutions of the labor-managed socialist system.

---

[4] More will be said about this in the following section.

The third and final point worth noting again involves a comparison between the labor-managed and the capitalist firm; however, this time —from the viewpoint of social desirability—the participatory firm has a distinct advantage over the capitalist one. Recall our conclusion that in the long run a fully competitive labor-managed firm operating under conditions of constant returns to scale can find its equilibrium at any scale of operation, its aim of maximizing income per laborer being attainable at all scales. The same holds regarding a capitalist firm only if the market price is such that profit is zero. With a higher price, the theoretical equilibrium level of output is infinity. While absurd when considered in the context of the real world, this result underscores the well-known conclusion that with constant returns to scale and positive profits a capitalist competitive market is impossible; either the profits or competition must give way, and, unfortunately, most often it turns out to be the latter.

Furthermore, basing our conclusion on the same argument, we may say that even with increasing returns to scale, the impetus to grow indefinitely, and thus to control a sizeable portion of the market, in the labor-managed firm can be expected to be considerably less than in the case of its capitalist equivalent. On the whole—and we will reach the same conclusion in many other instances and contexts—the capitalist alternative appears as more Darwinian and the labor-managed system —without being inefficient—as more consistent with the principle of "live and let live."

2.5: *Equilibrium of the Labor-Managed Firm and the Cost of Production*

In the preceding sections we have studied the equilibrium of a labor-managed firm in the context of its factor inputs and factor-input productivities. This procedure differs from that normally adopted when discussing a capitalist firm; in that case reference is customarily made to the level of output and to corresponding average and marginal costs. The purpose of this section is to show that, though preferable in many respects, the approach adopted above for the analysis of a labor-managed firm is not the only possible one; all of the results obtained thus far can be similarly derived from an analysis of costs and level of output. In fact, in many instances the cost analysis may serve to point up otherwise unobservable facts and, as a consequence, will be useful to us later.

It is essential to our task to recognize that because the labor-managed firm is to maximize income per laborer, the relevant cost functions must involve a relationship between cost and output per laborer, rather than the usual relationship between cost and total output. This may be demonstrated in the derivation of the equilibrium of a firm whose only variable input is labor and whose only other (fixed) input is the stock of capital, K_0. As before, the product price (p_X) and price of capital (p_K) are constants, given by the prevailing market conditions. Because labor-income does not constitute a cost, the only "usual" average cost of the firm is

$$AC = \frac{K_0 p_K}{X} \tag{1}$$

as illustrated in the first quadrant in Figure 2.5.1. Assuming always decreasing returns to labor (with a constant stock of capital) we obtain a relationship between X/L (output per laborer) and X shown in the fourth quadrant as $F(X)$. With the help of a 45° line in the third, it is now possible to construct (in the way indicated in the diagram) the

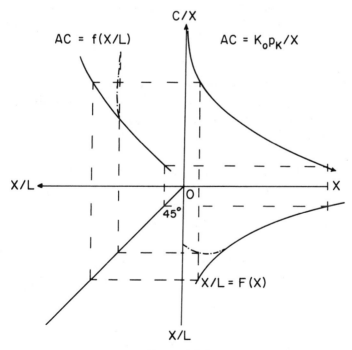

Figure 2.5.1

average cost function depending on X/L in the second quadrant.[5] This is illustrated by the solid line $f(X/L)$, and indicates the cost per unit of output which must be incurred by the labor-managed firm to produce the levels of output per laborer shown on the horizontal axis measured to the left from the origin. From this locus we are able to obtain in the customary fashion the marginal cost function, again related to product per laborer. The two are shown in Figure 2.5.2, together with the price p_X (competitive demand function) facing the labor-managed firm.

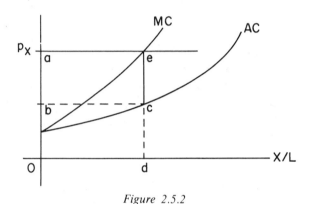

Figure 2.5.2

The short-run equilibrium of the firm is now obtained for that level of output per laborer $0d$, where price equals the marginal cost. At that level of output the income per laborer Y equals the area $abce$, the revenue per laborer is $a0de$, and the residual $b0dc$ is the corresponding cost per laborer. Actually, as will be easily verified by the reader, it is the cost per laborer (represented by the areas such as $b0dc$) from which the marginal cost line (MC) is derived. Clearly, the income per laborer will be at maximum when, for a (small) unitary increase in X/L, the resulting increment in gross revenue—i.e., p_X—equals the corresponding increment in cost per laborer, MC. Of necessity, the equilibrium condition obtained here must be equivalent to that obtained in section

[5]Note that if initially there are increasing returns to labor, then for low outputs the F-function in the fourth quadrant of Figure 2.5.1 will assume the form indicated by the broken line and the average cost curve for such outputs will be an almost vertical broken line in the second quadrant. But note also that we now have two average costs for single output per laborer (the AC curve no longer is single-valued), and, of course, only the lower average cost would pertain in the rationally managed firm.

2, namely that the income per laborer equals the marginal value product of labor.[6]

The derivation of a long-run equilibrium where not only labor, but all factors are variable inputs proceeds along similar lines. Recalling that in the labor-managed firm labor income should not be counted as a factor cost, it is possible to obtain a set of customary average cost functions, one function for each different level of labor employment, expressing costs in relation to the level of output. Now for each such cost curve it is possible to divide the scale of the output (horizontal) axis by the corresponding (constant) level of employment—so as to obtain on the horizontal axis outputs per laborer—and all the average cost functions (for all employments) now can be plotted in one diagram, with X/L on the horizontal axis. Three such average cost curves are shown in Figure 2.5.3, as AC_1^*, AC_2^* and AC_3^*, corresponding to three

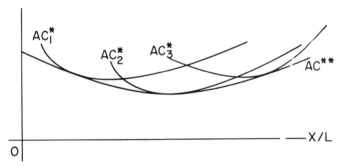

Figure 2.5.3

different levels of labor employment. It will be noted that the ranking of the underlying employment levels will generally be reflected by the relative positions of the AC^* curves.

[6]Except for the fact that we know that in both cases we are maximizing income per laborer, this correspondence is not immediately obvious from the mathematical statement of the two equilibrium conditions; however, using the notation of the main text, it can be established as follows: the condition $P_X = MC$ (as shown in Figure 2.5.2) implies

$$p_X = MC = AC + (X/L) \text{ times slope of AC} = K_0 p_K/X - (X/L) K_0 p_K X'/X^2,$$

wherefrom, realizing that $X' = dX/d(X/L) = \dfrac{(dX/dL)L^2}{L(dX/dL) - X}$, we get, after a substitution and a few simplifications, our original equilibrium condition $Y = p_X(dX/dL)$. We must realize, however, that in the above marginal cost analysis we have not considered a situation involving a nonsubstitutable factor.

Now for all possible levels of employment there would be an infinity of curves such as the AC^* contours, and this family of cost lines would have an envelope, such as AC^{**}. This latter is a locus of minimum average costs attainable for prescribed levels of output per laborer. As follows from the construction, to each point of AC^{**} will generally (but not necessarily) correspond a specific level of employment L; that L can be increasing or declining as we move from left to right. From the envelope AC^{**} the marginal cost curve—again a function of X/L —is obtained in the same way as it was above in the case of the short-run equilibrium. The long-run equilibrium output and income per laborer is then obtained from the condition $p_X = MC^{**}$, and the absolute scale of operation—if this is possible at all—is indicated by the employment level corresponding to the long-run equilibrium point on the average-cost curve.

In the context of the present analysis, the case of constant returns to scale (the "second form" discussed in the preceding section) represents a unique "median" situation. In this case, as is well known, the conventional average-cost curves (by conventional we mean plotted against the X-axis) corresponding to various levels of employment (and constant other factor prices) will look something like the AC contour in Figure 2.5.2 and will be moving further to the right as L increases. Now the transformation of the conventional cost functions into those related to output per laborer—similar to that leading to the AC^* curves in Figure 2.5.3—will lead in the case of constant returns to scale to a single AC^* line, applicable to all levels of employment, and, of course, identical with the envelope AC^{**}. This must be so because if at one level of X and L the minimum average cost is, say, dc in Figure 2.5.2, then the same minimum average cost must apply if output and all inputs are doubled or tripled. Taking now the AC and MC contours in Figure 2.5.2 as descriptive of a long-run situation with constant returns to scale, the derivation of the equilibrium point proceeds along the familiar lines illustrated in Figure 2.5.2. The only special result—reflecting what has been said in the preceding section— is that we can find a long-run equilibrium AC, MC output per laborer (and of course all equilibrium input coefficients) and the maximum income per laborer, but we cannot obtain the "optimum" level of output. The latter conclusion stems from the fact that point c on AC in the diagram corresponds to all possible levels of output and employment.

APPENDIX

In mathematical terms, the subject of the present chapter can be formulated as a special case of the following general problem:

Given a set of constant product prices p_i and factor prices w_j, the objective of a labor-managed firm is to maximize income per laborer

$$Y = (1/L)\left(\sum_i p_i X_i - \sum_j w_j V_j\right) \tag{A.1}$$

where X and V represent quantities of products and nonlabor inputs respectively; this is to be done subject to a continuous production function

$$F(X_1, X_2, \ldots; V_1, V_2, \ldots; L) = 0 \tag{A.2}$$

containing all the X's and all the V's appearing in relation (A.1). If nonsubstitutable factors are related through a factor of proportionality to one of the outputs X, such a situation can be taken care of (as it was done in the main text of this chapter) by redefining the appropriate p's in relation (A.1) to exclude the cost per unit of output of the non-substitutable factors.

The solutions of this constrained-maximum problem are obtained by postulating an extreme value ($dZ = 0$) of the expression

$$Z = Y - \phi F \tag{A.3}$$

where ϕ represents the Lagrangean multiplier. This implies, differentiating relation (A.3) with respect to all X's, V's, and L and putting them equal to zero,

$$p_i = \phi L \frac{\partial F}{\partial X_i} \tag{A.4}$$

$$i = 1, \ldots, m$$

$$w_j = -\phi L \frac{\partial F}{\partial V_j} \tag{A.5}$$

$$j = 1, \ldots, n$$

and

$$Y = \phi L \frac{\partial F}{\partial L} \tag{A.6}$$

Relations (A.2) and (A.4) through (A.6) are $2 + m + n$ in number and contain the variables V_j, X_i, Y, and L, also $2 + m + n$ in number.

Thus the system is consistent with a solution. That solution is the long-run equilibrium of the labor-managed firm. Supposing that factor V_1 stands for the capital stock, and postulating that it assumes a constant value, we obtain the short-run equilibrium values of the remaining $m + n + 1$ variables by solving the previous set of equations excluding the capital equation in the set (A.5).

The special one-product case dealt with in the main text is obtained, realizing that

$$F = X - X(K, M, L) = 0 \qquad (A.7)$$

and that instead of p_X in the above relations we have to write $p_X - np_N$ because of the nonsubstitutable factor N. Relation (A.4) thus becomes

$$\phi = (p_X - np_N)/L \qquad (A.4')$$

and substituting that equation into relations (A.5) and (A.6), after effecting the appropriate changes in notation, we obtain

$$p_K = (p_X - np_N)\frac{\partial X}{\partial K} \quad (= MVPA_K) \qquad (A.5')$$

$$p_M = (p_X - np_N)\frac{\partial X}{\partial M} \quad (= MVPA_M) \qquad (A.5'')$$

and

$$Y = (p_X - np_N)\frac{\partial X}{\partial L} \quad (= MVPA_L) \qquad (A.6')$$

These three "management rules" together with relation (A.7) lead to the long-run equilibrium solutions for X, L, K, and M. The short-run solution, as explained above, is obtained by eliminating relation (A.5') and holding K constant at K_0.

Now if we substitute the results A.5', A.5'' and A.6' into relation (A.1)—recalling that p_K and p_N in the former are the w_j's in the latter and that $p_X - np_N$ in the former is $p_i(i = 1)$ in the latter—we obtain after rearrangement and simplification

$$X = \frac{\partial X}{\partial L} L + \frac{\partial X}{\partial K} K + \frac{\partial X}{\partial M} M \qquad (A.8)$$

Now using the production function (A.7) in relation (A.8) we obtain a relation in L, K, and M defining the locus of "maximum physical efficiency" at which the labor-managed firm must operate in the long run. For the first form of technology (the increasing-decreasing-returns function, as discussed in the main text) the locus is a surface in the factor space, single-valued for any set of prescribed factor proportions. For the second form of technology—that is, the constant returns to scale function—through Euler's theorem the entire production function satisfies relation (A.8) and thus the locus of maximum physical efficiency becomes the entire production function. Clearly, for indefinitely increasing or diminishing returns the locus does not exist.

3. The Competitive Firm and Changing Market Conditions

3.1: *Introduction*

The analysis presented in this chapter is a logical continuation of that offered in the preceding one. In that chapter our principal concern was to identify and derive the equilibrium solution for a competitive labor-managed firm operating in an environment of labor abundance, on the principle of maximization of net income per laborer. In this chapter, while preserving all the general assumptions defining the firm, we want to study the impact of changing market conditions—that is, more specifically, of changing market prices—on the equilibrium of the firm. For example, we want to ask such questions as How will the output of the firm, or demand for a specific factor of production, be affected if the product-price declines? and ... if the cost of capital increases? In other words, we intend to study the main characteristics of the individual firm's supply and demand for products and factors of production.

The approach of the preceding chapter also suggests the organization of our present exposition. Basically, there are four relevant markets: (1) the market of the good produced by the firm, (2) the market of the nonsubstitutable factor N, (3) the market of the substitutable factor M, and finally, (4) the capital market. Because it is always possible to postulate (as we did in the preceding chapter) that the firm is selling its output ($-$added) at the price of the product diminished by the value of input of the nonsubstitutable factor (i.e., at the price $p_X - np_N$), the analysis of the impact of the firm of changes in p_X and np_N is quite analogous; and thus we treat the effects of these two prices together in the following section. The third and fourth sections will be concerned with the substitutable material input and capital respectively.

As might be expected, the comparative statics of this chapter is somewhat more complicated than the static analysis presented in the preceding chapter. Actually, in a number of instances we are able only to indicate the rationale of the various results rather than to prove them

42

fully. In the mathematical appendix to this chapter, however, we treat the questions at hand more rigorously.

3.2: *The Effects of a Change in the Product Price*

In this section we shall study the effects of changes in the product price p_X (and, by implication, of the price p_N—as explained above) on the amount of the product supplied, and on the amounts of the productive factors K, L, and M (N being proportional to X) demanded by the labor-managed firm. As before, we make the distinction between short and long-run adjustments, and study the problem in the context of the two basic forms of technology (it will be recalled that the first form is one generating the U-shaped long-run average cost function for a capitalist firm, while the second form corresponds to constant returns to scale).

Let us first consider the short-run situation where the stock of capital is fixed at K_0 leaving us with two variable and substitutable factors, M and L. The first question to be answered here is, What effects will a change in p_X have on M, L, and X? The answers are by no means simple or unambiguous, even in this case, where K is assumed constant. We have to work our way through to the answers gradually, and in order to do this, we must first simplify the problem even further. In this simplification and several other respects we follow quite closely work done by Ward in a contribution to which we have referred in the preceding chapter.[1]

The simplification resides in the assumption that even M, the substitutable intermediate input, is employed in a constant amount M_0. With this assumption our task becomes relatively easy, and what is more gratifying, the results turn out to be unambiguous. To carry out the necessary analysis, let us use one basic relation, and one basic diagram, both slight alterations of what is familiar from the preceding chapter. First, let us define a variable y as the income per laborer Y divided by $(p_X - np_N)$. Recalling further that the marginal value product-added of labor (used in the preceding chapter) is the product of the marginal physical product (MPP_L) and the factor $(p_X - np_N)$, we can write the following (triple) relation

$$y = X/L - (p_K K_0 + p_M M_0)/L(p_X - np_N) \overset{\text{"}e\text{"}}{=} MPP_L \qquad (1)$$

[1] See note 1, Chap. 2.

While the first equality stems from our definition, the second is true only in equilibrium—as indicated by "e"—and follows simply from the fact that dividing an equilibrium equation (i.e., $Y = MVPA_L$) by the same number on both sides will not alter the validity of the relation. With all prices and inputs except labor assumed constant, all three magnitudes entering relation (1) depend on L only. The variation of the relevant magnitudes with the level of employment is illustrated in Figure 3.2.1.

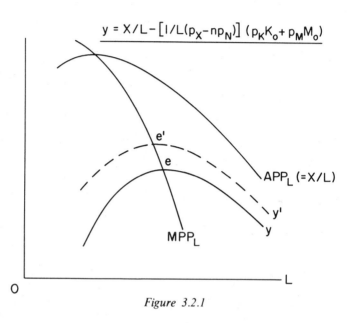

$$y = X/L - [I/L(p_X - np_N)] (p_K K_o + p_M M_o)$$

Figure 3.2.1

As postulated in relation (1), the initial equilibrium corresponding, among other parameters, to the price level p_X, is found at point e, where the MPP_L equals y. It will be observed from relation (1) that y is the difference of two variables, namely the average physical product of labor X/L, shown in the diagram, and another term, the capital and material cost per laborer deflated by ($p_X - np_N$), which appears in the diagram implicitly as the difference between APP_L and y.

Suppose now that the price of the product p_X increases to the level p'_X. Only the denominator of the second term just discussed will increase and thus the term itself will decline; that is, in terms of the diagram, the vertical distances between APP_L and y must decline. The y-contour shifts to the position y' indicated by a broken line and, as explained in the preceding chapter, the equilibrium (maximum) income per laborer again is attained (at e') where $MPP_L = y'$.

Three important conclusions follow for this simple case where p_X increases and where all substitutable inputs except labor are constant: (1) labor employment in the labor-managed firm will decline; (2) income per laborer will increase; (3) output must drop. This decline in output is measured by the area above the L-axis defined by e, e', and MPP_L. Conclusion (3) is perhaps the most important and also the most startling; it states that in the special case here considered the supply curve of the labor-managed firm must be backward-bending (negatively sloped).

Turning to the short-run situation where the management of the firm is permitted to adjust its use of the input M to the optimum level—rather than keeping that level constant—only the second of the above conclusions remains unchanged. Conclusions (1) and (3), as we will see presently, become only the "most likely outcomes." Moreover, it is also necessary to study the impact of an increase in p_X on the employment of M.

Leaving aside for the moment the question of how the supply of the product will be affected in the short run, let us first concern ourselves with the demand for the two variable and substitutable factors, L and M. Actually, the two demands are interconnected. Consider first the situation just discussed, and reflected in Figure 3.2.1 by the equilibrium e': labor employment has declined, while (by assumption) employment of M has remained unchanged. In that situation, how does the price of M, p_M compare with the marginal value product-added of M, $(p_X - np_N)MPP_M$? With an increase in p_X, obviously, $p_X - np_N$ must have increased, while MPP_M—M's marginal physical product—could have increased or declined with the decline in L, depending on whether L and M are substitute or complementary inputs. In the former case, the $MVPA_M$ would have increased on account of both p_X and MPP_M, and thus, with M variable, the employment of M would have increased. For a specific degree of complementarity between M and L the decline in MPP_M would just offset the increase in p_X and thus the $MVPA_M$ would remain unchanged. Consequently, the employment of M also would not have been altered. And finally, for a high degree of complementarity between L and M the decline in the marginal productivity of M could have been so strong as to make the $MVPA_M$ drop and, of course, employment of M would decline.

It is clear that these adjustments in employment of M would, in their turn, have a secondary impact on the employment of L, over and above the effects discussed. While not going into the detail of such secondary effects, let it be noted that they may either act to reinforce or to offset the initial decline in the employment of labor. While the total effect of a product price increase on labor employment still normally may be expected to be negative, it is no longer a necessary outcome. Actually —using results derived in the appendix to this chapter—it is now possible for the demand for labor to increase if M is "highly" complementary (with labor) and if the MPP_M is not very sensitive to changes in the employment of M.

From what has just been said about the employment of labor and the material M, it follows that the output of X may either increase or decline with an increase in the price of X. The latter alternative still may be taken as the more likely one—but this is an extremely crude and general statement. The factors that contribute to a negative supply elasticity of X are: (1) a low MPP_M, (2) a high MPP_L, (3) high average product of labor, (4) a steep MPP_M line, and (5) a flat MPP_L line.

It should also be recalled at this point that the employment of the nonsubstitutable material N is rigidly linked to the output of the firm and, consequently, whatever has been said about the direction of change in X also holds about the direction of change in N. On the other hand, because changes in the price of N are, in the context of the present analysis, equivalent to a change in p_X in the opposite direction, the above analysis actually also answers the question of how the price of N influences the level of output and the level of substitutable inputs. Note, for example, for the simple case where both K and M are constants, that a decline in p_N will increase y in relation (1) of this section, and thus, with a declining MPP_L, the employment of labor and hence the level of output must decline. This may be readily seen from Figure 3.2.1.

Let us now turn to the even more intricate problem of long-run adjustment of the equilibrium of the firm to changes in the product (and by implication, factor N-) price. Recalling our previous distinction of production functions, let us start here with the discussion of the problem in the context of the second kind (i.e., with constant returns to scale). As we have shown in the preceding chapter, in that case all short run equilibria are also long-run equilibria (in the sense that the long-run marginal conditions are fulfilled), the scale of operation of the firm is indeterminate in the long-run, and the long-run solution assumes the form of equilibrium factor and factor-product proportions.

The long-run effects of an increase in price can most easily be discussed in reference to Figures 2.5.1 and 2.5.2 of the preceding chapter. Because the latter diagram represents the determination of a long-run equilibrium of a firm operating under constant returns to scale, it is immediately apparent that an increase in price will increase the income per laborer Y and the output per laborer X/L. As for the two factor proportions K/L and M/L, only one very general and rather obvious conclusion can be stated at this stage of the argument: at least one of the two must increase as a result of the increase in the product price, as otherwise, indeed, X/L could not have gone up.

But to obtain a better insight into what will happen to the two factor proportions just stated, we can employ the already established fact that for the particular technology under study, the scale of operation is arbitrary. And thus, fixing the scale by postulating a given level of labor employment L_0, our problem is transformed into an equivalent and a good deal more familiar one: namely, what is the impact of an increase in product price on employment of the two variable factors in a competitive capitalist firm? Of course it is understood that the market prices of the two variable factors K and M are given constants.

It is immediately apparent that the increase in p_X will lead to an increase in employment of both M and K—and hence to a long-run equilibrium with higher K/L and M/L in the original problem—provided that neither K or L are inferior factors.[2] Using the mathematical analysis in the appendix to this chapter, two more rigorous statements can be derived regarding the impact of a price increase on the long-run capital-labor and M-labor proportions in a labor-managed firm operating under constant returns: (1) complementarity of K and M (as defined earlier in this section, that is, an increase in the MPP of one of the two factors with an increased input of the other) is a sufficient condition for both proportions to increase; and (2) substitutability of K and M is a necessary but not a sufficient condition for one of the two proportions to decline. Of course, it will be recalled that both proportions cannot decline in the situation considered here.

Before turning to the case involving technology of the first kind, a methodological remark is in order. The assimilation of the problem

[2]"Inferiority" here should be understood in the sense in which it is used in the theory of consumers' demand.

of a long-run equilibrium of a labor-managed firm using a homogeneous technology to that of a capitalist firm is a useful procedure that we will rely on at several occasions later in this study. In general terms the method (or procedure) can be described as follows: to study the effects of changing structural parameters on the long-run equilibrium of a labor-managed firm with a constant-returns technology employing three variable and substitutable factors including labor, it is perfectly correct to study such effects for a capitalist firm using the same technology, but with a constant amount of labor; the conclusions derived for the capitalist firm for output and nonlabor inputs then apply for the labor-managed firm's output-labor and input-labor coefficients in the long run.

When technology used by the firm is of the first kind it becomes more difficult to predict the effects of a change in the product price on the levels of output and factor employments. Actually, the exact relation between the effects sought and the data (parameters) defining the problem becomes so involved that a mathematical treatment is necessary; for this, the reader is referred to the appendix to this chapter. However, several useful observations of a more approximate nature can be made on the subject.

The most important derives from the fact—established in the preceding chapter—that with the technology of the first kind, the labor-managed firm must operate in the long run at the locus of maximum physical efficiency; that is, whatever the firm's input-proportions, it must be producing the maximum attainable physical output per unit of input. For example, if the firm uses only capital and labor, it can operate in the long run only at the locus EE in Figure 2.4.2; and an increase in the (competitive) product price, this can only move the input combination from one point on EE to another. If the locus of maximum efficiency has a negative slope (as in the diagram)—a situation that can be termed "normal" but is not necessary—and the firm uses only K and L, then an increase in the product price, leading to a relative increase of net income per laborer, will reduce the firm's demand for labor and increase its demand in the long run for capital; but of course the capital-labor ratio must always increase.

How these two offsetting effects will influence total output is a question to which a simple answer cannot be given. Actually, given the general nature of the locus of maximum physical efficiency, there is no strong a priori reason to expect that output should increase or decline:

as drawn in Figure 2.4.2, of course, the locus would yield an increase in output and thus an upward sloping long-run supply curve of the labor-managed firm. An extrapolation of what has just been shown for the two-factor case to a larger number of factors leads to similar conclusions: there is no unambiguous expectation for output to increase or to decline in the long run resulting from a price increase.

Perhaps one conjecture tilting the expectation in the direction of an increase in output (resulting from a higher product price) is in order before we conclude this section. As is suggested by the construction of Figure 2.4.2, and as is implied by the definition of the technology of the first kind, the locus of maximum physical efficiency must be single-valued with respect to a ray through the origin and thus the capital-labor ratio must increase with a higher product price; that is, the firm will move toward a relatively capital-intensive technology. But it can normally be expected that the more capital-intensive a technology becomes, the higher the firm's operation, and thus a positively sloped long-run supply curve appears as the more likely outcome. Innumerable real examples could be used to illustrate this point. Indeed, it is not an accident that we usually associate primitive labor-intensive industries with cottage industries, and modern automated industries with giant plants.

3.3: *Effects of a Change in p_M*

It is clear that a change in the price of the substitutable material M will disturb the equilibrium of the firm, whether considered in the short or long run. The purpose of this section is to study the effects of such a change. We can proceed with our discussion a good deal more quickly than we did in the preceding section. First of all, the present analysis is simpler because a change in p_M does not disturb the equilibrium marginal condition for capital (relation (4) in section 2.4) as did a change in p_X. Moreover, the analysis in this section is quite analogous to that of the preceding one and thus allows us to take several short cuts.

We can refer again to Figure 3.2.1 and consider—for the sake of exposition—the rather unrealistic case where both capital and M are fixed inputs. With only labor variable it immediately follows from the definition of y (also given in Figure 3.2.1) that under these conditions an increase in the price of M will unambiguously shift the y-contour downward, and thus employment of labor must increase. Consequently, the output of the firm will increase. What is even more obvious, the income per laborer will decline.[3]

Turning now to what is truly the short-run situation, with a variable input M and a constant capital stock, we can again, as in the preceding section, start from what we have just found. After the increase in employment and decline in MPP_L (see Figure 3.2.1 corresponding to the situation with constant M), the marginal equilibrium condition for M almost certainly will have been disturbed, the $MVPA_M$ having become either less or more than the price of M (of course we presuppose here that the M-market was in equilibrium before the change in p_M). Two forces must have been operative in producing such a disparity: the increase in p_M and the increase in employment of L which either increased the $MVPA_M$—if L and M were complementary—or reduced the $MVPA_M$—if L and M were substitute factors. If the latter were the case, both the increase in p_M and the decline in $MVPA_L$ would have cooperated in producing a decline in the employment of M. However, with what we may term the more likely case where M and L are complementary, the two forces would have been offsetting; but a decline in the employment of M would still be the normal outcome. Only with a very high degree of complementarity between labor and the material input M could an increase in the equilibrium use of the latter factor be expected in the short run.

With a little reflection it will be clear to the reader that an increase in equilibrium employment of labor is no longer a necessary outcome. However, it still remains by far the more likely one. Our mathematical results in the appendix indicate that independence or substitutability of L and M is a sufficient condition for an increase in the employment of L, while complementarity of the two factors certainly need not lead to a decline in L when the price of M increases.

From the fact that both L and M can increase or decline and that the "most likely" outcome is for the first to increase and for the second to decline, the broad conclusion is that output of the labor-managed firm may either increase or decline. Perhaps an even cruder conclusion is the expectation that, on balance, output will not change at all. A precise answer for each particular case again is obtainable from results presented in the mathematical appendix and a more precise specifica-

[3]The reader may find it interesting to establish for himself that these propositions and many others derived later can easily be verified using the cost analysis of section 2.5.

tion of the problem. One general conclusion derived from the mathematical analysis is that the likelihood for output to increase when p_M increases is the greater the more sensitive the MPP_M is to variations in M and the less sensitive the MPP_L to variations in L. But, upon reflection, this result becomes quite obvious even without mathematics.

Using our method of assimilation of a capitalist firm with constant labor employment (as explained in the preceding section), we can now turn briefly to the long-run comparative statics of a labor-managed firm using a technology of the second kind. The autonomous disturbance which we are considering is still a change in the price of M. It will also be recalled that in the situation at hand we are concerned only with the output-labor and input-labor ratios, the scale of operation being indeterminate.

For a (competitive) capitalist firm using a constant amount of L and variable amounts of substitutable K and M, we know that an increase in p_M will (1) reduce output, (2) reduce employment of M, and (3) reduce (increase) employment of K if K and M are complementary (substitutes). And consequently, with p_M increasing, the labor-managed firm will in the long run (1) reduce its output-labor ratio, (2) reduce employment of M per laborer, and (3) reduce or increase its equilibrium capital-labor ratio, depending on whether M and K are complementary or substitute. Moreover, it follows for the labor-managed firm that the income per laborer Y must decline. This is most easily seen by considering Figure 2.5.2 and realizing that both the MC and AC curves must shift upward with an increase in the price of M.

As for the case studied in the preceding section, the effects of a change in p_M in the long run are rather difficult to analyze in nonmathematical terms when the production function assumes the first form. However, a set of rigorous results is contained in the appendix. Here let it only be recalled again that the firm must always be operating on the locus of maximum physical efficiency before and after the change in the price of M. But as we have argued previously, there is no reason—except perhaps that connected with capital intensity, explained in concluding the preceding section—to expect that the locus should reveal a special correlation between the level of output and factor inputs. And consequently, whatever the effects of a change in p_M, there is no reason to expect that total output of the firm would increase or decline.

One thing that can be expected with certainty is that output per laborer will decline with an increase in the price of M. This is most easily seen by considering the analysis of section 5 of the preceding chapter, and in particular the discussion surrounding Figure 2.5.3. Note that in that diagram the AC^{**} contour must shift upward as a result of an increase in p_M—and so will the corresponding marginal curve (MC^{**}, not in the diagram). But with such a shift and a fixed price, of course, the output per laborer must decline. Another unambiguous conclusion to be derived from the same analysis is that income per laborer must decline.

But with a decline in Y (income per laborer) and, by assumption, an increase in p_M, further "normally expected" (rather than necessary) outcomes can be identified for the labor-managed firm (using technology of the first kind) in the long run: labor employment will tend to increase, and employment of M will tend to decline. As for the employment of capital, its adjustment will depend on the degree of complementarity or substitutability of capital with the other factors of production.

3.4: *Effects of a Change in p_K*

Because there exists a good deal of similarity between the analysis of a change in p_K and that of the preceding two sections, we may proceed rather rapidly. First, the reader will find it easy to verify—through one of the methods suggested previously—that in the case where only labor is variable, an increase in the price of capital must lead to an increase in employment and hence in output of the firm.

The first of the two conclusions—regarding employment of labor— will not be altered by the introduction of a variable and substitutable factor M into the production process (that is, in the context of a short-run analysis). Recalling the analysis in section 3 of the preceding chapter, and Figure 2.3.1, it will become clear that an increase in the price of capital cannot affect at all the position of the contour $MVPA^*_L$ because the latter depends only on the production function and the price of M, both of which remain unchanged. Therefore, observing that an increase in p_K must lower income per laborer, it immediately follows that employment in the labor-managed firm must rise with an increase in the cost at which it hires its capital.

Of course, employment of M in the short run can either increase or decline, the two alternatives depending on whether labor and M are complementary or substitutes in the production function. This being so, it is immediately apparent that a positive correlation between the price of capital and output must be present if M and labor are complementary; on the other hand, if the two factors are substitutes, a negative correlation is possible but not necessary. The absence of a negative relationship in the second case becomes more likely the higher the ratio L/M.

In the case of long-run equilibria and technology of the second kind, we shall once again employ our device of assimilating the labor-managed firm to a capitalist firm employing a constant number of laborers. The corresponding results for the labor-managed firm are that an increase in p_K will lead to a reduction in both the stock of capital per laborer and output per laborer, while use of M per laborer will increase or decline depending on the by now familiar conditions of complementarity between K and M.

Using the analytical tools of the last section of the preceding chapter, we can conclude that for technologies of the first kind, when the price of capital increases output and income per laborer must decline. Referring again, however, to the fact that the firm is bound to remain on the locus of maximum physical efficiency, there is no special reason to believe that the absolute level of output would increase or decline; except, of course, on grounds of the argument that the optimum scale of operation and relative capital-intensity are likely to be correlated. With respect to the absolute level of factor employment nothing definite can be said; however, the outcomes "normally" to be expected for an increase in p_K are a reduction in the employment of capital and an increase in the employment of labor. As for M, either can happen and the main conditions influencing the outcome are the degrees of substitutability among all factors.

3.5: *The Supply Elasticities and Joint Production*

Except in the appendix to Chapter 2, we have not dealt with production functions involving joint production. Instead, we have always assumed that a single product is produced in one productive process from several inputs. This has been done partly to keep the exposition simple, partly in order to conform to a conventional practice.

In the real world, of course, joint production is far more common than single-output activities. And what is of greater importance for our present analysis, the introduction of the assumption of joint production alters significantly some of the theoretical results obtained in the foregoing sections. Specifically, in activities producing jointly more than one product we will generally find product-supply elasticities in algebraic value far above those established in the earlier sections for single-product firms.

Although to a theoretically minded reader this conclusion may be

obvious at this stage of the argument, we should elaborate on it somewhat and provide a rigorous proof. Let us demonstrate the point by
means of the simplest case possible: namely, an activity producing
jointly two products, X_1 and X_2, from capital and labor, only the latter
of the two inputs being variable. The two products are selling in competitive markets at (constant) prices p_1 and p_2, and a fixed amount of
capital K_0 is hired at the constant unit cost p_K. As before, the operating
principle of the firm is to maximize the income per laborer Y.

The production function (involving the three variables L, X_1, and X_2)
is described by the concave[4] contours in Figure 3.5.1, contours further

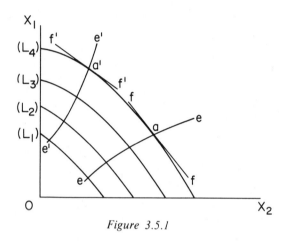

Figure 3.5.1

from the origin corresponding to higher (constant) inputs of labor
$L_i (L_1 < L_2 <$ etc.). It is clear that with a constant number of laborers,
say L_4, the firm will maximize the value of its product by producing on
the contour marked L_4, where the slope of the contour equals in
absolute value the ratio of product prices p_2/p_1. That ratio being
reflected in the slope of ff, the optimum point of production becomes point a on ff. Now letting L vary with product prices unchanged, we derive a whole locus of optimal product-mix points ee.
Clearly, to that locus we can make correspond loci of total, average,
and marginal value product of labor (note that at each point of ee both
product prices, both outputs, and the labor input are determinate). The
last of the three, MVP_L (corresponding to p_1 and p_2) is illustrated in
Figure 3.5.2. Similarly, for each point of ee the income per laborer can

---

[4]Note that the contours must be strictly concave at least in certain regions; otherwise
joint production in a competitive firm could hardly arise.

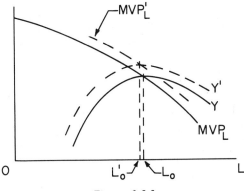

Figure 3.5.2

be computed (from AVP_L and $p_K K_0/L$) and the corresponding locus Y drawn. As before in the single-product situation, maximum Y—and thus the solution point—will be reached where $Y = MVP_L$.

Now suppose that p_1 increases to the level p_1'. Compared to the one-product situation studied in section 3.2, there will be two differences, both—but especially the first—leading to a higher supply elasticity of X_1. The first difference arises from the fact that with an increase of p_1 relative to p_2 the firm will tend to substitute in production X_1 for X_2, as indicated by the shift from a to a' in Figure 3.5.1. And thus on that account—without a change in employment—the supply of X_1 would have to increase and that of X_2 decline.

The second difference arises with respect to the employment effect. It will be recalled from our earlier discussion that with labor the only variable input, L had to decline with the increase of product price in a single-output firm. This is no longer a necessary outcome when more than one product is produced. As is indicated in Figure 3.5.1 the shift in the price of X_1 from p_1 to p_1' will generate a new "expansion-path" $e'e'$ and a new (corresponding) locus reflecting the income per laborer Y'. As is shown in Figure 3.5.2, the Y'-locus must be everywhere above Y and consequently the new equilibrium income per laborer must be higher than the old; however, the MVP locus (analogous to the $MVPA$ in section 3.2) may now shift by more or less than the Y-locus and thus employment may either decline or increase. The situation illustrated in the diagram, a slight decline in L, still remains the more likely outcome; but it is no longer a necessary one.

As we shall see over and over again in our subsequent chapters, the low supply elasticities emerging from the formal analysis of this chapter —the short-run elasticities in particular—are the main weak point of the decentralized labor-managed system. At the level of the firm, joint production—so frequently encountered in the real world—provides one important natural[5] escape from such a potential difficulty. Another escape, almost certainly even more significant in any realistic context, will be our subject in the next section.

3.6: *The Social Short- and Long-Run Adjustment*

As we have explained in Chapter 1, the main purpose of Part I is to develop the microeconomic theory of the labor-managed system, proceeding along similar lines and using concepts, categories, and tools similar to those of the conventional capitalist theory. Two such analytical categories are those of the short-run and the long-run equilibrium of the firm that we have used in this and the preceding chapters.

It should be clear that these two categories are tailored to, and have been developed in connection with, the analysis of a capitalist system where labor is a variable input, and where, consequently, no category involving a constant labor force is necessary. However, in a system where labor is not only the principal beneficiary but also the sole manager of the productive efforts of the enterprise, it makes a good deal of sense to speak and think in terms of categories involving a constant labor force (labor collective). For lack of better expressions I have termed these situations the "social short-run" and the "social long-run" respectively, the second halves of the expressions indicating whether the capital is or is not variable, while the adjective "social" is used to indicate that labor participation, for a time at least, is constant and not a variable of adjustment. Of course, except for the constancy just noted, the principle of maximization of income per laborer is maintained.

It is not our purpose here to elaborate on the rationale of the two new concepts; Part III will be a more appropriate place to do so. At present only a few technical observations are in order. The most basic —and almost trivial—is that with a constant participation, maximization of (net) income per laborer is identical to maximization of profit at any prescribed wage rate. Consequently, the social short- and long-run behavior is that of a capitalist firm which is bound to operate with a constant labor force. In particular, the social short- and long-run supply elasticities of labor-managed firms for a given product, whether they produce one or more goods, will be positive; the short-run variety,

[5]I am using here the term "natural" to distinguish from a number of possible policy actions to remedy the situation which will be discussed later on.

however, especially in cases of a single output firm, will be likely to be very low or zero because neither capital nor labor in that case can be adjusted to product-price variations.

Perhaps the most important observation is that in the case of technology of the second kind (i.e., constant returns to scale) the social long-run adjustment is fully consistent with the conventional long run. More specifically, a labor-managed firm undertaking a social long-run adjustment to a change in market conditions will also fulfill simultaneously the conditions of conventional long-run equilibrium; this is only a natural consequence of the indeterminacy of conventional long-run equilibrium of the labor-managed firm using a technology of the second kind, which is fulfilled as soon as the social long-run equilibrium condition is attained. In case of technology of the first kind, the firm must in the very long run eventually find itself at its locus of maximum physical efficiency; however, if such an adjustment calls for a reduction in the labor force, the social short run and/or long run is likely to prevail at first, and the subsequent adjustment to a conventional long-run equilibrium will proceed at the rate permitted by natural attrition.

In the real world, where as far as we know constant returns prevail[6] in a vast majority of firms for outputs in excess of a certain minimum scale of operation, the normal course of events subsequent to a market disturbance is that corresponding to a social long run (which also is consistent with the conventional long-run equilibrium). It is highly unlikely that in such real situations the conventional short-run adjustment would be operated by the labor-managed firm; note that if the firm did perform such an adjustment, this would imply an alteration of the working body for the sake of a short-run gain, in a situation where an even greater gain is in sight for each individual participant, after a somewhat longer period, without a change in the working body. Still remaining in a realistic situation, it can be inferred that negative supply elasticities will indeed be rare. Between the effects of joint production analyzed in the preceding section and the "social equilibrium behavior" suggested here in the context of the real world, we have more than enough justification for such a conclusion. Still another argument, based on the observation that in the short run input coefficients tend to be constant, will be developed in Chapter 7.

---

[6]Or at least a technology sufficiently near constant returns to be taken for such by the decision-makers, who of necessity operate under some degree of uncertainty and imperfect information.

APPENDIX

To keep the analysis realistic, yet operational, let us use as our point of departure the equilibrium structure summarized in relations (A.5'), (A.5'') and (A.6') of the appendix to the foregoing chapter. Dividing all three relations by $(p_X - np_N)$, recalling the definition of Y, and using the price notations

$$P_K = p_K/(p_X - np_N)$$

and

$$P_m = p_M/(p_X - np_N)$$

we obtain the following three equivalent relations

$$X_K - P_k = 0 \qquad (A.1)$$

$$X_M - P_m = 0 \qquad (A.2)$$

and

$$X_L - \frac{1}{L}(X - P_k K - P_m M) = 0 \qquad (A.3)$$

where capital subscripts are used to indicate first partial differentiation. The effects of autonomous changes in product or factor prices (as well as a technological change reflected in a decline in n) can now be calculated from the system (A.1) through (A.3). Differentiating with respect to the four price parameters and using double subscripts for second partial differentials we obtain (in an abridged form):

$$
\begin{bmatrix}
X_{KK} & X_{KM} & X_{KL} \\
\hline
X_{MK} & X_{MM} & X_{ML} \\
\hline
X_{LK} & X_{LM} & X_{LL}
\end{bmatrix}
\begin{bmatrix}
dK/d\ldots \\
\hline
dM/d\ldots \\
\hline
dL/d\ldots
\end{bmatrix}
=
$$

$$
=
\begin{array}{c|c|c|c}
\text{``}dp_X\text{''} & \text{``}dp_N\text{''} & \text{``}dp_M\text{''} & \text{``}dp_K\text{''} \\
\hline
\dfrac{-p_K}{(p_X - np_N)^2} & \dfrac{np_K}{(p_X - np_N)^2} & 0 & \dfrac{1}{p_X - np_N} \\
\hline
\dfrac{-p_M}{(p_X - np_N)^2} & \dfrac{np_M}{(p_X - np_N)^2} & \dfrac{L}{p_X - np_N} & 0 \\
\hline
\dfrac{Kp_X + MP_M}{L(p_X - np_N)^2} & \dfrac{-n(Kp_X + Mp_M)}{L(p_X - np_N)^2} & \dfrac{-M}{L(p_X - np_N)} & \dfrac{-K}{L(p_X - np_N)}
\end{array}
\qquad (A.4)
$$

The above expression actually represents four different systems of three linear equations in the three multipliers $dK/d\ldots$, $dM/d\ldots$ and $dL/d\ldots$, where for a specific "$d\ldots$" the right-hand side of the three equations is represented by the column-vector under the particular heading "$d\ldots$" For example, when the multipliers with respect to the price of capital are considered, the second equation of the system will read:

$$X_{MK}dK/dp_K + X_{MM}dM/dp_K + X_{ML}dL/dp_K = 0 \qquad (A.5)$$

From the system (A.4) the twelve different long-run multipliers are obtained by solving it by the conventional Cramer's method. Of course, these multipliers give only the changes in the equilibrium demand for the three substitutable factors. The corresponding change in supply of X is then obtained from

$$dX/d\ldots = X_K dK/d\ldots + X_M dM/d\ldots + X_L dL/d\ldots \qquad (A.6)$$

The short-run results are obtained by solving through the Cramer method a subsystem of two equations in $dM/d\ldots$ and $dL/d\ldots$, indicated by the outer broken line and obtained by dropping the first equation and variable of the system. A similar truncation—indicated by the inner broken line—leads to a one-variable equation in $dL/d\ldots$ yielding the unambiguous results discussed in the main text. Obviously, since X_{LL} is negative $dL/d\ldots$ in that situation will have a sign opposite to the sign of the bottom terms in the four column-vectors on the right-hand side of relations (A.4): that is, $(-)$, $(+)$, $(+)$, and $(+)$ for dp_X, dp_N, dp_M, and dp_K respectively. The same signs will be obtained for the corresponding $dX/d\ldots$'s from relation (A.6), recalling that, by definition, dK and dM both are zero.

The system (A.4) also lends itself to the analysis of long-run comparative statics of a labor-managed firm using capital and labor only. In that case one has only to substitute K for M in the above truncated short-run system in two equations and two variables, and omit M altogether. It must be remembered, however, that the long-run production function in L and K is likely to be different from the short-run production function in L and M.

Similarly, to study the long-run equilibrium changes for a firm using a linear-homogeneous production function through the assimilation of the labor-managed firm to a capitalist firm with a constant labor force, the system (A.4) can easily be adjusted. This adjustment consists of the elimination of the third row of both sides of the relation and of the third column in the coefficient matrix.

It would take an unwarranted amount of space to spell out all the particular solutions of the system (A.4) pertinent to the discussion of the main text of this chapter. Actually, the values of the different multipliers dZ_j/dp_i (where $j = 1,2,3$ and $i = 1,2,3,4$, and Z_j is the j'th variable among K, M, and L, and p_i the i'th parameter among p_X, p_N, p_M, and p_K) can easily be studied or obtained directly from the system (A.4), recalling that for stability the 3×3 coefficient determinant must be negative and its principal (2×2) minors positive,[7] and recalling the Cramer rule, namely,

$$dZ_j/dp_i = D^{ji}/D \qquad\qquad (A.7)$$

where D is the coefficient determinant (whether 3×3 in case of the "first-form" long-run analysis, or 2×2 in case of either the short-run analysis of the "second-form" long-run analysis) and where D^{ji} is a determinant derived from D by replacing D's j'th column by the vector under heading "dp_i" on the right hand side of (A.4). Of course, the j-numbering always remains 1, 2, 3 and based on the complete matrix D, so that even if the system is truncated and the coefficient matrix assumes the dimensions 2×2, the three variables retain their respective numerals. For example, in the context of the short-run analysis, the first column of the (truncated) coefficient matrix corresponds to $j = 2$.

[7]Note also that these signs are guaranteed by the usually postulated concavity of the production function in the vicinity of equilibrium.

4. Equilibrium Behavior of the Firm and Alternative Conditions of Labor Availability

4.1: *Introduction*

The careful reader of the preceding two chapters may have been startled by the virtual absence of specifications regarding labor supply in determining the equilibrium or comparative-static behavior of the labor-managed firm. An intuitive argument explaining this omission is that the competitive labor-managed firm really does not have a labor demand function (curve) as does its capitalist counterpart, but rather —as was shown previously—a demand point, containing both the equilibrium quantity of labor demanded and the corresponding remuneration. The supply of labor then can serve only as a check on the feasibility of a given demand point rather than as one half of the Marshallian market scissors.

Still relying on intuitive reasoning, the situation can further be clarified by analogy to the role of the supply of entrepreneurs to a capitalist firm. Such a supply is never introduced explicitly into the determination of equilibrium for a competitive capitalist firm, and yet the availability of entrepreneurship to the firm is a necessary condition of the firm's operation. In a similar manner availability of the "equilibrium" labor force at the income per laborer indicated by the demand point is a necessary condition of an equilibrium operation of the labor-managed firm. Accordingly in the preceding two chapters it was only necessary to stipulate that the equilibria—or supply and demand schedules —derived are consistent with labor availability. Possibly the most convenient and in many cases not unrealistic way to meet the availability postulate is to assume that unemployment of labor exists in the economy or industry being studied.

Even though, as we have seen, it is possible to study the equilibrium behavior of the labor-managed firm without ever mentioning the specific nature of the supply of labor, it would be unwise to omit a comprehensive consideration of that supply. Not only does such a consideration throw additional light on the theory of an individual labor-managed firm, but labor supply constitutes a vital link from the theory of the firm to broader frameworks, such as the theory of a competitive industry, price theory, and the theory of general equilibrium. All of these broader theories will be taken up in later chapters of Part I.

In the following section we will discuss various alternative forms of labor supply and their significance for the labor market in a competitive labor-managed economy. Of course we retain, here and in all of Part I, the assumption of a single and homogeneous type of labor. In section 4.3 we study the static equilibrium of the firm under alternative assumptions regarding the nature of the labor supply and of the firm. The remaining two sections are devoted to the analysis of the impact of labor supply on the labor-managed firm's product supply function (or functions) and demand for productive factors other than labor.

4.2: *The Labor-Supply Functions and Their Significance*

The immediate purpose of this section is to introduce several types of labor supply, to be used in the subsequent analysis of the equilibrium behavior of the firm. But as we have already noted the present discussion also has relevance for other and more general segments of the theory of competitive labor-managed systems.

In Figures 4.2.1-a through 4.2.1-d we find four different typical labor-supply functions. *From the point of view of the individuals or community generating these supplies* the meaning of the schedules is exactly the same as that of labor-supply curves in a capitalist economy: they indicate for a given level of employment L the wage (or income per laborer) that must be paid in order to secure that employment, or, vice versa, for a given wage the level of labor supply that will be forthcoming. But from the point of view of the labor market, as we will see presently, they generally will have a meaning different from that conventionally attached to them in the theory of a competitive market.

The supply function S_1, which is infinitely elastic at a very low level of labor remuneration—on the limit, it could have coincided with the horizontal axis—is typical of the supply relevant for a firm (or industry) in an economy with a labor surplus, that is, unemployment. In a less developed economy where such conditions may often prevail, the low level of S_1 may be thought of as a subsistence minimum. The situation illustrated by S_1, indicating a labor surplus of arbitrary size for all wage rates above S_1, is also the best illustration of the setting of the competitive firm as discussed in the preceding two chapters.

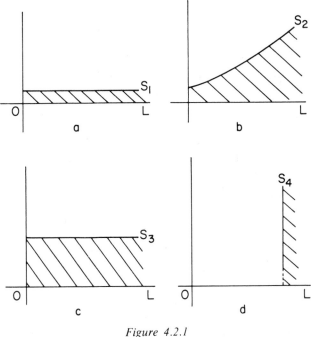

Figure 4.2.1

The labor supply S_2 having a positive and finite elasticity is probably the truest description of the *actual* labor environment faced by a large firm operating in a fully employed economy: to secure the services of larger numbers of laborers, higher labor returns must be paid in order to induce them to leave current jobs, in order to overcome the disutility of moving from one place to another, in order to cover costs of displacement, and so forth. Some readers might object that actually the supply function S_2, and for that matter S_4, does not belong in a discussion of the theory of a competitive firm because less than infinite elasticity of labor supply is bound to lead to a situation of monopsony. While this statement is correct for a capitalist firm it makes no sense in the context of the firm we are concerned with. Monopsonistic exploitation based on a less than infinitely elastic labor supply by a labor-managed firm practicing income sharing is impossible; the rationale of this—which will become evident in a more exact way in the subsequent sections—is that (1) the equilibrium labor income generally does not depend on the specific form of the labor-supply function, and (2) the employees and employers in our firm are one and the same group of people earning *all* the net income of the enterprise, that is, income which in a capitalist firm would fall into two parts, profits and the wage bill.

The infinitely elastic supply S_3 is the analogue of the labor supply faced by a perfectly competitive capitalist firm: At a given wage any amount of labor—of course within reasonable limits of conceivable operation of the firm—can be hired by the firm. The only difference between this locus and S_1 is the higher level of remuneration, presumably given by the general level of labor income in other firms and industries. Alternatively, the position of S_3 can be given by a government minimum-wage policy (of course, in situations where the true behavioral supply curve would find itself below S_3) or through a self-imposed statute of the enterprise, as is the case with firms in Yugoslavia.

The perfectly inelastic supply function S_4 does not have very much relevance for an individual competitive firm. We show it here for completeness because we will not return again to the specific discussion of labor supply. This supply curve best describes total national labor availability in the context of macroeconomic analysis where a single type of labor force is considered for the whole economy; as such it will be useful to us in Part II where we take up the macroeconomic theory of the labor-managed system.

We may now turn to the significance of all four schedules from the point of view of the market solution. It will be recalled that in a capitalist situation, under all circumstances—whether for a competitive or monopsonistic firm—the wage paid at a given employment level is that indicated by the supply schedule. In the determination of market solutions, the S-functions thus restrict the total number of conceivable solution points (some might call that number ∞^2) from the plane of each of our diagrams to a single line (a collection of only ∞^1 points). However, in the context of a labor-managed firm the role of the supply function is different: S merely divides the plane into two parts. The shaded areas represent a no-man's land where a market solution cannot arise, because at correspondingly low remuneration the labor supply will not be forthcoming. The clear areas, on the other hand, now take over the role played in the capitalist case exclusively by the S-contours: equilibrium market solutions for a firm can arise anywhere on S or in the clear area above and/or to the left of it. We now turn to a closer examination of such solutions.

4.3: *Equilibrium of the Firm and the Product Supply in the Light of Labor Availability*[1]

In this and the subsequent sections we seek to learn how the analysis of the preceding two chapters is affected when the assumption of un-limited labor availability is abandoned. To render our task as simple as possible, let us assume—contrary to the general setting of the preceding two chapters—that the firm whose behavior we are examining uses only two factors of production, labor and capital. In this section we will study the effects of labor-supply limitations on the equilibrium em-ployment and output of the firm, and also derive, as part of this analy-sis, the (conventional) short- and long-run supply functions for the firm's product.

Let us begin by considering the firm's behavior in the short run, that is, assuming that its capital stock is fixed. Therefore, labor is the only variable input. Given a fixed cost of capital, the constant stock of capi-tal K_0 and a product price p_X^0, we get the familiar relation $Y(p_X^0)$—see Chapter 2 and in particular relation (3) in section 2.3—showing the levels of income per laborer corresponding to various levels of employment L. The locus has been plotted in Figure 4.3.1-a. As we

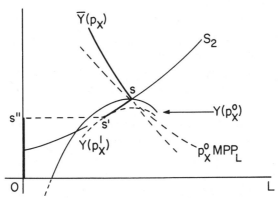

Figure 4.3.1-a

know from our previous discussion, the equilibrium of the firm is at-tained at point s where Y is at its maximum and where, at the same time, the income per laborer is equal to the value of the marginal physical product of labor, that is, where $Y(p_X^0) = p_X^0 MPP_L$.

---

[1]Some of the analysis developed here will also be found in E. Domar, "The Soviet Col-lective Farm," *American Economic Review*, September 1966.

It so happens that the equilibrium employment and level of remuneration corresponding to s is feasible because the point s lies exactly on the supply function S_2, also shown in the diagram. Point s in Figure 4.3.1-a thus represents an actual equilibrium of a labor-managed and income-per-laborer-maximizing firm operating in a labor market characterized by the supply function of labor S_2, selling in a perfectly competitive product market at the price p_X^0. From among the supplies of labor introduced in the preceding section we have chosen S_2 because the analysis developed for that schedule permits a very easy derivation of results for the other three supplies, S_1, S_3, and S_4.

We know from Chapter 3 that as the price of the product p_X increases above the level p_X^0, the points representing equilibrium employment and remuneration will move to the left and above point s in Figure 4.3.1-a. The line $\overline{Y}(p_X)$ is the locus of such points constructed on the assumption of alternative product prices exceeding p_X^0. It is clear that all such points represented by the heavily drawn line northwest of s are consistent with the availability of the labor force described by S_2. Actually, all the points with the exception of s involve, at the corresponding levels of labor remuneration, some degree of what we may refer to as involuntary unemployment.

As must be clear from the position of the supply of labor S_2 in Figure 4.3.1-a, matters become somewhat more complicated when the market price of the product drops below the level p_X^0. As we know from our earlier discussion, were it not for the supply function, the equilibrium levels of employment and remuneration would be moving downward from s along the dashed extension of $\overline{Y}(p_X)$. Such equilibrium points now are impossible because they would imply levels of employment and remuneration inconsistent with S_2. However, it is immediately apparent that, for prices only slightly below p_X^0, nonzero outputs and employment levels are possible along S_2 to the left and below s in the diagram. The labor-managed firm will maximize its income per laborer by moving along its $Y(p_X)$ line (with p_X below but not too different from p_X^0) as far to the right as it can, given S_2; and therefore the equilibrium point will be on S_2. As p_X assumes smaller and smaller values, eventually the contour indicating the income per laborer will become tangential to S_2. This happens for p_X^1 at point s' in Figure 4.3.1-a. All points between s and s' along S_2 are thus possible solutions or equilibria of this labor-managed firm. It follows from the nature of the construction that these equilibria involve (1) full employment of labor (given the supply function), (2) income per laborer and employment lower than the unconstrained optimum of the firm, and (3) remuneration (Y) less than the marginal value product of labor (recall that the negatively sloped marginal product curve passes through the maximum point of the Y-loci).

Now for product prices less than p_X^1 the income-per-laborer line and supply function do not meet at all, which means that there is no level of employment with the remuneration which it could earn and consequently the firm under consideration cannot operate any longer. Point s' in Figure 4.3.1-a—and as we shall see presently, also point s' in Figure 4.3.1-b—is therefore the *short-run* shutdown point.

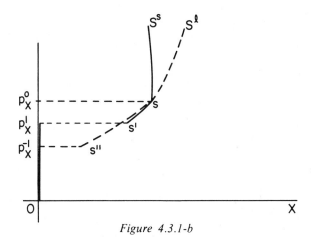

Figure 4.3.1-b

We can now translate what has been done thus far into the product-market plane shown in Figure 4.3.1-b. The heavily drawn contour S^s is the short-run supply curve of our labor-managed firm facing a labor-supply function S_2. In its upper part, corresponding to $\overline{Y}(p_X)$ above s in Figure 4.3.1-a, it is the old supply curve familiar to us from the preceding chapter; of course here we have simplified the problem by postulating labor to be the only variable factor, and thus with a negatively sloped $\overline{Y}$ we *must* have a negatively sloped corresponding segment of S^s. At the critical price p_X^0, S^s suddenly changes direction and becomes positively sloped, reflecting the declining equilibrium inputs of the only variable factor. As indicated already, at s' in Figure 4.3.1-b, for price p_X^1 output drops to zero and thus the corresponding remainder of the supply curve S^s coincides with the vertical axis.

Still remaining within the realm of short-run analysis, it is now easy to consider the other three situations, as outlined in the preceding section, corresponding to labor-supply functions S_1, S_3, and S_4. Since the only difference between the first and third labor supply is the level of wages (or income per laborer) from the point of our present analysis the two cases are equivalent. It is immediately apparent by inspecting Figure 4.3.1-a that were the supply curve in the vicinity of s horizontal, the point s'—defined as the point where $Y(p_x)$ is tangential to the labor supply curve—would have to coincide with the point s, defined as the point where $Y(p_x)$ reaches the labor-supply curve. Thus we can conclude that the segment ss' in both the wage-labor plane and in the price-output plane shrinks to a single point when the labor-supply function is infinitely elastic. This is shown by the solid-line contour S^s in Figure 4.3.2; measured from 0 we have the situation corresponding to

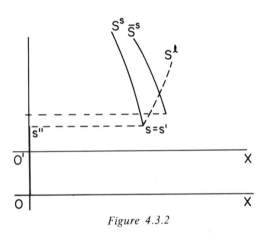

Figure 4.3.2

the labor supply S_3 and from $0'$ that corresponding to the "subsistence-wage" supply function S_1.

It can be said that just the opposite happens when the labor-supply curve—such as S_4 of the preceding section—is zero-elastic. Imagining a vertical supply-line passing through s in Figure 4.3.1-a, it is immediately apparent that when the price of the product drops below p_x^0 (the price at which labor employment first becomes equal to the fixed supply size), the firm remains in operation, with employment constant at the level given by the zero-elastic supply function of labor, but with reduced income per laborer. The critical tangency between the supply of labor and the contour showing the income per laborer can never occur;

however, there will be some price p_X^1 low enough to reduce the income per laborer at the constant level of labor supply to zero. Of course, with all factor inputs constant within the range ss' the supply of X must be vertical for the range of prices between p_X^1 and p_X^0. This is shown by the solid contour S^s in Figure 4.3.3. As before, all the equilibria cor-

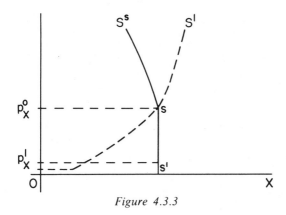

Figure 4.3.3

responding to points falling within the stretch ss' have the properties of full employment and income per laborer lower than the marginal value product (which would have been earned with the unconstrained maximum).

This completes our discussion of the short-run case, and we are ready to turn to the somewhat more complicated situation of long-run equilibrium and long-run supply of the labor-managed firm. We retain the assumption of only two factors, but the capital stock is now permitted to vary, adjusting optimally to product and capital prices and to income per laborer. As with the short-run case, the same four supply functions of labor will be considered.

Let us first recall the distinction between technologies of the first and second kind introduced in Chapter 2. The first involves a production function subject to increasing total returns (along a ray through the origin) for low levels of output and to diminishing total returns for high levels of output, with a dividing line (see *EE* in Figure 2.4.1) where the production function is "instantaneously" linear homogeneous or subject to constant returns to scale. The second kind simply refers to a production function everywhere subject to constant returns to scale. We will first consider the long-run equilibrium and supply of a labor-managed firm producing according to the technology of the first kind.

We know from our previous analysis that in the case where no labor-supply limitations are present, the long-run equilibrium must be on the locus of maximum physical efficiency—that is, the limiting locus EE in Figure 2.4.1, where the production function is subject to constant returns. With a given product price and price of capital (in our two-factor situation) a point on the locus of maximum physical efficiency is uniquely determined and to it also uniquely corresponds the long-run equilibrium levels of output and income per laborer. If the product price is reduced (with unchanged price of capital) the equilibrium point will travel along the locus of maximum physical efficiency in the direction of lower capital-labor ratios, and the level of supply of output may increase or decline. All this is shown in the preceding chapter where we also have argued that there may be some presumption for a lower long-run equilibrium output with lower product prices. It is also evident that with unchanged prices of capital and declining product price the equilibrium income per laborer will be declining.

Now consider the simplest situation where the supply of labor is infinitely elastic (see S_1 or S_3 in the preceding section). For some product price low enough, the equilibrium income per laborer will drop to the level given by the supply function of labor. For labor incomes and prices above that critical value the firm will have its "unconstrained" long-run supply function—as developed in Chapter 3—while for prices and incomes lower than the critical value the firm will have to cease to operate. This critical price is indicated by point s'' in Figure 4.3.2, and the corresponding long-run supply curve of the labor-managed firm, with labor supplies S_1 or S_3, is shown by the broken line S^1 and the segment of the vertical axis below s'.

Let it be noted now that the short-run supply function also shown in Figure 4.3.2 is the one corresponding to the same capital price as the long-run locus and to the constant level of capital stock reached on the locus of maximum physical efficiency when the income per laborer reaches the critical level given by the supply function of labor. It will also be recalled from the preceding chapter that S^s must have an elasticity in algebraic value less than that of S^1. Any short-run supply function for capital stock other than that underlying S^s in the diagram, such as $\bar{S}^s$, must have its shutdown point (price) above the shutdown point $s = s'$. As the reader may verify through a more careful analysis, this is the consequence of the fact that with a given capital cost and labor remuneration (the latter given by the supply function of labor) the lowest conceivable price is to be found on the locus of maximum physical efficiency, and of the fact that all points of the long-run supply function S^1 correspond to the locus of maximum physical efficiency, while S^s has only one point—that of intersection with S^1—fulfilling the maximum-efficiency condition.

Let us now turn to the other extreme situation where the supply of labor is perfectly inelastic, that is S_4 of the preceding section. With comparatively high product prices and a fixed price of capital the firm will be operating in the long run on the locus of maximum physical efficiency using relatively little labor—well below the limit imposed by S_4 —and a good deal of capital. As the product price is reduced, with declining or increasing output, more labor will be used as a general rule. For some level of prices low enough, the fixed labor supply will be exhausted. Calling K_0 the capital stock corresponding to that instance, the short-run supply S^s in Figure 4.3.3 is that based on K_0. For prices lower than p_X^0 in the diagram, labor supply cannot increase further and therefore, since capital stock cannot vary in the short run, S^s becomes vertical below s.

The unconstrained long-run supply function of our firm is again—similar to that in Figure 4.3.2—the broken line S^1 above s in Figure 4.3.3. But suppose now that price declines below p_X^0. It is clear that the firm interested in the maximization of income per laborer will not keep its capital stock unchanged. With income per laborer lower than that at point s in Figure 4.3.3, remaining at point s would clearly involve paying (the fixed price) to capital in excess of its marginal value product; and thus the employment of capital must be reduced to re-establish equilibrium at the fixed level of labor supply and utilization given by S_4 (of the preceding section). But this must lead to a reduced level of output for prices below p_X^0, as indicated by the broken line in Figure 4.3.3.

As in the case of short-run supply, the situation involving a positively sloped supply curve of labor is also the most complicated when we analyze the long-run product supply. Fortunately, we can learn a good deal from both the short-run analysis and the two extreme cases of long-run supply just examined. The long-run supply curve of X in question is illustrated in Figure 4.3.1-b as the broken contour passing through s, s'', and, for prices below the level corresponding to s'', collapsing into the vertical axis. As in our preceding analysis the point s which the short- and long-run schedules have in common presupposes that the capital stock underlying S^s is also the long-run equilibrium capital stock of the firm corresponding to p_X^0, the prescribed price of capital, and employment and income per laborer consistent with the labor-supply curve. We notice that at all points where the short-run supply is positive, the elasticity of S^s is less in algebraic value than that of S^1. While this fact is known to us for the unconstrained region above s, its rigorous proof for the region below s is fairly involved, and is left to the ingenuity of the reader. Only an intuitive argument is offered here: we have shown that in the case of a zero-elastic supply function of labor—see Figure 4.3.3—the elasticity of S^s below s is less than that of S^1. Now suppose that the elasticity of supply of labor turns from zero to very-small positive. This small change will increase the elasticities of both S^s and S^1 below s a little bit, but from the continuous nature of the situation it must follow that the comparative size of the two elasticities will not be reversed.

Another interesting characteristic of S^1 is that its shutdown point s'' lies below the shutdown point of S^s, s'. This must be so for the following reason:[2] consider the contour $Y(p_X^1)$ in Figure 4.3.1-a; we know from our discussion of the preceding chapter that it must be tangential to and never above another contour Y^* (not in the diagram) which reflects for p_X^1 and the given price of capital the maximum levels of income per laborer (for each prescribed level of employment) on the assumption that at all times the stock of capital is adjusted optimally. From the envelope property just stated it follows that if Y^* were drawn into Figure 4.3.1-a, it would intersect S_2—except in one case out of infinity where it would be tangential at s'—and consequently a price lower than p_X^1 would be consistent with S_2 and nonzero supply of product X; observe that reduction in the product price below p_X^1 would shift the (hypothetical) contour Y^* downward, until for some price $p_X^{-1} Y^*$ itself would become tangential to S_2. Beyond that point, as shown in Figure 4.3.1-b, the long-run supply would drop to zero.

Let us now turn to the analysis of equilibrium and product supply of the labor-managed firm using a technology of the second kind, that is, constant returns to scale. This can be done quickly because regarding the short run the technology of the second kind does not add much to the discussion of the technology of the first kind, and because in the context of the long run we will have to return to the subject extensively in the following chapter.

_____

[2]The argument presented here will also indicate to the reader the way in which the long-run supply function of X is constructed when labor supply assumes the form of S_2.

It will be recalled from our discussion in Chapters 2 and 3 that a competitive labor-managed firm maximizing income per laborer with unconstrained labor availability, and using a technology subject to constant returns to scale, does not have a definite long-run equilibrium. For a given price of the product and all nonlabor inputs, it has only a set of equilibrium factor proportions and factor-output proportions. The scale of operation of the firm is arbitrary and must be determined from other than the customary data (that is, factor and product prices and specification of the production function). It will also be recalled that the reason behind this indeterminacy of long-run equilibrium is the fact that the income per laborer for a prescribed set of factor-output coefficients is a constant, and thus, for a manager who desires to maximize the income per laborer, all scales of operation are equally desirable.

Now it should be clear that whenever the supply of labor has finite elasticity—contrary to the assumption of unlimited labor availability made in the preceding two chapters—this will establish an upper bound on the outputs that the competitive firm using a technology of second kind can attain in the long run. Letting Y_0^* stand for the income per laborer corresponding to the equilibrium set of factor-output coefficients, a horizontal line drawn at the level Y_0^* in Figure 4.2.1-b will immediately establish the maximum attainable level of employment corresponding to a supply of labor of the type S_2; for the supply function S_4 the problem is even simpler, labor remuneration not being a relevant factor of labor availability. What must be stressed here is that the level of employment thus determined *does not* lead to the equilibrium scale of operation of the firm, *but only* to the maximum possible scale of operation. For this to be necessarily the equilibrium, other behavioral postulates besides maximization of income per laborer, such as maximization of employment (elimination of involuntary unemployment) in the region or community described by the labor-supply function, or a positive value attached to "bigness" (even if size does not increase the income per laborer) would have to be assumed. Alternatively, as we will see in the following chapter, the full-employment solution, which here is only a *maximum*, may become the *necessary* equilibrium of a firm or of a group of firms representing a competitive industry with no barriers to entry into the industry.

It should go without saying that the analysis presented here on somewhat simplified assumptions regarding the number of products and productive factors can easily be generalized. Furthermore, such a generalization does not lead to anything substantially new or different from our previous findings. For example, from the analysis of the preceding two chapters we know that existence of joint products generally increases the algebraic value of the supply elasticity of a single product; this still holds here for the "labor-unconstrained" segment of the supply curve. However, if and when for a sufficiently low price of the product (one among the joint products) the income per laborer drops at the equilibrium level of employment to the level indicated by the labor-supply function, further reduction in the price will either cause a shutdown of the enterprise—this will happen with labor-supply functions S_1 and S_3—or alter the unconstrained supply curve of the product to one which is more elastic. What has just been said is valid in both the short- and the long-run contexts.

4.4: *The Labor-Supply Constraint and the Firm's Behavior with Respect to Changing Factor Prices*

It should not be difficult to understand that the labor-supply constraint plays a role equally important in the determination of the firm's responses to changes in the factor-market conditions as it does in the determination of the firm's supply curve. Actually, the analysis of the two aspects of theory of the labor-managed firm has a good deal in common. We therefore can proceed fairly rapidly with the subject matter of this section, relying on what has been done in the preceding two chapters and in the foregoing sections of this chapter.

For any perfectly competitive firm the only relevant information regarding the state of a factor market is the price ruling in that market. Consequently, our task is to relate the level of and variations in the factor price—to be referred to hereafter as p_f—to the behavior of a labor-managed firm whose labor availability is limited through a labor-supply function of one of the types presented in section 2. As in the preceding section, most of the time we will be thinking of the production function as one involving only two inputs, capital and labor, and consequently capital will be the only factor actually being hired at a fixed competitive price (in the conventional sense), and p_f will ordinarily refer to the price of capital.

What we want to present in this section is summarized diagrammatically in Figures 4.4.1-a, b, and c. In all three diagrams we find the price of the productive factor p_f on the vertical axis, and that price is

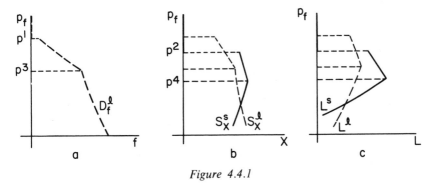

Figure 4.4.1

related in the figures a, b, and c to the demand for the factor f, to the supply of the product X, and to employment L respectively. All this is done in the context of both short- and long-run analysis, and—in the way to be better explained presently—for the four types of supply of labor previously discussed. Whereas for the short run—depicted in terms of solid contours in the diagrams—the analysis is pertinent for both technologies of the first and of the second kinds, in the long run, for reasons explained already in the preceding section, it pertains solely to the technology of the first kind (subject to increasing and then to diminishing returns).

It is clear that when the factor f is interpreted to be capital, there is no short-run demand function for that factor as the stock of capital is, *ex hypothesi*, constant and unalterable by the firm. Therefore, the only meaningful context regarding the demand for the capital factor is that of the long run. As indicated by the broken line of Figure 4.4.1-a, the conventional result of declining demand with increasing factor price is obtained throughout. For the segment of the demand function D_f^l below p^3, which corresponds to the (unconstrained) situation of involuntary labor unemployment, the negative slope is only the most likely and not an absolutely necessary outcome. It is obvious that as we keep increasing p_f from a very low level, the residual income per laborer must be gradually declining. If the labor supply is given by either of the infinitely elastic functions S_1 or S_3, when the (constant) level of income per laborer given by these functions is reached, the long-run demand for capital (here referred to as f) drops suddenly to zero and the firm's output X and employment L vanishes; as would be the case in Figure 4.4.1-b and c for the price p^3. If, however, the supply of labor has a finite elasticity—as is the case for S_2 and S_4 from section

4.2—the operation of the firm may continue even after full employment of labor has been reached for a price such as p^3. The rationale for
this is the same as that developed in detail in the preceding section (see
in particular Figures 4.3.1-a and b and the accompanying discussion) in
explaining the kink in the short- and long-run supply functions of X
with a supply of labor S_2. If such a continuation of the firm's operation takes place for prices p_f above p^3, clearly, employment in the labor
market can no longer increase; as is shown in Figure 4.4.1-c for S, employment and income per laborer will be declining with increasing p_f.
Of course, with a perfectly inelastic supply of labor, employment will
remain unchanged. In both situations, however, the elasticity of demand for f for prices above p^3 must not be less than it was below p^3
but must also be negative. With a declining long-run employment L^1,
clearly, output must drop with prices increasing above p^3 when there
are no other productive factors; this is shown in Figure 4.4.1-b. If other
factors are present—as may be the case when f is not capital and capital is among the "other" factors—the negative slope of D_f^1 in all its
ranges and of S_X^1 for prices above p^3 still remains by far the most likely
outcome. Of course as the factor price p_f reaches higher and higher
levels, a price p^1 will be reached when there will not be an income per
laborer high enough for any level of employment to guarantee the
willingness of that many laborers to join the firm. The situation depicted by s' in Figure 4.3.1-a is relevant here; it only has to be realized
that the factor shifting the Y-contour now is the price of a productive
factor, rather than the price of the product p_X. For factor prices higher
than p^1, the demand for f, the supply of X, and the employment L will
all drop to zero.

Referring again to f as capital, the short run is characterized by a
situation in which the utilization of f is fixed. The question now arises
as to how the product supply of the labor-managed firm and its labor
employment will vary with changing p_f when either of the additional
labor constraints S_1, S_2, S_3, or S_4 is imposed. The typical outcomes
are illustrated by the solid contours S_X^s and L^s in Figures 4.4.1-b and c
respectively. While the reader may want to study these cases in greater
detail, we will limit ourselves to a few general remarks. First we notice
that the shutdown price p^2 corresponding to the short run is below p^1,
the long-run shutdown price. This relation, the inverse of what we
found for analogous product prices, stems—as it did before—from the
greater efficiency of long-run over short-run adjustment; recall that in

the latter capital is not permitted to assume the level which would equalize its marginal value product and price.

We know already that with an increase in p_f and a corresponding decline in the income per laborer, with f fixed, the utilization of labor must increase in the labor-managed firm provided that this is consistent with labor-supply conditions. Once the price of f—i.e., of capital, as it is interpreted here—reaches a level where the income per laborer falls below an infinitely elastic supply of labor, the firm must cease operation. This happens, as indicated in the diagrams, at $p_f = p^4$. If the supply of labor is less than infinitely elastic, again, as in the long-run situation, full-employment operation of the firm is consistent with increasing p_f beyond the price—p^4 in the diagram—for which the income per laborer first reaches the supply function of labor. If the supply of labor has a finite but not zero elasticity, increases in p_f beyond p^4 must lead to lower incomes per laborer; this in turn generates reductions in employment, and because labor is the only variable input, reductions in the supply of X, as shown in Figures 4.4.1-b and c. Were the supply of labor zero-elastic, both S_X^s and L^s would become zero-elastic beyond p^4.

5. Theory of a Competitive Industry and Price Determination

5.1: *Introduction*

By now we have said enough about the competitive labor-managed firm to be able to start aggregating a large number of such firms to study the behavior of a competitive industry producing the same, or a set of identical, products. Some parts of this discussion will be closely related to what has been done before, and we will carry it out as briefly as possible to avoid redundance or triviality. Other parts—especially when the phenomenon of free entry into and exit from the industry is introduced—constitute a definite step forward on our road toward a complete theoretical description and explanation of the decentralized labor-managed economy.

It should be obvious that when by assumption firms are neither permitted to enter nor leave the industry, the problem of industry equilibrium and industry reaction to changing demand conditions becomes a very simple one. Only an aggregation of the behavior of individual firms, as studied previously, is necessary. This will be our task in the subsequent section. The one somewhat new and perhaps more interesting element of that section is that in it we are able to consider also the other side of the product market—that is, demand—and thus derive the Marshallian (partial) equilibrium price, and study the properties of the equilibrium.

Free entry into and exit from the industry is assumed in sections 5.3, 5.4, and 5.5. As the reader may visualize, the entire analysis of the preceding chapter bearing on labor-supply limitations is of paramount importance here. Indeed, it is the availability of labor to the competitive industry composed of labor-managed firms that takes over the role played in a capitalist industry by the positive-profit signal for entry. The main aim of sections 5.3 through 5.5 is the derivation of long-run industry supply functions for products and demand functions for factors of production respectively. These results again, as in section 5.2, are coupled with data on product-demand conditions in an analysis of equilibrium price determination for the industry.

Primarily in preparation for a formal general-equilibrium analysis of the decentralized labor-managed system, a special case—that involving identical technologies throughout the industry—is considered in detail in section 5.4. This is done not only to derive the corresponding special results regarding such an industry, but also to simplify the analysis. Among other instances, use is made of this simplification in section 5.5.

The last section of the chapter is devoted to considerations of efficiency of productive resource allocation within the industry. Two of the specific purposes of the analysis are the comparison—in theory, of course—of the performance of decentralized labor-managed industries against an absolute standard of Pareto-optimality and against the performance of capitalist industries. Contrary to some similar comparisons made earlier—in particular regarding monopolistic tendencies in the two systems—the capitalist case may, under some conditions, turn out to be superior in the present instance. Still another purpose is to prepare the ground for the derivation of policy instruments which would prevent the possible inefficiency just referred to; of course, the policy question itself will be taken up only in Part IV. Even at this point it should be stressed that the efficiency comparison undertaken in this chapter alludes to only one aspect of the two industries' operation and is not intended to have a general validity. Actually, a general appraisal of the efficiency of the system will be possible only at the end of the study, once all major aspects have been considered.

5.2: *Industry Supply and Market Equilibria with Restricted Entry into and No Exit from the Industry*

Like any other competitive industry, the competitive industry of labor-managed firms has a supply function, or a supply curve, showing how much of the product will be supplied at various prices. Again it is an aggregation of the supplies by individual firms forming the industry; graphically, this would correspond to a horizontal addition of supply schedules in a diagram where the quantity supplied is measured along the horizontal axis.

By "restricted entry" and "no exit" we understand that the industry is at all times composed of the same number of firms producing a non-zero output. If at all realistic, such a situation would be likely to prevail only in the short run. Our main reason for discussing this special case first is to distinguish it from the general case where the numbers in the industry can change and where significant new elements of analysis must be introduced. For sake of brevity, we restrict ourselves here to the case of excess labor availability, that is, we envisage the labor-managed firm as it was discussed in Chapters 2 and 3. The existence of an "active" labor constraint will play an important role in the later sections of this chapter.

With these observations in mind, and assuming at first (perhaps quite unrealistically) a single-product industry, we can now aggregate the long-run supply functions for all the firms of the industry and get the long-run competitive supply curve S^1 in Figure 5.2.1. The schedule's

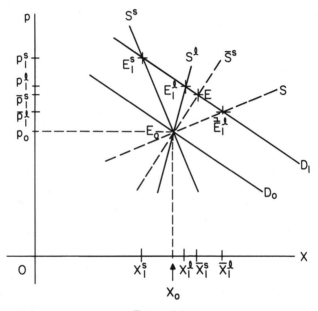

Figure 5.2.1

positive elasticity reflects the previously conjectured positive correlation between the optimum physical scale of operation of the firms in the industry (or at least of the majority of firms, noting that the technologies need not be identical) on the one hand and the capital-labor ratio on the other. Supposing further that D_0 is the aggregate competitive demand for product X, p_0 and X_0 are the long-run equilibrium price and quantity respectively. Because there is no reason to expect that the clearing operation of a market in our decentralized labor-managed economy should be any different from that in any other competitive market—that is, for $S > D$ prices will be competitively bid down, and vice versa—the equilibrium is a stable one. Even in the long-run situation considered thus far, however, there is no absolute guarantee that this would have to be so. Indeed, we know that S^1 can be negatively sloped; and thus, with the usual downward sloping demand curve, it is possible to have an excess supply for prices below p_0 and consequently a process of competitive bidding leading away from equilibrium. The short-run elasticity of supply being less in algebraic value than the long-run, it is equally clear that in the short run the possibility of market instability is comparatively stronger.

But even in the absence of explosively unstable markets, it is not difficult to realize that the supply conditions in a decentralized and labor-managed industry *without entry* and *exit* is likely to lead to wider price fluctuations from changing market conditions than would, *ceteris paribus*, its capitalist equivalent. It is for this reason, more than for the reason of an actual danger of market instability, that short-run price controls or other measures designed to render prices more "sticky" may be more justifiable in the decentralized labor-managed economy than in the capitalist economy. Using results derived here and subsequently, we will also argue later in Part IV that the comparative tendency toward wider price variation just identified provides the labor-managed system with a rationale for economic forecasting, planning, and deliberate policies tending to increase the supply elasticities.

Of course it must be emphasized that the results presented thus far are in a sense most unfavorable from the point of view of market stability. We know that S^s must be negatively sloped, as drawn, only if X is the only product of the industry and labor the only variable input; existence of other inputs, and *especially* of other outputs, is liable to increase the supply elasticities. The broken supply lines marked by $\bar{S}^s$ and $\bar{S}^1$ in Figure 5.2.1 are intended to illustrate the case of joint products, an occurrence which certainly is by far more frequently encountered on the assumption that the prices of products other than X are constant. If variations in demand and hence price variations for all joint products are strongly correlated, then again the individual supply functions $\bar{S}$ would become less elastic.

Of perhaps greater importance is the supply response which we have earlier identified as the social short run and the social long run. The two corresponding supply functions can also be described by the broken contours; we recall the important fact that the positive slopes of these contours become a necessary outcome. Accordingly, save for the most awkward and virtually impossible case of a positive demand elasticity, the market stability in the "social" case (as defined at the end of Chapter 3) is guaranteed. In practice, this is a very important result, because, as we have argued previously, the "social" adjustment is most likely to prevail in the real world.

Once we have made our step from abstract theory to conditions likely to prevail in the real world, it also ought to be noted that what we have termed the possibility of instability (of a market of a fixed number of labor-managed firms producing a single output) is the occurrence of unstable intersections of supply and demand schedules, and not actual equilibria at such intersections. Because any slightest disturbance would be bound to displace the equilibrium from an unstable position, the price and the volume sold have to settle soon at a stable equilibrium to one side or the other of the unstable one. Even in the "forced" situation of a constant number of firms in the industry, it can be expected that such "bordering" equilibria would exist—and they certainly must exist once free entry and exit are permitted.

More generally, it ought to be recalled that the analysis presented thus far involves a constant number of firms, adjustments to market variations through entry into or exit from the industry not being permitted *ex hypothesi*; again, this is not a realistic description, especially in the long run. Finally, the assumption made earlier in this section that members of the industry operate in a labor environment of excess availability need not necessarily be realized. There may be full employment, and with firms located in different locations it is possible that each firm draws on a local supply of labor, increased employment being securable only at higher incomes per laborer. As we know from the preceding chapter, if such is the case, the supply of X necessarily assumes a positive elasticity within its range corresponding to full employment (of labor). All in all, even if market instability cannot be ruled out on theoretical grounds, it is hardly something that a labor-managed economy ought to worry about in practice.

We may now turn briefly to the question of how variations in demand affect the market solutions for our industry without entry or exit. Assuming that a total demand for a product will generally have a finite elasticity, it is apparent from Figure 5.2.1 that with a stable market situation the price will increase more in the short run from an increased demand (D_1) than it will in the long run. This result is as necessary for our labor-managed industry as it is for its capitalist cousin. The novel, and in fact somewhat irritating, result is that in the short run the amount supplied can decline if there are no alternative outputs; if labor is the only variable input this is, as we know, a necessary outcome. On the other hand, existence of joint products, especially those which have a high elasticity of substitution with X, are liable to prevent the unorthodox result. Again, as indicated by equilibria $\bar{E}_1^s$ and $\bar{E}_1^l$ and the corresponding levels of prices and sales, the rectification of the unorthodox outcome through joint production is more pronounced in the long run—that is, when the capital stock is permitted to adjust optimally—than it is in the short run. The same conclusions can be drawn for the *social* short- and long-run adjustments, probably the most likely to occur in the real world.

5.3: *Industry Supply and Market Equilibrium with Free Entry and Exit*

The principal task facing us in this section is to introduce into our analysis of equilibrium behavior of the competitive industry the possibility for firms to enter or to leave. Of course, a rational motivation to enter or to leave the industry must be specified. The customary capitalist rule for a firm to enter and operate permanently within an industry is that of nonnegative profit; in the short run, this condition is usually amended to include situations where firms temporarily keep operating with negative profits—i.e., losses—not exceeding in absolute value their fixed costs.

The rule for permanent operation and entry into our labor-managed industry, where profits are not defined, is that the equilibrium income per laborer generated by the firm be at least so large as to guarantee the availability of the corresponding equilibrium level of employment. The labor-supply constraint known to us from the preceding chapter will clearly play a central role here. The condition for permanent absence or exit from an industry is the opposite—that is, an equilibrium income per laborer inconsistent with the labor supply constraint faced by the firm. For the purpose of the present "purely theoretical" discussion, these behavioral rules are perfectly sufficient and most of the rest of this chapter will be based on them. Of course, there are related interesting questions of a more practical and institutional nature—such as who actually decides on whether to enter or leave the industry, who is responsible for possible operation losses prior to an actual exit, and so on —but these are not essential here and we will take them up only in Part III.

Some may ask whether in the situation at hand the same distinction should not be made as in the conventional theory between short- and long-run exit (as mentioned a little while ago). Whereas some of the pertinent discussion and qualifications belong to Part III, it seems to me that at the present level of abstraction the distinction is unnecessary. For now, let it only be noted that all of the pure analysis conducted in Part I presupposes hiring the services of capital assets by the workers' cooperatives—or labor-managed enterprises—rather than ownership or lasting control of these capital assets. Consequently, if the actual income per laborer falls below supply price of labor, the firm can simply cease hiring the capital services as is the case with any other factor of production.

We may start our discussion by considering the long-run supply of our competitive industry with free entry and exit on the assumptions of identical technologies for all actual or potential firms of the industry and an infinitely elastic supply (availability) of labor. Moreover, we postulate that technology is of the conventional first kind for each firm, that is, subject to increasing and then diminishing returns. In choosing the long-run situation—that is, one where capital assets in each firm are permitted to adjust optimally to conditions prevailing in the capital market—we follow what is customary in the discussion of the capitalist supply function with free entry. Indeed, it appears rational to assume that entry or exit of firms is an even more time-consuming process than is optimum adjustment of the capital stock in each firm. Consequently, once we consider periods sufficiently long to allow the adjustment to changing market conditions via entry or exit of firms, it is certainly justifiable to postulate the *long run* for each individual firm. However, it is not inconceivable to speak of supply functions based on individual firms' *short run* coupled with free entry or exit; but that case is not defined unless the capital stock for each actual and potential firm is specified. Once this is done, the case becomes analogous to one involving the *long-run cum*-different technologies which we will speak about below.

The contour S^1 in Figure 5.3.1 passing through 0, p_0 and s is the long-run supply function of a representative firm (identical to all other firms) of the industry. As we know from the preceding chapter, it ef-

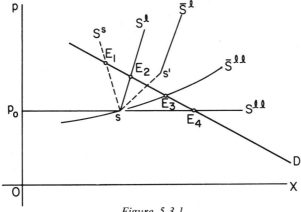

Figure 5.3.1

fectively reflects a situation where the supply of labor faced by the firm (as much as by the industry) is infinitely elastic. We also recall that when at point s the firm can exactly cover the income per laborer called for by the labor-supply function, it pays each laborer his marginal value product. Were the market price to be increased infinitesimally above p_0—the price corresponding to point s—the representative firm would produce a slightly higher amount of X, as indicated by the stretch of S^1 above s in the diagram. With this happening, the income per laborer in the representative firm would rise above the level called for by the supply of labor; but this, coupled with an infinitely elastic labor-supply for the industry and our behavioral rule for entry, would lead to an entry of an infinite number of firms and a corresponding infinite output. On the other hand, a price below p_0 would lead to the exit of all firms. Consequently, the long-run supply curve of the industry with free entry is the infinitely elastic supply function S^{11} in Figure 5.3.1. The first of the superscripts refers to the "long-run" postulate for each firm, while the second indicates the "long-run" nature of entry into and exit from the industry.

It is conceivable, though not very likely, that each firm, while sufficiently small in the product market to remain a perfect competitor, face a less than infinitely elastic supply of labor. In that case, as we know from the preceding chapter, the representative firm will operate, for a certain range of product prices, with full employment of its "local" labor supply. For that range of prices—corresponding to the range ss' in the diagram—the supply of the product will definitely have a positive elasticity, and the laborers will be paid less than their marginal revenue product. However, they will be paid exactly the supply price and thus there will be no inducement to entry. We can thus conclude that in the case where all firms in the industry are operating within the stretch ss'—that is, operating at full employment of their respective local markets—the situation actually is one with a constant number of firms and the industry supply function is that shown in Figure 5.3.1 as $\bar{S}^1$. Contrary to what it would be in the capitalist context, however, the situation still should be termed perfectly competitive because the less than infinitely elastic local supply functions faced by each firm cannot lead in our labor-managed economy to monopsonistic practices.

Let us now turn to two important fully competitive situations, both involving a positive slope of the free-entry supply function for the industry, such as that shown for $\bar{S}^{11}$ in Figure 5.3.1. The first is defined by identical technologies (still of the first kind) for all firms, but a positively sloped supply of labor for the industry as a whole. With a large number of firms, of course, the supply of labor for each individual firm within the industry is infinitely elastic. Suppose that at price p_0 and a constant cost of capital, one thousand (identical) firms supply the amount corresponding to s in the diagram; each firm being in a long-run equilibrium and paying each laborer just the supply price corresponding to the number of laborers needed by the industry. Now the price is increased above the level p_0. In the short run, while the initial capital stocks are unchanged, the industry will adjust its supply along S^s, as given by the representative firm. In the long run, still with one thousand firms, the industry supply will move to some point along S^1 while the new equilibrium labor force employed by the industry generally will be less than the old, and the new capital stock more than the old. Obviously, the new income per laborer in the industry will be considerably higher than the corresponding supply price (i.e., income per laborer as given by the labor-availability function for the number of laborers actually employed by the industry in the new equilibrium). The discrepancy in part is imputable to the fact that fewer laborers than before are employed, in part to the fact that the product price (and thus the residual income) now is higher. Given our rules for entry, there will thus be a strong influx of new firms. It will be terminated and the long-run equilibrium with free entry reached only when, with increasing supply price of labor, the industry will find itself in a situation where each firm reaches a long-run competitive equilibrium and pays the supply price to labor. The number of firms now must be in excess of one thousand and the new equilibrium will be established on the supply curve $\bar{S}^{11}$ in Figure 5.3.1, that is, at E_3.

Both in the situation just discussed and that based on an infinitely elastic supply of labor for the industry, the product-supply functions $\bar{S}^{11}$ and S^{11} are exactly the same as those that would be obtained *ceteris paribus* for capitalist industries composed of firms using identical techniques. This will not be so for the second important case which we are about to discuss. Other important properties which hold in the foregoing situations are the equality of laborers' remuneration to the marginal physical product of labor for each and every firm of the industry, and the equality of labor incomes among firms.

The second case is one in which the technologies of existing and potential members of the industry—still assumed to be of the first kind —are different. That case, usually associated with generation of quasi rents when the industry is capitalist, also leads to positively sloped industry supply curves with free entry such as $\bar{S}^{11}$ in Figure 5.3.1, whether the supply of labor is finitely or infinitely elastic. With a prescribed product price, a long-run equilibrium of the industry with free entry now will involve, as before, long-run equilibria of each and every operating firms; however, instead of all firms, it will now be only the marginal least efficient firm which will pay its workers the labor-supply price, that is, the price required by the over-all labor supply for the particular level of equilibrium industry employment. All the other firms in the industry will pay higher incomes per laborer than the marginal firm and, of course, with different technologies there will be different remunerations among all firms. But each and every firm in the industry will still be paying its laborers their marginal value product. Of course, this inequality of marginal productivities among firms will generate certain kinds of inefficiencies of resource allocation; these will be discussed in greater detail in the last section of this chapter, while the means of avoiding them through taxation will be taken up in Part IV of the study.

At this stage a few words ought to be said regarding the technology of the second kind—that is, a constant-returns-to-scale technology. First, it should be clear that with constant returns to scale and identical technologies the equilibrium number of firms is indeterminate and nonessential, as in the capitalist case; actually the whole industry can now be represented as a single firm using the common technology and paying all its factors of production the value of marginal physical product (*not* the marginal revenue product). We know already from our preceding discussion that for such a firm without a labor constraint the equilibrium capital-labor and output-labor ratios are known once the product price and nonlabor factor prices are prescribed. If we now postulate free entry and an infinitely elastic supply of labor, equilibrium in the industry will be reached through variation of the product price when the income per laborer equals labor's supply price. The product price thus obtained will then be—because of the infinite elasticity of all factor supplies and homogeneity of the technology—the long-run supply price of the industry with free entry. As usual the scale of operation of the industry will be determined by the demand for its product.

More generally, when the assumption of constant returns to scale and identical technologies is made, the results are not too different from those obtained for the technology of the first kind. The representation of Figure 5.3.1 still obtains, with one important modification. The modification is that the conventional long-run supply with limited entry, S^1, does not exist. As we know from the preceding chapter, this is so because the scale of operation of a perfectly competitive labor-managed firm is indeterminate in the long run—that is, when both labor and capital (and possibly other productive factors) are permitted to be hired in optimal amounts.[1] However, the short-run supply function S^s and the two long-run supply functions S^{11} and S^{11} will still obtain, *ceteris paribus*, when we substitute the technology of the second for that of the first kind for each of the firms in the industry.

This allows us now to state briefly the conditions of market equilibrium and market adjustment for all the cases discussed thus far. Suppose that an initial long-run equilibrium is established at the long-run equilibrium price p_0, at point s in Figure 5.3.1; that is, a demand function (not in the diagram) passes through that point. If now the demand function shifts to the position indicated by D, in the short run —and with no new firms entering—a conventional equilibrium will be established at a point such as E_1 at a considerably higher price, and a reduced output, provided that there are no alternative products and/or variable nonlabor factors. In the long run, still with restricted entry,

---

[1]Of course, as we have argued in Chapter 3 in connection with the social long run, the long run for each of the competitive firms might be determined by solidarity considerations of the working collective; specifically, the scale of operation could be selected by each firm not involving any changes in employment.

the price would have to drop to the level indicated by E_2, and the industry output very likely but not necessarily would increase to a level above the initial equilibrium output (at S). We know that this holds only when the technology is of the first kind. If the technology were of the second kind and, in addition, the workers-managers decided not to reduce the labor force, the resulting social equilibrium would be comparable to that just described, except that the increase in output from the initial equilibrium at s would now be of greater magnitude, and moreover, it would be *necessary* instead of only *most likely*. If free entry is permitted and the industry uses a single technology (of first or second kind) the new long-run equilibrium will be attained at E_4 when the supply of labor is infinitely elastic and at E_3 when the elasticity of labor supply facing the industry is positive. Both of these adjustments are exactly the same as those that would be obtained, *ceteris paribus*, for an ideal capitalist industry. The adjustment to an equilibrium such as E_3 would also prevail with different technologies of the first kind for different firms of the industry. The solution, however, is no longer identical to its capitalist analogue; note, for one thing, that in the capitalist case all laborers in the industry still keep receiving identical wages while this is not true in the labor-managed instance.

As for stability, it should be clear from Figure 5.3.1 that with a declining demand function the long-run equilibrium with free entry must be stable. With restricted entry the long-run equilibrium with the technology of the first kind will very likely—but not necessarily—be stable, and in the short run, market instability becomes at least a theoretical possibility if there are no substitute products and the firms adhere strictly to short-run maximization of income per laborer. Of course, observing the simple fact that there would generally be no price high enough to reduce supply to zero, while there certainly must be a price high enough to eliminate all demand, we can be certain that even if a particular short-run equilibrium were unstable, it would be bordered by another one at a higher price which would be stable. Similarly, there would have to be some stable equilibrium for the industry at a price below the unstable solution for the simple reason that the firms of the industry could not operate for too long with incomes per laborer below the income at which labor is available;[2] but this brings us back to the long-run equilibrium with free entry (and exit), which is at p_0 in the diagram and, as we have pointed out already, must be stable.

[2]Of course, in any realistic context, such a lower limit could be well below the income necessary to induce entry.

5.4: *Identical Technologies, Freedom of Entry, and Constant Returns to Scale in a Competitive Industry*

In this section I want to state and elaborate on a very useful proposition applicable in a decentralized labor-managed world. The proposition runs as follows: "A long-run equilibrium with free entry of a competitive industry composed of labor-managed firms using identical technologies of first or second kind, is equivalent in all respects to the equilibrium of a single firm using a technology of the second kind (i.e., unit-homogeneous), paying productive factors, including labor, their value of marginal product and selling at a price equal to average cost; the technology of the hypothetical single firm being either the common technology of the second kind or, when the individual firms are using the technology of the first kind (i.e. increasing and then diminishing returns), a technology (unit-homogeneous) having for each set of factor proportions the maximum physical efficiency of the individual firms' technologies."

While the part of the proposition bearing on the case in which the individual firms of the industry use technologies of the second kind is self-evident and, moreover, was explained in the foregoing section, the case in which the individual technologies are of the first kind calls for explanation. A typical locus of maximum physical efficiency corresponding to the common technology of the first kind was shown in Figure 2.4.1 as *EE*. We know that along that locus marginal physical products exactly exhaust the corresponding output. We also know that in the long run each competitive firms must be at that locus paying *all* its factors (in terms of the output) these marginal products. Since factor and product prices for all firms in a competitive industry are the same, all firms will use the same point on *EE*, and thus the entire industry will use a single set of factor proportions. With given product and nonlabor factor prices, expansions and contractions of output will thus, with free entry and exit, solely take the form of, and be proportional to, movements along a given ray in Figure 2.4.1. But all these conditions (all factors earning their marginal products; expansion and contraction of output with, and proportional to, a movement along a constant factor-input ray) would be exactly replicated by a single firm (representing the industry) using a linear homogeneous technology consistent with EE^3 and hiring factors at cost = value of marginal product and selling at average cost = average revenue.

[3] That is, a production function tangential to the underlying production function of the first kind along a locus whose projection into the factor plane (space) is the locus of maximum physical efficiency.

There may be greater applicability for our proposition in the context of a socialist labor-managed economy than in the context of other economies. Indeed, the crucial assumption of identical—and presumably most advanced—technologies will be less likely to be met in a basically individualistic situation than in one where the society is the owner and supplier of capital assets or their services.

5.5: *Long-Run Industry Demand for Productive Factors*

Not to spend undue time on the subject of industry demand for factors of production, let us assume throughout this section that firms of the industry are using the same technology (of the first or second kind), and use for our analysis the proposition of the preceding section. The case of different technologies can be easily handled by the reader himself. Also we will consider here only the situation of long-run equilibria with free entry, recalling that when the entry is limited—whether in the short or the long run—the industry market schedules are just (horizontal) aggregations of the individual firms' schedules.

Suppose that the supplies of all productive factors, including labor, faced by our competitive labor-managed industry are infinitely elastic. Under such conditions the long-run supply of the industry with free entry will also be infinitely elastic because the supply of our hypothetical firm introduced in the preceding section would be infinitely elastic. Such a supply function is illustrated by S_1 in Figure 5.5.1, drawn at the price p_1. That price, as we know, exactly exhausts the factor remunerations, all factors being paid their supply price (or, more descriptively, availability-income); note that with free entry even labor must be receiving its supply price. The equilibrium price for the industry thus is p_1, and given a prescribed demand function D, the equilibrium level of output is that corresponding to e_1.

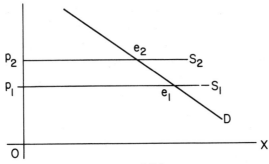

Figure 5.5.1

When the industry is producing at e_1 in Figure 5.5.1, it is hiring specific amounts of productive factors at the prescribed factor supply prices. Now consider one of the factors, say capital. Letting F stand for the capital factor and w_1 for its prescribed supply price, the equilibrium employment of capital (corresponding to e_1 in Figure 5.5.1) is F_1 in Figure 5.5.2. Point e_2 in that diagram is a point of demand—or

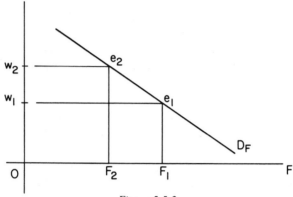

Figure 5.5.2

more exactly, derived demand—for capital of our industry operating under conditions of free entry.

With an increase of the supply price of capital from w_1 to w_2, the long-run equilibrium price charged by the industry must increase; it does so to, say, p_2. As shown in Figure 5.5.2, this leads to a new market equilibrium at e_2 involving a reduced supply of product X. But we also know that with an increased price of one factor of production and all other factor prices unchanged the equilibrium capital-output ratio in our hypothetical firm operating under constant returns to scale (as introduced in the preceding section) must decline. And thus on both accounts—reduction of X and reduction of the F-X ratio—the long-run demand for F must decline. This is indicated by e_2 in Figure 5.5.2; the entire derived demand for F then must be negatively sloped as shown by D_F in the diagram. It should also be clear from the derivation of D_F that its elasticity will vary with the elasticity of the product demand D (in Figure 5.5.1) as well as with the elasticity of substitution of the homogeneous technology of our hypothetical firm. It should also be clear that what has been said thus far about demand for capital must be equally true for the demand for any other nonlabor factor of production.

The rather remarkable thing—perhaps by now evident to the reader —is that in the competitive labor-managed industry *with free entry* even labor now has its definite demand function which can be used in all respects in determining the labor-market equilibrium. In particular, whenever there is an excess supply (demand), given such a demand function, the remuneration per laborer must decline (increase). We recall that without free entry this was not the case for the individual firm or the industry.

The demand function for labor, clearly, is derived in exactly the same way as that just derived for capital; actually we have only to let F stand for labor instead of capital. It should also be clear to the reader that provided that the assumption of identical technologies is maintained— and, of course, retaining the "dehumanized" framework of Part I—the demand of the competitive industry (with free entry) for any productive factor is exactly the same in the labor-managed and income-sharing world as it is, *ceteris paribus*, in the case known to us from conventional microeconomic theory.

5.6: *The Equilibrium of a Competitive Labor-Managed Industry and the Efficiency of Productive Resource Allocation*

One important subject remains to be taken up in this chapter. We must answer the question: How efficient is the competitive labor-managed industry composed of labor-managed firms maximizing income per laborer in using given productive resources? A related question is: How does its efficiency compare with that of capitalist industry? In what follows we will answer these questions restricting ourselves to the consideration of long-run equilibria prevailing with free entry, relegating other aspects of the problem to our general equilibrium analysis in Chapter 7.

We must consider two alternative sets of assumptions, namely (1) identical and (2) different technologies among the firms of the industry. Case (1) presents no difficulties, for we know that, given identical technologies, *ceteris paribus*, the labor-managed industry—as conceived of here in Part I—performs in the long run and with free entry exactly in the same manner as an ideal capitalist industry and, moreover, we know that such a capitalist industry—whether it uses technology of first or second kind—will maximize output from a prescribed set of factor inputs. In case (2), on the other hand, we know that the solutions generated by the labor-managed industry and by the capitalist industry are different. Let us now turn to the efficiency evaluation and comparison of the two.

Suppose that the industry producing product X is given fixed supplies of capital and labor, represented by the dimensions of the box in Figure 5.6.1. Free entry and competitive bidding for capital guarantee

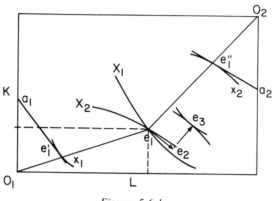

Figure 5.6.1

full employment of these resources. The money price of the product, p_X, is an arbitrary constant, determined by and maintained through monetary policy. Moreover, we assume that a limited number of producers, say one hundred of them, are endowed with an identical superior technology while all other actual or potential firms have available to them an inferior technology.

We thus have two segments of the industry, segment "one" and segment "two," the first having a better technology. It should be clear that in a long-run equilibrium where the selling price and competitive capital cost are identical for everyone, the long-run equilibrium factor proportions and income per laborer within each segment will be identical. We also know that each firm in the industry must in the long run be at the locus of maximum physical efficiency, and consequently—using a reasoning similar to that offered in the preceding section—each segment of the industry can be represented in our box diagram by a linear-homogeneous production function defined by its locus of maximum physical efficiency (as it was done in Section 5.4). Because the remuneration of labor on the first segment must be higher than in the second segment on account of the superior technology, and because all factors everywhere are receiving their respective marginal value products, the marginal rates of substitution in the two segments (i.e., for the two-unit homogeneous production functions representing the two segments) must be different at the equilibrium point of employment. Such a point is represented by e_1 in Figure 5.6.1, and we notice that, as required, at that point marginal productivity of labor is more relative to capital in the first segment than it is in the second. As indicated by the two isoquants of the representative homogeneous technologies passing through e_1 (each measured from its origin, 0_1 and 0_2 respectively), the two segments' outputs are X_1 and X_2 respectively, and total output of the industry is $X_1 + X_2$. It will also be noted that prices of X charged by the two segments are identical, and measured in terms of capital by the segments 0_1a_1 and 0_2a_2 respectively.[4]

It is immediately apparent that the industry, while allocating its resources among the two segments in the manner indicated by e_1, does not produce the maximum level of output. First of all, output of both segments and thus of the industry could be increased by moving the allocation point to a point such as e_2, where the marginal rates of substitution for all firms in both segments of the industry would be identical. But at such a point, in greatest likelihood, the marginal factor productivities of both factors would be higher in segment one than they are in segment two, and thus transfer of both resources from segment two to segment one would be warranted—proceeding along a kind of a contract curve—until point e_3 would be reached where not only equality of the marginal rates of substitution would be reached for each and every firm of the two segments, but also an equality of absolute marginal productivities. At that point the aggregate output X would be maximized. Note that the isoquant representing the first segment at point e_3 no longer belongs to the unit-homogeneous representative technology of segment one based on the locus of maximum physical efficiency. Rather, it is a hundredfold blow-up (recall that we have assumed that there are a hundred identical firms in segment one) of an actual isoquant of the basic technology used by segment one of the industry, for which the physical efficiency of factor-employment is not at its maximum but rather at a level equal to the maximum efficiency in the second segment.

The optimal point e_3 is characterized by equality of marginal physical productivities of identical factors in the two segments of the industry. Therefore, because we know that there is only one such point in the box-diagram, we also know that e_3 is the point of resource allocation generated, *ceteris paribus*, by an ideal competitive and profit-maximizing industry. Note also that implicit in the derivation of point e_3 was the assumption of technology of the first kind. Were all the hundred firms of the first segment of the industry using a technology of the second kind, the allocation point would, through competition, be pushed all the way to 0_2 in the capitalist case. We know, on the other hand, that the inefficient equilibrium at e_1 is permissible in the labor-managed situation whether technology is of the first or the second kind. The only distinction that can be made between the cases implied by the two technologies in the labor-managed world is that with technology of the first kind the equilibrium must be at e_1, whereas it only *may* be there when the technology is of the second kind; recall that the long-run equilibrium of a firm operating under constant returns to scale is indeterminate. Actually, with technologies of the second kind, the industry equilibrium might just as well have been established at 0_2 in the diagram in which case the inefficient segment would cease to exist.

A planning authority interested in the most efficient solution actually would have a very easy job to obtain it from the hundred efficient producers provided that they were endowed with a linear-homogeneous technology; just a word pointing out the social preferability of the solution would suffice because no real cost (or loss) would be involved on the part of the producers. On the other hand, with technologies of the first kind, the optimum solution at e_3 could be attained only through a set of fiscal and/or pricing policies in a labor-managed system. Of course, in a realistic context, especially in a socialist economy, the optimal long-range policy would be to let everyone in the industry share the same optimal techniques.

6. The Labor-Managed Firm and Imperfect Market Conditions

6.1: *Introduction*

Thus far we have been concerned exclusively with firms and industries operating in perfectly competitive markets. In this chapter, we abandon that assumption and study the equilibrium behavior of firms and industries under imperfect market conditions. Because in the economy under study—by definition—monopsonistic exploitation of labor is impossible (if it is conceivable in some environments, such environments are not our concern) and because the effects of monopsony in other factor markets are almost identical to those known to us from capitalist analysis, we devote ourselves here entirely to the study of monopolistic and oligopolistic forces in the product markets. As a guide for the organization of the material we use the various customary categories taken from conventional microeconomic theory.

We begin in the subsequent section with the analysis of the equilibrium—short and long run—of a pure labor-managed and income-per-laborer maximizing monopoly. Effects of changes in (competitive) markets for factors of production other than labor, and in demand conditions, are derived in section 6.3. In the subsequent section we transpose Chamberlin's theory of monopolistic competition—originally cast for a capitalist situation—into the environment of an industry composed of labor-managed and income-sharing firms. In particular we consider the existence and stability of monopolistically competitive equilibria. In the fifth section, we discuss the operation of some other oligopolistic market structures, such as the cases originally suggested and analyzed by Cournot, Stackleberg, and Bertrand. Following some realistic remarks in the sixth section, the seventh and last section is devoted to product differentiation, sales promotion, and advertising.

Conventionally, public control is an integral part of study of monopoly and oligopoly. We omit this subject in this chapter, however, because economic policy and plan implementation in general will be our topic in Part IV. In other words, we are conforming in this chapter to the purely theoretical framework adopted in all of the preceding chapters.

6.2: *The Equilibrium of a Labor-Managed and Income-Sharing Monopoly*

Clearly, the first topic belonging to a discussion of the labor-managed firm under imperfect market conditions is the case of a pure product-market monopoly. The equilibrium of a monopolistic firm—both in the short and in the long run—will be examined in the present section, whereas the comparative statics—that is, analysis of change—of that market situation will be discussed in section 6.3. As we have pointed out in the introduction, we can proceed comparatively fast because the basic logic of the discussion is quite analogous to that used in studying the competitive situation; moreover, the transition from the competitive to monopolistic case is quite analogous to that known to us from the conventional analysis of monopoly.

Let us first consider the short-run situation, and, in order to make the analysis as simple as possible—while preserving, of course, the essentials of the case—let us postulate only two factors of production, capital and labor.[1] The first of the two factors is considered to be a given constant K_0. The amount of labor employed thus becomes the only variable input. As usual, the market conditions are specified by a given less than infinitely elastic demand for the output of the firm, written for convenience as

$$p_X = p_X(X) \tag{1}$$

by a constant price of capital p_K, and—along the lines of the analysis of Chapter 4—by a specification that the equilibrium monopoly income per laborer must be at least as large as the labor-supply price faced by the monopoly. Finally, the technology used by the firm is described by a production function of the first or second kind (as defined in the previous chapters)

$$X = X(K, L) \tag{2}$$

where, for the moment, K is held constant at K_0.

The operating principle of the firm is the same as in the competitive situation, that is, maximization of the income per laborer Y. That mag-

[1]The reader should find it easy to introduce the two intermediate inputs into the analysis, as we have done in Chapters 2 and 3 for the competitive situation.

nitude is defined for all levels of output and employment as

$$Y = (Xp_X - K_0 p_K)/L \tag{3}$$

where p_X and X are given by relations (1) and (2), respectively. Recalling that the input of capital is fixed, it becomes clear that Y is a function of—or depends on—only the employment of labor L. As such it is reproduced in Figure 6.2.1. Except for the fact that the product price

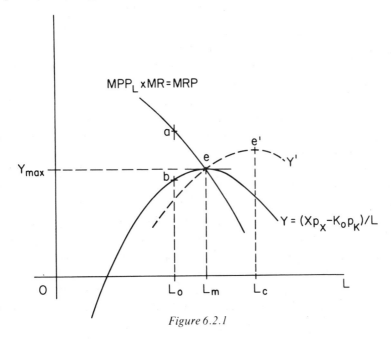

Figure 6.2.1

now is variable, it is very much like the Y-function which we have studied in Chapter 2. For very low levels of employment it assumes negative values because the very heavy capital charges per laborer more than offset revenue from corresponding sales, even though the product price is comparatively high. As we move to higher levels of employment and output, price declines, but the gains from spreading fixed costs over a larger number of laborers and possibly from increasing returns are so strong as more than to compensate for such declines, and thus the Y-function is increasing. With diminishing returns necessarily setting in at some point and continuously declining average revenue (price), the upward trend of Y must eventually be reversed because the function (hyperbola) reflecting fixed cost per laborer for high levels of employment must become quasi parallel to the L-axis and thus can no longer exercise any strong positive effect on Y. The maximum reached between the increasing and declining stages, at e, is the solution sought by the labor management of the monopolistic firm; L_m is the equilibrium employment and the corresponding equilibrium output and prices are then known from relations (2) and (1).

As in the competitive case, the point e has an important property providing the managers with a set of operational rules for finding that point: namely, at e the equilibrium maximum income per laborer Y_{max} is equal to the marginal revenue product of labor. In other words, when in equilibrium the monopolistic firm is paying each laborer exactly his marginal contribution to the revenue of the enterprise, that is, the physical increment in output valued at the additional revenue generated by adding to sales one unit of output at the actual level of output. Note that the equilibrium can take place only within the elastic range of the demand curve because only within such a range is the marginal revenue positive.

The derivation of the operational rule just stated is quite simple. Suppose that employment is temporarily at the level L_o in Figure 6.2.1. The corresponding income per laborer generated by the monopoly is then given by point b. On the other hand, employment of the L_o-plus-first laborer generates an incremental revenue given by the MRP-contour, that is, revenue equivalent to the segment $L_o a$. It would thus be possible to pay an income equal to $L_o a$ to all $L_o + 1$ laborers and retain a "surplus" of ba in the diagram. But instead of retaining that surplus, ba divided by $L_o + 1$ can be added to the income of each of the $L + 1$ laborers; and thus employment of the L_o-plus-first laborer in our monopolistic firm distributing all its net income benefits everyone in the enterprise. And consequently—on grounds of an analogous reasoning—it will pay to increase employment all the way to L_m, where the MRP-contour intersects the Y-contour, that is, where the segment ab is reduced to a single point. For points to the right of L_m the operational rule is to reduce employment because each incremental employee adds to the firm's revenue less than he earns, and thus his leaving the firm must increase the income of those remaining.

Two additional remarks are called for before we turn to the discussion of the long-run equilibrium of our monopolistic firm. First it will be observed that the labor-managed monopoly will be producing less than would the competitive firm, all other things (including the equilibrium price) remaining unchanged. This follows from the fact that Y', the locus of income per laborer of a competitive firm selling at the equilibrium monopoly price, must pass through e in Figure 6.2.1 and have a slope higher than that of Y; this is so because in the definition of income per laborer (see relation 3) p_x is a constant for Y' while it is declining for Y. Thus e' is to the right of e and the competitive equilibrium employment L_c exceeds that of monopoly, L_m.

The other remark we want to make concerns the "operational rules" derived here for the labor-managed monopoly and similar ones derived several chapters back for the competitive firm. The rules are the same as those to be used by the manager of a capitalistic monopoly or competitive firm facing a competitive labor market: "Hire or discharge to the point where the marginal revenue product equals remuneration of each laborer." This similarity may lead to the conclusion that there is no difference between the equilibria of the firm under the two alternative systems. But such a conclusion would be incorrect here, as it was for the competitive case, unless the incomes per laborer (wages) are identical under the two systems. Whenever the capitalist counterpart of a labor-managed and profit-sharing firm makes a positive profit, its equilibrium will be different. More specifically, with positive (negative) profits in the capitalist equivalent, and thus comparatively higher (lower) remuneration of labor in the labor-managed firm, the latter will generally have a comparatively higher (lower) capital-labor ratio.

Relying on all that we have done here and in the preceding chapters, the analysis of a long-run equilibrium of a labor-managed monopoly is quite straightforward. It must be clear that in the short-run equilibrium, when the income per laborer and employment are those given by point e in Figure 6.2.1, the marginal revenue product of capital (that is, the marginal physical product of capital valued at the marginal revenue corresponding to point e) MRP_K generally will not be equal to the price (cost) of capital p_K. As in the capitalist situation, if $MRP_K > p_K$ it will pay to hire more capital—that is, the income per laborer will be increased by employing more capital—and vice versa. The long-run equilibrium characterized by a maximum income per laborer attainable through both variation of labor and capital employment will thus be reached when

$$MRP_L (= MPP_L MR) = Y \qquad (4)$$

and

$$MRP_K (= MPP_K MR) = p_K \qquad (5)$$

It is clear that the conditions derived earlier for the competitive situation are nothing but a special case of the two just stated, with $MR =$

p_X. We recall also from the competitive situation that the long-run equilibrium solutions were restricted to a special locus on the production function: we have referred to it as the locus of maximum physical efficiency. An analogous locus is defined for a long-run equilibrium of a monopolistic firm. In other words, given a demand function faced by the monopolist and given the specification of long-run equilibrium, there will be a locus on the production function of the firm to which all conceivable equilibria of the monopolistic firm are restricted. Actually, as the reader may suspect, the previously explained locus of maximal physical efficiency corresponding to an infinite elasticity of demand will turn out to be just a special case of the locus we want to consider here.

We remain in the simple situation where only capital and labor are used as inputs. In the long-run equilibrium we know that each factor is paid its marginal revenue product and also—this being the peculiarity of the labor-managed firm—that all revenue of productive factors is always distributed in full to productive factors. Thus

$$L \cdot MPP_L \cdot MR + K \cdot MPP_K \cdot MR = X \cdot p_X (= X \cdot AR) \qquad (6)$$

Dividing both sides of the equation by marginal revenue, we obtain $X \cdot AR/MR$ on the right-hand side, while the left-hand side contains only terms pertaining to the technology (or the production function). Assuming a declining demand curve, AR/MR must be larger than one. Also the reader will easily be able to verify that

$$AR/MR = d/(1 + d) \qquad (7)$$

where d is the elasticity of demand. This also indicates that the left-hand side must be larger than one whenever the firm has any monopoly power (i.e., $-1 > d > -\infty$). When demand is infinitely elastic, as is well known, $AR/MR = 1$, and relation (6) divided by MR then reduces to the relation defining the locus of maximum physical efficiency known to us from Chapter 2. That locus is illustrated by $E_c E_c$ (c standing for "competitive conditions") in Figure 6.2.2 for the technology of the first kind (that is, technology subject first to increasing and then to diminishing returns). We know that in the case of constant returns to scale (i.e., technology of the second kind) $E_c E_c$ degenerates into the whole production function (production surface).

Now suppose that d is less than infinite in absolute value and, moreover, that it is a constant at all points of the demand function; from relation (6) we then get

$$K \cdot MPP_K + L \cdot MPP_L = X \cdot \left(\frac{d}{1 + d}\right) \qquad (6')$$

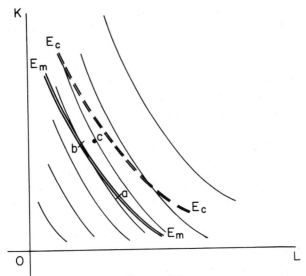

Figure 6.2.2

where the bracketed term is a positive constant larger than one (it must be positive because the equilibrium marginal revenue cannot be negative, that is, the demand function must be elastic at equilibrium). In other words, at the locus of monopolistic long-run equilibria the payment of marginal products to factors more than exhausts total output. This is a condition encountered with increasing returns—that is, for technologies of the first kind to the left and below the locus of maximum physical efficiency $E_c E_c$. The locus of long-run monopolistic equilibria $E_m E_m$ thus falls to the left and below $E_c E_c$, as indicated in Figure 6.2.2. It is given exactly as an implicit function of K and L by expressing the marginal physical products and the output X as functions of the two inputs in equation (6′); of course, we are still assuming that the demand elasticity d is a constant. If d is variable, one way of deriving the locus of monopolistic long-run equilibria is to express AR and MR as functions of X, and thus of K and L, and then carry these expressions into relation (6).

The first thing to be observed is that with technologies of the first kind the labor-managed monopoly must always produce at a scale below that which is physically most efficient. This is not, we recall, true for a capitalist monopoly which can produce at, beyond, or below $E_c E_c$. Second, we can conclude that monopolies using the same technology will all have the same locus $E_m E_m$ provided that the elasticity of demand they are facing is the same—the position of the demand curve is arbitrary. Third, we observe that the degree of physical inefficiency encountered with technologies of the first kind varies inversely with the absolute value of the demand elasticity. As with the competitive case, the equilibria of a capitalist and a labor-managed monopoly will be identical—*ceteris paribus*—provided that the capitalist "analogue" earns no profit (over and above the contractual remuneration of capital p_K). This is so because in that case both firms pay both factors the same marginal revenue products. In other words, with zero profits in the capitalist monopoly, both monopolies will find themselves on $E_m E_m$ in Figure 6.2.2. Supposing now that from such a position the demand function facing the monopoly shifts to the right, the labor-managed "twin" monopoly will remain on $E_m E_m$ while the capitalist "twin," as is well known, will move its point of factor employment to the right and above $E_m E_m$ to a point such as c. And thus, since capitalist monopolies generally make positive profits, using the criterion of physical efficiency (note that this is not the only criterion in evaluating social desirability), it can be said that the labor-managed monopoly is even more inefficient than its capitalist twin. But as we are about to show, some important qualifications ought to be appended to this statement.

The case in which the technology is of the second kind—that is, subject to constant returns to scale—is quite interesting. We recall that for the competitive situation, with such a technology the equilibrium was indeterminate. In the monopolistic situation, the solution is determinate but degenerate; specifically the equilibrium output of a monopoly using the technology of the second kind is zero. This results from the fact that anywhere on the linear-homogeneous production surface total product is exactly distributed among factors paid their marginal physical products; whereas, as we have shown through equation (6), a labor-managed monopoly calls for overdistribution of the total product. More generally and more realistically, even with mildly increasing returns (for technologies of the first kind) and comparatively inelastic demand functions, the locus of monopolistic long-run equilibria will be likely to degenerate into, or somewhere very near, the origin in Figure 6.2.2.

What is the moral of the story? In the strict case of technology of the second kind, with a monopolistic equilibrium at a zero level, the economy just could not produce a product under such market conditions; to produce, some kind of monopoly regulation would be necessary (this will be one of our topics in Part IV). On the other hand it can be argued that in a decentralized labor-managed economy, and especially in a socialist one, the case cannot be real except perhaps where unique natural resources are involved. The society, as owner of capital assets, could always prevent other types of monopoly through what we may call technological proliferation.

In the more realistic case where the force just identified will tend to result in a very low level, rather than an actual nullification of output, the technological inefficiency relative to the capitalist case will be offset, however, by another force. Because the equilibrium size of a labor-managed firm is considerably smaller than that of a capitalist firm, the degree of monopoly power in, and the structure of, a given industry will tend to be far worse in the capitalist alternative.

6.3: *The Labor-Managed Monopoly and Changing Market Conditions*

Our next task is to see how the labor-managed monopoly whose equilibrium conditions we have studied in the preceding section behaves under changing market conditions. As before, our analysis will be quite analogous to what has been done with regard to a competitive firm. Not to run the risk of making the reading too repetitive because of this analogy, we will change somewhat the analytical tools along the lines suggested in Section 2.2. The change we want to introduce is the substitution of "total" for the "average" and "marginal" variables used previously. This will be most useful to us in our discussion of economic policies in Part IV.

Let us start by considering the short-run situation. The monopoly has a fixed capital stock K_0 and uses technology of the first or second kind; its only other factor of production is labor, capital is hired at a constant price p_K, and, by definition, the demand function is less than infinitely elastic. In Figure 6.3.1, D represents such a demand function

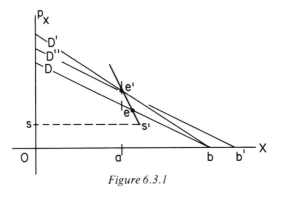

Figure 6.3.1

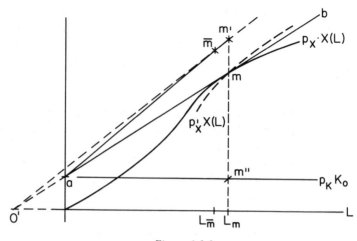

Figure 6.3.2

and the point e on it is the initial equilibrium of the monopoly. The "anatomy" of the equilibrium is shown in Figure 6.3.2. The two components entering the total net income of the firm (see relation (3) of section 6.2), namely $p_X X$ and $p_K K_0$, are shown in that diagram. The net income of the enterprise is measured as the vertical distance between the first and the second of these aggregates. For example, mm'' is the net income with an employment of L_m laborers. Now it is equally clear that the magnitude which the management of our firm wants to maximize, Y, is given by the slope of a line originating at point a and leading to the point of $p_X X$, for which Y is sought. The maximum Y will be reached when the slope of $p_X X$, that is, the marginal revenue product, is equal to the slope of the ray through a. The equilibrium monopoly output, employment, and price are thus given by point m for the case considered, and mm''/Lm is the (equilibrium) maximum income per laborer.

To study the impact of a change in demand on the monopolistic labor-managed firm, let us consider a "central" case, illustrated by D' in Figure 6.3.1, characterized by a proportional *upward* shift of the monopoly demand. Such a shift can also be referred to as elasticity-preserving because for each level of sales the elasticities of D and D' are the same. Recall that the elasticity of, say, D' at e' is given by $ab/0a$.

The elasticity-preserving shift of D upward will proportionately increase p_X for each level of sales and employment and thus the total revenue $p_x X$ in Figure 6.3.2 will shift proportionately upward. As is well known, this will also increase proportionately all its slopes and thus, at the initial equilibrium employment L_m, the new marginal revenue product (i.e., the slope of $p_x X$) will—for a proportional upward shift in the demand function equivalent to mm' in Figure 6.3.2—be given by the slope of $0'm$. As is immediately apparent from the diagram, the ray through a whose slope measures the income per laborer must be tangential to the new total-revenue curve to the left of m', at a point such as $\bar{m}$. And consequently, the elasticity-preserving increase in demand *must* reduce the equilibrium output and employment of our labor-managed monopoly in the short run. This is shown by e and e' in Figure 6.3.1 and the solid line defined by these two points; the line shows all possible equilibria corresponding to elasticity-preserving shifts of D. It is truncated at s' (below which point the monopoly would go out of business) because the income per laborer corresponding to that point is equal to the supply price of labor. The supply of labor is assumed here to be infinitely elastic (such as S_1 and S_3 in Chapter 4); were it otherwise, there would be a positively sloped locus of equilibria below s', as was the case in the competitive situation. Of course, it must be pointed out that the whole locus $0ss'ee'$ is a locus of equilibria determined, among other things, by the demand conditions and is not a supply curve in the traditional sense.

Next, it ought to be observed that an increase in elasticity of the demand function in the vicinity of an equilibrium must increase—*ceteris paribus*—the equilibrium output of the monopoly. This follows immediately from the fact that a counterclockwise rotation of D around e in Figure 6.3.1 will make the total-revenue curve $p_x X$ rotate to $p'_x X$ in Figure 6.3.2, and this in turn must shift the point of tangency of the total-revenue contour with a ray through point a to the right of m in the latter diagram. This finding is useful in showing that a parallel shift of the demand function—a shift which is elasticity-increasing if upward—can either increase or reduce the supply of the labor-managed monopoly in the short run. For example, a parallel shift upward from D to D'' can be decomposed into an elasticity-preserving shift from D to D' and then an elasticity-increasing rotation from D to D''; and we know that the effect of the first on output and employment must be negative while that of the second must be positive. Only the exact knowledge of the comparative size of the two offsetting effects, as given by each particular situation, will allow us to decide whether the aggregate effect is positive or negative.

Still remaining with the analysis of the short-run equilibrium, the next question we can ask is: What effect will there be from an increase in the price of capital p_K? The answer is the same as that obtained for a competitive, labor-managed firm and just the opposite, again, from the corresponding result in the capitalist situation: an increase in p_K must increase the equilibrium output of the monopoly. This is so because in Figure 6.3.2 the line $p_K K_0$ including point a must now shift upward, and the line such as ab will now "roll" along $p_X X$ (which remains unchanged) to a point above and to the right of m. Of course, the effect of the increase in p_K on the income per laborer will be negative.

Our study of the long-run equilibrium of the labor-managed monopoly in the preceding section makes it easy for us to establish the long-run effects of changing market conditions on such a firm. Of course, we know that from now on the assumption of technology of the second kind must be discarded as leading to degenerate solutions. Supposing first a constant and unchanging elasticity of the demand function, upward shifts of demand will produce movements along the $E_m E_m$ locus in Figure 6.2.2 in the northwest direction; this must be so because the increased demand will generate increased income per laborer and thus substitution of capital for labor in the long run.[2] As for the competitive case, there is no unambiguous sign that the change in output should assume. We only can repeat our previous "weaker" postulate that more capital-intensive technologies are likely to involve increased scales of operation, and thus that an increase in demand without a change in demand elasticity would be more likely to lead to increased sales by the monopoly. As for the factor markets, the normal—but not necessary—outcome is that indicated by $E_m E_m$ in Figure 6.2.2, namely, a reduced employment of labor and an increased employment of capital.

To obtain the correct conclusions about the direction of change in situations other than the constant-elasticity case just discussed, we have only to recall our previous conclusions that, *ceteris paribus*, reductions in elasticity shift the locus of monopolistic equilibria in the northeast direction, and vice versa. And thus, for example, a parallel shift in demand upward, which, as we know, is elasticity-reducing, should pro-

[2]Strictly speaking, this conclusion could (but would not have to) be vitiated if either capital or labor were inferior inputs; but this situation, implying that $E_c E_c$ is not single-valued with respect to a ray through the origin, can safely be discarded as not being a real possibility.

duce an over-all movement in Figure 6.2.2 such as ac, composed of a movement along $E_m E_m$, ab, and then an outward movement, bc.

In concluding, it should be noted that all the analysis of this and the preceding sections was based on the assumptions of (1) no joint production, and (2) no "social" behavior (i.e., no respect for the existing size of the working collective). If relaxed, the two assumptions would change the solutions in the same direction as they did for the competitive situation discussed in Chapter 3; the reader should find it easy to verify this proposition. The only major difference to be retained here is that now, with the technology of the second kind disappearing from the scene, the identity between *social* and *conventional* long runs becomes an impossibility; and thus, we can conclude that the labor-managed monopoly—if and when it arises—has an additional drawback of not permitting what we have termed the social behavior in the long run, or at least of permitting it only at the expense of conflict between the income-per-laborer maximizing principle and that of the stable, or exogenously given, size of the working body.

6.4: *Monopolistic Competition among Labor-Managed Firms*

Although the purely competitive and the purely monopolistic situations discussed so far constitute the two all-important boundaries—or cornerstones—of our theoretical analysis, it is a well-known fact that in the real world situations "somewhere in between" are frequent, if not predominant. It is equally well known that in many instances the solutions of these in-between cases are very complicated—or do not even exist—for a capitalist economy. Without attempting to push further the general theory of oligopoly, the purpose of the present section and of the rest of this chapter is to transpose some of the most important theories of imperfect (intermediate) market structures into our world of labor management and profit sharing. Product differentiation is a phenomenon bound to arise in a decentralized labor-managed economy as often as, if not more often than, it does in the capitalist economy. Therefore, we choose as our first topic Professor Chamberlin's theory of monopolistic competition dealing with this type of market structures.[3] In the next section we will discuss some of the other intermediate situations.

We follow Chamberlin's procedure in presenting first—mostly for expositional purposes—the "symmetrical" case which can be analyzed

[3]See E. H. Chamberlin, *The Theory of Monopolistic Competition* (Cambridge: Harvard University Press, 1956).

in terms of a single "representative" firm, and turn only then to the discussion of the general case. Suppose that there is an industry of n firms, all using identical technologies and subject to—in the sense to be spelled out presently—identical demand conditions. The products they sell, $X_1, \ldots, X_n$, are differentiated so that each firm is facing a market in which it exercises some degree of monopoly power. The cross-elasticity of demand for a particular product with respect to another particular product is very low; however, the cross-elasticity with respect to all other products (of the differentiated industry) combined is significant.

The technologies (production functions) shared by all firms are of the first or second kind in the context of short-run analysis, and can be only of the first kind in the context of long-run analysis because, as we know already, a nondegenerate long-run equilibrium of a labor-managed income-sharing firm operating under constant returns to scale is incompatible (inconsistent) with any degree of market power. The demand functions faced by all the firms are

$$X^j = X^j(p_1, \ldots, p_j, \ldots, p_n) \qquad (8)$$

and in the symmetrical case studied here they have the special property that when all prices but the j'th are fixed at the level p_o, they look, when plotted against their own j'th price, exactly alike—having a negative elasticity high in absolute value. Such a demand function defined by relation (8) and with all but the j'th price equal to p_o is illustrated in Figure 6.4.1 by the line dd. A significant point on it is point a, corre-

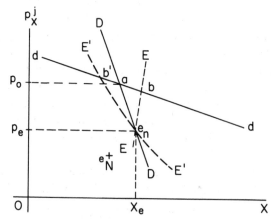

Figure 6.4.1

sponding to the common price of all the other firms in the industry, p_0. It tells us what each of the identical firms in the industry would be selling if prices charged by all were p_o. Now it must be clear that with a significant (and, of course, positive) cross-elasticity between the j'th product and the prices of all the other products combined, the demand function such as dd in our diagram will keep sinking (drifting downward) with a declining common price of all the other firms, such as p_o. The point such as a on the sinking demand function and corresponding to the prescribed common price (such as p_o) will then trace the other demand curve in the diagram, DD. We can refer to it as the *mutatis mutandis* demand, by contrast to the *ceteris paribus* demand curve dd.

Beyond this point, we can rely on our previous work regarding the behavior of a labor-managed and profit-sharing monopoly. Suppose that the j'th representative firm (for which the diagram in Figure 6.4.1 was drawn) finds itself temporarily at point a, all firms in the industry charging the price p_o. Knowing its own *ceteris paribus* demand function dd, the j'th firm will attempt to adjust its price and output in such a way as to maximize its income per laborer. The maximizing equilibrium conditions are at b on dd—it is immaterial for the present analysis whether the equilibrium sought is one of long- or short-run character. But starting from a this movement toward b will not be undertaken only by the j'th firm, but by all the firms of which the j'th is the representative—and this implies price reductions by all firms. Assuming that prices are being reduced at the same rate by all, the sales of all firms will be changing according to DD—instead of, as intended by each of the firms, along dd. For each price level, there will be a point such as b on the corresponding *ceteris paribus* demand line indicating the desired equilibrium; the locus of these points is illustrated by EE in Figure 6.4.1. The movement along DD can be arrested only once the point on DD is also a point on EE, that is, at a point such as e_n in the diagram, where the two important loci interest. It is only at such a point that each of the firms in the industry will subjectively consider itself in equilibrium (i.e., maximizing Y) and thus not engage in any further price and sale alterations.

The subscript used in describing our equilibrium point e_n is intended to emphasize the fact that the equilibrium obtained thus far is one corresponding to the fixed number n of firms in the industry. If for one reason or another the entry is limited, and the equilibrium income per laborer is consistent with the labor-availabity (supply) function faced by the industry, e_n effectively is the equilibrium solution sought. If either or both of these conditions are not met, further adjustment must take place.

Suppose that the equilibrium described by e_n in Figure 6.4.1 involves an income per laborer higher than the supply (or availability) price of labor for that level of employment by the industry. Using the same rule for entry as we did for the perfectly competitive industry, then, new firms will be entering, and new equilibrium points, $e_{n+1}, e_{n+2}, \ldots$, will be obtained—most likely moving in the southwest direction in the diagram as more and more firms enter. For some number of firms, say N, equilibrium will finally be reached for which the income per laborer is just about equal but not below the corresponding labor-supply price. The corresponding levels of output and price for each of the N firms is illustrated by point e_N in Figure 6.4.1. Should the equilibrium at e_n have been inconsistent with the labor supply faced by the industry, the opposite process from that just described—that is, exit from the industry—would lead to a solution point somewhere to the northeast of e_n in the diagram. At such a point, again, the equilibrium income per laborer would have been just about equal but not below the supply price of labor.

Thus far we have spoken only about the properties, derivation, and existence of equilibrium in a labor-managed monopolistically competitive industry, without touching on the important question of stability. It is an implicitly or explicitly accepted fact that the Chamberlinean monopolistically competitive equilibria in a capitalist environment are stable, or at least that possibilities of instability are so remote that there is nothing to worry about in any real situation. This is not quite so in our labor-managed and income-sharing world. Note that the locus EE in Figure 6.4.1 not only need not be positively sloped, but, in the short-run context, almost necessarily will be negatively sloped. This follows from the fact that, as we know from the preceding section, if all the shifting *ceteris paribus* lines such as dd had the same elasticity at the equilibrium points such as b, the short-run locus of equilibrium supplies would *have* to be negatively sloped (see the locus passing through e and e' in Figure 6.3.1). In the context of long-run equilibria the locus EE has only a slightly better chance to have a positive slope than to have a negative one. On the other hand, the locus DD is generally expected to have a negative slope—implying that more of differentiated products will be sold *in toto* at a lower uniform price. However, the elasticity may be quite low in absolute value. And thus it is not excluded, especially with groups of differentiated products which have *in toto* a low demand elasticity, that the slope of *EE* in the vicinity of an equilibrium point may be less, in algebraic value, than that of *DD*. Such is the case, for example, with *E'E'* in Figure 6.4.1. Were the representative firm now at *a* (as in the previous exposition), it would desire to increase price and lower sales in order to move towards *b'*. But with all firms doing the same, the system would move along *DD* away from e_n rather than toward it. Thus, whenever an initial equilibrium at e_n were disturbed, destabilizing forces would set in. The danger of this happening is far less in the long run with a limited number of firms and, of course, once free entry and exit are posited, the possibility of instability disappears altogether. Similarly, joint production and "social" behavior both reduce, if not eliminate, the possibility of instability; and in the real world, this is of decisive importance.

It will now be recalled that, in the conventional Chamberlinean world, in the long-run equilibrium with free entry all extra profits are paid their respective marginal revenue products and, with competition in the factor markets, all factors receive supply prices. But this is exactly what happens in our labor-managed world with free entry in the long run. Consequently, *ceteris paribus*, the monopolistically competitive—as much as the perfectly competitive—long-run equilibria with free entry are identical under both regimes.

We shall now turn briefly to the general, or asymmetrical, case where production as well as demand conditions are permitted to be different for different firms. The equilibrium can now be visualized as the intersection of so-called price reaction functions (or reaction-surfaces), one for each firm and each showing the monopolistic equilibrium prices of a particular firm on the condition that all other prices in the industry are constant at levels indicated by the other coordinates of the function. Clearly, the intersection of all *n* such surfaces for an industry of *n* firms is a solution, similar in character to e_n in Figure 6.4.1—except that the solution prices now need not, and very likely will not, be identical. Also the corresponding incomes per laborer are unlikely to be the same. A similar possibility of instability, especially in the short run, is present as that identified earlier in this section for the symmetrical case under restricted entry.

The assumption of free entry in the general asymmetrical situation constitutes a major difficulty here as much as it does in the context of a conventional monopolistically competitive industry (even if this may not be fully realized for the capitalistic case). With a prescribed very large number of potential entrants and specified individual production and joint demand conditions for every firm's differentiated product, the final selection of firms actually in the industry and the price and output solutions for each will only in part be the outcome of supply and demand conditions, another important role being played by chance, or what we may refer to as "accident." Of course, the incomes per laborer in different firms will be different, the only restriction being that all must be no less than the income of labor at which the corresponding labor participation is available.

6.5: *Other Oligopolistic Structures*

The title of this section may surprise the reader, since the preceding section was devoted to the discussion of monopolistic competition among producers of differentiated products. But in fact the title is permissible because in the situation where the number of firms (n in the preceding section) is small, entry is limited, and products are differentiated, we are actually facing a case of oligopoly—and the logic of its resolution offered above, while presupposing some degree of naïveté on the part of the labor management, is not entirely unrealistic. But to turn to the subject of this section, our task here is to go briefly over some of the other theories offered in explaining market behavior when the number of participants on the selling side is small, but larger than one. Of course, we again want to look at the subject assuming that the basic behavioral principle of individual firms is maximization of income per laborer.

Not only is it desirable to start with Cournot's theory of duopoly—or oligopoly—because it comes first, as far as I know, in the chronology of economic doctrine, but it is convenient because the formal solution of that case has a good deal in common with Chamberlin's small-numbers "naïve" situation pointed out above. The underlying idea in both instances is that of "reaction" of one partner assuming the behavior of another partner (or other partners) constant. In the Chamberlinean case the variables acted on are prices, while in Cournot's situation they are quantities of output.

For a short-run duopolistic situation not involving any product differentiation, two Cournot-type reaction functions are shown in Figure 6.5.1 as solid lines. Their significance is customary; for example, point a' on the reaction function marked (1 on 2) indicates the equilibrium output of firm one, behaving as a pure income-per-laborer maximizing monopolist, on the assumption that the current output X_2^0 of

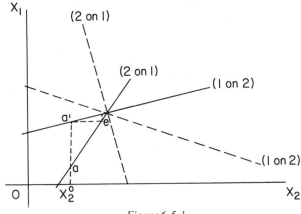

Figure 6.5.1

the second duoplist remains unchanged. Contrary to the capitalist situation, the two contours are positively sloped. Because the Cournot-type mechanism of market sharing involves (with linear demand functions) parallel demand shifts for each of the duopolists—rather than elasticity-preserving ones—there is a possibility that either or both of the short-run reaction curves would be negatively sloped. This outcome, which can be termed conventional and which is illustrated by the broken lines in Figure 6.5.1, is more likely but not necessary when we consider a duopoly of labor-managed firms in the long run.

As shown by the broken contour leading from *a* to *e*, the short-run situation illustrated in the diagram is one involving a stable equilibrium solution. And so is the long-run situation described by the dashed contours, as the reader may easily verify. Passing from two to a larger number of firms supplying the same product presents no difficulties, and the solution then is obtained at the intersection of reaction surfaces (or hypersurfaces) rather than lines. The situation with a larger number of firms, however, may be more realistic than that of a duopoly because with many firms the absence of recognition of interdependence postulated as a behavioral premise for each of the partners becomes more likely. It is also easy to establish the conventional result that as the number of firms increases, other things remaining unchanged, the equilibrium income per laborer of an individual oligopolist declines.

Perhaps one interesting point should be made before we leave our transplantation of Cournot's theory. We know already that in the short run the reaction functions should generally be positively sloped;

in the long-run setting they can be positively or negatively sloped and cannot be expected to have a significant elasticity, whether positive or negative. As a "central" tendency, it can thus be expected that they will be just about perpendicular to the axes in Figure 6.5.1. But if this is so, it really means that the first producer will produce a constant amount in the long run, whatever the other producer does, and vice versa. In other words, the situation of a Cournot duopoly of labor-managed and profit-sharing firms will tend to be much more stable than its capitalist equivalent in the sense that deviations of output from equilibrium by one firm will not tend to produce, as a repercussion, deviations by the other; but, of course, the levels of income per laborer will change in both firms.

The next and related subject is the case of duopoly (or oligopoly) first dealt with by Stackleberg, and involving sophistication on the part of one of the partners. The sophisticated duopolist is expected to be aware, and to have exact knowledge, of the other duopolist's reaction function. If such is the case, of course, he can scrutinize and compute his own income per laborer for each point of the other partners' reaction function and choose the highest. This is usually done for the capitalist case by means of so called iso-profit contours in the $X_1 - X_2$ plane of Figure 6.5.1 constructed by the sophisticated duopolist, the tangency of one of the contours with the opponent's reaction function giving the maximal (constrained) solution. The same can be done here by constructing iso-income-per-laborer contours; as with the iso-profit contours, they would resemble, when constructed for the second producer (of X_2), superimposed haystacks placed on the X_2-axis in the diagram, and corresponding to declining levels of income per laborer as we move upward. The reader may use this or any other technique in analyzing the situation of Stackleberg asymmetrical duopoly in detail. We will content ourselves only with a few general conjectures. The first is that the Stackleberg equilibrium will generally be different from the Cournot equilibrium in the labor-managed world just as it is in the capitalist world. The second is that, unlike the outcome of the capitalist situation, the sophisticated partner may find himself producing less in the Stackleberg equilibrium than he would produce in the Cournot situation; but of course, his income per laborer will be higher.

Instead of assuming that the other duopolist keeps his physical output constant—as is done in the case of solutions suggested by Cournot—it is possible to make an analogous assumption, but this time with respect to price. Actually we have done precisely that in the Chamberlinean case of differentiated products (recall that the *dd* line was based on the assumption that all other members of the industry hold their prices unchanged). In the present instance, analyzed by Bertrand for the capitalist case, we assume that the product is identical (or undifferentiated) for both, or all, producers of the industry.

The Bertrand solution in the labor-managed and profit-sharing world is quite different from its capitalist counterpart, and actually is much better behaved. Restricting ourselves to the assumption of identical technologies and constant returns to scale (i.e., horizontal cost-curves in the capitalist case), we have for the capitalist Bertrand duopoly the well-known cutthroat solution involving output variations, which can be terminated (of course, besides through regulation) only by elimination of one of the partners and thus by return to monopoly; this may offer greater stability, but will be extremely inefficient on other accounts. On the other hand, Bertrand transposed from capitalism into labor management and profit sharing turns from an unstable and dangerous choleric into a calm sleeper whose main desire is never to move or change—something comparable to the phenomenon usually associated in the capitalist context with the kinked demand curve, to which we will presently turn.

Suppose that there are two producers maximizing incomes per laborer, producing an identical product under conditions of constant returns to scale and jointly facing a downward sloping demand curve. Initially both are established in the market and each sells his output at an identical price. At one point one of the duopolists takes his partner's price for given—as he does in the capitalist Bertrand situation—and decides to capture all the market by undercutting the original price by a little bit. This will, it is true, increase his sales considerably (actually by a little more than the initial output of the other duopolist who now goes out of the market), but because the price is less and because his technology is of the second kind, his income per laborer must decline. And consequently he will not undercut the initial price. Nor will he attempt to sell at a higher price because, with a homogeneous product, this would, at least potentially, yield all of the market to the other duopolist.

But at this point one ought perhaps to leave the Bertrand world in order to remain realistic. In fact, the second duopolist, maximizing his income per laborer, might not want to take all of the market abandoned through sales at a higher price by the first. He might find out that by following the leadership of the first and also increasing his price, his income per laborer will increase with no, or only a slight, reduction in his sales. If this avenue is followed through, we end up, after a cutthroat "competition upward"—of course, the cutthroat now regards the workers eliminated in the process—at the monopolistic solution corresponding to the technology of the first kind in the long run, namely, zero output for the duopoly. Actually, on the assumptions made, a more realistic outcome would be one employee left in each firm. Of course, the assumptions are unrealistic and so are the conclusions of the situation just discussed, but they may illustrate correctly the general tendency of a real Bertrand situation: there is certainly no danger of competitive undercutting, and if the solution is not a stable one, as outlined above, the over-all tendency would be in the direction of a monopolistic solution, rather than that of a competitive world (i.e., selling at average and marginal cost). Whether stable or not, however, the case at hand again calls for some public control for the sake of a greater social efficiency. But this will be our topic only in Part IV.

Let us conclude this section by discussing briefly the phenomen of the so-called kinked demand curve. In the capitalist context, as is well known, it is used to explain one aspect of oligopolistic behavior—namely, a comparative price rigidity. The actual level of price and of sales for each of the oligopolists is usually left unexplained—or must be explained through a different theory. To state our conclusions under both sets of assumptions; whether the world is capitalist or labor managed, oligopoly prices will tend to be rigid as a result of a kinked demand curve. For the labor-managed case this is immediately apparent from Figure 6.5.2. It contains the same type of total revenue curve pX as we have introduced in Section 6.3, with the important difference that the total-revenue contour has a kink at the level of employment L_m, and the corresponding level of output, for which the "kink," or discontinuity in the demand function, occurs.[4] It will be recalled that—as the theory goes—such a "subjective" kink is visualized by each of the oligopolists because he feels that his own price reductions would be followed by his competitors, while price increases would not be followed. It is clear from the construction in Figure 6.5.2 that an equilibrium (maximum income per laborer reached at the tangency solution) is highly likely to occur at m. Moreover, within a wide range,

---

[4] A kinked demand function in both its logic and appearance is well illustrated by dd to the left of and DD below a in Figure 6.4.1.

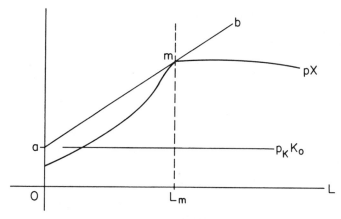

Figure 6.5.2

variations in p_k will leave the equilibrium point *m* unaltered. Also, realizing that the kink always arises at a given price and output, even changes in total capital stock, or in technology, will, within broad ranges, leave the equilibrium price and output unchanged. This is so because with an invariant *p* and *X* (at the kink) the kink in Figure 6.5.2 must always arise at the same distance $L_m m$ from the horizontal axis —only shifting to the right or left of *m* in the diagram—and a line such as *ab* still will remain tangential to *pX* at the kink for a wide range of positions of *pX* and/or of point *a* (such positions depending on the technological changes or changes in capital stock).

6.6: *Some Realistic Remarks*

Having considered the various main cases of market imperfection, we may ask what concrete lesson—if any—can be drawn from our analysis for the actual performance of imperfectly competitive labor-managed industries. The question is highly relevant because the ideal competitive conditions presupposing a very large number of firms are only rarely encountered in the real world.

Perhaps the most important conclusion is a far lesser danger of gigantism—and a corresponding far greater likelihood of competitive conditions—in labor-managed market structures than in just about any other economic regime. By gigantism we understand existence of firms of a size far beyond the minimum size warranted by an efficient scale of operation, firms often operating well beyond the range of maximum physical efficiency and enjoying a monopoly power and aggregate profits well beyond what is reasonable. The conclusion follows from the fact, already noted, that a labor-managed firm with any degree of control over its own price must operate on its production function within the range of increasing returns. In the real world, where normally increasing returns are present at first and then followed by a sizeable or virtually limitless zone of constant returns, this result can lead to market structures with dozens of firms where, for example, in a capitalist situation, only a few could survive the pressure of oligopolistic market warfare. But with a considerable number of firms in the labor-managed instance, the elasticity of demand, even if finite, will be very large, and thus the long-run equilibria will be quite near the maximum efficiency. It can thus be postulated that regarding the efficiency of use of resources the labor-managed industry can be as efficient as any other; note here that the gigantic firms of capitalist market structures often are already beyond maximum efficiency, and thus in the respect just mentioned they may have no advantage on balance. On the other hand, regarding the allocation of produce to final consumers, the labor-managed industry can be far more efficient because of its far lesser degree of monopoly power. The latter in fact, in any real situation, can be so small that the labor-managed firms in the industry will act in the long run as if they were in the lower portion of the constant-returns range, facing an approximately infinitely elastic demand curve. In particular, they will be able to behave in a *social* manner, leaving the size of the collective (of course, within limits) outside the category of variables of adjustment, and at the same time not being in serious conflict with long-run maximizing principles.

6.7: *Sales Promotion, Advertising, and the Equilibrium of a Labor-Managed Firm*

One very important subject remains to be discussed in this chapter. It is the phenomenon of sales promotion and advertising, so often encountered in connection with oligopolistic market structures. We will first concentrate on the purely technical aspects of the problem, and then try to appraise the effects of sales promotion on the labor-managed economy.

To make matters as simple as possible, let us postulate that an oligopolistic firm produces only one product, X, and that it uses only one factor of production, labor, L: if we want, we may think of the equilibrium as one in the short run. The product of the firm is differentiated from other products supplied by the industry, and thus it is possible to shift the demand function for it by an appropriate sales promotion program, involving an outlay (cost) C. It is thus possible to write the demand function for X as

$$p = p(C,X) \qquad (1)$$

where the product X itself is a function of L, that is

$$X = X(L) \qquad (2)$$

The labor-managed firm is interested in maximizing its income per laborer y, that is

$$y = (1/L)[p(C,X)X - C] \quad (= y(C,L)) \qquad (3)$$

The customary differentiation procedure gives us two necessary conditions for an extreme value of y, namely

$$y_L = 0 = (1/L^2)[(p_X X + p)X_L L - (pX - C)] \qquad (4)$$

and

$$y_C = 0 = (1/L)(p_C X - 1) \qquad (5)$$

where subscripts are used to indicate partial differentiation. The two equations can be thought of as two implicit functions of the promotion cost C and employment L, $F(C,L) = 0$ and $f(C,L) = 0$ respectively; recall that the former is nothing but the expression of the fact that when the income per laborer is to be maximized, the marginal revenue product must equal income per laborer. A more careful consideration of the two relations, or simple differentiation, will convince the reader that the first contour, the one based on F, can be positively or negatively sloped, while the second, based on f, must have a positive slope. They are illustrated by the two solid lines in Figure 6.7.1, $F = 0$ being drawn with a positive slope. The equilibrium is found at point e for $L = L_0$ and $C = C_0$. Noting that whenever the firm operates at a point below $f = 0$ it will increase the promotion costs, and vice versa, and noting that whenever it produces less than what is called for by $F = 0$ it will increase output (and employment), and vice versa, it becomes immediately apparent that the equilibrium at e will be dynamically stable; the dynamic forces of adjustment are indicated by the double arrows in the four quadrants defined by $F = 0$ and $f = 0$.

Reversing the reasoning—that is, using the correspondence principle —the configuration of the two contours in the diagram is a necessary

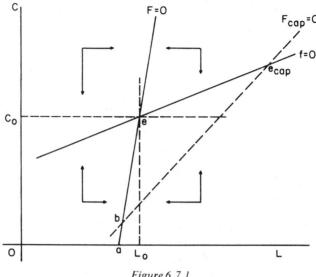

Figure 6.7.1

one once stability is postulated. Of course, such a postulate is necessary in the context of any realistic analysis.

At the foot of $F = 0$ in the diagram we identify the no-advertising solution of the oligopolistic firm corresponding to employment $L = 0a$. Comparing the positions of points a and e it is immediately apparent that in the situation illustrated sales promotion activities lead to an expansion of employment and output. But we recall that this is by no means a necessary outcome; in fact, in the context of a labor-managed firm it might be more accurate to speak of price and income-per-laborer promotion rather than sales promotion.

It ought also to be realized that not every labor-managed oligopolistic firm must engage in sales promotion. The intersection of $F = 0$ and $f = 0$ might just as well never have occurred, and then advertising could only reduce the income per laborer.

Of great importance is the comparison between sales promotion in a labor-managed and a capitalist oligopoly: again, the labor-managed alternative comes out considerably superior from the social point of view. Recalling that a profit-maximizing capitalist firm will also—as much as the labor-managed firm—equalize the marginal return of sales promotion $p_c X$ to unit promotion cost; that is, to one unit of currency, relation (5) and contour $f = 0$ in the diagram still obtain for such a firm. The employment condition now changes, however, postulating that the marginal revenue product of labor must be equal to competitive wage w_0. We thus have

$$W_0 = (p_X X + p)X_L \quad (= \phi(C,L)) \tag{4'}$$

again a relation between C and L. The corresponding contour $F_{cap} = 0$ will now be almost necessarily positively sloped (in fact a negative slope would imply that sales promotion leads to a reduction in equilibrium sales) and certainly the slope will be less than that of $F = 0$ if the latter contour is positively sloped. For stability, $F_{cap} = 0$ must again intersect $f = 0$ from below as we move from left to right. The two contours $F = 0$ and $F_{cap} = 0$ will intersect at the point where the competitive capitalist wage equals the income per laborer. Such a point is b in the diagram; but it must be realized that most often it will not exist, because even with zero promotion effort the capitalist firm will make positive profits.

The equilibrium of the capitalist firm is now found at e_{cap}, indicating a higher level of output and employment and a higher level of promotional spending than in the labor-managed firm. It is clear from the derivation that the outcome is a necessary one provided that the differentiating capitalist oligopolist makes a profit—a situation encountered virtually without exception in the real world. It should also be clear that in many instances the labor-managed firm will not engage in promotion at all while the capitalist firm will. Such would be the case, for example, if the L-axis shifted up to the position $C_o e$ in Figure 6.7.1. The general conclusions which can be derived follow the same lines as those obtained earlier for oligopolies in the absence of sales promotion: with sales promotion and advertising the average size of the labor-managed oligopolists will tend to be smaller and thus market structures will tend to be more competitive than in the capitalist situation. Moreover, advertising and promotion being socially wasteful beyond a certain minimum of purely informational activity, the misallocation of resources in the labor-managed situation will tend to be less than in the capitalist situation. Especially if we realize that the most vicious forms of advertising—aggressive, mind-twisting, often immoral and deceitful—arise at the more extreme stages of promotion somewhere within or near the range of ee_{cap} in the diagram, the social advantage of the labor-managed situation emerges as quite considerable.

7. The General Equilibrium in a Labor-Managed Market Economy

7.1: *Introduction*

We have now come to the final and perhaps most important subject in the pure theory of decentralized economies based on labor management and income sharing; namely, the general equilibrium representation of the system. There are at least three basic questions to be answered by such an analysis. First, and most basic, do the component parts studied in the preceding chapters actually hang together in forming the whole of the economy, and, if so, how? Second, how does the economy adjust to changes in structural parameters such as demand conditions, factor supplies, technology, or man-controlled policy instruments? Third, how efficient is the economic organization based on markets, labor management, and income sharing, and how inefficient are certain economic imperfections in such a system?

In the context of conventional western analysis, by general equilibrium we customarily understand the study of a system involving a structure consisting of several sectors—or industries—the principal concern being the allocation of resources among, and outputs from, these sectors. While recognizing the structural aspects of general equilibrium as of central importance, we will start our discussion of the labor-managed economy by considering a one-sector situation. This will allow us to identify and understand some "global" characteristics and properties of our system and treat them separately from the more conventional questions of structure. However, in both the global and the subsequent structural analysis we deal, as customary, with a barter situation where money, securities, and investment markets are absent. It is only in Part II that such markets are integrated with the product markets (studied in Part I) to form the macroeconomic theory of the system. Of course, the one-sector analysis—presented in the subsequent section—will be useful as a starting point in Part II.

In section 7.3 we examine the structural long-run equilibrium of the

124

decentralized labor-managed economy together with its adjustment to changing conditions. In section 7.4 we make a realistic departure from the customary general equilibrium approach and introduce intermediate products into the analysis. Short- and intermediate-run equilibria and adjustment are studied in section 7.5. In the subsequent section we examine inefficiencies resulting from monopolistic forces, and in section 7.7 those resulting from differences in technology, factor immobility, and the like. The eighth and final section contains a set of remarks designed to bring closer together any realistic situations of labor management with the theoretical analysis of this chapter.

At all stages of the analysis, besides trying to answer the three basic questions of general equilibrium outlined at the outset of this section, we find it instructive and thus desirable to draw comparisons with either an absolute Pareto-optimal standard or an "ideal" capitalist system. The reader must again be warned, however, that such comparisons are not final conclusions regarding the real viability and efficiency of the two systems. For one thing, reality is far less perfect and far more complex than the idealized world we are presenting here. For another, as we have pointed out in Chapter 1, we are studying a system analogous to the capitalist one in all respects except for the assumptions of labor management and maximization of income per laborer; for example, we are assuming that labor in its quality, efficiency, motivation, and aspirations is the same in the two systems—which is patently unrealistic. And thus the comparisons made in this chapter must be taken only as partial inputs into some final, more comprehensive evaluation, which we will attempt at the end of the study.

7.2: The Aggregate General Equilibrium of a Barter Economy

As the reader may suspect, the labor-managed competitive economy will perform, even in its global attributes, differently from the conventional western-type market economies.

The important reasons for this are the absence in most contexts of a conventional labor market and the income-per-laborer maximizing, rather than profit-maximizing, behavior of individual decision-making units. The purpose of the present section is to bring to light as carefully and rigorously as possible the global characteristics of the labor-managed economy. As we have pointed out in the introduction, we assume that money is absent from the system.

We further assume that a large number of firms in the economy produce a single product X, representative of national product, and because there is no intention at this stage of our argument to study structural phenomena, we postulate that a single technology is employed by all firms. The technology has positive marginal productivities of all factors everywhere and is of the first or second kind, as the case may require. Capital K and labor L are the only two factors of production used. While the equilibrium national income per laborer is one of the key variables to be determined, we will be making—in this and several subsequent sections—two alternative assumptions regarding the remuneration of capital. The first and more conventional in general equilibrium analysis is the assumption that the price of capital p_K (or of services of capital) is set through competitive bidding among a large number of firms. The other assumption is that p_K is an institutionally fixed constant. The latter alternative is considered because in any realistic case of a labor-managed economy it is perhaps more likely to occur than the competitive capital price-setting. Moreover, p_K will in any realistic context depend on other markets than those considered thus far in our barter analysis, and thus it must be supplied as an exogenous parameter.

To consider the operation of our highly idealized economy in greater detail let us turn to Figure 7.2.1. Points K_o and L_o together with the

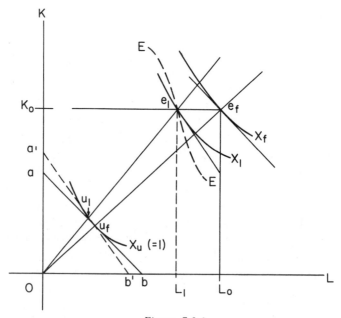

Figure 7.2.1

two coordinate axes define the resource availabilities of the economy. We will first consider what turns out to be the simplest situation, namely, the long-run (competitive) equilibrium with free entry and exit of firms. As we know from our previous analysis, these conditions are best approximated in our single-production-function world by the assumption that the national aggregate production function is of the second kind, that is, subject to constant returns to scale. From our previous analysis we also know that under the assumed conditions factors of production will be paid their respective marginal value products; but in a barter economy where the output X is taken as a numeraire the value products are nothing but the marginal physical products. With perfect market conditions (including factor mobility), p_K is equalized among firms—actually this is already implied in the above assertion of a single "national" technology of the second kind—and the same conditions also guarantee full employment of the K_o units of capital available to the economy. Note that if there were unemployed capital on the assumption of positive marginal products, it would always pay for existing or newly entering firms to compete for, and thus fully employ, all of the existing capital.

With free entry and exit of firms the available labor force must also be fully employed, and everyone in it must earn the same income. This is so because if there were workers earning either zero incomes—being unemployed—or less than some other workers being employed in firms using less advantageous factor combinations, they could always form new or join other existing firms and this would keep happening until an equilibrium were reached with full employment and equality of labor returns. Of course the equality of labor returns here argued is implied again in the postulate of a single aggregate technology for the economy.

All these results can now be quantified using Figure 7.2.1. With perfect competition and freedom of entry, the economy will be producing at the full-employment point e_f a national product X_f. The equal-product line X_f in the diagram is representative of the national aggregate production function of the second kind; that production function is derived from the individual firms' production functions in the way explained in Section 5.4. Its unit-isoquant (indicating the minimum combinations of inputs necessary to produce one unit of output) is X_u and thus the level of national product is measured by the ratio of $0e_f/0u_f$. Because the factors are being paid their respective marginal value products (in terms of the numeraire X), the line tangential to X_u in the diagram at u_f (having the same slope as the tangency at e_f) is a locus of factor combinations worth the same as the actual unit-input point u_f; but because all income is distributed to factors of production, every point of ab—including a and b—is also worth the price of X corresponding to the full-employment equilibrium at e_f. And thus the segments $0a$ and $0b$ measure the equilibrium price of X, in terms of capital and labor respectively—more specifically, $0a = p_X/p_K$ and $0b = p_X/p_L$ (i.e., $= p_X/Y$), where the p's are money (or abstract-numeraire) prices. But because we have selected the output X as our numeraire, the equilibrium remunerations (prices) of capital and labor are nothing but the inverse of these magnitudes, that is, $\overline{p_K} = 1/(0a)$ and $p_L = Y = 1/(0b)$. We recall also that these magnitudes are the marginal physical (or in terms of the X-numeraire, the marginal value) products of the two factors of production.

This completes our exposition of the finding of solutions for the long-run general equilibrium of a competitive and labor-managed economy, using a single technology (for all firms) in producing a single product, and enjoying perfect freedom of entry (and exit). As the reader will have realized already, all the solutions obtained are perfectly identical to those customarily obtained for a capitalist economy under identical assumptions (save, of course, for the assumptions of maximization of income per laborer and labor management). It is this identity of solutions—not unknown to us from the foregoing chapters —that leads us to start our analysis with the case of long-run competitive equilibrium under free entry; as we will see from the subsequent analysis, the identity of solutions disappears in most other instances.

As the next step, let us retain all the previously made assumptions except for that of freedom of entry; we also restrict, for the moment, the (identical) technologies used by each firm to the first kind; that is, in the capitalist context to technologies leading to the conventional U-shaped long-run cost functions. Under such conditions we know that factors of production will still be receiving their marginal products. Moreover, with a competitive and free capital market, p_K will be the same and all capital will be fully employed. In terms of Figure 7.2.1 this tells us that the economy must be producing somewhere along the horizontal line passing through K_o. The long-run equilibrium condition tells us that each firm must be operating at its locus of maximum physical efficiency; with, say, one thousand firms, we can thus enlarge a thousand times the maximum efficiency locus of a single firm and plot it in the diagram representing the whole economy. EE in Figure 7.2.1 is such an enlargement. Provided that all firms in equilibrium must resemble each other, the equilibrium point for the economy must be found on that locus; but this resemblance is guaranteed—as we know from Chapter 2—by the already established condition that all firms (in addition to having identical technologies) pay the same equilibrium price for capital.

And thus the solution for our long-run equilibrium without free entry must be at the intersection between EE and the line $K_o e_f$ in the diagram, that is, at point e_1. It is immediately apparent that the solution involves less than full employment of labor, the unemployment being measured by the distance $e_1 e_f$. The corresponding national product X_1 is measured by the ratio $0e_1/0u_1$. Those employed now are better off than they were under the full-employment situation, their real income (per laborer) $\overline{Y}$ being measured by $1/(0b')$. The reverse is true about capital, which now earns in real terms $\overline{p}_K = 1/(0a')$. It will be noted that the equal-product contour defining the new equilibrium national product, X_1, belongs to the same aggregate production function of the second kind as do X_u and X_f, and consequently the qualifications just made are correct.

While in the foregoing situation with free entry the economy performed in a Pareto-optimal way in the sense that it produced the producible maximum given its technology and its resources, it now performs less than optimally, some of its resources being unemployed. As is well known, the optimal solution for our economy with one thousand firms would be again to produce at point e_f, each firm again paying its factors the value of marginal product which is equal for all firms, but this time the output would be less than X_f. This reduction in full-employment output is imputable to the diminishing returns realized by each of the one thousand firms when we find ourselves in the region beyond EE in the diagram. Actually, on our assumption of technology of the first kind for each firm, there will now be a new equal-product line passing through e_f, derived as a thousandfold blow-up of an isoquant of the underlying single-firm technology.

As is well known, the system just identified as optimal in the case of restricted entry and technology of the first kind is an ideal, fully competitive capitalist barter economy. The key reason the labor-managed economy does not reach the optimum is the absence of a conventional labor market where unemployed laborers could compete with those who are employed. In fact—as we have realized at several occasions already—the laborers in the labor-managed economy need freedom of entry as a vehicle of their competitive power. Of course, we must recall that these conclusions hold only for, and critically depend on, the assumption of a unique optimum size for the existing firms, that is, of technology of the first kind.

Turning now to the long-run equilibrium of the economy with restricted entry and technology of the second kind, we will find our conclusions to be different. We know that with constant returns to scale the efficient locus EE degenerates for all firms and thus for the economy as a whole into the whole production function. Capital still will be fully employed because of competition among the thousand firms, and thus the economy again must operate on the frontier $K_o e_f$ in Figure 7.2.1; however, because of the degeneracy of the EE locus, the exact location of the equilibrium—strictly speaking—is indeterminate. This is so—as we recall from the analysis of the preceding chapters—because at any particular equilbrium on $K_o e_f$ each of the thousand firms is actually maximizing its income per laborer at the going competitive prices of X and K whatever its output, and, at the same time, the management of each firm would realize that (at those prices) expansion or contraction of output would leave the income per laborer unchanged. Of course, once interference of public authorities into the operation of the economy is permitted, it is clear that the full-employment optimal point e_f can easily be attained; actually, given the frictionless (or indeterminate) nature of the system just explained, it would take only a suggestion—and not an actual economic policy instrument—to secure the desired optimum results. Alternatively, in a more realistic context, it can be argued that confronted with the indeterminacy, the thousand firms would adopt what we have earlier termed a "social" behavior, and simply employ everyone who wanted to be employed. In fact, with second-kind technologies more relevant in the real world, this can be termed the most likely outcome.

Finally let us consider the short-run situation. As in our partial-equilibrium analysis, the important characteristic of the "short run" is that the capital stock of each and every firm is fixed (over the span of time considered), presumably given by past accumulations of plant and equipment—and nontransferable to other firms because of the specific physical nature of the capital assets. With a given amount of capital in the economy, K_o, the assumption of the short run then means for our analysis: first, that capital is nontransferable and rigidly allocated among firms; second, that there is no capital market wherein the price of capital, or the rate of interest, would be endogenously determined; and third, entry is limited, only the firms already in existence being permitted to operate.

Of the three, perhaps the most serious implication is that regarding the indeterminateness of the price of capital p_K, because, as we know from Chapter 2, without p_K the short-run equilibrium of any of the operating firms cannot be determined. Fortunately, this is not so serious a hindrance as might at first appear. Indeed, the "short run" is not something completely independent and pulled out from nowhere; it is only a point of view—or time horizon—in contemplating a single reality which has both short- and long-run aspects. And thus one way out of our impasse is to say that the p_K which we need for the short-run analysis is, so to speak, inherited or taken over from the "long run." In a more realistic context, even though firms cannot trade capital or services of it among themselves in the short run, there is still a price of capital, that is, a payment which the firms are called on to pay and which was contracted for at some previous date. An alternative assumption is that p_K is an institutionally set constant. Actually, in our macroanalysis of the labor-managed competitive economy in Part II, the latter will be our principal assumption for the short-run operation of the economy. The assumption is a realistic one not only in the sense that in the one concrete instance of the system here considered—that is, in Yugoslavia—such a fixed capital charge actually is levied, but also because normally it can be expected that the capital employed by the firms is social capital and thus a compensation set by the society is called for. But more will be said about all these and related matters later on. For the moment, let us just assume that we have, for the purpose of our short-run general equilibrium analysis, a given price of capital—and actually, since we still are in a barter economy, that price is fixed in real terms, that is in terms of the output X; we shall refer to that constant as $\overline{p}_K$.

In addition to the assumption of a common technology, we now also assume identical capital stocks for all firms, that is, identical shares of the total national capital stock K_o. This simplifies our analysis a good deal without affecting much, if at all, the generality of the conclusions. It is obvious that since the firms cannot divest themselves of their capital in the short run, and since we postulate always positive marginal productivities, K_o will always be fully employed. The economy thus is constrained to the line $K_o e_f$ in the diagram. However, contrary to the long-run case with limited entry, it now can operate, within a wide range of that locus, with technologies of the first kind. Due to the nontransferability of capital, as we know, the equalization of $\overline{p}_K$ to the marginal physical product now ceases to be operative (this actually makes it possible to assume equilibria at various points of $K_o e_f$), but $\bar{p}_K$ retains its determining influence. Specifically—as we know from Chapter 3—for a prescribed $\bar{p}_K{}^o$ there will be a corresponding maximum real income per laborer $\bar{Y}^o$ for a certain level of employment L^o and output X^o, which are the solutions of the system. Because the real equilibrium incomes per laborer must equal the marginal productivity, increases in the real price of capital $\bar{p}_K$ unambiguously imply increases of employment in the short run; and of course for some capital price high enough, the full-employment solution at e_f will be reached.

As is well known, the full-employment solution at e_f would always be reached (*ceteris paribus*) in a capitalist economy in the short run through the automatic forces of the labor market. In the labor-managed economy the policy-makers have the power to produce such a solution in the short run through an appropriate selection of $\bar{p}_K$. As is clear from our analysis, if the technologies of the individual firms are of the second kind, the authorities have well accomplished the task because the equilibrium will remain at e_f even in the long run. If, on the other hand, the optimum sizes of the existing firms are not arbitrary— that is, if we are facing technologies of the first kind—the $\bar{p}_K$ set at a high level (to attain e_f) will backfire if entry of new firms is sluggish or not permitted at all. This is so because in the long run without free entry the economy must revert to Ee in Figure 7.2.1—and it will do so to a point below the line $K_o e_f$. Actually, to be more precise, with competition in the capital market the authorities could indefinitely enforce an abnormally high $\bar{p}_K$ only by withholding some of the total stock K_o from the market. But in several respects we are touching here on subjects belonging to later chapters, and therefore let us return to our main concern.

We have already determined in quantitative terms all the solutions of long-run equilibria with and without free entry. Let us now do the same for the short run, using Figure 7.2.1. We know already that a prescribed $\bar{p}_K$ uniquely determines, in conjunction with the national production function (which now is a thousandfold enlargement of the production function of the individual firm), the equilibrium short-run level of national product. If the production functions of the individual firms are of the second kind and characterized by X_u in the diagram, the equilibrium real income of labor will be determined as before; for example, for a short-run equilibrium at e_f, $\bar{Y} = 1/(0b)$. If the technologies of individual firms are of the first kind, the quantitative answers will be found by considering the representative firm—one identical with all the one thousand—in the same way as we did in Chapter 2; but of course it is postulated here that labor is the only variable input.

If we were to end this section here, a careful reader might justifiably object that what we have discussed is something which, at most, is a "truncated" general equilibrium and not what was promised at the outset. Indeed, a general equilibrium theory must always include the conditions of demand, as embodied in social or private preferences, as well as the conditions of supply which have been emphasized thus far. To give a summary explanation first, let it be pointed out that the emphasis on the supply side was warranted by the fact that in going from traditional general equilibrium analysis to that of a labor-managed economy most of the changes occur on the side of supply, that is, more specifically, in the conditions of production. Let it also be noted that supply of labor—that is, demand for leisure—was assumed away (in a not fully justifiable, but quite common manner) by postulating a fixed supply of labor L_o, unrelated to what labor receives as remuneration. On the other hand, we have disposed of the demand for the single product of the economy by invoking—implicitly, as is done so often—the Walras law. But we must now turn to some of the questions just raised in somewhat greater detail, not only because we want to cover some of the ground not yet considered in this section, but also to dispose of some problems which otherwise would keep reappearing later on.

It should be clear that the system of labor management cannot affect the conventional theory of demand; it can only affect—presumably through a different income distribution—the specific form of the demand functions actually obtained. And thus we can postulate, as a summary of conventional demand analysis,[1] a labor-supply function of the form

$$L^s = L^s(\overline{Y}) \qquad (1)$$

which is nothing but a mirror-image of a demand function for national product X; the latter can be written as

$$X^d = X^d(1/\overline{Y}) \qquad (2)$$

The long-run general equilibrium with free entry is easiest to handle.

[1] By this we understand a derivation based on the maximization of utility by society or individuals, constrained by total availability of leisure, and yielding, for any prescribed real income per laborer, $\overline{Y} = Y/p_X$, the amounts of X demanded and L supplied (i.e., residual leisure demanded).

Under these conditions, entry must occur as long as the actual real income per laborer, as obtained earlier in this section, is above the corresponding supply price, as given by relation (1). The general equilibrium will be realized when the supply price equals the remuneration actually paid by all the (identical) firms in the economy.[2] When this happens the product market must be in equilibrium also. This is so because at the equilibrium income per laborer the laborers demand exactly their wage bill in terms of the real good, and the remainder of total supply of X is paid out, at the equilibrium price $\bar{p}_K$, as remuneration of capital.[3]

Now consider either the short- or the long-run situation where entry is limited. We know already that in that situation full employment need not be attained in equilibrium except by a deliberate policy or social behavior of labor-managed firms. At first this would imply that the labor market and consequently—through Walras' law —the product market may not be in equilibrium. This cannot be said, however, because, even though relations (1) and (2) still are meaningful and defined, the labor market and hence (in our barter economy) the product market do not exist in their conventional form. Specifically, there is no mechanism of adjustment which would make $\bar{Y}$ decline when the supply finds itself (for the corresponding employment) below it, and vice versa.[4] In the absence of free entry, we may thus have a highly unorthodox situation where the system finds itself in a general equilibrium, all its variables being defined at a given level which perpetuates itself once attained, yet the supply and demand for labor are not equalized.

7.3: *The Structural General Equilibrium in the Long Run with Free Entry Guaranteed*

In this section we will discuss the long-run operation of a labor-managed economy wherein freedom of entry is guaranteed but which contains, in contrast to the assumptions made in the preceding section,

---

[2]If the firms had different technologies, the conditions would be that the marginal (least efficient) firm would pay the supply price of labor.

[3]In fact we are postulating here that in our barter economy the market for physical capital (or its services) is always cleared, as a matter of an identity; however, it would not be difficult, and would not change the analysis substantially, to introduce the fixed capital stock as a part of society's or of individuals' endowment, and thus to incorporate it directly as one of the factors of total national demand for X.

[4]To a degree these equilibrating forces will be restored when money is introduced in Part II.

more than one productive sector. Specifically, in most of our discussion we will assume that two products, X_1 and X_2, are produced by a large number of firms, using identical technologies, that buy and sell in perfectly competitive markets. All firms are labor managed and maximize their respective incomes per laborer in the long run. The reader who has carefully reflected on the foregoing six chapters may by now become suspicious, and with good reason, whether at all it was necessary to write this section. Indeed, we strongly suspect—even if we are not sure of it—that, on the assumptions made, the labor-managed competitive economy should perform in exactly the same way as does its capitalist counterpart, that is, Pareto-optimally. We recall that this analogy held for the assumptions of free entry and identical technologies both for a single industry and for the global general equilibrium studied in the preceding section.

Nonetheless, if for no other reason than completeness, we have to go briefly over the proposed subject. It may not be a complete waste of time because in this way we can clarify some minor "procedural" points which otherwise could bother us later on. Also we ought not to overlook the important fact that in this section we are actually proving one of the most important properties of the "pure" labor-managed economy: namely, that a multisectoral perfectly competitive general equilibrium of that economy is Pareto-optimal in the long run provided that free entry is guaranteed. In other words, under these conditions no one in the economy can conceivably be made better off without reducing the welfare of someone else. Therefore, there is another structure besides the "ideal" capitalist one which is maximally efficient *through its automatic operation*—a conclusion which is usually neglected implicitly or explicitly.

Let us now go briefly through the underlying analysis: From section 5.4 we know the equilibrium operation of a perfectly competitive industry composed of firms each using a single common technology—whether of the first or the second kind—can be fully "simulated" by the operation of a single firm using the maximally efficient linear homogeneous technology consistent with the underlying (common) technology[5] and buying factors and selling its produce as if a perfect competitor, that is, with *average* factor cost = marginal value product. Thus it is possible to represent our labor-managed economy

[5] By "consistent with" we understand here a technology either identical with the underlying firms' technologies, if these are of the second kind, or given by the locus of maximum physical efficiency of the underlying technologies, if the latter are of the first kind.

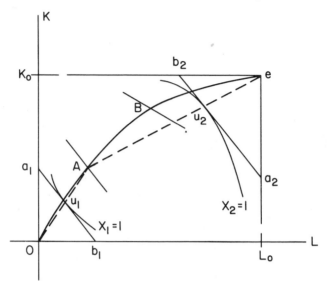

Figure 7.3.1

through the customary box-diagram technique, illustrated in Figure 7.3.1, where the two linear homogeneous isoquant maps are measured from 0 and e for products X_1 and X_2 respectively. Because for technologies of this type a single isoquant is sufficient to describe the technology, we have drawn only the two unit-isoquants marked $X_1 = 1$ and $X_2 = 1$. For the moment it is assumed that the supplies of productive resources, K_0 and L_0 are fixed.

The postulate of freedom of entry guarantees that the full amounts of these supplies will be employed. Indeed, if some were not, their corresponding zero-income would induce them—on our basic entry-principle—to form new labor-managed firms and thereby secure a higher income. In the long run, moreover, the price of capital will be equalized for all users through competition among firms and between industries; such conditions involve, among others, the postulate of perfect factor mobility. That same postulate, applied to labor, guarantees the equalization of incomes per laborer between the two industries (the equalization within an industry already being contained in the derivation of the "simulated" industry-technologies). Actually what we have just termed perfect mobility of labor is nothing but a slight generalization or modification of our basic entry-principle: in the long run, workers will always leave their employment and form new firms provided that the equilibrium operation of the latter leads to increased incomes per laborer.

Now recalling the equilibrium behavior of the two "simulating" industry-firms, and using what has just been said about employment and remuneration of productive factors, it becomes clear not only that all the factor endowments given by point e in the diagram will be fully employed, but also that the marginal rates of substitution will be equalized in the two industries. That is, we must find ourselves at the conventional Pareto-optimal contract curve $0ABe$ (recall that the contract-curve is the locus of points of tangency between isoquants of the two linearly homogeneous technologies descriptive of the two industries).

As usual, to that contract locus corresponds a production-possibility locus (the diagram of which is not shown). The important and almost self-evident fact is that the slope of the production-possibility locus, while entirely dependent on technological data, also reflects, under perfectly competitive conditions, the equilibrium product-price ratio. While this could be proven directly for the labor-managed situation in a more roundabout manner, we will content ourselves to prove it here using the analogy with the capitalist pure general equilibrium. Indeed, we know that in a fully competitive capitalist economy production will be taking place on a production-possibility locus which, *ceteris paribus*, will be exactly the same as that for the labor-managed economy just derived. But because under the "perfect" capitalist conditions relative product prices must equal the slope of the production-possibility locus, and because factor remunerations under both regimes must (*ceteris paribus*) be the same, and because under both regimes total value of output is distributed to productive factors, the slope of the production-possibility locus of the labor-managed economy must also reflect relative prices of products X_1 and X_2.

It thus follows that under perfect competition in the product market, the general equilibrium price ratio and the corresponding production point will be obtained—again in the conventional manner—at the point of tangency between a social indifference curve and the production-possibility function; more exactly, in a pluralistic society, the equilibrium point on the production-possibility locus will be found where the implied product supplies equal the aggregate demands for such products, each individual demand entering the aggregate being obtained from a household's preference function and budget constraint.

Suppose that the demand conditions are such as to lead to the allocation of productive resources in the economy indicated by A in Figure 7.3.1. Using the construction shown in the preceding section (observing that the slopes or marginal rates of substitution at u_1, A, and u_2 are the same) we immediately get the corresponding quantitative general equilibrium solutions. Using a superscript "0" for such solutions, we have: $X_1^0 = (0A)/(0u_1)$, $X_2^0 = (eA)/(eu_2)$, $p_{X_1}^0/p_{X_2}^0 = (0a_1)/(ea_2) = (0b_1)/(eb_2)$, $Y^0/p_K^0 = (0a_1)/(0b_1)$, and finally $Y^0/p_{X_1} = 1/(0b_1)$ and $Y^0/p_{X_2} = 1/(eb_2)$. Note that we no longer can speak unambiguously about real income and use the sign $\overline{Y}$ because we now have two products; and thus, as shown by the last two equalities, we now have to speak of "real" solutions expressed alternatively in terms of X_1 and X_2.

The comparative statics of the long run with free entry is most simple, and obviously again identical to that known to us from the theory of capitalist economies. Suppose that the demand conditions change, perhaps as a result of introduction of international exchange, and that product X_1 becomes more expensive. The new (long-run and free-entry) equilibrium allocation point again must be on the contract curve but to the northeast of A, and all the quantitative solutions will be obtained as above for A. A point that must be stressed here is that B will be reached only in the long run, and provided that freedom of entry prevails. How B will actually be reached, in stages where either or both of these assumptions is not made, will be our subject later in this chapter. At this stage let it only be mentioned that the analogy between the capitalist and labor-managed economies then disappears entirely. The analogy also ceases when technologies are permitted to be different within an industry. This situation will also be taken up at a later stage.

Before leaving this section, a few words should be said about the properties of the general equilibrium just derived. It is a well-known fact that the production possibility function arrived at here is generally concave and never convex—it can be linear only when X_1 and X_2 are produced using identical technologies (i.e., defined by an identical equal-product line). And thus if a single nonintersecting social-indifference map is postulated, the equilibrium must be unique. In that case, as the reader can easily verify by considering variations in supply and demand in the vicinity of equilibrium, the equilibrium will also be a stable one. If demand conditions are derived from individual preferences and incomes, the two conclusions just obtained need not hold; especially with important differences in tastes among individuals and strong income-redistributional effects of relative price variation, there can be several solutions along the production-possibility contour, stable ones alternating with unstable ones.[6]

It also should be clear that the analysis presented here for two products and two primary factors can be extended, without any change in our main conclusions, to situations involving many products and many factors as well as the existence of intermediate (input-output) product flows. The latter generalization will be presented briefly in the following section.

7.4: Long-Run General Equilibrium and Interindustry Flows in the Labor-Managed Economy

The general equilibrium analysis carried out thus far is unrealistic in one important respect: final products are produced from primary products only and do not use any goods as inputs. The purpose of this section is to amend this imperfection and show both that the analysis can readily be altered to include input-output relationships and that the main conclusions obtained in the preceding section remain unaltered. We remain—for the moment—within the sphere of long-run analysis with free entry of firms; similarly, we retain all other assumptions of the preceding section excepting that of no intermediate products.

As in the preceding section, perfect competition, free entry and perfect factor mobility guarantee full employment of national resources and equalization of prices of inputs and outputs to all users and producers. Identity of technologies among firms within a single industry, in turn, guarantees a linearly homogeneous production function for each industry, that is, a situation where proportional variation of all inputs implies proportional variation of output (or outputs). The primary factors of production, capital and labor, are continuously substitutable, as they were in all of our previous analysis, while the material input—that is, the other product X (in our two-product economy)— enters the productive process always in a constant proportion, a_{12} for X_1, and a_{21} for X_2. In other words, we are now returning to the more general production function which was used in Chapter 2.

Let us first make the unrealistic, but expositionally useful assumption that each of the two industries is always given (say, by imports) whatever amounts of raw materials it needs for its operation. Then, with the box-diagram of the preceding section (see Figure 7.3.1) repre-

---

[6]A simple exposition of these conclusions will be found in my *International Trade: Theory and Economic Policy* (Homewood, Ill., 1962), Chapter 14. The analysis there presented describes a capitalist economy, but we know that there is no difference in the long run and with free entry between the two systems.

senting the economy's endowments and the primary-factor requirements of the two industries (given by the equal-product lines), the
economy will—on the assumptions made—operate again at the contract curve. The latter locus then generates the locus of maximum gross
outputs attainable by the economy, illustrated by AEB in Figure 7.4.1.

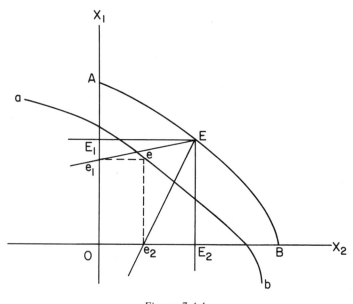

Figure 7.4.1

This locus, for the moment, also represents the availability of the two
products to the economy, because we have assumed that the two industries are given whatever material inputs they may need.

   The true availability, or production-possibility locus of the economy
is then derived from AEB simply by diminishing the amounts implied
by AEB by the necessary interindustry requirements (which, until now,
were freely given). This is easily done, as shown by the broken-line
construction in Figure 7.4.1. Suppose that we want to derive the *net*
outputs of the two products for the gross-output point E. Through E
passes a line Ee_1 whose slope, measured from (the axis) EE_1, is a_{12}.
Consequently, at any point of Ee_1, including e_1, the vertical distance
from EE_1 shows how much of X_2 will be required for a gross output
of X_2 measured to the left from E. E_1e_1 thus is the interindustry consumption of X_1 needed by the economy producing gross outputs at E.

Similarly, e_2E_2 is the interindustry requirement of X_2. And because these requirements no longer are assumed to be given to the economy, they must be withdrawn from gross output, as is shown by the construction (derivation) of point e. The latter point is the maximum *net* output of the two products attainable, given national resources of primary factors, the technologies, and resource allocation leading to gross output at A. The locus aeb shows all the *net*-output points. It passes through the second and fourth quadrant because net outputs can be negative in an open economy where raw materials can be imported. Recall that import of intermediate product is nothing but a negative output from the economy's point of view. For example, when the economy produces gross output at point A, it has available to itself a net output of X_1 equal to the vertical coordinate of point a, provided that it imports X_2 as an input in the amount equivalent to the horizontal coordinate of a.

Again, because the long-run situation with free entry here described is perfectly analogous to that of a capitalist economy, results for the latter obtained elsewhere can be used in completing our exposition.[7] First, it has been shown that the slope of aeb reflects the ratio of product prices. The relative prices (remunerations) of capital and labor are, as they were in the absence of interindustry flows, reflected by the common marginal rate of substitution (see Figure 7.3.1) at the equilibrium points on the contract curve. Thus the only price ratios (recall that only price ratios concern us in our barter economy) which remain to be determined are those of real factor earnings in terms of both products, say Y/p_{X_1} and Y/p_{X_2}. Referring back to Figure 7.3.1, suppose that the economy is producing at A, but now the two industries call for material inputs, as explained above. $X_1 = 1$ and $X_2 = 1$ still being unit-isoquants (with respect to the substitutable primary factors), $0b_1$ and eb_2 now are the primary-factor (rather than total) unit costs measured in terms of labor. To obtain prices of the two products, the costs of material inputs now must be added, so that we have

$$(p_{X_1}/Y) = 0b_1 + a_{21}(p_{X_2}/Y) \tag{3}$$

and similarly

$$(p_{X_2}/Y) = eb_2 + a_{12}(p_{X_1}/Y) \tag{4}$$

[7]In particular, see my paper, "Pure Theory of International Trade and Interindustry Flows," *Quarterly Journal of Economics*, 77 (March 1963).

These are two linear equations in the two product prices (each price expressed in terms of labor units) which can readily be solved to yield

$$p_{X_1}/Y = \frac{0b_1 - a_{21}(eb_2)}{1 - a_{21}a_{12}}$$ (5)

and

$$p_{X_2}/Y = \frac{eb_2 - a_{12}(0b_1)}{1 - a_{12}a_{21}}$$ (6)

Therefore, all solutions of the general equilibrium corresponding to a prescribed allocation of resources are determined. The result of the analysis follows the lines of, and comes to the same conclusion as, the preceding section. In particular, the operation of the competitive labor-managed economy with input-output flows is again Pareto-optimal, with free entry in the long run, and the properties of the equilibria are the same as without interindustry flows (note, for one thing, that the derivation of the net from the gross-production possibility cannot reverse the convexity of the former locus). The only novel thing now is the possibility of negative net (not gross) outputs when international trade is permitted.

7.5: Short-Run Adjustment of General Equilibrium to Changing Market Conditions

In the preceding four sections we have shown the principal aspects of long-run general equilibrium of a labor-managed economy in which free entry and exit of firms is permitted. We also know now how a general equilibrium will adjust to changing demand under these conditions. What we do not know yet is the exact path through which the general equilibrium will proceed from one long-run—or permanent—equilibrium to another. From what we have shown in the context of partial equilibrium analysis we can expect that the adjustment in the short run, and in the long run without free entry, will tend to be difficult and very likely less smooth than in an ideal capitalist situation. The purpose of the present section is to take up the first half of the problem, namely, the adjustment in the short run. It is the "strict," or *conventional*, short run that we have in mind in most of this discussion. Only at the end of the section and in section 8 will we say more about the *social* short run adjustment and some other realistic aspects of the problem.

In order to keep the analysis as simple as possible, we now abandon again the assumption of interindustry flows—noting, however, that

just as in the preceding section, such a simplification cannot significantly affect our conclusions. We retain the assumptions of a two-
sector, two-factor economy with identical technologies and a single
output in each sector (this assumption will be relaxed in a later section.)
Our point of departure—that is, the initial general equilibrium—is the
long-run situation with free entry established in section 7.3. Our
present task is to show the displacement of the general equilibrium
from that initial situation in the short run, resulting from changed demand conditions. Regarding the change in demand conditions, all we
have to do is to specify that the new equilibrium barter-exchange ratio
between the two products (i.e., the terms of trade) is different from the
old one; specifically, we will postulate that X_1 becomes more expensive
relative to X_2 in the new situation. Clearly, this change, in turn, can be
the consequence of a shift in national preferences, or a change in international trading conditions—but this distinction will not concern us
here.

The technologies can be of either the first or the second kind. In
either case, in the initial equilibrium (which is Pareto-optimal) the factor proportions in all firms within one industry are identical, and so
are the marginal rates of substitution. Point E in Figure 7.5.1 illustrates

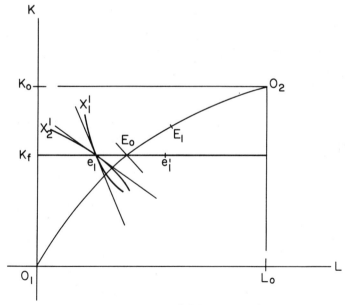

Figure 7.5.1

the initial allocation of (fully employed) resources L_0 and K_0 between the two industries and the (common) factor proportions in each industry; the line passing through E_0 indicates the common marginal rate of substitution in the initial equilibrium. The important characteristic of the short-run transitional equilibrium which we are seeking here is that the capital stocks employed by each firm are fixed, and consequently so is the capital available to the industry. In terms of our diagram (Figure 7.5.1) the short-run equilibrium—or equilibria—must be somewhere on the line passing through K_f and E_0 in Figure 7.5.1.

We say "equilibria" because we do not know whether there will be full employment of labor in the new situation; and if there were not, there would be two equilibrium points on the line $K_f E_0$. Actually, as we have seen in Section 7.2, full employment, even with one sector only, is not guaranteed in the short-run general equilibrium except if the long-run market forces, or the central authorities, set the price of capital p_K at an appropriate level. The structural disturbance which we are considering here can clearly involve such changes in $p_K/p_{X_i} (i = 1, 2)$ as would not guarantee full employment of labor. This, however, we could think of as a global rather than structural aspect of the disturbance—and the global, one-sector situation has already been examined.

In order to bring out our principal concern here (that is, the structural effects), let us postulate that the authorities at all times set the supply of money and p_K (i.e., the money price of capital charged to both industries) in such a way as to guarantee full employment of labor at incomes per laborer equal to the marginal value product in each industry. At the same time, however, we must remember that if such a deliberate policy is not pursued—and, for example, the initial real price of capital is fixed in terms of any product-price index whatsoever (note that an index-number problem is involved here)—underemployment of labor can be the result; actually, overemployment (as explained and defined through the inequality of income per laborer and the marginal value product of labor in Chapter 5) then is equally unlikely. With all these remarks and assumptions in mind, let us now examine the new short-run solution in Figure 7.5.1. We already know that it must be on the line $K_f E_0$ and that it will be represented by a single point. But we also know from our earlier partial equilibrium analysis that with an increase in the price of X_1 and reduction in the price of X_2, both being measured in terms of capital (note that these relative prices cannot move in the same direction given the postulated full-employment policy of the authorities), the employment and hence output in the first industry will be reduced and the employment and output in the second industry increased. In other words and with reference to Figure 7.5.1, the new equilibrium will be established to the left of E_0, at a point such as e_1. The income per laborer—equal to the marginal value product of labor—will now be higher in the first than in the second industry. Realizing also that the movement from E_0 to e_1 must involve a decline in the marginal productivity of capital in the first industry and an increase in the second, the marginal rates of substitution in the two industries must be different at e_1 in the way indicated by the isoquants X_1^1 and X_2^1. This inequality implies one inefficiency of the short-run solution; another will emerge when we consider the production-possibilities plane.

Before making that step, let us consider two other points in the box-diagram of Figure 7.5.1. First, the reader will recall that with an increase in relative price of X_1, the long-run allocation of resources with free entry will be somewhere at a Pareto-optimal point such as E_1, whether in a labor-managed or a capitalist economy. The position of e_1 relative to E_1 suggests the importance of a short-run distortion of the process of general equilibrium adjustment. The reader will also recall that in the short run an ideal fully competitive capitalist economy—also constrained (by definition) to the locus $K_f E_0$—will move to a point such as e_1'. That point is subject to a shortcoming similar to e_1 in one respect: the marginal rates of substitution are not equal at that location. However, in another respect, as we will soon see more clearly, the e_1' is superior to the conventional short-run equilibrium e_1 because it is located in the general direction of E_1.

Let us now turn to Figure 7.5.2, entirely based on the box-diagram which we have just considered, but revealing the allocation of outputs and product prices rather than the allocation of inputs and factor prices. The solid contour passing through E_0 and E_1 is the customary (long-run and free-entry) production-possibility frontier of the labor-managed economy, and the two points just mentioned are the long-run and free-entry equilibria corresponding to the price lines $t_0 t_0$ and $t_1 t_1$. In a closed economy, E_0 and E_1 are also points indicating the national allocation of consumption of the two products. The question which concerns us here is the movement of the equilibrium point, in the conventional short run, from the initial equilibrium at E_0, brought about by a change in the relative price-ratio from the level indicated by $t_0 t_0$ to the level indicated by $t_1 t_1$. Note that in the new situation X_1 becomes more expensive. As indicated in the diagram, the new equilibrium must

be within the area enclosed by the Pareto-optimal production possibility locus, and southeast of E_0. It is immediately apparent that the
short-run equilibrium of the labor-managed economy is considerably
inferior to the equilibrium which will be attained in the long run and
with free entry. As indicated in the diagram, the equilibrium is also
inferior to the short-run equilibrium of the ideal capitalist economy at e_1', which, while not on $E_0 E_1$, is the best possible solution under
the constraint of capital immobility; note that, as is well known, e_1' is at
a point of tangency between a price line parallel to $t_1 t_1$ and the production-possibility locus corresponding to the fixed allocation of capital at K_f, as shown in Figure 7.5.1.

In terms of index numbers, consideration of Figure 7.5.2 leads immediately to the following conclusions: $(e_1 < E_0)_{L,P'}$ $(e_1 < e_1' < E_1)_L$

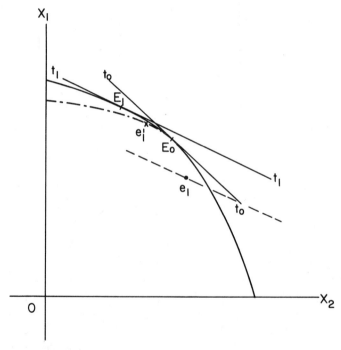

Figure 7.5.2

and $(e_1 \gtrless e_1' \gtrless E_1)_P$, where L and P—the initials of names appearing
in customary terminology—correspond to valuation at the initial (i.e.,
$t_0 t_0$) and the terminal (i.e., $t_1 t_1$) prices respectively.

In concluding this section, it must be noted that what we have presented here is the analysis of what we have earlier referred to as the *conventional* short-run adjustment in labor-managed general equilibria, one based on the assumption of single-product industries. Both the introduction of *social* short-run behavior and the postulated joint production alter the results, and make the case of labor-managed economies unambiguously more favorable than that just examined. Because a more careful analysis of these alternative assumptions overlaps to some extent with the long-run case to be discussed in the next section, we will postpone it for the present. Just a few remarks may be useful. Note for example that in the *social* short run there could be no flow of resources from one industry to the other, and thus the general equilibrium solution corresponding to the change in relative prices from those indicated by $t_0 t_1$ to those indicated by $t_1 t_1$ would still be at E_0 in Figure 7.5.2—a result clearly and unambiguously superior to e_1. If, on the other hand, X_1 and X_2 were jointly produced by a single industry, the change in relative prices would normally lead to a short-run adjustment such as $E_0 e_1'$ in the diagram.

7.6: *Long-Run Adjustment of General Equilibrium to Changing Market Conditions*

In this section we use the general setting of the preceding section, but ask a new question: what will be the long-run effect of a change in demand conditions on the general equilibrium of the labor-managed economy? In other words, we want to study the adjustment from an initial equilibrium such as E_0 in the preceding section when the relative product price-ratio changes and, at the same time, capital is mobile among, and competed for by, firms and industries. As the reader may infer from our previous discussion, the distinction between technologies of the first and of the second kinds now is critical. First we will postulate the first kind, that is, a production function subject first to increasing and then to diminishing returns; later in the section, we will alter this assumption and show the corresponding results together with the solutions pertaining to *social* adjustment and joint production. It must also be stressed that, as in the preceding section, the number of firms is fixed in each industry, entry and exit not being permitted (note that if entry were permitted we would have the long-run Pareto-optimal solution known to us already from section 7.3).

The endowments of capital and labor again are fixed for the economy

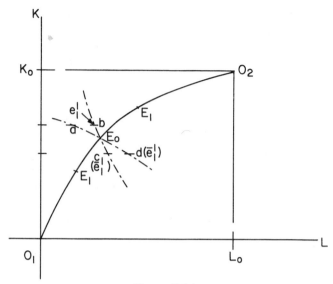

Figure 7.6.1

and given by points L_0 and K_0 in Figure 7.6.1. Capital must now be fully employed at all times because it is perfectly mobile and subject to competitive bidding by firms whose technology, as we have always assumed, never comes to a point of zero marginal productivity of capital. As for the employment of labor, the solution will emerge presently from our discussion of general equilibrium adjustment.

Since we have technologies of the first kind, we know that in the absence of limitations of labor availability each of the existing (and only conceivable) firms must operate at all times at the locus of maximum physical efficiency. Moreover, because the price of capital p_K must be equal through competition for all users of capital, the factor proportions will be the same at all times within each industry. The common factor proportions and the allocation of national resources in an initial equilibria are illustrated by point E_0 in Figure 7.6.1; the equilibrium again is Pareto-optimal and corresponds to a prescribed initial product-price ratio.

Now suppose that the relative price ratio changes in favor of X_2. We consider this price change first because, as we will soon see, it is easier to handle. With ad and bc in Figure 7.6.1 representing the aggregated loci of maximum physical efficiency for the second and the first industry respectively, the postulated price change will lead to an equilibrium production point in the first industry such as c and in the second industry such as d. This is so because (1) capital must be fully employed at all times, and (2) with an increase of the relative price of X_2, income per laborer must increase in the second industry relative to that in the first and, given an identical price of capital for both industries, this implies an increase in the capital-labor ratio in the second industry and a decline of that ratio in the first industry.

Recalling that the factor inputs in the second industry are measured from 0_2, this immediately implies that there will be unemployment of labor equivalent to the distance cd. Given the configuration of the loci of maximum physical efficiency, unemployment is a necessary outcome of an improvement in the relative price of X_2 in the vicinity of E_0. Of course, full employment could (again) be reached at some point where the two dashed-and-dotted lines would intersect; but this would be one possibility out of infinity. Even if this happened, and points such as c and d coincided, the new solution would still be nonoptimal because the marginal rates of substitution in the two industries still would have to be different. Beyond such an intersection—as much as for factor allocations northwest of E_0 in Figure 7.6.1—full employment of labor will be the result of product-price alterations; however, other inefficiencies still will remain. Before turning to such situations involving an increase in the relative price of X_1, let us translate what we have done thus far into the plane of production possibilities.

Our initial equilibrium E_0 again is found on the Pareto-optimal production frontier E_1E_0 in Figure 7.6.2; as indicated, it corresponds to the

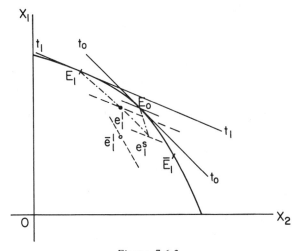

Figure 7.6.2

relative price ratio shown by the slope of $t_0 t_0$. It is clear that in the long run, and with free entry guaranteed, an improvement in the relative price of X_2 must result in an equilibrium such as $\overline{E}_1$ in either diagram. Without freedom of entry, however, the equilibrium will be reached in Figure 7.6.2 at a point such as $\overline{e}_1^1$, involving at least two types of inefficiency, labor unemployment and different rates of factor substitution. There is no special reason for factor proportions to change, except that which we have suggested in our partial equilibrium analysis to the effect that increased capital-labor ratios may correspond to larger optimum sizes of firms. If this hypothesis is correct, the new equilibrium point $\overline{e}_1^1$, as shown in Figure 7.6.2, should reveal a higher proportion of X_2 relative to the initial equilibrium at E_0.

Still retaining the assumption of technology of the first kind, let us now consider what happens when the disturbance of the initial general equilibrium stems from—or is accompanied by—an increase in the relative price of X_1. This price change must lead to a relative increase in labor remuneration in the first industry, and this, with full employment and identical prices of capital should lead to factor-allocation points in the two industries at points such as a and b in Figure 7.6.1. But this, obviously, is impossible because these points imply an excess demand for labor equivalent to the distance ab. Thus, in the absence of labor immigration (not postulated here) something must give way. It is quite clear that in the new equilibrium both factors of production will be fully employed. The equilibrium full-employment allocation will be established at b in Figure 7.5.1 on the locus of maximum physical efficiency of the industry producing X_1. This must be so because with an increase in its relative price, the first industry not only tends to reduce its labor employment, but also pays its laborers better than the other industry. Consequently, it is in a position to retain the optimum level of employment it needs (at b measured from 0_1). The other industry, on the other hand, while gladly hiring all the laborers released by the first industry, does not find enough laborers to settle at its equilibrium locus of maximum physical efficiency—that is, at a point such as a in the diagram. This tends to produce a reduction in output of X_2 relative to that of X_1. This is indicated by point e_1^1 in Figure 7.6.2 which is the long-run general equilibrium solution for the labor-managed economy without free entry, corresponding to initial conditions at E_0 and a new price ratio implied by $t_1 t_1$. It is clear that the point is suboptimal—that is, lies below the locus $E_1 E_0$. In spite of its full-employment operation, the economy is not at its optimum for two reasons. First, the marginal rates of substitution in the two industries cannot be all identical, and second, most or all of the firms in one of the two industries cannot operate with maximum physical efficiency.

This nearly completes our discussion of the case in which technologies in each industry are identical and of the first kind. By way of summing up, we are in a position to answer the original question regarding the various stages of general equilibrium adjustment: a disturbance associated in Figure 7.6.2 with a change in relative prices from those implicit in $t_0 t_0$ to those implicit in $t_1 t_1$ will make the economy's equilibrium point travel from E_0 first to e_1^s, in the short run, then to e_1^1, in the long run without free entry and exit of firms, and finally to the new Pareto-optimal solution at E_1 once entry and exit of firms governed by income-per-laborer motivation is allowed. It will be recalled that a similar trajectory for an ideal capitalist economy, also leading from E_0 to E_1, would be smoother, proceeding along an approximately straight line from the first to the second permanent (and Pareto-optimal) equilibrium.

Of course, what has just been said presupposes a technology of the first kind. If, on the other hand, each of the firms operates under constant returns to scale, the outcome will generally be different. We know that under these conditions the loci ad and bc in Figure 7.6.1 degenerate into the entire factor-input plane defined by 0_1 and 0_2. In other words, any specific factor allocation is technologically just as efficient, for each industry, as all factor allocations having the same factor proportions. Under such conditions, strictly speaking, the general equilibrium still should move in the *short run* from E_0 to a point such as e_1^s (in Figure 7.6.2) as a result of an improvement of price for the first industry. However, if the managements of the firms in the two industries consider the price change as lasting, and especially if they are reluctant to release their fellow laborers, they may now skip the short run (or, if we want, adopt what we earlier referred to as the *social* short run) and, with all scales of operation being now equally efficient, start performing the *social* long-run adjustment through competitive hiring and firing of capital. This would then involve (again in terms of Figure 7.6.2) staying at E_0 in the short run—but with a new price ratio, as shown by the flatter line passing through that point—and then proceeding more directly (but still slightly less than optimally) in the over-all direction of E_1 through long-run relocation of capital assets and by-and-large unchanged allocation of labor among the two industries. This solution, then, although different, would bring about the adjustment in the general equilibrium with an efficiency a good deal more comparable to that of an ideal capitalist economy.

Actually, carrying this argument to its logical conclusion, it can be said that if the managers of all the firms operating under constant returns to scale were even more farsighted, they would adjust their scale of operation (upward or downward) as long as they could see differences between their own and other industry's incomes per laborer, knowing that competition and free entry eventually would bring about income equalization anyway. In that case the new Pareto-optimal equilibrium at E_1 could be reached even more directly, and in fact, more efficiently, than in the ideal capitalist situation. Note that even with this high degree of foresight, such is not the case with technologies of the first kind because the optimal scale of operation is uniquely given for each firm in the industry in the long run.

Of course, once we postulate joint production, there is very little reason for the short- and long-run adjustment in the labor-managed economy to proceed away from the most efficient contour $E_0 E_1$ in Figure 7.6.2.

7.7: *General Equilibrium and Various Market Imperfections*

Our discussion of the general equilibrium of an economy based on workers' management would not be complete if we did not consider some major market imperfections. These, in the real world, may be closer to the "rules of the game" than the pure model studied thus far. The analysis is useful not only because it shows exactly the effects of the imperfections on the general equilibrium solution, but also because it establishes an indispensable basis for a subsequent analysis (see Part IV) of policy instruments which could cope with such imperfections. Throughout this section, we will consider only long-run equilibria, and most of the time—unless the very imperfection considered explicitly precludes it—we will postulate freedom of entry and exit. The relevant motivation is the same as in all of our preceding analysis: attainment of a higher income per laborer through entry by those leaving either unemployment or a less well remunerated activity.

Monopoly. The first situation which we propose to discuss is that of a monopoly in the products market. Suppose that in a world very much like that which we have discussed thus far, one of the two industries, let us say that producing X_2, is a perfect monopolist; that is, for one reason or another X_2 is and can be supplied by only one firm. That firm, however, is labor-managed as are all the others (in the sec-

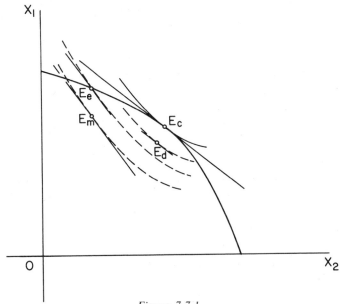

Figure 7.7.1

ond industry) and attempts to maximize its income per laborer. The situation can conveniently be described by Figure 7.7.1. We find in the diagram the Pareto-optimal production frontier, and on it the perfectly competitive solution E_c.

Another point on that frontier is well known at least to students of the capitalist economy, namely E_e, which represents the general equilibrium solution for a capitalist situation in which the producer of X_2 is a monopolist. Note that the point E_e is on the frontier of productive capability because it is based on full employment of national resources and equality of marginal rates of factor-substitution in the two industries (i.e., the factor-allocation point is on the contract curve). The only inefficiency of E_e resides in the difference between the marginal rate of transformation (slope of the production locus) and the marginal rate of substitution in demand (slope of a social-indifference curve). In the labor-managed economy one of two other inefficiencies will generally arise: (1) With no free entry (by definition) into the industry producing X_2, it is highly likely that incomes per laborer in the two industries will not be equalized, and thus (with a necessary long-run equalization of capital charges to both industries) the factor-allocation point for the economy will be off the contract curve. And consequently in the product plane the economy will operate at a point such as E_m, below E_eE_c.

(2) If the technology of producing X_2 is one of the second kind, as we have shown already, the only conceivable equilibrium production point of the second industry is zero. And thus, while returning in this instance to the production-possibility locus, we do so at a point where the "capitalist" inefficiency is at its maximum, that is, at the intercept with the vertical axis in Figure 7.7.1.

The over-all conclusion regarding the situation of monopoly—and, by now, an emerging general theorem—is that while complete "market-perfection" leads to equally perfect (or optimal) solutions in both the labor-managed and the capitalist economy, *identical* market imperfections carry comparatively greater penalties in the former. But again it must be recalled that market structures will not be identical, those under capitalism being considerably more concentrated. And thus a greater inefficiency in one context will tend to be offset by a lesser inefficiency in another.

Factor-immobility. Only a few words are necessary regarding the case of factor immobility. Our previous discussion of the short run is nothing but a discussion of an instance of complete capital immobility, and the inefficiencies involved in it have been sufficiently well explained already. On the other hand, the inefficiency arising in an otherwise competitive world leads to exactly the same results in the labor-managed economy in the long run as it does in a capitalist one. To see this, it need only be pointed out that, with labor fixed in each industry and firm, the income-per-laborer maximizing and the profit-maximizing worlds become—in the context of our present discussion—one and the same. And the corresponding well-known solution is that, say, an improvement in relative price of X_2 will lead from an initial equilibrium at E_c in Figure 7.7.1 to a solution somewhere southeast of E_c and below the production function through an interindustry transfer of capital; however, the relative price ratio at such an equilibrium still must be equal to the marginal rate of transformation along a production frontier constructed on the assumption of labor immobility.

External economies and diseconomies in production. For a variety of reasons, usually classified under the headings of external economies and diseconomies, marginal private and marginal social costs may be different in the capitalist economy. In the labor-managed economy similar phenomena are possible—only it is a little more difficult to speak of marginal costs, private or social, because labor remuneration does not really constitute a production cost. It is clear that whether we are in a labor-managed or a capitalist situation, a locus of maximum attainable outputs by the economy (i.e., the production-possibility frontier) is defined. If the employment of factors is full and remuneration of factors is the same in both industries—a condition guaranteed by mobility, free entry, and perfect competition in the labor-managed economy —the production point must be on the frontier of production possibilities, whether externalities are present or not. However, with an external economy present in the second industry or an external diseconomy in the first, a transfer of productive resources on the margin from the first to the second industry will be more productive in real terms than is indicated by the equilibrium price ratio. Such a situation is illustrated in Figure 7.7.1 by point E_c and it resembles the instance of a capitalist monopoly referred to above or, for that matter, a presence of externalities in a capitalist economy. The general conclusion is that externalities will have the same distorting effects in a labor-managed economy with free entry in the long run as those familiar to us from a competitive capitalist model. It is another matter that the labor-managed system will normally be in a much better position to correct such inefficiencies. But to this "special dimension" we will turn only in Part III.

Differences in technology. Thus far we have assumed that within each competitive industry each firm has access to the same pool of technological knowledge, and consequently that all firms have the same production function. For a number of reasons, which need not concern us here, such a situation only rarely arises in the real world; we must see, however, how differences in technology affect the general equilibrium solution. The analysis need not be very extensive because we have already presented its principal ingredient in the last section of Chapter 5.

It should be clear that to have two or more different sets of technologies used by a large number of firms producing the same product under competitive conditions, entry into the segment of the industry using the more efficient technology (at going factor and product prices) must be restricted. For if it were not, all firms would, in the long run, adopt the better technique. But under these conditions, the equilibrium income per laborer in the more efficient segment must be higher than in the other segment or segments of an industry. And with perfectly competitive conditions in the capital markets, and with long-run equilibrium behavior of the labor-managed firms, this necessarily implies differences in marginal rates of factor substitution in different segments of a single industry. Finally, such differences, as we have seen in Chapter 5, imply the possibility of increasing the output of the industry without a reduction in resources available to—and thus in output of—the other industry (or industries). In other words, with differences in technology within one industry, the economy as a whole cannot be at its production-possibilities frontier (this frontier including as one of its restrictions the technological difference or differences). This inefficiency does not arise in a capitalist economy. In terms of Figure 7.7.1, we thus have a solution such as E_d for the labor-managed economy and one such as E_c—both corresponding to the same relative price ratios—for the capitalist situation. It must be kept in mind, however, that the locus passing through E_e and E_c now incorporates the postulate of technological differences in at least one of the two industries.

7.8: *Some Realistic Concluding Remarks*

Thus far, in the present chapter and in fact in most of Part I, we have been filling in boxes, or analytical categories, given to us by (1) conventional microeconomic theory and (2) our general definitions of the labor-managed economy. It can be said that this procedure was rather indiscriminate—in fact, pedantic—when viewed in the context of conceivable real situations. Even though the purpose of Part I has been the formulation of an abstract microeconomic theory of the labor-managed system, and even though some of the more realistic aspects of that economy will be our concern in Part III, I feel that it would be incorrect to close our discussion without drawing a few conclusions filtered, so to speak, through the screen of real relevance.

Perhaps the best way of starting our discussion is to observe the twofold social advantage of what we have termed the *social* adjustment to changing conditions, that is, an adjustment not including variations in the size of the working collective among the variables of adjustment. The first advantage is that the collective as a social body is not disrupted—in fact, it was this consideration that initially led us to the adoption of the category of "social" adjustment. The second advantage is that which we have established here through the general equilibrium analysis: an increased efficiency of the short-run and long-run adjustment in the absence of, or with delayed exit and entry of firms.

It can thus be argued that whether the *social* short-run and long-run behavior can be justified on grounds of individual firms' narrowly economic maximizing objectives or not, from the broader point of view of the national economy it always leads to superior social welfare (i.e., a higher level of social utility and satisfaction). And consequently, the *social* adjustment can always be recommended to individual labor-managed firms as a matter of national economic policy.

Our next point, perhaps the most important of the present section, is that the conflict between *social* and *conventional* adjustment on the part of individual firms is a theoretical possibility which very often disappears once some additional pieces of information are brought in from the real world. Consequently, a good deal of the comparative inefficiency of conventional general equilibrium adjustment, in the absence of free entry and joint production (shown in some of the earlier sections), also turns out to be not much of a danger in a real situation. Also, and for the same reasons, a national economic policy of recommending employment stability to firms will only seldom prove a real necessity.

The reasoning behind these conclusions is as follows. What we refer to as the *short run* is a situation wherein the firm has a fixed capital stock—more specifically, a fixed installed productive capacity of buildings and equipment. That capacity normally calls for a specific number of laborers, each of whom has a specific assigned job. Increasing the labor force beyond that number, L_0, can add only very little if anything to the total product. Assuming a competitive firm and facing a product price p_0 we thus get, as a limiting case, a total-value-product line such as that shown to the right of point a in Figure 7.8.1. If the productive process is perfectly divisible, the total-value product for employments less than L_0 is given by $0a$ in the diagram. At the other end of the spectrum, if the process is perfectly indivisible, the total-value product is given by the broken contour $0L_0a$. In either case, the maximum income per laborer corresponding to these conditions and a fixed capital cost $p_K K_0$, reflected in Figure 7.8.1 by the segment $0e$, is given (as we recall from our earlier analysis) by the slope of ea, and the corresponding equilibrium employment is L_0; the short-run equilibrium output of the firm then is $X(L_0, K_0)$. It is now apparent that a change in the product price, or a change in the price of capital, will not affect equilibrium or output. For example, an increase in the product price from p_0 to p_1 leads to a new vertex at a', a new equilibrium income per laborer reflected by the slope of ea', but no change in employment or output. Similarly, changes in p_K reflected by vertical shifts of point e will also not affect the physical characteristics of the firm's equilibrium.

And thus, in our "realistic case," the *conventional* short-run adjustment coincides with, or is the same as, the *social* adjustment. And in

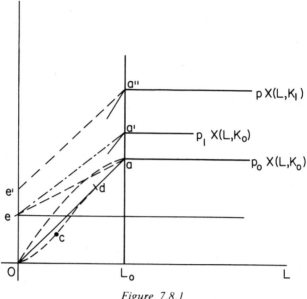

Figure 7.8.1

the context of our general equilibrium analysis an economy finding itself at a point such as E_0 in Figure 7.6.2 will tend to remain at that point
in the short run following a change in relative prices; it will tend to
remain there even if it bases its decisions on strictly income-maximizing
(conventional) criteria.

Still retaining the assumption of perfect competition, we can now
turn briefly to the "most realistic" long-run situation: in fact, we only
have to dwell here on some observations made earlier. The normal expectation is that in the real world when both the capital stock and labor
can be varied, the technology reflecting the various efficient combinations of these factors is likely to be of the second kind (i.e., subject to
constant returns to scale), at least beyond a certain minimum scale of
operation of the firm. But if this is so, and if—as we have just argued—
the working collective preserved its size on ground of short-run efficiency, there is no reason why a subsequent adjustment in labor participation should be undertaken in the long run (where all scales are
efficient) as a result of a product or factor price change. It is only the
factor proportions that the firm must now adjust. As shown in Figure
7.8.1, for an increase in product price from p_0 to p_1, this adjustment will
lead to an increase in the capital stock to K_1, an increase in output
measured by the distance $a'a''$, and an increase in the income per

laborer to that indicated by the slope of $e'a''$. And thus, even if social motivation is entirely absent from the decision-making of our competitive labor-managed firm, the firm will behave—or at least tend to behave—under realistic conditions in a *social* manner when faced with changing market conditions.

Taking a step further in the direction of a realistic representation of the labor-managed economy, we have to abandon the assumption of perfect competition for many industries. We have to do so even though we have shown earlier that the tendency toward competitive market structures will be much more pronounced in the labor-managed world than in other situations. Some small degree of monopoly power is likely to prevail in many industries. If such is the case, the identity between *social* and *conventional* behavior shown above for the competitive case is likely to be preserved. This is immediately apparent for the short run, noting that a "low degree of monopoly power" will make the value-product lines rotate slightly clockwise around such vertexes as a and a'. Consequently, changes in product prices or factor prices, reflected as before by shifts of such points as a or e, are unlikely to change employment or output. Only a significant degree of monopoly power could change this expectation.

In the long run, of course, the labor-managed firms enjoying some degree of monopoly will have to operate somewhere near and to the left of a point such as d in Figure 7.8.1 on the broken contour $0cd$ corresponding to the increasing-returns stretch of the production function. Under such conditions, changes in demand conditions may call for alterations of *conventional* equilibrium labor inputs; but these changes, since they are to be undertaken in the long run, can be entirely free of social friction. Moreover, with a low degree of monopoly power the proximity of the constant-returns range of the production function can be such that in a real situation, where information and knowledge are less than perfect, gains from adjustment in employment may be imperceptible. Under such conditions no adjustment may be undertaken when market schedules facing the firm undergo long-run changes.

We should also note that in the short run, whether with or without perfect competition, the identity of *social* and *conventional* adjustment will be maintained even if the firm operates in the zone of long-run increasing returns. This is easily seen if we realize that at a point such as c in Figure 7.8.1—corresponding to low output and employment and lesser efficiency than at a—the *short-run* value-product line forms a vertex as it did at point a.

The approach of the present section also contains an important message for the macroeconomic analysis of the subsequent part of the study: the zero elasticity of supply of an individual labor-managed firm in the short run will be directly reflected in a zero elasticity—or, more realistically, a very low elasticity—of short-run supply of aggregate national product. Note that the aggregate elasticity we have in mind is defined in terms of variations in physical output and money product-prices, with the money price of capital constant. Moreover, in the macroeconomic context the full-employment constraint will act as an important stabilizer of the supply elasticity of national product.

Perhaps the only significant real instance where a negative supply could be possible for a competitive labor-managed firm in the *conventional* short run is when the fixed capital stock K_0 and the corresponding productive processes are divisible, but instead of being all of equal quality, the productive capacity (measured by K_0) has a diminishing efficiency. Under such conditions, the short-run total-value product corresponding to K_0 will be represented by a concave contour short of full capacity (as shown in Figure 7.8.1) and the equilibrium may be reached at c', corresponding to an employment smaller than L_0. It is in this situation that conventional adjustment behavior leads to a backward-bending short-run supply function. The employment may be maintained by the labor-managed firm facing product-price variations only as a matter of a *social* adjustment behavior, in expectation of a long-run adjustment of scale to the size of the working collective.

PART II
MACROECONOMIC
THEORY

8. The Aggregate Market for Goods and Services

8.1: *Introduction*

Whereas in Part I we were concerned with the behavior of individual firms and industries and the structural interdependences among them, the purpose of Part II is to elucidate the global—or aggregative—properties of the labor-managed system. Thus instead of studying how prices and outputs of one sector of the economy behave relative to prices and outputs of another sector, we now want to determine the aggregate level of prices or the aggregate level of national product for the whole economy.

Clearly, this process requires—at least conceptually—a high degree of aggregation. But as is well known, economists are not overly bothered by it, whether in dealing with capitalist or labor-managed systems. Following the customary procedure, we simply assume that our idealized economy has only one representative product—or, more generally, one economic quantitative variable—for each distinct category of markets. Thus all the real goods and services are to be represented by a single good, call it X, where the physical quantity X measures the real national product of the labor-managed economy. Similarly, all bonds are to be represented by a magnitude B, or all money (here the aggregation probably being most legitimate) by the quantity M. As in Part I, there still is only a single type of homogeneous labor in the economy, and we use for its aggregate measure the symbol L.

As in any aggregative or so-called macroeconomic theory, we are thus asked to determine for the labor-managed economy the equilibrium levels of the four major quantitative aggregates X, B, M, and L and the corresponding prices (or remunerations), conventionally expressed in terms of money, p, p_B, 1 and Y. Let it be noted that in an open economy there would be other aggregate variables, but these will not concern us in this study.

The correct and consistent procedure leading to the solutions is the

163

general equilibrium procedure, comparable in its over-all nature to that used in Chapter 7, wherein all the variables are determined simultaneously. This procedure simply recognizes the interdependence of all segments, or components of the system, an interdependence obvious even from a most casual reflection concerning any actual case of a market economy. Among the conceivable general equilibrium procedures we choose one which is most illuminating and which, probably for that reason, is most frequently employed today. The basic idea of this particular approach is to organize the analysis according to, or under the headings of, the different specific markets.

Thus in the present chapter we will discuss the real goods and services market and in the following chapter the money and bond markets. In Chapter 10, finally, we review earlier results regarding the labor market or, more accurately, the "labor equation," and combine all the component parts into one general equilibrium analysis.

In the present discussion of the market for goods and services, we will be able to follow the approach customary in "western" macroeconomic theory not only in respect to organization of the material, but also, to a large extent, in respect to the individual behavioral functions defining the particular market. We can thus proceed fairly quickly, relying on some familiarity of the reader with conventional macroeconomic theory.

The one component entering the real goods market which is quite different from its capitalist counterpart is the demand for investment goods, more commonly known as the investment function. Because of this difference, we will assign a special section (8.4) to the subject. The analysis of investment behavior, however, deserves also a special attention for another reason and in another context. In the "pure" model of Part I, investment was treated in a rather summary manner on the assumption that capital is a factor similar to any other being hired at some contractual wage (price). This short-cut method can be highly unrealistic, and consequently we are using the discussion of section 8.4 also to remedy this imperfection of Part I.

8.2: *The Supply of Goods and Services*

Having adopted the approach of general equilibrium analysis organized around the principal markets, and having decided first to study the market of goods and services, let us first consider the supply side of that market. For reasons which we will be able to explain fully only in Chapter 10, we adopt a trivially simple function for the supply of national product $\overline{X}$—note that the superscribed bar indicates supply. The supply function is no other but the well known 45-degree line used in conventional macroeconomic theory, namely

$$\overline{X} = \overline{X} \tag{1}$$

The fact that we treat the supply of goods and services in the same way as in the conventional theory of national income determination may serve as a provisional justification for that functional form. But a little more can be said here. Many readers may ask why the price which was always introduced into a supply function for a competitive firm or industry (in Part I) is not used also here as an explanatory variable of aggregate supply of national product. The provisional answer is that if we did so here—in the context of general equilibrium—we would actually be discarding one of the key dynamic moving forces inherent in the general equilibrium, guaranteeing adjustment of the solution following a disturbance. More picturesquely, if we introduced prices into the supply function, it would be as if we were to take a wheel out of an otherwise perfectly functioning machine.

8.3: *The Demand for Goods and Services: Consumption and Government*

We will assume that total demand for goods and services can be decomposed into three component parts; namely, consumption demand C, autonomous demand A—including all demands determined exogenously, primarily government demand—and finally investment demand I. As we have pointed out already in section 8.1, we reserve for the latter a separate section; and consequently we are left here with the aggregates C and A. Actually it is only C which interests us in the sense that we want to find a behavioral function explaining the variation in that aggregate. As for A, by definition, no such behavioral function needs to be sought because A is a prescribed constant. That constant can be changed as a result of a government decision, but this type of problem will concern us only in Part IV. To sum up, we can write for aggregate demand for goods and services (noting that no bars are used here to indicate demand)

$$X = C + A + I \tag{2}$$

and what we want to speak about in this section is the consumption aggregate C. Let it be stressed that C is measured, or expressed, in terms of real units, and not in terms of money or wage units, as is frequently done in conventional national-income analysis.

The fact that a given household lives in an environment of a labor-managed economy should not make the *desired* economic behavior of the household fundamentally different from what it would be in any other environment where the household is not under external coercion. And thus we can start our discussion with the conventional form or forms of the consumption function, and only then ask the question whether some new elements should be introduced into it on the grounds that the economy which we now consider is of the labor-managed and income-sharing variety.

Unquestionably the most significant determinant of real consumption of an individual household is the level of real income earned by that household. The relation between the two magnitudes generally is expected to be positive, a real dollar's worth of additional income leading normally to less than one dollar's worth of real consumption. For the nation as a whole a similar type of relation can thus be expected to prevail between national real income and consumption, some variation in the slope of the aggregate function generally being permissible depending on the distribution of income. We can thus write, as the first part of the aggregate real consumption function

$$C = C(\overline{X}, \ldots), 0 < C_{\overline{X}} < 1 \qquad (3)$$

with the dots in the brackets expressing the fact that there will be other determining factors, and the bar on top of X expressing the fact that the real income earned on which consumption depends in a given period is real income produced—that is, real product supplied in that period. The expression $C_{\overline{X}}$ is used to express the slope of the consumption function with respect to real income, that is, $\Delta C/\Delta \overline{X}$, or the marginal propensity to consume.

Next in line of customary explanations of consumers' behavior is the rate of interest, hereafter to be designated by i, and measuring the amount of currency received by a lender (i.e., saver or buyer of bonds) per one unit of the same currency currently invested per annum. More will have to be said about this rate of interest in the following section when we discuss the capital and money markets. For the moment, however, our definition of i and of its role in consumers' behavior is sufficient.

It is usually recognized that the sign of the slope of C with respect to i, that is, the sign of C_i, can be positive or negative. The customary argument is that a change in the rate of interest will—in the context of choices between present and future consumption—produce income and price effects of opposite signs.

Finally, the general price level p is very often introduced as an argument of the consumption function. This is done on the grounds that an individual who in each period owns not only his real income but also given nominal money and bond balances will see his real buying power changed through variations in p affecting the real value of these balances. Of course, it must be assumed that asset-holding consumers are not exactly matched by debtor consumers, because if they were, and spending habits between debtors and creditors were by and large similar, the real-balance effects would cancel out. But normally money balances will constitute a debt on the part of the central authorities, as we will see in the following section, and an analogous postulate for interest-bearing debt is highly plausible for a labor-managed economy. Consequently, p should be retained as a factor of consumption behavior. Moreover, it will be noted that C_p, the rate of change of C with respect to p, can generally be expected to be negative, higher p leading to consumer-creditors' impoverishment and thus to less consumption spending.

Although this will be more our concern in Part IV, let it only be noted here that in a labor-managed economy changes in p can have another impact on consumption, stemming from the operation of the productive sector of the economy. For example, if charges for use of social capital are fixed in terms of money rates, inflation of prices may lead to an increase in real income withheld by the workers, and thus to an increase in consumption. It should also be noted, however, that the price-consumption effects, whether based on the real-balance argument or any other, can never be very important in a realistic context except in a situation of hyperinflation (or, if such a thing exists in the real world, in a case of hyperdeflation).

To sum up, we have a consumption function, containing three of our endogenous variables as explanatory factors, namely,

$$C = C(\overline{X}, i, p) \qquad (4)$$

with

$$0 < C_{\overline{X}} < 1; \quad C_i \gtrless 0 \quad \text{and} \quad C_p < 0$$

The function also depends on two parameters, the total supply of money, and the number of bonds outstanding, but these, again, will only be of direct concern to us later on.

8.4: *The Investment Function*

As is customary in microeconomic theory, we have treated capital in Part I in the same way as any other substitutable factor of production. Specifically, the investment decision on the part of the labor-managed firm was reduced merely to the decision as to what degree the services of capital assets should be hired, on a current basis, in a given period. Elimination of this oversimplification is the very basis and *raison d'être* of the theory of investment. The fact that capital assets generally are acquired by a firm for a substantial period and thereafter become virtually nontransferable and nonsalable produces all sorts of complications and problems which must be resolved by the theorist. In the context of our analysis, in particular, these problems must be resolved before we can write a behavioral function explaining the national demand for investment goods. The analysis proceeds along similar lines to that underlying the well-known function of marginal efficiency of capital. There is, however, one important difference: the labor-managed firm, rather than considering an index of internal return as its key decision indicator, must be concerned with some measure reflecting the returns per unit of employment. The question then presents itself whether and to what extent this alteration of the problem changes the customary properties of an aggregate investment function.

Before we can turn to the essence of our topic, a few words must be said about the general setting in which the labor-managed system arrives at its investment decisions. We recall that the labor-managed firm never can have full ownership of the capital assets which it uses in production. As we have explained in Chapter 1, it only has the usufruct of the assets. Nonetheless, with existing firms, management is the sole body empowered to make investment decisions, and, even with potential entrants, whoever deliberates on the act of entry must pursue motives similar to those of existing labor-managed firms.

The key question, therefore, is what the worker managers, or, more realistically, the elected management of the firm, consider their investment costs on the one hand and benefits on the other, and how do they combine these elements in arriving at a workable criterion for investment. The rational principle of maximization of income per laborer, already used in Part I, again will serve us as a basis in deriving the investment criteria. The only complication which presents itself now is that the capital assets to be acquired in a given year will be productive over a number of future years and that in such future years new workers will join the enterprise or old workers leave the enterprise. The almost philosophical question therefore arises as to how to introduce the incomes of those who are not currently employed into the decision-making criteria.

More will be said in the following section and also in Part IV about the type or types of capital market in a labor-managed economy. For the moment, let it suffice to make the simplest assumption, most customary in discussions of the marginal efficiency function: namely, that there is a perfect capital market (bond market, if we want) where an individual firm can lend or borrow unlimited amounts at the going rate of interest, i. Let it also be assumed that there may be another cost factor p_K (zero, positive, or negative) charge per real dollars' worth of capital assets (i.e., per physical unit of capital) actually utilized by the firm. The factor p_K can be thought of as a capital-tax rate, and as such it will be of interest to us in our discussion of policy and planning instruments in Part IV. But even in the context of a pure system, p_K, as distinct from the current rate i, must be introduced as a predetermined variable reflecting an average unit interest charge for plant and equipment installed in the past. Of course, in some special situations of long-run equilibrium, the current rate i and the average past unit charge p_K might be identical.

Now let us transpose the principle of maximization of income per laborer from a one-period to a multi-period setting by postulating that what the labor-management is interested in is the maximization of an equal income for everyone, whatever the period in which that income is earned and whether the laborer is currently employed or not. We recall here from Chapter 1 that in Part II we still retain the assumption of a perfectly homogeneous labor force. The management also could build into its decision function a specification of an escalation of income per laborer over time, but this would not change substantially the nature of the problem. Given the assumed conditions of the capital market, the income per laborer, A, which can be disbursed to each employee while he is employed is given by the relation

$$A \left[\sum_{t=0}^{T} n_t (1 + i)^{-t} \right] = \sum_{t=0}^{T} R_t (1 + i)^{-t} - C_0 \qquad (5)$$

where t indicates the time period, n_t the total number of employees in the enterprise in that period, C_0 the initial capital cost (if any), and R_t the net return from the operation of the enterprise in period t resulting from both employment of old (i.e., preperiod zero) and new capital assets (if any) procured in the planning period. It is possible to construct for prescribed levels of the market rate of interest i^0 and of the charge on old investment p_K^0 a locus $A(i^0, p_K^0; C_0)$ reflecting, for each specified level of initial capital cost C_0, the corresponding maximum conceivable level of A attainable. The "maximum conceivable" is to be interpreted here as "maximum among all combinations of projects procurable with the given C_0."

In Figure 8.4.1 we show the contour. Its intercept with the vertical axis at a, corresponding to zero current investment, simply reflects the firm's long-range income-generating capability if no new investments are undertaken and, presumably, the firm just keeps replacing its existing capacity. The slope of the curve in the vicinity of point a reflects the marginal contribution to income per laborer of the first and most productive project. Of course, were the slope zero or negative, there would be no impetus for any further investment. As the value of initial investment increases, each additional dollar's worth at first keeps adding to A, normally but not necessarily at a diminishing rate. A diminishing rate must set in at some point, leading to an eventual decline to zero at a point such as c in the diagram, and beyond that point it will be negative—that is, A will be declining. Clearly, the equilibrium solution which the labor managers will choose is that at the point of maximum c, corresponding to a total value of investment in the current period C_0^0.

Now suppose that the market rate of interest increases from i^0 to i^1. What can we expect to happen to the A-contour? The normal outcome is illustrated by $A(i^1, p_K^0; C_0)$ in Figure 8.4.1; the effect is approximately one of pivoting of the A-schedule downward around point a. Point a can be expected to be a pivotal point because—referring to relation (5)—when we are at the vertical axis, C_0 is zero and thus changes in the rate of interest will cancel each other out, by and large, on the two sides of the relation, leaving A approximately unchanged. Moreover, with no new investment, it can be assumed that future interest charges (entering the R_t's) will have been determined prior to the planning period $t = 0$, and thus the R_t's, for $C_0 = 0$, should be independent of i. As C_0 assumes higher and higher values, an increase in i will tend to reduce both sides of relation (5), but the right-hand side relatively more so—this comparative effect being the more pronounced the higher C_0 is. And thus with the downward shift in the A schedule, we can normally also expect a leftward shift in the equilibrium (maximum) point to the position indicated by b in Figure 8.4.1. With further increases in

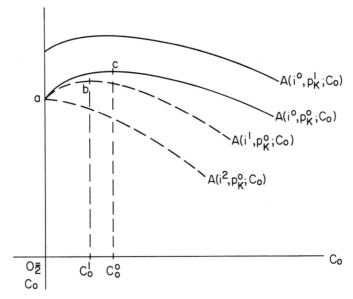

Figure 8.4.1

i, such as from i^1 to i^2, using a perfectly analogous argument, the A schedule will further rotate clockwise around a and reach a position such that all new investment becomes undesirable because it does not promise any further increments in the income per laborer. Beyond that point, any additional investment will cease, and, actually, even reductions in plant and equipment through nonreplacement and retirement of debt can be expected.

What interests us most in the context of our present subject is that the maximum point on the three schedules has traveled leftward—from c to b to a in the diagram; in other words, as in the traditional theory of marginal efficiency of capital, increases in the rate of interest have curtailed investment activity for the firm considered. In consequence, the same impact can be expected on the total value of national investment. And assuming either that prices are constant throughout or that if they vary they do so in proportion at present and in the future, a price factor can be canceled out on both sides of relation (5), and C_0 now can be replaced by I—the real demand for investment goods—in both relation (5) and Figure 8.4.1. This then directly permits the construction of a relation of the form

$$I = I(i) \qquad\qquad (6)$$

with $I_i < 0$. More generally, with prices at present being permitted to vary with future prices constant, and with the obvious effect that the level of real national income must have on expectations and investment, we can write

$$I = I(i, p, \overline{X}) \qquad (6')$$

with $I_i < 0$, $I_p < 0$, and $I_{\overline{X}} > 0$.

As far as the endogenous variables are concerned, this completes our task for this section. There remains only one minor matter to be cleared up regarding the factor p_K. As we have pointed out already, its main relevance is with respect to questions of economic policy; in the context of "pure" theory p_K must be a constant predetermined parameter. However, it is convenient to discuss it here, once we have developed the A-schedule. A change in p_K, the average rate due per real dollar's worth of existing (and undepreciated) plant and equipment, will shift—rather than rotate—the A-schedule. For example, decline from p_K^0 to p_K^1 will produce an upward shift of the schedule. This is so because in relation (5) the p_K enters only on the right-hand side as a negative component of the R_i's, and the latter will be changed whether C_0 is zero or not, that is, whether we are at the vertical axis intercept or not. Such being the case, there also is no special presumption that the maximum point on the A-schedule should shift to the right or to the left as the schedule itself shifts. Consequently, we can now write our generalized investment function depending on three endogenous variables and one predetermined, or policy parameter in the form

$$I = I(i, p, X; p_K) \qquad (7)$$

with $I_i < 0$, $I_p < 0$, $I_X > 0$, and $I_{p_K} \gtrless 0$, the last of the four slopes presumably being very small in most cases.

8.5: The Market Equilibrium and Its Characteristics

Having discussed the supply and demand sides of the market of goods and services, we are now in a position to combine the two and examine the equilibrium in that market. Postulating equilibrium, that is

$$\overline{X} \overset{e}{=} X \qquad (8)$$

("e" is used here to indicate an equilibrium condition rather than an identity) and using relations (1), (2), (4), and (6'), we can write

$$\overline{X} \overset{e}{=} X(i, p, \overline{X}) \qquad (9)$$

where
$$X(i, p, \overline{X}) \equiv C(i, p, \overline{X}) + A + I(i, p, \overline{X}) \qquad (10)$$

the latter being an identity. Because both slopes of C and of I with respect to $\overline{X}$ will generally be positive, so will be the total slope, that is, the marginal propensity to spend on goods and services. However, that propensity may now exceed unity, even though this outcome still can be deemed unlikely. In symbols,

$$1 \gtrless X_{\overline{X}} > 0 \qquad (11)$$

where the doubled inequality sign indicates a more likely outcome. The change in total demand for goods and services with respect to the rate of interest can usually, but not necessarily, be expected to be negative because the slope of the investment demand function is unambiguously negative while that of consumption function can be either positive or negative, and in general it will be small. On the other hand, as can be concluded from relations (4) and (6'), the rate of change of total demand for goods and services with respect to product price .is unambiguously negative. Summarizing these two conclusions, we have

$$X_i \lessgtr 0 \quad \text{and} \quad X_p < 0 \qquad (12)$$

where the doubling of one of the inequality signs again indicates a more likely outcome.

Now considering relation (9), we find a function connecting three variables, $\overline{X}$, i, and p. In other words, when relation (9) is satisfied—that is, when the real goods market is in equilibrium—the three endogenous variables just mentioned must be in a specific configuration—or relationship—to each other. We will learn a good deal about the particular market—and this knowledge will be important to us later on—if we study some of the general properties of the relationship between i, p, and $\overline{X}$. Let us first pick any set of specific values of these variables, such as i_0, p_0, and $\overline{X}_0$, satisfying relation (9). In other words, when $i = i_0, p = p_0$, and $\overline{X} = \overline{X}_0$, the equilibrium in the goods and services market is fulfilled. The three coordinates and the point E_0 which they define are illustrated in Figure 8.5.1. Clearly, there will be an infinite number of points such as E_0 satisfying relation (9). The normally expected pattern of the surface containing all the "equilibrium" points such as E_0 is also illustrated in Figure 8.5.1. It looks very much like one-fourth of a tent, indicating that for any two variables—with the remaining variable held constant—one must increase one of the two and reduce the other if one wants to preserve the state of equilibrium in the market for goods and services.

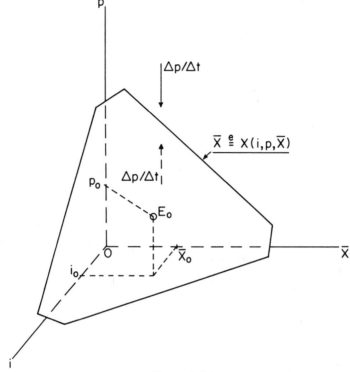

Figure 8.5.1

This conclusion is most readily demonstrable if the variable to be held constant is taken to be $\overline{X}$. In that case the left-hand side of relation (9) is a constant and, with X_i and X_p both negative, one clearly must increase i if one reduces p and one wants to keep the right-hand side— that is, total demand—constant. Now suppose that the rate of interest is kept constant, and assume that the general price level p is increased. This will—as we know from our consideration of slopes—reduce demand X (that is the right-hand side of (9)) and thus, if $\overline{X}$ did not change, the market would be out of equilibrium; thus $\overline{X}$ must adjust. But in what direction? The answer is "downward" because with declining $\overline{X}$ the left-hand side of (9) will be decreasing faster than the right-hand side (of course this is on the normal assumption that $X_{\overline{X}} < 1$) and thus the left-hand side will, so to speak, catch up with the right-hand side, which was smaller in the initial state of disequilibrium (caused by the increase in p). Consequently, to preserve equilibrium with unchanged i and increased p, one must reduce $\overline{X}$, if the more likely double inequality relation (11) holds.   The opposite is the result when the marginal propensity to spend is larger than unity. Transcribed in geometry, the more likely result just obtained is reflected in Figure 8.5.1 by the negative slope of the intercept of the equilibrium surface with the vertical coordinates plane p-$\overline{X}$ or, for that matter, with any parallel vertical plane (not in the diagram). A perfectly analogous argument—*mutatis mutandis*—leads to the remaining conclusion to the effect that one must reduce i if $\overline{X}$ is increased and p kept constant. Note that with the less likely inequality in relation (11) the equilibrium surface would retain the intercept with the p-i plane in the diagram but the intercepts in the $\overline{X}$-i and $\overline{X}$-p planes would be diverging from (rather than converging towards) the $\overline{X}$ axis with increasing $\overline{X}$.

This nearly completes what we have to say in this chapter about the equilibrium in the real goods market. A few words remain to be said, however, about states of disequilibria and the nature of dynamic adjustment to such disequilibria in that market. Suppose that the market in question is out of equilibrium; what are the forces, if any, which will restore the equilibrium?   More specifically, which of our three endogenous variables, $\overline{X}$, i, and p, will be directly affected by the state of disequilibrium and change in one direction or the other?   The answer is that, as in any competitive market, it is the price of goods and services, p, that will be the immediate variable of adjustment in cases of disequilibrium of the market for goods and services; it will tend to increase over time when $\overline{X} < X$ and decline when $\overline{X} > X$.

It should be noted that contrary to the Keynesian system describing the capitalist economy, no rigidity is to be expected here which would prevent prices from adjusting. Competitive bidding should always produce the dynamic changes in p postulated.[1] It is important to note that in the total general equilibrium system other variables besides p normally will also adjust; however, their adjustment must be brought about by disequilibria in other than the goods and services market. It is convenient to summarize the dynamic postulates made: Taking a to be a negative number, we can write

$$\Delta p/\Delta t = a(\overline{X} - X) \tag{13}$$

where the fraction on the left-hand side is the rate of change in the general price level per unit increment (i.e., Δt) of time—for example, per second, minute, day, or year.

[1]Of course, price controls imposed by the authorities or other causes might change the picture; but this should not concern us at this point, in the context of a "pure" macroeconomic theory of the labor-managed economy.

As the reader may easily verify, the tentlike surface in Figure 8.5.1 has not only the property of being an "equilibrium surface" but also the property of separating the region of excess supplies (above the tent) from the region of excess demands (below the tent). With our dynamic adjustment postulate we can thus associate any point above the surface with a downward movement—that is, reductions in p—and vice versa for points below the surface. This is indicated by the solid (visible) arrow pointing downward in the diagram and the broken (covered by the tent, or invisible) arrow pointing up.

9. The Money and Bond Markets

9.1: *Introduction*

There are several reasons for combining the discussion of the money market with that of the bond market. For one thing, both really are bond markets—the only difference being that money does not carry a coupon, that is, it is noninterest-bearing. A more important reason is that, historically and in part erroneously, these two markets were used alternatively as determinants of the rate of interest. The main reason, however, is the fact that the correct way of deriving the demand functions in the two markets is through a simultaneous (or "joint") procedure. This is explained and developed in section 9.3.

Before coming to the more technical analysis, however, it is imperative to spend some time in discussing the actual institutional forms, operation, and functions of the two markets—especially those of the bond market. This will be done in section 9.2. Note that such a discussion was unnecessary in the preceding chapter because there is no difficulty in visualizing a competitive market in goods and services, whether it is located in a labor-managed or a capitalist economy. By contrast, in a labor-managed economy where producers do not enjoy full ownership and where the "true" owner is someone else, entirely new legal and institutional forms must be designed, and these, to the extent that they bear on the economics of the securities markets, must be explained and incorporated into our analysis. Of course, because we are still in the realm of pure theory, we will confine ourselves here to what we may refer to as "minimal assumptions," not only to bring to light what is essential, but also to conform to accepted practice. In Part IV, on the other hand, we will discuss several sets of realistic assumptions defining the forms of the capital and money markets.

As we have noted above, joint determination of demand for both bonds and money will be our topic in section 9.3. In section 9.4, we will use the results thus obtained for the bond market and combine them

177

with an analysis of the supply of bonds; the determination of equilibrium and study of the dynamic forces of adjustment in the bond market are the ultimate purpose of that section. Our task in the concluding section of the chapter is analogous to that in section 9.4, except that we deal with money instead of bonds.

Although the institutions and legal forms in many respects are different for the labor-managed economy, once we have gone through the process of theoretical abstraction, the two markets which we propose to study here and the behavioral functions underlying them become remarkably similar to the "idealized" capitalist markets as we know them from theoretical discussions by western economists. The similarity will permit us again, as it did in the preceding chapter, to cover the gound just outlined comparatively quickly.

9.2: *The Legal and Institutional Setting*

Before turning to the theory of the two markets we propose to study, let us see what these markets should look like in a labor-managed economy. Of course, they could have a virtually infinite number of characteristics—but most of these will not interest us here since they are not essential. It is only the "minimal" characteristics of—or minimal assumptions underlying—the two markets consistent with the labor-managed economy that belong to our purely theoretical discussion. Let us first consider the simpler of the two markets, the money market.

First, what exactly is the commodity traded in the money market? We postulate that there is only one type of money, paper money, not having any value *per se*—value which gold or silver money would have, for example. That money is issued (printed) by a central bank, and enters circulation as a liability of the central bank through open market operations. These operations are conducted exclusively in the securities market (to be discussed presently), that is, in exchange for securities. The central bank thus cannot hold any other assets besides securities. The totality of the money market, however, comprises not only the securities market but also the goods and services market and the "labor market"—the quotes being used here to recall that if we can speak of a labor market in a labor-managed economy at all, it is a different species from that which we are acquainted with in a capitalist or a Soviet-type economy.

Since every market should also have a price, we should ask what price corresponds to the money market. Because money is the numeraire used in all commercial transactions, clearly there is not a single price of money but rather as many such prices as there are markets other than the money market—three in our case. One price is the price of money in terms of commodities, which is $1/p$; another, to be derived later, is in terms of bonds; and the third is in terms of labor, $1/Y$. But the last of the three again should be considered merely as a definitional value-ratio rather than a relative price in the sense that one unit of currency cannot be sold for $1/Y$ units of labor services in the conventional sense. The conventional meaning of selling is exchanging with "no strings attached"; in the labor-managed economy, however, selling for labor means that the other party in the transaction accepts the labor received as an active and equal member of the labor-managed enterprise.

We can now turn to the bond market. Actually, usage of the term "bond market" anticipates part of our exposition. We really should start speaking about the "securities market" and only then, if it is warranted, end up with a securities market in which bonds are transacted exclusively. We will follow this procedure here—primarily to underscore a basic difference between the theory of a labor-managed system and the conventional macroeconomic theory. Note that in the latter the assumption of a single security (that is, bond) market is made for convenience as a matter of theoretical simplification. In the present theory, while the simplifying quality of a bonds-only approach is appreciated, that approach closely reflects the fundamental nature of the labor-managed system. Indeed, there is no place for ownership shares (i.e., equity, common stock, etc., as they are usually referred to) in the system discussed here.

Among the several arguments which could be raised in this context, probably the most fundamental is that ownership of shares implies the control of productive activities stemming from the use of the corresponding capital assets. This is clearly impossible because it contradicts one of the central characteristics of the labor-managed system, namely that the power to control and manage a productive activity belongs exclusively to those who participate in it. The second most important argument is that share-ownership constitutes a claim on profits of an enterprise, either in the form of dividends or in the form of stock appreciation. Again, in a labor-managed economy the portion of income which might be called profit belongs to the members of an enterprise. In brief, we are fully justified, for the labor-managed economy, in reducing the category of "securities" to that of "bonds"—that is, securities not implying either ownership of real assets of claim on profits. Correspondingly, we can from now on speak exclusively about a bond market. In the definition of the merchandise actually traded in that market, we can follow the established practice of conventional theory. There is only one type of bonds in our economy and they are consoles —that is, bonds never coming to maturity—whose coupon, or fixed annual return (payable forever), is one unit of currency. The number of such bonds we denote by "b." As is well known, the price of such a bond in terms of money is $p_b = 1/i$, and in terms of real goods (and services), $P_b = 1/pi$, so that the real value of bonds B can be written as $B = b/pi$.

How do such bonds come into being in the labor-managed economy and what exactly is their function and—in some sense—their legal status? As was implied in our discussion of the investment decision and of the investment function in the preceding chapter, it is the individual labor-managed firms that decide on investment projects in a decentralized manner.[1] Alternatively, with new entrants into an industry, the decision to invest is taken by the entry-sponsoring group or institution. In either case, the current costs of the investment project—the C_0 in section 8.4—are to be procured in full by the sale of bonds in the open market, at the going bond price. This does not preclude the members of the enterprise from "ploughing back" some of their income; but if so, they do it as a matter of a separate savings decision leading to a purchase of bonds in the open market at the going competitive price.

Ideally, and more realistically, the central government or a National Labor Management Agency such as that defined in Chapter 15—representing the society—should protect the public interest by controlling or verifying the credit-worthiness of the investment projects whose financing is being effected through the bond market. In a socialist economy—a form probably best fitting the labor-managed system—it would be only natural for the government to serve as an underwriter of all the consoles. More concretely, all the consoles, whoever their initial seller might be, should assume the form of government securities of equal quality and free of the possibility of default. Of course, the initial seller would be liable to honor the coupon payments associated with the debt, the central authorities serving only, so to speak, as an insurance agency to cover the holder

---

[1]Of course, the central authorities can influence investments in various sectors of the economy, but they have to do it respecting the market forces and the sovereignty of the firms where the investment is to be effected.

of the console against default of coupon payments. Termination of and retirement of debt would, of course, be performed by the initial seller through an open market purchase. Even more conveniently, all the consoles might be perfectly identical, not even carrying the name of the initial seller, the latter being only registered with a government agency; the initial seller then would settle its coupon dues and perform debt retirement with such an agency (by supplying the required number of consoles purchased in the open market).

We can turn now to the demand side of the bond market. We have already indicated that one possible type of buyer (saver) could be the employees of an investing firm. More generally, the only possibility of saving at interest offered to the income earners (households) would be through purchases in our single-bond market. Of course, especially in less developed countries, the savings volume thus generated might be deemed inadequate from the standpoint of the society. In such situations, the government itself, acting in behalf of the society and as a result of a political—rather than an economic—decision-making process, will purchase bonds in the open market using the proceeds of current budgetary surpluses. Moreover, as we have already argued in this section, the central bank will, through its monetary open market operations, at times act as a buyer of bonds. For one thing, all expansions in the supply of money—presumably necessary in any growing economy—must come about in this manner. Finally, the labor-managed firms may be buyers in the bond market, not only for purposes of debt retirement (and gradual or total liquidation), but also as an outlet for, say, depreciation funds and reserve funds of all sorts.

9.3: *The Joint Determination of Demand for Money and Bonds*

The demand for bonds and money has been explained in economic literature in a variety of ways. For the purposes of our analysis, we select the explanation most modern and theoretically most consistent with a general equilibrium analysis. It is based on the postulate that a rational individual—here representative of all the individuals or households in a labor-managed economy—makes a joint set of utility-maximizing demand decisions under the constraint of resources available to him, the latter depending, among other things, on market prices. The purpose of the present section is to carry out rigorously and in a step-by-step fashion the analysis implied in this statement of rational behavior to arrive at a set of demand functions for bonds and money respectively. We shall also seek to establish some of the important properties of such functions.

First, let us postulate that our representative individual has a set of preferences with regard to present real consumption C, the real amount of bonds he wants to hold and the real amount of money. The utility of both types of real assets is derived from the expected utility of corresponding future consumption, and that of money balances individually resides in the riskless liquidity of such balances. We thus can write a utility function of the form

$$U = U(B, M, C) \tag{1}$$

On the other hand, the real resources of our individual representative of the whole society, R^0, are given as the sum of real income (national income produced) $\overline{X}$, the real value of bonds he actually holds, b^0/ip, and finally, the real value of his money balances, m^0/p. Thus for given m^0 and b^0 the resources R^0 become a function of the current interest rate i, current general price level of goods and services p, and of the real income $\overline{X}$. Furthermore, R^0 must be equal to the sum of B, M, and C. In symbols,

$$R^0(i, p, \overline{X}) = B + M + C \tag{2}$$

The right-hand side is nothing but a plane in the B-M-C space of Figure 9.3.1, such as the plane anchored at points r, s, and t (equidistant from the origin measured in terms of the respective scales of the axes) and corresponding to a particular combination of the variables i, p, and $\overline{X}$. The point e, surrounded by two illustrative iso-utility (indifference) contours u and u', is the optimal point chosen by the society. With changing R^0—that is, changing i, p, and $\overline{X}$, there will be a whole locus such as E in the three-dimensional space generated by points of tangency between highest indifference surfaces of the U-function and planes parallel to that drawn in the diagram. Because we have disposed already of the demand for current consumption of goods and services in the preceding chapter, all that really interests us here is the horizontal-leftward projection of the E locus into the B-M coordinate plane, illustrated by E' in the diagram. To any prescribed set of i, p, and $\overline{X}$ corresponds a unique point on E', and its two (nonzero) coordinates provide us with the magnitudes sought, that is, the total demand for real bonds

$$B = B(i, p, \overline{X}) \tag{3}$$

and the total demand for real money balances

$$M = M(i, p, \overline{X}) \tag{4}$$

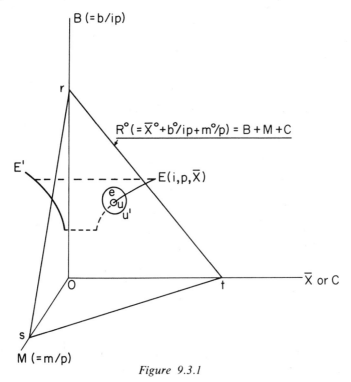

Figure 9.3.1

The corresponding two nominal demands are readily obtainable, re-calling that $b = ipB$ and $m = pM$.

Our next task is to learn something about the slopes, or rates of change of these functions with respect to changes in their arguments i, p, and $\overline{X}$. We begin with an *a-priori* postulate which is so intro-spectively plausible that it is stated without further elaboration: Both real balances, and real bonds are not inferior goods. This means that the E' contour (i.e., the Engel's line) in Figure 9.3.1 is positively sloped (with respect to its M and B axes). Using the conventional notation for slopes known to us already from the preceding chapter, we thus can write $B_{R^0} > 0$ and $M_{R^0} > 0$. But recalling the definition of real re-sources R^0, we know that R^0 increases with increasing $\overline{X}$ and declining i and p (see the definition of R^0 given in the diagram). And con-sequently, we have

$$M_i < 0 \qquad M_p < 0 \qquad M_{\overline{X}} > 0 \qquad (5)$$

and

$$B_i < 0 \qquad B_p < 0 \qquad B_{\overline{X}} > 0 \qquad (6)$$

The slopes of nominal rather than real demand functions are readily obtainable from the definitions of the nominal variables in terms of real magnitudes. It is immediately apparent that $m_{\bar{X}}$ and $b_{\bar{X}}$ are both positive and m_i is negative, because in these three cases the changing arguments ($\bar{X}$ and i) are not contained as a coefficient in the definition of the nominal demands. In the other three cases—m_p, b_i, and b_p—the problem becomes a little more complicated. It is easily resolved, however, provided that another highly plausible assumption is made, namely that both the price and interest elasticities of demand for real bonds and real money balances are less than unity (note that this is not a necessary consequence of the positive resource-elasticities for all C, B, and M). As the reader may easily verify, with this assumption we find that the three relevant inequalities are reversed from what they were in relations (5) and (6), that is, we have $m_p > 0$, $b_i > 0$ and $b_p > 0$—results hardly surprising to common sense. The reasoning behind this reversal can be illustrated as follows: Take for example $m = pM$; when p increases by one percent, M declines—assuming a less than unitary elasticity—by less than one percent. And thus in the product pM one term increases by a higher percentage than the other declines, a situation which, as is well known, leads to an increase in the product as a whole; more specifically, m increases with p.—Q.E.D.

9.4: *The Money Market*

Only very little remains to be done to complete our theoretical analysis of the money market. Since the supply of money is entirely controlled by the central bank and since there are no intermediaries and there is only one kind of money, the nominal supply of money can be taken as an exogenously prescribed constant, $\bar{m}^0$. As usual, the bar on top is used to indicate the supply side of the market, and the superscript 0 denotes that we are dealing with a constant. The market equilibrium condition can therefore be written in either of two equivalent forms:

$$\bar{M}^0 \; (= \bar{m}^0/p) \; = \; M(i,p,\bar{X}) \tag{7}$$

or

$$\bar{m}^0 \; = \; m(i,p,\bar{X}) \qquad (=pM) \tag{8}$$

The second formulation is more convenient for us because it involves a constant on the left side, and all the slopes of the nominal demand m

are known to us from the preceding section, namely

$$m_i < 0 \qquad m_p > 0 \quad \text{and} \quad m_{\overline{X}} > 0 \qquad\qquad (9)$$

The market-equilibrium relation (8) is one among three endogenous variables i, p, and $\overline{X}$. The locus describing it—that is, the locus fulfilling the condition of equilibrium—is shown in Figure 9.4.1. Since we

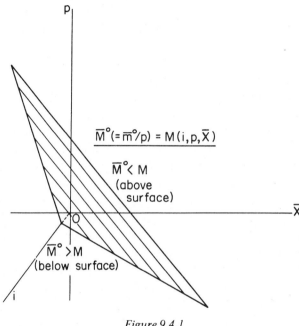

Figure 9.4.1

have no special reason to assume it to be convex in one way or another, and also because in reality only a small portion of it will be relevant in describing any real situation, we have drawn the surface as a plane.[2] Its general inclination is a necessary result of the slopes of the demand for money which we have established previously. Considering relations (8) and (9), it becomes immediately apparent that an increase in i with unchanged $\overline{X}$ must be matched by an increase in p if the market

[2]The Keynesian liquidity trap, involving a nonlinearity, may be a possibility, but we do not have to be greatly concerned about it because the speculative motive on which the trap is based should not be expected to be a powerful one in a labor-managed economy; also, the conditions in which a country is likely to face the danger of a liquidity trap are those of advanced countries—and these countries are unlikely to adopt the labor-managed system.

equilibrium (involving a constant nominal supply of money $\bar{m}^0$) is to be preserved. And thus the intercept of the equilibrium plane with the *p-i* coordinate plane in Figure 9.4.1 is positively sloped. A perfectly analogous argument, but substituting $\bar{X}$ for p, leads to a positive intercept-line in the $i\text{-}\bar{X}$ coordinate plane. Finally, (as is implied by the two slopes just established) preservation of equilibrium in the money market must require reductions in p simultaneous with increases in $\bar{X}$ and no change in i, because an increase in real income $\bar{X}$ leads to an increase in money demand which must be offset by the effect of a reduced general price level.

As before, the equilibrium plane divides the $i\text{-}p\text{-}\bar{X}$ space into two parts; that above the plane involves excess demands for money—as indicated in the diagram and as can be easily verified by considering relations (8) and (9)—while that below involves excess supplies of money. While this situation is analogous to that encountered with respect to the goods market in the preceding chapter, similar conclusions regarding the variable of adjustment are impossible here. Recall that when we discussed the goods market, the excess demands or supplies on one or the other side of the equilibrium plane led to dynamic adjustments in the general price level; there is no such unique and unambiguous adjustment process in the market presently discussed —and consequently it is impossible to draw directional arrows as we did in Figure 8.5.1. The only thing that we can say is that when the labor-managed economy finds itself at a point off the money-equilibrium plane, we cannot be in general equilibrium and thus the whole system—and generally all the endogenous variables—will have to adjust.

This absence of a unique variable of adjustment in the money market makes the money market, in a sense, an inferior tool of economic analysis, especially in situations of more advanced analysis where disequilibria, and dynamic adjustments resulting from such states, are considered. It is primarily for this reason that the money market should be eliminated from the analysis, wherever possible. But this brings us to a subject which will concern us only in Chapter 10.

9.5: *The Bond Market*

Some work remains to be done before we can study the equilibrium in the bond market. From section 9.3 we have derived the demand function; however, we have said very little thus far regarding the supply of bonds. Only our discussion of the investment function in the preceding chapter can offer us a set of partial clues in that respect. To begin with, let us summarize what we know about the real and nominal demands for bonds. We have

$$B \ (=b/ip) = B \ (i, p, \bar{X}) \tag{10}$$

and, on the "very plausible" assumptions made in section 9.3, we have the slopes

$$B_i < 0 \quad B_p < 0 \quad B_{\bar{X}} > 0 \tag{11}$$

and

$$b_i > 0 \quad b_p > 0 \quad b_{\bar{X}} > 0 \tag{12}$$

As for the supply function, which can be written as

$$\bar{B} \ (=\bar{b}/ip) = \bar{B} \ (i, p, \bar{X}) \tag{13}$$

(the superscribed bars again indicating supply), there are two sets of effects, or forces, determining its over-all shape. We can refer to one of these as stock effects and to the other as flow effects. Recall that $\bar{B}$ is a stock of outstanding consoles constituting (exclusively, in our idealized economy) the debt of the productive sector, that is, of all the labor-managed firms combined. Changes in any one of the variables (i, p, or $\bar{X}$) will act on the structure of the firms' assets and liabilities on the one hand and, on the other hand, on the firms' current behavior—primarily with respect to investment—thereby affecting the supply of new bonds. It is in the latter respects that our earlier discussion of the investment function can be useful to us.

Let us first consider the effect of a change in national product $\bar{X}$. There is hardly any doubt about $\bar{B}_{\bar{X}}$, the rate of change of real supply of bonds with respect to real income; it will be nonnegative. Normally, one would expect it to be positive but not too large. Rising national product is likely both to improve investors' expectations and to increase their willingness to go into debt. It should be expected, however, that this effect will be less powerful than the corresponding effect on the real demand for bonds B, the latter being conditioned by the savings motive, that is, the desire to transfer some of the gains in real income into future consumption. We can thus write, as a normal expectation,

$$B_{\bar{X}} \geqq \bar{B}_{\bar{X}} > 0 \tag{14}$$

Next we consider the effect of a change in the general price level. The stock or structural effect on nominal debt ($\bar{b}$) is unambiguous. With increased prices the real value of outstanding debt declines, and so does the real value of money balances; on the margin, the firms will thus find it desirable to expand their nominal money balances by increasing the nominal supply of bonds. On the other hand, the current flow effect of a price increase on the real supply of bonds $\bar{B}$ will be just about nil if the increase is expected to last into the future; the nominal supply $\bar{b}$ thus would increase in proportion with p. This increase will be less, but it will almost certainly not turn into a decline, if future prices are not expected to move up by as much as current prices. The one "almost" unambiguous result therefore is that nominal bond supply will be increased if the general price level increases. Whether such an increase will be stronger or weaker than the corresponding (and necessary) increase in nominal demand for bonds cannot be answered in a unique way. In the case of zero-elastic price-expectation, perhaps, the supply effect will be stronger—but this will, among other things, depend on the proportion of money to debt on the part of the productive sector. Using the double-line inequality again to indicate a stronger expectation, we thus can write

$$b_p \;\overset{\ll}{\underset{>}{}}\; \bar{b}_p > 0 \tag{15}$$

As for the real rates of change, we know that B_p is negative and $\bar{B}_p$— from the above discussion—also should, but need not necessarily, be negative. This "necessary" versus "most likely" formulation also lends support to the double inequality sign in relation (15).

Finally, the real supply of bonds, $\bar{B}$, should be expected to decline as the result of an increase in the rate of interest (with a reduced volume of investment) on account of what we have termed the flow effect. But because bond prices now have declined, the nominal supply of bonds on account of the flow effect will decline by less, or even may increase. The normal expectation is that it will decline somewhat. The stock effect almost certainly will be in the same direction because, with a decline in the price of the outstanding debt, producers may want to retire some of that debt (or incur less new debt) while the price is low, using their money balances or inventories. On the limit, with inventories and operating balances closely linked to the productive activity, this effect could be very small or nil. Whatever the case, a strong presumption still remains that the nominal supply of bonds b will decline with an increase in i (that is, a decline in the price of bonds $1/i$). And there is an equally strong, or even stronger, presumption that the impact on nominal demand will be the opposite. Thus we can write

$$\bar{b}_i < 0 < b_i \qquad (16)$$

and because the inequalities must be the same for real as well as nominal variables, and recalling the sign of B_i,

$$\bar{B}_i < B_i < 0 \qquad (17)$$

With all these conclusions in mind, we are now in a position to derive the "equilibrium plane" or equilibrium surface reflecting the combinations of the endogenous variables consistent with equilibrium in the bond market. We will do so for the most plausible slopes as they were obtained above, leaving it to the reader to study the alterations which would be produced by the occurrence of some of the "less likely" slope configurations. The equilibrium condition defining our surface is

$$\bar{B}(i, p, \bar{X}) = B(i, p, \bar{X}) \qquad (18)$$

Suppose now that we are in an equilibrium situation and that p and $\bar{X}$ are kept temporarily constant. This allows us to draw partial demand and supply curves for real bonds depending on the rate of interest. Both curves will be downward sloping, as indicated by relation (17), and the supply function will appear flatter; the equilibrium rate of interest is at the intersection of these two schedules. Now suppose that real income $\bar{X}$ increases (p remaining unchanged). According to relation (14), this will shift both schedules to the right, but with a greater shift in the real demand for bonds. Therefore, the rate of interest must decline as a result of an increase in real income, with unchanged general price level, if we postulate preservation of equilibrium in the bond market. This is indicated in Figure 9.5.1 by the negative slope of the intercept of the equilibrium plane with the i-$\bar{X}$ coordinate plane, or with any plane (not in the diagram) parallel to that coordinate plane.

An analogous construction in partial equilibrium with $\bar{X}$ held constant and p increasing by a prescribed amount will, using the more plausible inequality in relation (15), lead to an increase in the rate of interest consistent with market equilibrium. Therefore we have a positively sloped intercept of the equilibrium plane with the i-p coordinate plane. As is easily seen in the diagram, these two slopes determine the third—that is, the intercept with the p-$\bar{X}$ must also be positively sloped.

Contrary to the previously discussed case of the money market, we are again in a position to derive some important dynamic results re-

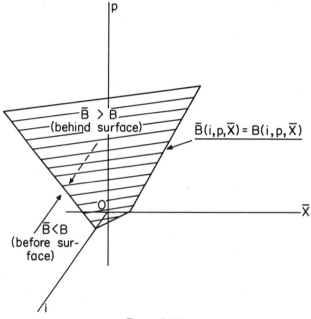

Figure 9.5.1

garding the process of adjustment to states of disequilibria. As is indicated in the diagram, and as the reader will find easy to verify, behind the equilibrium surface we encounter all disequilibrium points (combinations of i, p, and $\overline{X}$) leading to an excess supply of bonds, while points leading to an excess demand occur in front of the surface. The market being competitive—actually highly competitive given our general and institutional assumptions of section 9.2—there will be a tendency for the rate of interest to increase (i.e., price of bonds to decline) behind the equilibrium surface and to decline in front of it. This is shown by the two arrows in the left-hand side of the diagram. More formally, and by analogy to relation (13) of the preceding chapter, we can write

$$\Delta i / \Delta t = c(B - \overline{B}) \qquad (19)$$

where, as before, the coefficient on the right-hand side is a negative number whose absolute value reflects the dynamic speed of adjustment. Of course, the bracketed expression now is the excess demand because the variable of adjustment is the rate of interest rather than the price of bonds.

10. The "Labor Market" and the Aggregate General Equilibrium in a Labor-Managed Economy

10.1: *The Labor Market*

As was indicated in section 8.1, the principal purpose of this chapter is to bring together the various pieces of analysis worked out previously and derive and study the properties of the aggregative general equilibrium solutions for a labor-managed economy. Before doing it, however, we must refresh our memory on, and assimilate for our present purposes, one important subject not as yet discussed in Part II but which was, so to speak, the cornerstone of our analysis in Part I. That subject is the "labor market" or, more properly termed, the labor condition together with the behavioral forces influencing that condition.

Following accepted practice, the aggregative general equilibrium in which we are interested is of a short-run nature. This means, in more specific terms, that we postulate that the physical capital stock available to the economy is constant at the level K_0 (in very much the same way as we did in section 7.2) and that technology also is invariant. The latter thus can be written as

$$\overline{X} = \overline{X}(L) \quad [= X(L, K_0)] \tag{1}$$

meaning that supply of national product uniquely depends on the level of national employment. The function is subject to the law of diminishing returns and, as is usually assumed, has a positive slope at all points. The function thus has a unique inverse; this means, in common language, that we also can write

$$L = L(\overline{X}) \tag{2}$$

The slope of this function also must be positive, but always increasing.

Now from Chapter 2 we recall that the short-run equilibrium of a competitive labor-managed firm is given by the condition that the value of marginal physical productivity of labor be equal to the income per laborer. As the reader can easily verify, this condition can be ex-

191

tended to the whole economy provided that it is assumed—as is usual in macro-theory—that all the firms in the economy are identical, that is, use the same technology and are endowed with the same fraction of total real national capital stock K_0. We thus can write

$$(F=)\frac{p\overline{X} - p_K K_0}{L(\overline{X})} - pMPP[L(\overline{X})] = 0 \tag{3}$$

utilizing relation (2) to express the national employment of labor as a function of national product $\overline{X}$. The term p_K, known to us already from previous analysis, expresses the unit money-cost of capital, and is a constant given by previous financing commitments of the labor-managed firms and possibly by government fiscal policy. Also it will be noted that, as is apparent from the second term on the left-hand side of relation (3), the marginal physical productivity of labor is, via relation (2), a unique function of the national product. With given K_0 and p_K, relation (3) becomes a relation between two of our three endogenous variables, that is p and $\overline{X}$. In terms of our analysis of Part I it is nothing but a "national" competitive and short-run supply curve. Since it does not contain the rate of interest i, the equilibrium surface representing relation (3) is perpendicular to the p-$\overline{X}$ plane, and as we know from our partial equilibrium analysis of industry supply, the intercept with that plane is negatively sloped. Such a surface is illustrated in Figure 10.1.1.

We further recall from Chapter 2 that if there is a positive excess of the income per laborer over his marginal value product—that is, if F in relation (3) is positive—the firms and hence the national economy will tend to reduce employment and vice versa when $F < 0$. And hence, because we know that F is positive to the right of the equilibrium plane and negative to the left of the plane, we can draw two centripetal arrows to the right and left of the plane. In other words, the labor condition or quasi labor market provides us with the third dynamic force of adjustment for the third endogenous aggregative variable $\overline{X}$.

Especially in the very short run, the inclination of the equilibrium plane in Figure 10.1.1 may be very slight or nil, the labor-managed firms being reluctant, for one reason or another—some of these reasons were discussed extensively in Part I, and we will return to them more systematically in Part III—to adjust employment and output.[1] None-

---

[1] In particular we recall here the arguments of a "social" short-run behavior of the labor-managed firms, and of a high degree of short-run complementarity between employment and existing plant and equipment.

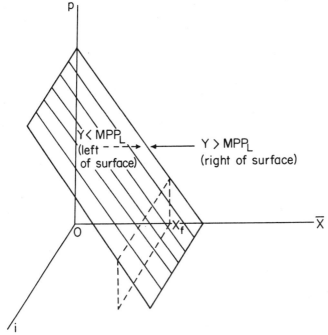

Figure 10.1.1

theless, we must retain here the negative slope of the short-run national supply function, however low the elasticity, to be consistent with the pure theory of the labor-managed system. Once full employment of labor is attained, the supply surface becomes absolutely inelastic with respect to price.

10.2: *The General Equilibrium Determination of the Aggregate Variables in a Labor-Managed Economy*

We are finally in a position to put all our building blocks together and derive the general equilibrium solution for the labor-managed economy. Using first numbers to indicate the particular chapter in which an equation appears, relations (8.9), (9.18), and (10.3) are three equations, each corresponding to one market (or quasi market) equilibrium, in three endogenous variables, i, p, and $\overline{X}$. The system defines our general equilibrium, and any combination of the three variables, i_0, p_0, and $\overline{X}_0$, simultaneously satisfying all three equilibrium conditions is a general equilibrium solution. The solutions for the other endogenous variables, such as C_0, I_0, and L_0, are then obtainable from the particular definitions of these aggregates. Generally there can be expected a finite number of such sets, and most frequently there will be only one solution.

Such a unique solution is obtained as a necessary outcome if the three equilibrium surfaces are planes, as we have assumed them to be in the graphical representations of Figures 8.5.1, 9.5.1, and 10.1.1. For such a situation we show the complete general equilibrium determination in Figure 10.2.1. The three-dimensional configuration of the three equilibrium planes is, we hope, apparent from the diagram. Since being at any one of the three planes implies equilibrium (i.e., absence of motion), for one of the variables, each plane corresponding to a different variable, at the intersection of the three planes (i.e., their unique common point) E_0 all three variables must be at rest. The three coordinates of E_0, i_0, p_0, and $\bar{X}_0$ are then the general equilibrium solutions for the labor-managed economy. In the rest of the chapter we will

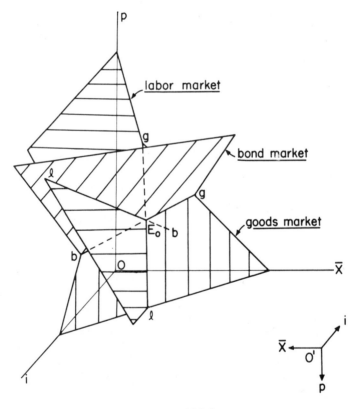

Figure 10.2.1

determining the positions of the three spears are unambiguous, and only the remaining one can assume both positive and negative signs. Specifically, using + and − signs for coordinate changes corresponding to movements indicated by the arrows, we have, from Figure 10.2.1:

Table 10.3.1

Locus	Change in Coordinate		
	i	p	$\overline{X}$
$\overset{--\rightarrow}{bg}$	−	±	+
$\overset{--\rightarrow}{bl}$	+	+	−
$\overset{--\rightarrow}{lg}$	−	+	−

Perhaps the autonomous shift easiest to establish is that resulting from an autonomous increase in demand for goods and services— whether stemming from changed investors' or consumers' behavior (we recall here that considerations of government-induced shifts are relegated to Part IV). Suppose that such an increase in demand for goods and services takes place, starting from a situation of market equilibrium, that is, starting from a point on the goods-market plane in Figure 10.2.1. Now postulate that we momentarily hold the price, the rate of interest, and real national product constant; the shift in demand will have generated a (disequilibrium) excess-demand situation. And the latter, with, say, interest rate and national product unchanged, can be eliminated only through an increase in the general price level. Translated in terms of our diagram, the goods-market plane must move upward (downward) as a result of an increase (decline) in demand for goods and services—a conclusion hardly in conflict with common sense. The mobile (goods-market) plane moves along the fixed spear $\overset{--\rightarrow}{bl}$ in the direction of the arrow; consequently, the impacts of the autonomous disturbance on our three endogenous variables have the same signs as those shown in Table 10.3.1 for the row marked "$\overset{--\rightarrow}{bl}$." In words, an increase in consumers' and/or investors' demand for goods and services will, in a stable labor-managed economy, increase the rate of interest and the general price level and reduce the level of national product (and employment) in the short run. But the last of the three effects can be expected to be very small or nil on account of a very steep slope of the labor-market plane.

Given the normal slopes for the bond supply and demand schedules, as presented in the foregoing chapter, the reader will easily establish— using a method similar to that just employed for the real goods market

—that an autonomous increase in the demand for bonds will shift the bond-market equilibrium plane forward; in other words, with unchanged p and X the rate of interest must now increase in order to preserve market equilibrium. This movement again is in the direction of the fixed spear $\overrightarrow{lg}$. Consequently, the signs in Table 10.3.1 again obtain as an indication of corresponding changes in the three endogenous variables. Specifically, resulting from an increase in the demand for bonds, we will witness in the labor-managed economy a short-run increase in the price level and a decline in the rate of interest and national product. The last of the three changes, again, can be expected to be insignificant.

Let us now turn to the quasi labor market, and ask the question how autonomous changes in it affect the general equilibrium solution. But before we come to the technical aspects of the problem, a few general remarks are necessary. First, it must be recalled that the aggregate theory of national-income determination is one of short-run nature. By contrast, the two autonomous disturbances which can take place in our quasi labor market—those stemming from changes in technology and those stemming from changes in the capital stock—usually are considered of the long-run variety. Therefore, they are not customarily included as concerns of macroeconomic theory. With respect to our study of the labor-managed system, such an exclusion is unwarranted, because the impacts of changing technology and capital stock certainly are very important and relevant facts. However, because these forces are of long-run character, the story which we can write on their behalf within the present setting is only a partial one. There will be other adjustments to changes in technology and capital stock taking place, but we will turn to these only in Section 10.5.

To study the short-run tendencies resulting in a labor-managed economy from autonomous changes in the quasi labor market, it will be convenient to restate here the corresponding equilibrium condition (relation (3) of this chapter); it is

$$\frac{p\bar{X} - p_K K_0}{L(\bar{X})} - pMPP[L(\bar{X})] = 0 \tag{3}$$

As we have pointed out already, the two autonomous changes that can affect this condition are (1) a change in K_0 and (2) a change in the technology, that is, a shift in the function on $L(X)$. Let us start with the first disturbance.

As a central case, suppose that the production function is of the Cobb-Douglas variety, that is, has a unitary elasticity of factor substitution. In that case, as is well known, the average productivity of labor remains in constant proportion to the marginal productivity of labor at all times.[3] Now suppose that K_0 increases by 10 per cent while L remains constant. Assuming (at least approximately) constant returns to scale, this would increase output by 10 per cent if labor also increased by 10 per cent; but because labor remained constant, the corresponding increase of $\overline{X}$ must be less than 10 percent, and so must be the increase in APP_L. On the assumptions made and with unchanged p and p_K, in relation (3) $p\overline{X}/L(\overline{X})$ and $pMPP[L(\overline{X})]$ would increase by the same percentage smaller than 10 per cent and $p_K K_0/L(\overline{X})$ would increase by 10 per cent. Consequently the whole left hand side of relation 3, that is F, would become negative. But with F negative, we know that to reach equilibrium L must increase and thus $\overline{X}$ will further increase on account of employment. Consequently, with a unitary elasticity of substitution, the labor-market plane in Figure 10.2.1 must shift to the right a good deal. That movement again is in the direction of the "spear" $\overrightarrow{bg}$, and consequently the corresponding changes will have the signs given in Table 10.3.1; specifically, the increase in capital stock will lead to a decline in the rate of interest, an increase in gross national product, and an ambiguous change in the price level. With prices ambiguous, and recalling that if they were constant employment would have to increase, the general equilibrium effect on employment on the whole also can be expected to be positive. Defining the elasticity of factor substitution as the per cent change in K/L per one per cent change in the relative price of capital in terms of labor, it is easily established that elastic production functions will tend to reduce or reverse the shift in the equilibrium plane while inelastic functions will lead to an accentuation of the effects just stated for the Cobb-Douglas function. It will also be noted that the effects on employment will be in the same direction as, and roughly proportional to, the effects on national product. Of course, throughout we must assume that if full employment is reached in the course of adjustment, the employment and product will settle at such a point while the rate of interest and the price level will undergo further equilibrating adjustments. This situation will be studied in section 10.4.

[3]The reader may want to recall at this point that for any linear-homogeneous function, MPP_L/APP_L is equal to one income share of labor, and that the latter is constant for a Cobb-Douglas function.

Let us turn to the case of technological change. Again, to consider a central situation, suppose that the national aggregate technology, as given in relation (1), improves in a Hicks-neutral fashion, that is, for an unchanged capital-labor ratio, the marginal productivities of capital and labor increase proportionately. Now suppose that technological progress occurs at a rate of 10 per cent. Postulating the production function (at least approximately) subject to constant returns to scale—that is, of the second kind—this will, for an unchanged use of capital and labor, increase both the $\overline{X}$ and MPP terms in relation (3) by 10 per cent; but because $p_K K_0$ remains constant, F, the left-hand side of relation (3), will become positive. And this, as we know, will lead necessarily to downward adjustment in equilibrium employment. And thus if we would have constructed our equilibrium plane in Figure 10.2.1 in terms of L rather than $\overline{X}$, such a plane necessarily would have shifted to the left. This downward shift, however, being offset by an increase in productivity, the actual plane describing the labor market in Figure 10.2.1 may shift to the right or left. The exact outcome will depend on some more specific properties of the production function, as much as on the nature of the technological progress if the latter is other than neutral; but the resolution of these refined points we leave to the interested and patient reader. It may only be noted here that in case of a predominantly "social" behavior the decline in employment should be insignificant, and thus the national product would increase.

To sum up, let us show the signs of the changes in endogenous variables corresponding to the four autonomous disturbances which we have examined. This is done in Table 10.3.2:

Table 10.3.2

Effect of increase in:	On variable:			
	i	p	$\overline{X}$	L
Demand for goods (C or I)	+	+	−	−
Demand for bonds	−	+	−	−
Capital stock ($C.$-$D.$ function)	−	±	+	+ *
Total productivity (neutral technical progress)	±	±	±	− *

*Not an absolutely necessary outcome.

10.4: *Full Employment and Some Other Special Aspects of the General Equilibrium*

In all of our discussion thus far in this chapter, the implicit assumption has been that the equilibrium employment L_0, linked through relation (2) to the equilibrium output $\overline{X}_0$, actually is attainable. In other words, it has been assumed that $\overline{X}_0 = \overline{X}_f$ and $L_0 \leqq L_f$, where the subscript "f" is used to indicate the level of the variables corresponding to full employment. Obviously, nothing guarantees that such inequalities would have to hold in the real world. For certain values of structural parameters the general equilibrium solution, as obtained and discussed thus far, would have to fall outside the boundary of full-employment output. Alternatively, for some autonomous changes of the type discussed in the preceding section, the equilibrium would have to move into the region beyond full-employment output.

We are thus facing the question of what will happen if the condition of over-full employment just identified should arise. Fortunately the answer is rather simple, especially if we recall our analysis of industry-supply functions under conditions of "effective" labor-supply constraint. The present concept of full employment is, it will be noted, what we have referred to in Chapter 4 as the labor supply (availability locus) S_4. From that analysis, or just from common sense, we know that the corresponding *short-run* supply of product (here $\overline{X}$) simply becomes truncated—and turns into a perfectly inelastic locus—when the full-employment labor constraint is reached. The corresponding labor-market equilibrium plane is shown by the broken-line construction in Figure 10.1.1. It should be clear that if we used such a truncated equilibrium plane in Figure 10.2.1, the problem of over-full employment would not have arisen; indeed the point E_0 now could have been located in either region of the labor-market equilibrium surface. In Part IV one of our important concerns will be the question of how to keep near the truncated region through government policy. Later in this chapter we will show that existence of the equilibrium at full employment guarantees stability of the general equilibrium, a condition which need not hold—in theory at least—otherwise.

There is another set of observations which we must take up in this section. They follow from, or are related to, the Walras law discussed previously and to the existence of the fourth market for money which has been omitted. We know that the equilibrium plane of the money market must pass at all times through the general equilibrium point such as E_0 in Figure 10.2.1. Consequently, in the process of adjustment to disturbances discussed in the preceding section, the money-market plane must (implicitly, or behind the scenes) be shifting together with the market plane wherein the disturbance has occurred. In other words, in our analysis where a plane is moving along a fixed line—we have referred to it as a "spear"—really two equilibrium planes are moving and two other planes remain invariant, the intersection (line) of the two moving planes (by Walras' law) always passing through (intersecting) the fixed line (i.e., the "spear" of the preceding section). Thus, an autonomous change in one market not affecting the other two markets considered must always also be viewed as an autonomous change in the market not considered (such as the money market in our general equilibrium derivation). More specifically, using an example, the comparative static results which we have obtained in the preceding section for an increased demand for bonds are the same thing as results obtained (within the same general equilibrium structure) for a reduction in demand for money. Indeed, in an all-inclusive economic system (which the general equilibrium system is) one cannot increase autonomously the demand for one commodity without reducing the demand for some other commodity or commodities; and the situation which we have been discussing thus far is one involving a compensating autonomous change only in one other market. That other market happens to be the market left out by Walras' law—in our case the money market. We may refer to such autonomous changes as "pure" changes; in the same breath, we should also say that pure changes are hardly ever encountered in the real world. For example, an increase in demand for bonds will not be compensated for exclusively by a repercussion in the money market, but there will generally be a compensating autonomous shift in the demand for goods and services or for leisure. Obviously, if we have any evidence on what the compensating effects are, we should include it into the comparative statics analysis. This can be done using the "pure" effects established in the preceding section. For example, a shift in demand for bonds compensated for by not only a money-demand adjustment but also by a goods-demand adjustment can be traced through the general equilibrium system as a composite movement, one along an $\overrightarrow{lg}$ "spear" (as before) and another along a (new) $\overrightarrow{bl}$ "spear."

In the context of general equilibrium analysis these remarks are extremely important. Yet, in most instances of applied comparative statics in aggregative general equilibrium their content is disregarded and only what we have called here the "pure" effects are considered. For example, in the well-known Keynesian multiplier analysis no one ever worries about what might have been the compensating shift corresponding to an autonomous increase in investment demand.

10.5: *The Short and the Long Run Considered Simultaneously*

It should be clear that, in any economic analysis, the separation of the short from the long run and analysis of the former in isolation is nothing more than a methodological convenience. In any real situation, both the so-called short run and the so-called long run forces will be operative simultaneously; only it can sometimes be ascertained that the long-run forces and corresponding adjustment are comparatively unimportant and thus, as a first approximation, they can be omitted. While such a justification is fairly plausible in the context of western-type Keynesian or other theories of national-income determination, it is rather inadequate for the case at hand. In fact, we should consider what we have done thus far only as an isolation of forces defined as short run—or of short-run effects of long-run changes, such as those in technology or capital stock—in a world where simultaneously long-run adjustment is taking place; the latter process often proceeding at a rapid pace.

While the analysis of Part I contains most of the relevant analysis with regard to long-run adjustment, at least a few of the most important implications of the long-run forces for the theory of national-income determination should be made explicit here. It may be useful to set the present case against the conventional western-type macroeconomic theory; the resulting contrast may be quite illuminating. One of the important findings of the foregoing sections is that in the labor-managed economy a state of unemployment can arise, and that there is nothing in the nature of short-run forces that would automatically correct such a state. The same conclusion is the crux of the western-type (or Keynesian) macro-theory. In the latter, however, unemployment "equilibrium" is necessarily—it will be recalled—a result of some kind of price rigidity in the system; most often the rigidity of money wages is blamed for the outcome. If the wages are permanently rigid, with a given volume of effective demand (as is well known from both theory and practice) the state of unemployment can last indefinitely. Potential new entrants into the productive sector, who could absorb the unemployed labor force, really cannot enter because at the given rigid wages and level of effective demand they would be bound to lose money.

In the labor-managed system it is not so, and in this particular respect, the system has a definite advantage. As soon as short-run labor unemployment (of the type discussed thus far) develops, entry of new

firms automatically sets in and starts absorbing such unemployment.[4]
The essential ingredient of this phenomenon is that wage or income-
per-laborer rigidity cannot be present in the system at hand.[5] The equilibrium income per laborer under unemployment established within the
short-run system by no means constitutes a constraint on incomes of
new entrants; the latter in their newly opened firms can earn somewhat
less. But such lower incomes will always be in excess of what they
would have to live on if unemployed. We will return to the problems
of multiple remuneration and economic policy toward entry in Parts III
and IV respectively; therefore, we do not have to elaborate any further
on these subjects.

It must also be recalled in the present context that labor incomes
are established as a residual, and hence can hardly be rigid as is the
Keynesian institutional wage. It is this phenomenon, together with the
desire of labor-managed firms to increase output with declining demand and the reluctance to fire fellow workers with increasing demand
in the short run, that will make departures from full employment unlikely, once such employment is established.

Finally, one more related point must be made, falling within the
scope of the present analysis. It concerns the general price level. The
anomalous result of the present short-run analysis is that short-run
disturbances leading to less than full employment will tend to produce,
at the same time, inflation of the general price level. The long-run
forces of entry pointed out earlier in this section as beneficial in respect
to unemployment will, by the same token, tend to counteract the inflation of the price level.

10.6: *On the Stability of the Aggregate General Equilibrium*

As we have indicated already, the question of stability is just as important as the derivation of the equilibrium solution. All of the comparative static analysis carried out in the preceding sections would be
quite meaningless if we could not ascertain that the equilibrium in
question is a stable one. We will approach the problem of stability in
two different stages. First we will discuss the matter in a more general
but also much simpler and more intelligible manner, relying primarily

----

[4]The new entry, it will be recalled, can be substituted for by expansion of existing firms
operating under long-run constant returns to scale.

[5]Of course, the government could impose a minimum labor income, but this should
not concern us here in the context of a purely theoretical analysis. Also it can easily be
assumed that such minimum remunerations would always be less than the income per
laborer of the potential entrants.

on some of the graphic representations known to us already. But because this approach, however straightforward, is not really rigorous—and not even complete—we will supplement it in the following section by a rigorous mathematical statement of necessary and sufficient conditions for stability of the equilibrium at hand.

Our point of departure is the dynamic forces of adjustment (from states of disequilibrium) of our three endogenous variables—p, i, and $\overline{X}$—studied previously in connection with the three individual markets of goods, bonds, and labor. In Figure 10.2.1, we have indicated the over-all directions of adjustment associated with each particular equilibrium plane; thus, for example, the vertical lines drawn on the goods-market plane indicate that, depending on the position regarding that plane, the price variable measured along the vertical axis will adjust.

It must be clear that any point away from equilibrium E_0 can be associated with a dynamic adjustment of some or all of the three endogenous variables. The lines drawn in Figure 10.2.1 and arrows drawn in Figures 8.5.1, 9.5.1, and 10.1.1 tell us a good deal about such dynamic adjustments. More specifically, they restrict the direction of the dynamic adjustment to one-eighth of all possible directions. This can tell us a good deal—even if not everything—about the dynamic stability of the general equilibrium E_0. For example, suppose that we are temporarily at a point (in space) in front of the "model" in Figure 10.2.1. "Being in front" means that the real goods market is in excess supply and hence $\overline{X}$ must be declining, the bond market is in excess demand and hence the rate of interest must be declining, and finally, the quasi labor market is in a situation where F is negative and hence $\overline{X}$ must also be declining. All this is summarized by the three arrows originating at $0'$ in Figure 10.2.1, corresponding to a point in space "in front." The composite movement of a disequilibrium point from a point such as $0'$ must proceed within this octant. With only a little spatial imagination, the reader will realize how much such a composite movement originating "in front" points in the over-all direction of E_0. Actually, from many points "in front" it would be easy to hit E_0, and thus settle at the general equilibrium directly.

But a direct approach to E_0 is not necessary. Given the configuration of the three equilibrium planes, even if the composite movement of adjustment crosses one or more of the equilibrium planes—once or several times—forces are present which in general will tend to direct the movement toward a final position at E_0; in other words, there will be what we may refer to as equilibrium forces and thus E_0 will tend to be stable. Suppose that, from a point such as $0'$, E_0 is not reached directly, but the goods-market plane is reached first. Given our dynamic rules of the game, the path of adjustment can cross that plane only with stationary general price level p; that is, the crossing must be embedded in a horizontal plane. And once on the other side, the vertical arrow associated with the adjustment path will suddenly turn upward. Another useful, even if only partial, observation is that the octant "behind the model" (hidden in our drawing) will have all the arrows reversed compared to those originating at $0'$. Therefore, E_0 will again tend to find itself in the aiming range of the adjustment path.

This analysis should be sufficient to enable the reader, if he so desires, to carry out further steps of this intuitive demonstration (not a proof) of stability (that is, convergence toward equilibrium from points of disequilibrium) of the point E_0. Consequently, we shall conclude our intuitive and qualitative discussion here in expectation of a rigorous statement in the next section.

Let it only be noted, using some of the results to be shown in the following section, that actually the equilibrium depicted in Figure 10.2.1 is stable in the vicinity of E_0 provided that the moving forces of adjustment are those which we have assumed in Chapters 8, 9, and 10 (i.e., provided that the speeds of adjustment are constants and adjustment of one endogenous variable depends exclusively on the state of a single market). Actually, under these conditions the equilibrium depicted is "too stable." In fact, stability could even be consistent with the goods and labor markets' intercepts with the p-X plane having slopes reversed with respect to each other.

10.7: *The Comparative Statics and Stability of Aggregate General*
        Equilibrium in a Labor-Managed Economy: Mathematical Analysis

In several of the foregoing sections we have discussed macroeconomic general equilibrium and its stability and adjustment to changing conditions in nonmathematical terms. If that analysis had been complete and fully rigorous, we could have relegated the mathematical treatment of these subjects, as a specialists' curiosum, to a mathematical appendix. But because this was not the case, we feel that a more rigorous treatment of comparative statics and stability should be offered in the main text; only in this way can we verify some of the previous propositions which otherwise would remain little more than conjectures.

Relying on the three markets for goods, bonds, and labor (omitting the money market), our general equilibrium is defined by

$$\overline{X} - X(i, p, \overline{X}) = a \tag{4}$$

$$B(i, p, \overline{X}) - \overline{B}(i, p, \overline{X}) = -b \tag{5}$$

and

$$\overline{X}/L - p_K K_0/Lp - c\overline{X}_L = 0 \tag{6}$$

where X_L stands for a partial differential, that is, the marginal physical productivity of labor and c, in initial equilibrium assuming the value of unity, is a shift parameter reflecting a Hicks-neutral technological change. The terms a and b also are shift parameters, their small increments indicating autonomous changes in demand (excess demand) for goods and bonds respectively. Differentiating the system of equations (4) through (6) totally with respect to a, b, and c respectively, we obtain, using matrix notation and subscripts to indicate partial differentials (a double subscript stands for second partial differential):

$$
\begin{array}{ccc}
& z = \quad a \quad b \quad c
\end{array}
$$

$$
\begin{bmatrix}
-X_p & -X_i & (1 - X_{\overline{X}}) \\
(B_p - \overline{B}_p) & (B_i - \overline{B}_i) & (B_{\overline{X}} - \overline{B}_{\overline{X}}) \\
p_K K_0/Lp^2 & 0 & L_{\overline{X}\overline{X}}/L_{\overline{X}}^2{}^*
\end{bmatrix}
\begin{bmatrix}
(dp/dz) \\
(di/dz) \\
(d\overline{X}/dz)
\end{bmatrix}
=
\begin{bmatrix} 1 \\ 0 \\ 0 \end{bmatrix}
\begin{bmatrix} 0 \\ -1 \\ 0 \end{bmatrix}
\begin{bmatrix} 0 \\ 0 \\ \overline{X}_L \end{bmatrix}
\tag{7}
$$

Relation (7) is an abridged way of writing three sets of three simultaneous linear equations, each set corresponding to a given $z(=a$ or b or $c)$. As is well known, the nine solutions of the system for the three variables and four changing parameters are obtainable through Cramer's method and can be written as:

$$dp/da = (1/D)(B_i - \overline{B}_i)L_{\overline{X}\overline{X}}/L_{\overline{X}}^2 \qquad (+) \tag{8}$$

$$di/da = (1/D)[(B_{\overline{X}} - B_{\overline{X}})p_K K_0/Lp^2 - (B_p - \overline{B}_p)L_{\overline{X}\overline{X}}/L_{\overline{X}}^2] \quad (+) \tag{9}$$

$$d\overline{X}/da = -(1/D)(B_i - \overline{B}_i)p_K K_0/Lp^2 \qquad (-) \tag{10}$$

*The function whose first and second differentials appear in this fraction is that given in relation (2) of this chapter. The reader who wants to verify the mathematical procedure may find it useful to know that this term is obtained after some simplifying manipulation from the definition of real income per laborer.

$$dp/db = -(1/D)X_i L_{\overline{XX}}/L_{\overline{X}}^2 \qquad\qquad (+)\quad (11)$$

$$di/db = (1/D)[X_p L_{\overline{XX}}/L_{\overline{X}}^2 + (1 - X_{\overline{X}})p_K K_0/Lp^2 \qquad (\pm)\quad (12)$$

$$d\overline{X}/db = (1/D)X_i p_K K_0/Lp^2 \qquad\qquad (-)\quad (13)$$

$$dp/dc = -(1/D)(\overline{X}_L)[X_i(B_{\overline{X}} - \overline{B}_{\overline{X}}) + (1 - X_{\overline{X}})(B_i - \overline{B}_i)] \qquad (\pm)\quad (14)$$

$$di/dc = (1/D)(\overline{X}_L)[X_p(B_{\overline{X}} - \overline{B}_{\overline{X}}) + (1 - X_{\overline{X}})(B_p - \overline{B}_p)] \qquad (\pm)\quad (15)$$

$$d\overline{X}/dc = (1/D)(\overline{X}_L)[X_i(B_p - \overline{B}_p) - X_p(B_i - \overline{B}_i)] \qquad (\pm)\quad (16)$$

One of the conditions necessary for stability of the general equilibrium is that $D > 0$, where D is the coefficients determinant in relation (7). Therefore, if it is ascertained that the system is a stable one (indeed, if such an assumption were not made, the problem of adjustment to disturbances would not make any sense since any disturbance would be bound to have either constrained or unconstrained explosive effects), the multipliers shown in relations (8) through (16) have, given our "expected" slopes of the behavioral functions, the signs indicated in brackets on the right-hand side. As the reader can verify, the signs are precisely those obtained through our graphical analysis with the exception of di/db, which here is shown as negative or positive. Only the former outcome came out from the geometrical study; but as the reader may easily verify, this absence of ambiguity was imputable to the fact that the intercept of the goods-market plane with the p-$\overline{X}$ coordinate plane was less steep than the intercept of the labor-market plane. However, this configuration is not necessarily required for stability of the general equilibrium. If the reverse configuration prevails, clearly, the rate of interest must increase as a result of an increased demand for bonds.

We can now turn to the question of stability. Provided that the dynamic mechanism at all times governing the movements of our three endogenous variables is that described by relations (8.13), (9.23), and an analogous relation for the movements of $\overline{X}$ holds, namely

$$\Delta\overline{X}/\Delta t = gF \qquad (17)$$

where F is defined in relation (3) of this chapter and g is a negative constant (speed of adjustment), then the necessary and sufficient conditions (known as Routhian) for stability in the vicinity of a general equilibrium solution are[6]

$$a_3 \equiv D > 0 \qquad (18)$$

---

[6]For a not too lucid derivation, see P. A. Samuelson, *Foundations of Economic Analysis* (Cambridge, Mass., 1953), pp. 432–433.

as stated already,

$$a_2 \equiv D_{11} + D_{22} + D_{33} > 0 \tag{19}$$

$$a_1 \equiv A_{11} + A_{22} + A_{33} > 0 \tag{20}$$

and

$$a_1 a_2 - a_3 > 0 \tag{21}$$

where the D_{ii}'s are principal minors of D and A_{ii}'s the diagonal terms of D.

The question must be asked as to how well these conditions are fulfilled, given the expected most likely slopes of the behavioral functions. By inspection of D in relation 7 we find the following most likely signs of the eight nonzero terms entering D:

$$
\begin{array}{ccc}
+ & + & + \\
- & + & + \\
+ & 0 & +
\end{array}
$$

Developing this into the four nonzero terms of the determinant, we have three positive products and one negative, the latter being formed by the terms of the second diagonal. This may give us some comfort, but it does not guarantee stability. However, were any of the three terms just mentioned small or zero, D would be positive and thus stability at least on account of relation (18) would be guaranteed. In fact, relation (18) does appear to be of crucial importance because D governs the sign and size of the multipliers of relations (8) through (16).

Turning now briefly to the other necessary conditions, we immediately find that, given our expected slopes, relation (20) must be satisfied, and relation (19) contains two positive and one negative principal minors. If A_{31} were zero or very small, again, relation (19) will be satisfied. We leave the examination of condition (21) to the reader. The sign and size of A_{31}, the term in the third row and first column, is of central importance for stability. As the reader may suspect, manipulation of that term through economic policy will be a powerful tool of stabilization; but this subject we leave until Part IV. Also, it must be noted from equation (6) that A_{31} very small or zero simply implies a highly inelastic supply of national product, a case that we have found plausible on several accounts.

10.8: *Summary of Main Findings*

The unavoidable technicality of the three chapters of Part II may blur—for some readers at least—the key conclusions of these chapters. Especially because the results concern the most important aggregate variables pertaining to the entire economy, it appears desirable to go over the most significant among them.

In the three chapters, we have considered, one by one, four aggregate markets—for goods, money, bonds, and labor—and combined these into a general equilibrium system within which such variables as national product, the price level, and employment are determined for the economy as a whole. Following the customary procedure, this analysis has been primarily short-run in nature. Compared to western-type macroeconomic theory, significant differences arose only in the goods and (quasi) labor markets. In the former, the short-run investment function, not incorporating possibilities of entry, was found to be similar to a Keynesian investment function, although the behavioral forces underlying it are quite different. The short-run quasi labor market, of course, is quite different from the labor market encountered in capitalist analysis.

Turning now to the results, the short-run aggregate equilibrium of a labor-managed economy can involve unemployment of labor, and if this happens, it is so not because of price-wage inflexibility (the latter being ruled out in a labor-managed system) but because—if one can speak at all of a single cause—of the special nature of the labor market; actually what we have just referred to as the labor market is not at all, in the short run, a market in the conventional sense, and for that reason we have suggested the term "quasi labor market."

Among the results in the sphere of comparative statics, probably the most important and unorthodox is that an increase in aggregate demand, while leading to higher prices, generally will produce a reduction in income and employment in the short run. However, such a reduction should be quite small, and moreover, as soon as short-run unemployment arises, long-run forces (largely absent in a capitalist economy) will become operative in the labor-managed system, offsetting both the initial short-run impacts on prices and employment. Everything considered, it can be said that the labor-managed economy will be very little susceptible to spontaneous short-run variations in employment and income; most of the impact of changing market conditions will be translated into variations in the general price level.

Strictly in the short run, the stability of the aggregate general equilibrium is not fully guaranteed, although for realistic values of the structural parameters it can be expected to be by far the most likely outcome. Even if the equilibrium is stable in the sense that small displacements will not lead to explosive alterations, the comparatively low elasticities involved may lead to significant variations, especially in the general price level in conjunction with autonomous changes in effective aggregate demand for goods, or for bonds or money. But the long-run corrective forces based on entry (suggested above) can counteract such variations. Also, the central authorities will have an important role to play, through indirect policy action, as a stabilizing agent. However, we will return to this subject only in Part IV as a part of a general discussion of aggregate government policy.

Finally, it can be expected that on the whole there will be less long-run inflationary pressure in the labor-managed economy, *ceteris paribus*, than we are accustomed to in western market economies. This is a result of a comparatively higher degree of downward price flexibility in the labor-managed economy.

PART III
SPECIAL ASPECTS OF THE
LABOR-MANAGED ECONOMY

11. The Labor-Managed Firm and a Diversified Labor Force

11.1: *Preliminary Considerations*

Throughout Parts I and II, we have worked with an extremely simple —in the context of any real labor-managed system, oversimplified— concept of labor. The rationale behind this approach was explained in detail in Chapter I. Here let us just recall that in the preceding nine chapters, labor was (1) perfectly homogeneous, (2) of constant quality, and (3) acting exclusively in its capacity as a factor of production. Especially in a labor-managed economy, these assumptions are extremely unrealistic. Labor now assumes a very large number of new dimensions, all in conflict with the three assumptions just stated. In Part III, our principal task will be to relax the simplifying assumptions and thus arrive at a representation of the labor-managed system far more in harmony with a real situation. Because many of the new dimensions that we are about to discuss are specific to the labor-managed system, Part III is, in a sense, central to the entire study.

The three simplifying assumptions stated above suggest a useful organization of Part III. In the present chapter we will relax the first assumption and postulate a labor force composed of several types of skills, or qualities, of labor. However, assumptions two (for each category of the labor force) and three will be retained. In the subsequent chapter, the second simplifying assumption will be relinquished in an analysis of incentives and of the relationship between income and management participation on the one hand and the quality and/or intensity of labor effort on the other. Finally, in the third and fourth chapters of Part III, we will abandon the third simplifying assumption and discuss the principal new roles of labor in the system under study. The second of the two chapters just mentioned—the last of Part III—is entirely devoted to problems connected with entry, expansion, and exit of firms in an industry.

We may now say a few more preliminary words about the scope and organization of the present chapter. The newly introduced diversity of the labor force must be considered in two different contexts. First, of course, we must see how it will be handled within an individual firm and how it will affect its behavior. Drawing on such results, we will then want to see how the "modified" equilibrium behavior of an individual firm affects the solution for a whole industry or the entire economic system.

Because the essence of the problem is the same whether two or more qualities of labor are considered, we will adopt the two-labor situation to facilitate a clear exposition; however, we will briefly explain the generalization to an arbitrary number of types of labor. In addition, we will provide a mathematical appendix containing the general solution.

Although the case with multiple categories of labor does not involve consideration of the new capacities of labor (in a labor-managed system) as endogenous factors, it must be based on a "constant" or datum derived from a new—specifically, the decision-making—role of those working in the enterprise. This datum is an income-distribution schedule, specifying for each employment category (defined by skills, seniority, or other characteristics) the relative share of total income to be given to a member of that category. More will be said about such schedules in the following section.

At present let it be noted that it is only at this stage of our analysis that we have come to a situation where democratic decision-making is called for to reconcile the interests of diverse groups. Previously, with homogeneous labor, it was easy to accept that equal efforts would earn equal retribution. The same principle can be postulated within each labor category. But what about share-setting among categories? Clearly, the answer will be the result of an interaction between factors internal and external to the enterprise. We will be able to discuss only some of these—the more economic, or objective ones—in the present chapter, leaving the rest of the subject for Chapter 13.

11.2: *The Income Distribution Schedule and the Equilibrium of a Labor-Managed Firm*

One of the most important self-management acts of the labor-managed firm is the decision on how to distribute net income among its participants. The problem of how to distribute income between, on the one hand, personal income and, on the other hand, reserve funds, investment funds, collective consumption, and the like may also arise, but we leave this subject for later in Part III and Part IV. As we have suggested in the preceding section, all we have to do at this stage of the argument is to postulate a given (personal) income-distribution schedule, stemming from the democratic process of labor management.

Of course, the distribution schedule could assume a virtually un-limited number of distinct forms, constrained only by the imagination of those submitting it for vote before the labor-management body. It could contain provisions for income in kind, or in terms of leisure, and it could stipulate distributive shares variable with the level of aggregate income. For our purposes, however, we will restrict ourselves to the analysis of the simplest and, from the practical point of view, by far most realistic alternative. We will assume that each type of labor L_i (defined by skill, job description, or otherwise) is to earn a constant number a_i of basic remuneration units, the latter being determined only once the total net income of the enterprise is known. Clearly, the ab-solute levels of the a_i's are arbitrary, the only relevant information being contained in the relationships (ratios) of the different a_i's to each other. In simple terms, what really counts is whether the first category of skills earns two or three times more than another. It is, therefore, possible to choose some convenient scale for all the a_i's. For example, the least remunerated job in the enterprise can be defined as one carry-ing income of one remuneration unit; that is, starting the job classifica-tion from that job description, we have $a_1 = 1$. The entire income dis-tribution schedule is now given by (a vector)

$$(1, a_2, a_3, \ldots, a_n) \tag{1}$$

where all the a's (larger than unity) are expressed in units of income of the least qualified position.

Once the director of the labor-managed firm is equipped with such an income-distribution schedule, his task again—at least in our idealized theoretical world—becomes quite simple and manageable. It will be in the interest of all the firm's employees, including himself, to maximize the size of the basic remuneration unit. For if this is done, the income of each participant—given, and subject to the income-distribution schedule—will also be maximized. The rest of the present section is devoted to a theoretical analysis of what this new (or modified) maxi-mization problem implies for the equilibrium of the labor-managed firm. Because basically the problem remains the same whether two or a large number of labor types is present, we will restrict ourselves here to the case where $n = 2$.

Let us first consider a short-run competitive equilibrium of the firm. The technology used by the firm in producing a single product X is, for the moment, one permitting of (smooth) continuous substitution among all factors and can be written as $X = X(L_1, L_2; K_0)$, where K_0 is a constant. The technology in all three inputs is either of the first or of the second kind—that is, either subject to increasing-diminishing returns, or to constant returns to scale. Three of its equal-product lines, corresponding to outputs X_1, X_2 and X_3, are illustrated in Figure 11.2.1.

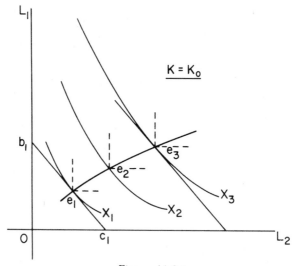

Figure 11.2.1

Suppose further that the income-distribution schedule is (approximately)

$$(1, 1.15) \tag{1'}$$

that is, whatever the equilibrium of the firm, the income of each member belonging to L_2 must be about 15 per cent higher than the income (per unit) of the other employees of the enterprise. The line $b_1 c_1$—whose slope reflects the assumed relative remuneration of L_1 and L_2—thus represents a locus of combinations of the two employments L_1 and L_2 attainable with a given level of net income of A_1 basic remuneration units and consistent with the income-distribution schedule (1'). The equation defining that line thus is $A_1 = L_1 + 1.15 L_2$. A_1 is a given number and is measured as the distance $0b_1$ in Figure 11.2.1 because the remuneration of L_1 is one remuneration unit per laborer and because at point b_1 only L_1 is employed. As we move along b_1c_1 in the southeast direction, increasing amounts of output and hence of gross money-income can be secured until the maximum is reached at e_1. At e_1 the gross money-income pX and hence the net money-income $pX - p_KK_0$ are maximized for a constant number of remuneration units A_1. And consequently, the basic remuneration unit

$$y = \frac{pX - p_KK_0}{L_1 + 1.15\,L_2} \tag{2}$$

corresponding to A_1 $(= L_1 + 1.15\,L_2)$ also is maximized.

This completes the first half of our derivation. The conclusion is that the firm must operate at a point where the marginal rate of substitution between L_1 and L_2 (i.e., the slope of the isoquant) is equal (except for sign) to the ratio between the remunerations stipulated by the income-distribution schedule, in our case 1.15/1. This restricts the conceivable points of equilibrium of the firm to the locus e_1e_3. We must now find where the actual equilibrium of the firm on that locus will be—that is, at what point the income of everyone will be maximized.

The question is not difficult to answer. With each point of e_1e_3, we can associate uniquely a basic remuneration unit, and the equilibrium will be attained at the point where that unit (defined in terms of money) is at its maximum. Now suppose that at e_1 the basic remuneration unit y_1 is such that the laborers in the first category (L_1) earn less than their marginal value product, that is $y_1 < MPPP_{L_1}p$. Because of the equality between the relative remuneration rates and the marginal rate of substitution at e_1, the inequality just stated also necessarily implies that $1.15\,y_1 < MPP_{L_2}p$—that is, that the second category of labor also earns less than its marginal value product. It will thus be in the interest of everyone in the labor-managed enterprise to increase employment of both L_1 and L_2 (starting from e_1 in the diagram) and move along e_1e_3 in the northeast direction, because such a movement will increase the income of everyone. Clearly, the impetus for such a movement will disappear—as it did in Part I in the single-labor firm—once the marginal value product of any laborer (and hence of all laborers) is equal to the remuneration that the laborer actually receives.

Let us sum up in a shorthand manner the procedure whereby a labor-managed firm employing a diversified labor force finds its short-run equilibrium: The a_i's of the distribution schedule determine a unique slope and thus a unique expansion path on the production function ($e_1 e_3$ in the diagram), and on that path the acutal equilibrium of the firm is obtained wherever any one category of labor earns its marginal value product.

To obtain the long-run equilibrium of the firm, only a minor step is necessary. In the short-run situation, it will be recalled, the capital stock was a constant and hence—save for a pure accident—the marginal value product of capital was expected to be different from p_K, the competitive price of capital. Once the firm is permitted to adjust the size of its capacity, that is, once K becomes a variable, it will clearly seek a situation where p_K actually equals $pMPP_K$. And this then uniquely determines, for the technology of the first kind, a single long-run equilibrium solution for the firm. That solution again must be (as it was in the single-labor case) on the locus of maximum physical efficiency characterized (as we recall) by "local" constant returns to scale. If the technology is of the second kind, again, the actual level of operation of the firm becomes indeterminate, but all factor-output ratios are uniquely determined.

Drawing on both the analysis of the present chapter and on our extensive work on Part I, we now turn briefly to some of the most important effects of changing market conditions on the equilibrium of a labor-managed pluralistic firm. Let us consider the effects of changes in the product price, and thus establish the expected elasticity of the supply curve of the pluralistic firm or industry. The first thing to be realized is that the expansion path such as $e_1 e_3$ in Figure 11.2.1 is entirely independent of the product price p and is determined for any short-run situation only by the income-distribution schedule and the production function. Consequently, the short-run effect of a change in price can only be reflected—if by any change at all—by a movement along the $e_1 e_3$ locus. What expectation is there as to the direction? As in the single-labor case, in the short run the output must decline in the firm studied thus far resulting in an increase in p; that is, we will move toward the origin in Figure 11.2.1. To prove this, suppose that initially we are at a point such as e_2 where, say, the first type of labor earns

$$(a_1 y_{max} =) \; 1 \; \frac{pX_2 - p_K K_0}{L_1 + 1.15 L_2} = pMPP_{L_2} \tag{3}$$

With an increase in p both the right- and the left-hand sides of the equation increase, but the left-hand side more so because it contains a negative constant term (i.e., a term independent of p). Without an adjustment in employment of the two labor inputs, the marginal value product of L_1 would fall short of the remuneration of L_1 and consequently, the level of output must decline; the new equilibrium point in Figure 11.2.1 will again be on e_1e_3, but somewhere to the left and below e_2.

Turning now to the long-run situation, we recall that the equilibrium of the firm must find itself at the locus of maximum physical efficiency. For technology of the first kind, the locus is necessarily single-valued with respect to any ray through the origin (in the L_1-L_2-K- space); and consequently, an increase in the price level leading necessarily to an increase in equilibrium marginal products of labor will generally result in a higher employment of capital and less employment of labor (of both kinds). Again there is no single expectation as to the change in output, but an increase in output can be considered more likely on account of the argument (used already in Part I) that a higher degree of capital intensity generally presupposes a larger scale of optimal operation. What has just been said for the technology of the first kind also holds in the case of constant returns to scale with respect to input-output ratios. Thus, for example, with a higher product price, the competitive labor-managed firm is liable to use more capital per unit of output in the long run. But of course, as we are well aware by now, the absolute scale of operation for the firm remains indeterminate.

Let us further consider the effects of changes in the price of capital and in the income-distribution schedule on the equilibrium operation of the labor-managed firm. We will perform all of the analysis assuming technology of the first kind with long-run equilibria (recall that for the short run the distinction is unnecessary) while noting that, as usual, with constant returns to scale, long-run scales of operation are indeterminate while all input-output ratios behave as those of a profit-maximizing firm using a technology of the first kind.

The easier of the two effects to understand is that of changes in p_K. Both in the short and in the long run, employment of labor will tend to be increased (we will move up along e_1e_3 in Figure 11.2.1 in the short-run case) with a higher return to capital, because less income is left over for labor, and thus the marginal physical products of labor must decline; and such a decline naturally calls for an expansion of employment of labor. In the short run, where the capital stock is fixed, this immediately leads to an increase in output. In the long run, employment of capital generally will be reduced. However, the level of output can either increase or decline (recall that labor employment has gone up), the latter alternative again being more likely because the process of production now is relatively less capital-intensive and thus can be expected to be consistent with a reduced optimum scale of operation.

Finally, what will happen if the worker-managers decide on an alteration of the income-distribution schedule? Suppose that one of the share coefficients a_i is increased. Obviously this will imply a substitution of L_j for L_i, whether in the short run or in the long run. The impact on capital stock in the short run, of course, is zero and, in the long run, it will depend primarily on whether capital is complementary to or a substitute for L_j. The level of output can either increase or decline, there being no special presumption in either direction. We can only say in the context of a long-run situation that if the utilization of capital increases (K and L_j being complementary), total output may be more likely to increase. But on the whole, since changes in the income-distribution schedule increase one type of employment and reduce the other, and are ambiguous with respect to K, the effect on X is likely to be small.

To summarize all of our findings, using double signs to indicate a stronger presumption, we have constructed Table 11.2.1. The sign "$+$" indicates a positive relation between the change in p, p_K, or a_i, on the one hand, and one of the variables indicated on top of the table, on the other; the sign "$-$" indicates a negative relationship. Two signs of one type together with one sign of another type indicate a stronger likelihood in an ambiguous situation.

Table 11.2.1

Effect on:	X		K		L_i		L_j	
of:	short run	long run	short run	long run	short run	long run	short run	long run
dp	$-$	$++-$	0	$+$	$-$	$-$	$-$	$-$
dp_K	$+$	$+--$	0	$-$	$+$	$+$	$+$	$+$
da_i	$+-$ small	$+-$ small	0	$+-$	$-$	$-$	$+$	$+$

The assumption which we have made thus far of a smooth substitutability between different types of labor may not be the most realistic. Often different skills will have to be combined in a highly complementary manner, that is, in more or less given proportions. An extreme in-

stance of such a situation—pertaining to the short run—is illustrated by
the three broken equal-product lines passing through e_1, e_2, and e_3 in
Figure 11.2.1. In this situation, as is easy to see, the expansion path e_1e_3
remains the same as before; it is independent of the income-distribution
schedule. Furthermore, the marginal productivities of the two types of
labor are undefined. However, a "joint" marginal productivity corresponding to a movement along e_1e_3, reckoned per basic remuneration
unit, still is defined. It is the marginal value product based on this joint
productivity that must equal the actual basic remuneration unit (actually disbursed) for short-run equilibrium. The effects of changing market conditions on the equilibrium with perfect complementarity of
labor are the same as those summarized in Table 11.2.1, except for the
impacts of changes in the income-distribution schedule on L_1 and L_2.
The latter now will simultaneously assume a positive or a negative sign,
the crucial relation determining whether one or the other outcome will
take place—and thus whether X will increase or not—being that between the slope of the e_1e_3 line in the vicinity of equilibrium and the
corresponding L_1-L_2 ratio.[1]

The short-run maximum is then obtained from

$$\frac{d}{dL_1}\left[\frac{pX(L_1, L_2(L_1)) - p_K K_0}{a_1 L_1 + a_2 L_2(L_1)}\right] = 0 \tag{5}$$

which yields

$$\frac{pX - p_K K_0}{L_1[1 + (L_2/L_1)(a_2/a_1)]} = \frac{(1 + [X_{L_1} + X_{L_2}(dL_2/dL_1)]}{1 + (dL_2/dL_1)(a_2/a_1)} \tag{6}$$

whence it is immediately apparent that the right-hand side will remain
equal to the left-hand side resulting from changes in a_2/a_1 if $L_2/L_1 =
dL_2/dL_1$. And consequently, if the latter equality (between average and
marginal factor-proportions) holds, output and employment will not be
affected by a change in the income-distribution schedule. If this is not
the case, and, say, $L_2/L_1 > dL_2/dL_1$, an increase in a_1 (higher pay to
the first labor group) will reduce the right-hand side of relation (6) relative to the left-hand side; and thus the basic remuneration, the level of
output and employment, will have to be reduced.

We should also recall briefly at this stage some of the realistic alterations considered in Part I in the context of a single-labor situation.
For one thing, the marginal productivity of all types of labor can drop

[1]With an invariant e_1e_3 line, we can write

$$L_2 = L_2(L_1) \tag{4}$$

to zero over a very small range of variation of employment at the full-capacity output level; under such conditions, the short-run supply function will be zero-elastic rather than backward bending. Moreover, the unorthodox short-run supply elasticity will again generally be eliminated in case of joint production. Perhaps most important, *social* rather than *conventional* behavior may be preferred and in that case, perverse responses to changing market conditions will become impossible. Especially where the (long-run) technology is of the second kind, social behavior will be the most likely outcome, and even more realistically, the size of the firm will not belong to the complex of maximizing business decisions.

11.3: *A Diversified Labor Force and the Industry and General Equilibrium*

Having understood how a diversified labor force in conjunction with a given income-distribution schedule affects the equilibrium of the firm, let us now go a step further and ask how these factors influence the equilibrium of a competitive industry or of the whole economy. Because the emphasis here is on the income-distribution schedule, let us assume identical technologies for all firms, of the first or second kind, and let us first examine the short-run equilibrium.

Clearly, if it happens that all the labor-managed firms in the industry decide on the same distribution schedule and all capital stocks (K_0) are the same for all firms, the short-run equilibrium for the industry is adequately described by what has been done in the preceding section, provided that we agree that the product price p is, instead of a constant, an equilibrium price corresponding to equilibrium sales of the industry and a prescribed industry demand curve. The really interesting case—conceivable in an unregulated economy—is one where different labor-managed firms decide on different income-distribution schedules. This may be the result of a variety of reasons which need not detain us here. For the moment let us examine the theoretical implications of the situation.

Suppose that there are two segments of the industry, the distribution schedules in each being identical. Both segments utilize two skills, L_1 and L_2, and the first segment values L_2 relatively more highly than does the second segment. Assuming the same size of capital stock for all firms in the industry, a single equilibrium equal-product line can be made representative of each segment. Corresponding to equilibrium outputs of X_1 and X_2 units respectively, two such representative

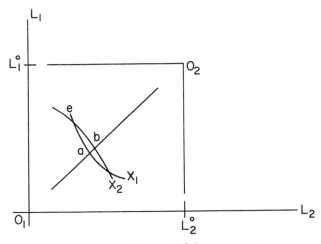

Figure 11.3.1

isoquants have been drawn for the two segments in Figure 11.3.1, the former measuring inputs of L_1 and L_2 from 0_1, the latter from 0_2. A resource-allocation point fully exhausting labor resources indicated by 0_2 is given by e. As claimed, the marginal rate of substitution in the first segment of the industry indicates a comparatively higher valuation of L_2 in that segment.

As is immediately apparent, the diversity of distribution schedules is inefficient in the sense that the same output $X = X_1 + X_2$ could be produced with fewer laborers or in the sense that, with the same labor-endowments L_1^0 and L_2^0, more output could be secured. For example, with identical income-distribution schedules, the two segments could produce somewhere between a and b on the locus of identical marginal rates of substitution. Alternatively, labor resources equivalent to the segment ab could be saved for expanded output of the industry, or for other uses.

If we now consider the situation in the long run, where capital also becomes a variable and where the earnings of capital everywhere must equal its marginal value product, the situation does not change very much from the short-run case just discussed. We can visualize a third dimension of our box-diagram for capital and the two isoquants X_1 and X_2 transformed into two soup-plate-type surfaces turned with their hollow parts against each other. All allocation points between the two soup plates, including those defined by identical distribution schedules and identical productivities of capital, are more efficient than an allocation point on the edge of the two plates.

Thus we can conclude that identical income-distribution schedules within an industry are efficient from the point of view of efficient resource allocation, whether in the short run or in the long run. The next important question is whether and how an industry can move from an inefficient point (such as e in our diagram) to an efficient one. The answer in part belongs to the discussion of economic policy—and for this we have to wait until Part IV. At this stage of our analysis we should see whether there is anything in the autonomous mechanism of the labor-managed system that can be expected to produce an optimal, or at least a more efficient solution, starting from an inefficient one.

There is every reason to suspect that such an autonomous mechanism is present: actually, several forms of it can be envisaged. Its central element is the entry of new firms, which has already played such an important role in our analysis in Part I. It should be clear that, in the situation we have described earlier in this section, the equilibrium income of L_2 will be higher in the first segment of the industry (at point e in Figure 11.3.1) than it is in the second segment, and *vice versa* for L_1. Supposing first that the two segments are in a state of long-run equilibrium (i.e., have already attained their respective optimum sizes at the locus of maximum physical efficiency), some of the laborers having the second skill can leave the second segment of the industry, and some of those endowed with the first skill can leave the first industry, together forming a third segment of the industry where both skills receive a higher remuneration than before. Under ideal conditions at least, with perfectly mobile and transferable capital, this process could continue until the two initial segments would completely disappear and only one segment with more efficient income-distribution schedules than the two initial ones would emerge.

Of course, such a process is much too roundabout in the context of any real situation, and could require an extremely long period of time to become fully effective. But in the real world we can expect a short cut, operating much faster and not depending on the condition of mobility of physical assets. Merely an initial tendency to leave present employment and form new firms (of the type just explained) would put pressure on the labor management of the two original segments to reconsider their income-distribution schedules in such a way as to stem the exodus; and clearly, such revisions would have to be in the direction of a greater equality of the a_i's defining the distribution schedules. If, as we have assumed, the initial state is one in which all firms experience a long-run equilibrium, the exit of some laborers would necessarily lead to less efficient operation of the firms concerned, and thus the pressure to revise the schedules and thus retain the potential "deserters" would be the strongest. But even if the initial equilibria are short run, the same basic argument for homogenization of the distribution schedules still obtains.[2]

Actually, even in an unregulated labor-managed economy, it would be entirely in the interest of a competitive industry—and not at all in restraint of competition—to form industry conferences with the aim of homogenization of the income-distribution schedules. The industry's interest coincides here, it should be emphasized, with the interest of the entire society because the equalization of remunerations of different skills leads to a more efficient allocation and utilization of national resources.

All that has been said thus far with regard to an individual industry also holds for the entire productive sector of the economy to the extent that identical skills—that is, types of labor L_i—are used by several industries. As the reader may verify for himself, schedules in different industries leading to different remunerations of identical skills again are inefficient, and the same process of exit and entry—though somewhat more intricate—or threat of such a process, would tend to bring labor remunerations to at least approximate equality. The same argument as that used in respect to intraindustry consultation now also holds in the interindustry context: such nationwide consultation again would be in the interest of national efficiency, and should in no way hamper competition.

Of course, what has been said thus far presupposes a perfect labor situation involving, among other conditions, perfect interregional and interindustry mobility, as well as perfect information. If such conditions are not fulfilled, it may be more efficient to have different income-distribution schedules in different environments. For example, if a certain type of labor in a given region is extremely abundant and that labor can move only with a good deal of difficulty to other regions, it may be both in the regional and national interest to value that type of labor comparatively lower in the distribution schedules applicable in that region. Indeed, if it were not done, regional unemployment would have to result.

It should also be noted that in the present chapter we are emphasizing

---

[2]Note that especially with a high degree of complementarity between skills, the pressures for equalization could be enormous because departure of the underpaid members of the enterprise might lead to less than full capacity operation and underemployment of those remaining in the firm. Note also that with complementarity the Pareto inefficiency vanishes.

the structural, rather than the global, aspects of employment. As for the latter, nothing much really changes from the analysis of Part II once multiple skills, or types of labor, are introduced. The aggregate changes in the national economy will have their global effects on all types of employment in the short run. In the long (or "longer") run, however, forces primarily based on—or analogous to (in the case of technologies of the second kind where entry can take the form of expansion of existing firms)—free entry are liable to absorb unemployed labor, whether the unemployment is in all or just some of the labor categories. If the unemployment is general, the long-run process of its absorption will probably be smoother and faster.

11.4: *A Diversified Labor Force and Pareto-Optimality of the Labor-Managed Economy*

One of our important concerns in Chapter 7 was whether and under what conditions the labor force would operate with optimal—that is, Pareto-type—efficiency. Assuming a single homogeneous labor force, our conclusion then was that Pareto-optimality would effectively be the outcome in the long run provided that perfect competition and free entry were guaranteed. We are now in a position to ask and seek answers to the same question with respect to a situation involving a diversified labor force—that is, many different types of labor. The foregoing analysis in this chapter provides us with the necessary analytical background.

The first thing that follows from the preceding section is that with free entry and perfect competition in all markets, irrespective of the number of labor skills, all national resources will be employed in the long-run equilibrium. Moreover, we know from section 11.2 that in each firm labor remuneration will be equal to the marginal value product of each skill category. But as we have argued in the preceding section, there will be autonomous forces (based on freedom of entry and exit) tending to equalize returns of identical labor categories among firms and industries. And in an ideal frictionless system this tendency would be transformed into an actual equality of identical factor returns. Hence, the marginal value products of identical factors would be equalized throughout the labor-managed economy. But this guarantees Pareto-optimality in production—of course, on the customary postulate of no externalities. With perfect competition among buyers, a "global" Pareto-optimality then must be the property of long-run general equilibrium of a labor-managed economy with several types of labor.

Turning from the ideal theoretical world, it is perhaps useful to say that the perfect optimum will never be attained exactly in the real world —in fact it will not be attained by any economic system. However, it can be conjectured that a "realistic" labor-managed system with a diversified labor force is likely to approach the optimum more closely than a "realistic" modern capitalist economy. This seems to be so because of the different nature of imperfections in the diversified labor markets. While the imperfections in the labor-managed system can be described as frictional, and thus tending to disappear over time, those in a modern capitalist system, beset by varying degrees of conflicting and countervailing powers of employers and unions, appear as more permanent and often increasing in intensity over time. A word of caution uttered several times before is again in order: the comparison just made is only a partial one, bearing on only one of the many aspects of the systems compared.

11.5: *Some Other Aspects of Labor and Skill Diversification*

All of the analysis of the preceding four sections was cast in terms of a competitive model. But the reader should not have much difficulty to extend this analysis to situations where some degree of market power is given to the producers. For example, it will be noted that the important locus e_1e_3 of Figure 11.2.1 is defined, independently of the situation prevailing in the product market, by the production function and the income-distribution schedule. A less than infinitely elastic demand for X characterizing a monopolistic situation can thus influence only the location of the final equilibrium point on e_1e_3. And it should be easy to understand that, at the point of equilibrium, any one labor category's income should be equal to the marginal revenue product of that category. Note that if such an equality did not prevail, variation of employment increasing everyone's income would be possible.

We do not have to spend more time in elaborating on technical points such as the one just made regarding monopolistic situations. With what has been said about labor diversification in the present chapter and about the general one-labor situation in Part I, the reader should be in a position to reconstruct other theoretical situations involving diverse labor skills. What seems to be more important in this concluding section is to place the material of Chapter 11 in its proper perspective in relation to the whole of the study and, in particular, to the rest of Part III.

From Chapter 1, let us recall that Part III is reserved for what we have termed the "specifics" of the labor-managed system. In this sense, our present analysis of situations involving a diversified labor force is only marginal to Part III. Indeed, labor diversification is something quite general and not specific to the system concerning us here. Actually, it was only the new (or specific) income-distribution schedule, originating in the management function of the working community, that made us incorporate the present discussion into Part III.

But as we have pointed out in section 11.1, the concept of labor has, in the context of the system studied, many other dimensions which were not treated in this chapter. While, for obvious reasons of organization, such other dimensions are examined in full in the subsequent chapters of Part III, I consider it desirable to outline at this stage a few of the limitations of the present analysis, deriving from the neglect of the other dimensions.

For example, we have found the "optimum" within a given industry to require identical income-distribution schedules. But, it will be recalled, this type of optimality is defined in the traditional "western" sense of "producing the maximum from given resources." But what if one workers' collective decides that it wants to have all a_i's defining the income-distribution schedule equal, whether for the director or the janitor, while another firm adheres to a distribution schedule based on "proportionality to qualification"? As we have shown, the industry now cannot produce the maximum amount of output from given resources (e.g., see Figure 11.3.1); but can we really say that the situation is inferior? The imposition on the first workers' collective of a differentiated income schedule, or an egalitarian schedule on the second firm, might involve hardships far in excess of those implied by a (presumably small) loss in physical output for the society.[3] We cannot resolve the problem here nor shall we fully resolve it later in Part III— in fact no one has yet given it a satisfactory treatment; however, it serves us as an illustration of a very wide class of similar problems, or limitations, of the analysis of the present chapter.

Another illustration, typical of a somewhat different class of problems, should be in order. Pareto-optimality based on equality of factor returns, as we have concluded, in a way worthy of a "western"

[3] Especially with complementarity of different skills, so frequent in the real world, the Pareto inefficiencies should be negligible.

economic theorist, is the best of all possible worlds. But what if returns vary with intensity, quality, or duration of work? This variability
may be the most crucial element of economic efficiency of the labor-
managed system and, if it leads to differences of remuneration among
firms or industries, they really should be deemed desirable. Of course,
a theoretical economist might argue that we can get out of this difficulty
by defining a sufficient number of labor categories, for each of which
equalization of returns is still necessary for optimality. But once we
realize that with the two attributes of "intensity" and "quality" we
have ∞^2 as the number of categories necessary for each single skill—
referred to thus far as L_i—the approach along these lines becomes of
rather limited value.

APPENDIX

Consider product X produced from capital K and n different types
of labor $L_1, \ldots, L_n$, according to a smooth production function of the
first or the second kind (as defined in Part I), written as

$$X = X(L_1 L_2, \ldots, L_n, K) \qquad (A.1)$$

Each member of the i'th labor group is to receive a_i basic remuneration
units as his income, all the $a_1, \ldots, a_n$ being constants given by the
income-distribution schedule. The firm will be in equilibrium when its
remuneration unit

$$y = \frac{pX - p_K K}{\sum_i a_i L_i} = y(L_1, \ldots, L_n K) \qquad (A.2)$$

is at its maximum, that is when

$$\frac{\partial y}{\partial L_i} = 0 \qquad i = 1, 2, \ldots, n \qquad (A.3)$$

and

$$\frac{\partial y}{\partial K} = 0 \qquad (A.4)$$

and

$$d^2 y < 0 \qquad (A.5)$$

Carrying out the differentiation in (A.3) and (A.4) we finally obtain
for the competitive case (p and p_K constant) the necessary conditions

$$pX_i = a_i y \qquad i = 1, 2, \ldots, n \qquad (A.6)$$

and

$$pX_K = p_K \tag{A.7}$$

where X_i and X_K stand for partial differentials of X with respect to L_i and K respectively. (A.6) and (A.7) are $n + 1$ relations determining the $n + 1$ long-run equilibrium values of $L_1, \ldots, L_n$ and K. In the short run, with $K = K_0$, relation (A.7) is irrelevant and we have n relations in variables $L_1, \ldots, L_n$. In words, we end up again with the familiar condition that each factor, including each distinct labor group, must in equilibrium earn the value of its marginal physical product.

12. Incentives and Efficiency in a Labor-Managed Firm

12.1: *Introduction*

If, in the preceding chapter, we have remained on the periphery of what is specific to the labor-managed system, in this chapter we penetrate to the very heart of the matter. At two successive stages of our argument we will abandon the two remaining simplifying assumptions (identified in the introduction to Chapter 11) regarding the nature of the working community, and thus arrive at what we may term a "final" or "most comprehensive" theoretical representation of the labor-managed firm and of the labor-managed system as a whole. We recall that the two important assumptions which we want to relax—and will relax for the rest of Part III—are (1) constant quality and efficiency of each type of labor (or skill), and (2) labor's exclusive role as a factor of production.[1]

Once the two simplifying assumptions are relaxed, a virtually unlimited number of new dimensions and corresponding new problems arise within the theory of a labor-managed firm. The most important among these will occupy our attention here and in the remaining chapters of Part III. For the present chapter we have assigned the consideration of the most important question of all: What is the relation between the productivity of labor, on the one hand, and the income-sharing and labor-management principles inherent in our system on the other hand? More specifically, and using somewhat more technical language, the question which we are asking is whether, and to what extent, are the principles of income sharing and self-management likely to influence the technology used by a given firm? It will be recalled that thus far, in the many comparisons we have drawn between the capitalist and labor-managed systems, technology was always classified within the category of *ceteris paribus*. Our present contention is that such a classi-

[1] The principle of maximization of income per laborer and the income-distribution schedule, it will be recalled, were taken as given, without any analysis of a management process which might lead to them.

233

fication may not be fully justifiable because the organizational and de-cision-making characteristics within the two systems really must be included as a part of the technological data underlying any productive activity.

As the reader must have realized from the outset, we are suddenly plunging into rather unfamiliar waters—unfamiliar at least to the economist. We would be much more comfortable with at least one psychologist and one group-behavior sociologist at our side. Actually, one might even want to give such experts the lead and let them con-struct a general theory of motivation and behavior of the workers' councils, and then proceed from such a theory to the solution of spe-cific problems. Unfortunately, all this is impossible, at least at this stage of the argument, and we must proceed unassisted.

For obvious reasons, we choose to build the theory around what is most familiar to us, the economic content of our "amalgamated" be-havioral theory. In the following section, we begin our discussion by defining the principal variables with which we want to deal in this chap-ter, and study the problem of incentives and productivity in the case of a one-man production unit. In section 3, we carry the analysis a step further and consider situations involving more than one individual in the absence of self-determination through labor management. The lat-ter assumption is then relaxed in section 4 and we arrive at what we have termed previously the most comprehensive theoretical representa-tion. Because the general approach of the present chapter is quite dif-ferent from the "pure theory" of Part I, in section 5 we find it desirable to reconcile the two approaches; in particular, it is necessary to show what meaning should be attached to the various marginal equilibrium conditions (derived in Part I) once the quality of each individual labor category becomes itself an endogenous variable. The remaining sec-tions then are devoted to the discussion of some of the less exact and more qualitative aspects of the problem at hand.

12.2: *Effort and Income in a One-Man Firm*

The instance of a self-employed producer is one where the relation-ships between incentives, productivity, and income can most easily be studied. This is so because in this particular case a single mind and a single will are involved, and thus no complications of the "social" variety can arise. At the same time, the one-man situation contains a number of elements common to itself and to the pluralistic case, and thus makes it possible for us to learn about some aspects of what primarily concerns us here—the problem of incentives in a labor-managed social environment.

Of central importance to the present analysis is a new variable—held constant or entirely disregarded in the preceding ten chapters—reflecting the variability within such labor or skill category L_i. Let us denote that variable by E_i, and let it represent the "effort"—a term to be further elaborated on below—expended by each member of the homogeneous skill category L_i per unit of L_i. If L measures the number of units of time, say, hours, the effort variable E (note that we are now dropping the subscript i because the *interskill* differentiation is not of interest to us here) can be thought of as measuring either or both (1) work intensity and (2) work quality. If L measures merely the number of men, E can, in addition, also represent (3) the number of hours worked.

In a more detailed analysis, one might want to distinguish between the three possible ingredients of E as between three different variables. We do not do so in the present analysis for two practical reasons: first, in most of what follows, we want to show that the distinction between the three elements is really not essential; and second, even without the distinction our analysis becomes fairly voluminous and any further extension would be beyond the scope and resources of this study.

The reader may want to ask about the units of measurement in terms of which E is reckoned. When time is involved in E, the answer is simple; when work intensity or quality is involved, the problem is more difficult—but it is possible to think of E as either measured in terms of some cardinal variable related uniformly to effort, such as the calory content, or in terms of an ordinal index permitting only of the comparisons "more than," "less than," and "equal." In either case, the problem is not crucial for most or all of our subsequent analysis, and thus can be disregarded.

Having defined our new variable, the problem which we want to treat in this section is quite simple. There is only one type of labor skill, L, and provided that we measure L in terms of numbers of workers belonging to the category, L is a constant equal to unity; indeed, we have postulated a single self-employed producer. L thus ceases to be a variable (this will be the case for most of this chapter), and E takes over its role. The value of output, pX, and consequently the net income of our self-employed producer, Y, thus becomes a function of E. Obviously, at least for a certain range of levels of E starting from $E = 0$, the function is an increasing one. This is so either because increased effort implies increased working hours or an increased labor intensity, thus affecting X, or because increased effort implies improved quality of product and thus affects p.

It is thus possible to think of a transformation curve (function) between various levels of effort and the corresponding levels of net income accruing to the individual producer. Such a locus is illustrated in Figure 12.2.1 by the contour $F(M, T)$ starting from $0'$ and moving leftward from that point with increasing E. The expression $F(M, T)$ is intended to indicate that (besides E) F depends on conditions in the markets for the product X and the nonlabor inputs, and the technology which the individual producer uses.

Measured from the origin 0 to the right is the reverse of effort, $(-E)$; we may call it "ease" (for lack of a better term). $(-E)$ and Y are two positive goods—such as apples and bananas in conventional demand analysis—combinations of which can be ordered ordinally or cardinally according to the degree of utility or desirability. Three conventional indifference curves, $u_1, u_2,$ and u_3, are shown in the diagram.

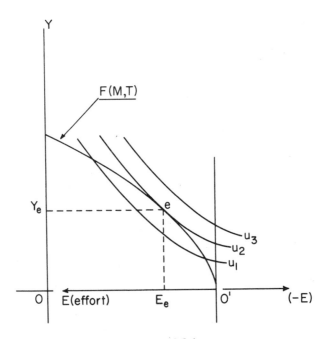

Figure 12.2.1

Clearly, our self-employed producer will select from among all the alternatives offered to him by the transformation locus F the point of maximum satisfaction e. To this point also correspond all the other solutions of our production problem, in particular the equilibrium level of income Y_e, the equilibrium level of effort expended E_e, and, by implication, the equilibrium levels of sales and product and factor prices.

Before concluding this section, it is imperative to elaborate on the comparative importance of the effort variable here introduced for the first time into our analysis. The discussion is equally relevant for the one-man case and for the large-number situations of labor management which will occupy us in the rest of this chapter. It must be realized that the range of variation of effort (E) between what we may term its minimum and maximum "reasonable" levels is considerable. For example, it is not an exaggeration to say that (irrespective of technological factors) just for one attribute of effort, intensity of work (as noted above), a reasonable range is between 100 and 200 per cent. Anyone who has had the opportunity to observe and compare different working situations must agree. Nor is it an exaggeration to say that the other two attributes of effort, duration of work and its quality, also can reasonably vary between similar limits of 100 and 200 per cent each. But realizing that to work with double intensity twice as long and with double quality implies producing an octuple effort, our global reasonable range for effort taken as an aggregate is between 100 and 800 per cent, or realistically, one of several hundreds of per cent.

Now it appears to the present writer—and this is a general observation not confined to labor-managed systems—that such a range, and consequently its economic importance and relevance, is far more significant than the "reasonable" ranges of variation imputable to suboptimal operation of firms, industries, or systems on account of greater or lesser perfection of resource allocation in the Pareto-marginalist context, where quality of labor is treated as a constant. For example, it can be shown that the gross gain to the union imputable to the European Common Market is far less than one per cent (the net gain being just about zero), and similar other results have been derived in the sphere of international economics. But even if the Pareto-marginalist ranges were ten, twenty, or thirty times higher, we still would be comparing ten, twenty, or thirty per cent magnitudes with one as high as eight hundred. And yet, let it be noted, the time and concern of economists devoted to the study of what we have identified here as effort is

of the order of one-thousandth of that devoted to the Pareto-marginalist analysis. Indeed, a good portion of the totality of modern economic
theory is of the second variety.

The ranges of reasonable (or likely) variation of effort can be visualized as further augmented in the context of the poor and developing
countries where such variations may be not only a matter of motivation
or incentives but also and often primarily a matter of sheer physical
capability of the worker. In the longer run an initial increase in effort
may lead to an increase in income and this in turn to a reduction in
malnutrition, which in its turn can engender new increases in effort.
Systems and solutions capable of putting into effect such a beneficial (as
opposed to vicious) circle may then be preferred by far by the developing countries.

12.3: *Income Sharing without Labor Management*

Let us now relax the assumption that there is only one man in the
enterprise, but still concentrate—as we did in the preceding section—
on the position of an individual employee. It is expositionally convenient to consider first, as a special case, the position of a worker or
employee in a typical capitalist firm (or, for that matter, Soviet-type
firm) where income or profit sharing is not present. Rather, the laborer
is paid a fixed contractual weekly wage w_0, represented in Figure 12.3.1
by the length of the segment $0\,Y_0$. Note that the diagram represents
the same E-Y plane as that in Figure 12.2.1.

If w_0 is independent of effort E, our typical laborer will face a
transformation function which is horizontal, such as the broken line
$Y_0 Y_0'$. With a marginal utility of ease $(-E)$ always positive, that is,
marginal utility of effort always negative, our laborer would naturally
proceed along the horizontal line as far as possible to the right; if un-
restricted, he would prefer to move all the way and settle at the zero-
effort point Y_0'. As is well known, this effectively happens in the
absence of any coercion, and not only in large government admin-
istrations.

It follows that if the private employer wants to produce anything,
while paying a fixed contractual wage, the contract must explicitly or at
least implicitly contain a provision regarding a minimum acceptable
performance standard. Such a minimum standard is represented by the
distance $0'E_0$ in Figure 12.3.1, and in terms of our three ingredients
of E can be thought of as containing a provision for minimum effort,
minimum acceptable quality of work, and, of course, a given number of

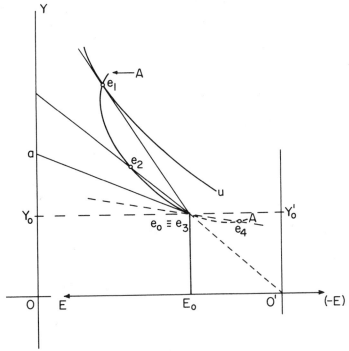

Figure 12.3.1

working hours. In terms of our diagrammatic analysis, this means that the laborer cannot proceed along $Y_0 Y_0'$ all the way to Y_0' but rather that he will be constrained by a "degenerate" transformation curve $Y_0 e_0 E_0$ in the diagram. With indifference curves always downward sloping, he must settle at e_0, where his satisfaction will be maximized.

While this "degenerate" situation which we are associating with a capitalist firm may have many disadvantages to which we will turn later, it has one important analytical advantage: It makes it possible to speak of a homogeneous labor factor and thus assimilate that factor to other, nonhuman inputs. This is so because E_0 is a given constant applicable equally to all members of a specific labor skill in a capitalist enterprise and because it will be in the interest of all laborers to operate at e_0, that is, at the contractual terms Y_0 and the minimum acceptable standard E_0. It should also be clearer now why at several previous occasions we have argued that the analysis offered in Parts I and II really is much better suited for a capitalist system and not fully adequate for the labor-managed economy.

There is a possibility that the indifference map with respect to Y and $(-E)$ would not always be negatively sloped, implying that effort in certain ranges of the map is associated with a positive rather than a negative marginal utility. If this is the case, as is sometimes argued for executives and intellectual workers, a tangency could occur at $Y_0 Y_0'$ in Figure 12.3.1. But as long as this would happen to the right of point e_0, the above argument regarding skill homogeneity and constancy in a capitalist situation still would hold.[2]

Let us now consider a hypothetical firm which distributes all its net income to the workers according to a prescribed income-distribution schedule (of the type introduced in the previous chapter), but which is not labor managed. Instead, it is individualistic, each worker being motivated exclusively by the results of his own effort and considering his fellow workers' effort a constant, independent of what he himself does. We may assume that all the workers have the same skill (i.e., that there is only one L_i category). Moreover, we assume that the firm, like its capitalist cousin discussed above, imposes a minimum acceptable effort requirement equivalent to $0'E_0$ in Figure 12.3.1, and the corresponding net income per laborer is Y_0 measured by $0 Y_0$.

If there were only one laborer in our hypothetical firm, all the returns resulting from his increasing his effort would accrue to him, and thus it could be expected that beyond e_0, to the left of that point, his effort-income transformation locus would be quite steep. Assuming for simplicity that such locus is a linear one, $e_0 e_1$ (we know that it need not be), the single worker would move to his optimum equilibrium point e_1, earning a corresponding high income. Introducing a second worker, then a third, a fourth, and so on, on the individualistic assumptions made, the transformation locus for our representative single laborer will become flatter and flatter, and the equilibrium points will proceed along the locus AA downward and to the right until, for some comparatively low number of employees—say, four in our case—the equilibrium will coincide with e_0, at e_3. Having reached the minimum acceptable effort limit, the process will be arrested at that point, and for any larger number of workers each worker's equilibrium solution will be at e_0. Thus, except for very low levels of employment, our hypothetical firm will perform in the same way as the capitalist firm described above.

[2] Professor Galbraith argues in his study *The New Industrial State* (Boston, 1967), that for the highest echelon of the executive in large modern corporations the equilibrium generally arises to the left of e_o on $Y_0 Y'_0$.

It should be clear that the state of affairs in our hypothetical firm is quite unsatisfactory. It would be possible for each worker (assuming of course that the firm's size does not have any impact on the price of its product), given the technology and economic environment of the firm, to produce at e_1 in the diagram an output far in excess of (or of better quality than) that corresponding to $e_0 = e_3$ and, what is more important, at the level of satisfaction u, well above that corresponding to e_0. And yet, given the organizational and psychological conditions, this does not happen in our hypothetical firm—nor does it happen as a general rule in a capitalist firm.

The true labor-managed firm—as distinguished from the hypothetical one just discussed—is in a very good position, however, to attain the optimum identified at e_1, or at least to approach it quite closely. Using the hypothetical case as a point of departure, this can be shown in two different stages; we may refer to the first, which we will discuss in the subsequent section, as the "mechanistic" approach, and to the second, discussed in section 12.5, as the "group-behavioral" approach. The distinction just made is convenient for several reasons; one of these is that the former approach can, to a degree, be emulated by a capitalist firm while the latter is quite specific to the labor-managed situation.

12.4: *The Mechanistic Approaches to Optimal Productivity in a Labor-Managed Firm*

We do not have to spend an excessive amount of time in discussing what we have termed the mechanistic approach; indeed, the ground is quite familiar from conventional economic analysis. Perhaps the most familiar case in point, taken from the capitalist situation, is that of overtime work. With E representing hours of work and the overtime wage somewhat more than the regular wage, we have, in terms of Figure 12.3.1, a solution at e_0 without overtime, and a solution somewhere along $e_0 e_1$ with overtime. If the laborers are free to determine how much overtime they want to work, they clearly would select the effort-income configuration indicated by e_1 where their satisfaction is maximized. On the other hand, were the required overtime work outside the range of the indifference curve passing through e_0, on the line defined by $e_0 e_1$, the workers should reject an opportunity for overtime work.

The example just given applies not only to the capitalist but also to a labor-managed firm. Actually, the labor-managed alternative could yield, *ceteris paribus*, better results for the workers whenever the capitalist distributed anything less than the totality of the incremental income from overtime work.

The notion of a "mechanistic" approach derives from the fact that, as in the overtime example just given, performance of an individual worker can be tied contractually, in one way or another, to his returns, and thus he can be assimilated to the individual producer of section 12.2. It should be clear that the mechanistic approach to effort optimization is not always possible. Some special conditions generally will have to be fulfilled for it to work. The most important among them is that either the effort or the output of an individual member of the working community be imputable to that particular worker. In the overtime example, it was the input E, expressing the number of hours worked, that could exactly be imputed to each worker. On the other side of the spectrum, we have the piecework form of remuneration, where the output is perfectly imputable and where, in the context of a labor-managed firm, the total net return per unit of output is distributed to the members of the firm.

In the first extreme example, we observe that the variable to which remuneration is linked is cardinally measurable—in terms of hours worked. But the case where E stands for hours worked is perhaps the least interesting. The cases where effort E represents either intensity of work or work quality are far more important; indeed, it is a well-known fact that both quality and intensity of work can vary enormously for an individual man, and thus losses of output and satisfaction resulting from a fixed hourly wage—or fixed income per laborer or per hour worked—of the type indicated by the solution at e_0 in Figure 12.3.1 can be quite substantial. But neither quality nor intensity of work can easily be measured in terms of cardinal units to which remuneration would be attached. It would be absurd to try to pay a worker per calory of energy expended on his job.

When E is not cardinally measurable, one way is that of the piecework arrangement where output is used as a "proxy" for effort E. But as we have noted already, this presupposes the imputability of output to individual workers. And imputability is impossible unless we have a perfectly divisible process of production, a process which, almost by definition, does not seem to require a collective production by a number of workers in a single firm. If, as is most often the case, the productive process or processes engaged in by the enterprise are complex and involve joint production and extensive division of labor, it is generally very difficult or quite impossible to impute definite shares of productive contribution to individual members of the labor force. And thus the "escape" from a lack of cardinal measurability of E generally disappears.

It is only in situations involving cooperation of very small numbers —such as four or less, as identified in section 12.3—and only for some types of technology, that the incentive to work at a higher level of E than that indicated by E_0 (or e_0) in Figure 12.3.1 may be present in a completely individualistic environment (of the type described in section 12.3) even in the absence of imputability. And we know from the preceding section that even in the rare instances where this could happen, the gains in satisfaction and output will generally be far less than those in the individual producer case. Compare, for example, the solution at e_2 corresponding to a two-man fully individualistic team to that at e_1 in Figure 12.3.1.

The conclusion is that in most real situations what we have referred to here as the mechanistic approach does not suffice—or is entirely inadequate—for the attainment of an optimal effort-income combination on the part of the working community. To attain such a solution, or come anywhere near it, one has to rely in one way or another on the social, or collective (i.e., nonindividualistic) behavior of the workers' community. Labor management—or self-determination if we want to be more descriptive—now becomes a powerful vehicle of such a social, or "collective-mind" approach, a vehicle that is fundamentally out of the reach of a capitalist firm, or for that matter, out of the reach of Galbraith's management-controlled giant corporation. But this brings us to the subject of the next section.

12.5: Group Behavioral Approaches to Optimal Productivity in a Labor-Managed Firm

The avenues leading to effort optimization in a labor-managed firm are manyfold, and consequently must be discussed on a number of different levels. First, a general introductory observation: in the preceding section we have established, it will be recalled, that the stumbling block of the "individualistic-mechanistic" approach was the absence of cardinal measurability of effort, coupled with nonimputability of output. In the context of the present discussion, by contrast, imputability is always guaranteed for the entire working community taken as a unit; indeed, it is a trivial fact that the output of the whole enterprise is always imputable to the labor force which has produced it. And we know that with imputability of output, cardinal measurability of effort becomes unnecessary as a means toward effort optimization. Consequently, as long as the working community of an enterprise can be made to act as a single-mind behavioral unit, the problem of optimization becomes solvable, irrespective of cardinal measurability of effort.

It should be clear that perhaps the most important function of labor management is precisely to produce the conditions of a single collective mind. The solidarity and unity of spirit of a labor union which in a capitalist environment is expended (wasted?) predominantly in generating the countervailing power, that is, in more common language, in fighting the opposing—and very often hostile—employer, can now more constructively be used in running the enterprise and working to the greatest advantage of everyone. The identification which a voter experiences in a full political democracy with his government and the running of public affairs is experienced, in a far more immediate and concrete manner, by a member of a labor-managed firm which is essentially and necessarily a producers' democracy.

It is true that as the enterprise becomes larger and larger, relationships become more and more impersonal, as they generally are in a political democracy where the large numbers of regular citizens remain at a great distance from those who run affairs. However, as much as in a political democracy, it is possible to gain a good deal by the application of the subsidiarity principle—that is, in the context of a productive firm, by an atomization of the productive process into smaller more or less autonomous producing and decision-making units. This is possible only on the condition that imputability of product be preserved. And this is possible—even if only rarely with full perfection—in most productive processes, through horizontal and vertical atomization.[3] Each of the units then is rewarded for its output, which varies with, and is used as a proxy for the effort—generally not cardinally measurable—of the workers' collective.

Of course, there is the problem of sharing of total returns, whatever the basic unit—whether it is the whole enterprise or one of its workshops. But this problem, which we have already dealt with in the pre-

---

[3] By horizontal atomization, we understand subdivision of a firm into units at a similar level of the productive process, while by vertical atomization, we understand a chainlike subdivision into consecutive elements (workshops) of the productive process.

ceding chapter, is mostly, although not entirely, solved by the demo-cratic establishment of an income-distribution schedule. Within each autonomous unit, even with given distribution coefficients (a_i) allotted each skill, imperfections and conflicts of interest still may result from unequal application by individual members of the productive unit. It is at this juncture that income participation and the over-all cooperative nature of the undertaking play a very important role. This role can be seen in two different forms. The first is that within a given workshop, or in any situation where men work side by side, there will be a natural constraint—as always in a team—for everyone to do his part. Even if only rarely required, the well-known sanctions applied to "loafers" range from a friendly reprimand by one's fellow workers to outright discharge. Note that in a firm where the workers and employees are hired at a constant wage by a capitalist employer, on grounds of the mentality of conflict already noted, covering up of the fellow worker who does not do his part will most often be considered the thing to do among members of a community of workers. The second form stems from the capacity of the cooperative arrangement to engender ex-tremely subtle and intangible instances of income distribution some of which, we may suggest, have a good deal in common with acts of hero-ism. For example, a lesser effort by a very young or a very old mem-ber of a working community, or by one who is ill or weak, may be not only accepted but explicitly recommended by the other members. And such transfers almost by definition benefit everyone, even if the form of benefit is of widely different kinds for the two parties involved.

Less abstractly, optimization or even full optimization of effort can be obtained in the labor-managed firm directly as a result, or product, of the very self-governing activity—such as deliberations of the work-ers' council or others—in the form of an agreement on the general cadence at which the productive operations are to proceed. Especially in more modern and complex productive processes, there is a good deal of rigid linkage among the various partial activities (e.g., one depart-ment may deliver semifinished products to another for further pro-cessing, or the whole sequence of productive activities be linked rigidly through an assembly line), and under such conditions, there must be a general endorsement by the members of the working community on the over-all rate at which the operations are to proceed. Translated into our diagrammatic representation of Figure 12.3.1 this means a simultaneous movement from e_0 left and upward along a steep path comparable to $e_0 e_1$; it is steep on account of the simultaneous increase in effort on the part of the whole working community conditioned by what we have termed above the "rigid linkage."

But this is not the only way in which the labor-managed firm becomes capable of approximating the collective optimum solution. Suppose that there are many workers, say one thousand, in a firm which, to begin with, practices a fixed-wage policy. We know already that everyone will be at the point of minimum acceptable effort, that is, at e_0 in Figure 12.3.1. From the point of view of each of the thousand workers, the situation is somewhat similar to that of a competitive industry with a thousand firms: each of the firms sells at the competitive price, call it p_0, knowing that increasing its price even by very little would make it lose all income while a small reduction in price would make it slightly less well off because it already sells all it can produce and its sales at the lower price cannot be increased. Similarly, each of our thousand workers in the hypothetical firm will not reduce E below E_0, because that would imply loss of all his income, and he will not increase E beyond E_0, because that would imply a slight reduction in his real income (i.e., satisfaction).

Suppose that the thousand firms which operated thus far as perfect competitors now form a monopolistic coalition and each reduces its sales by a certain percentage. It is a well-known fact that for a wide range of such reductions each and every one in the industry will benefit. Let us now ask why this hardly ever happens in the real world. The answer is (1) because in most cases the coalition is legally or practically (with a large number of firms) impossible; and (2) because with a large number of firms it may be difficult to establish or enforce the distributive shares for the thousand participants. But if it were not for (1) and (2) every rational competitive industry would transform itself into a monopolistic coalition.

Pursuing further our analogy between the thousand-firm industry and a thousand-man firm, it is clear that a coalition among the thousand men is equally as desirable and beneficial from their point of view as was the monopolistic collusion for the thousand firms. The coalition can make everyone move along a locus such as $e_0 e_1$ in Figure 12.3.1. And what about the hindrances (1) and (2) mentioned in respect to the industry situation; are these also present here? As for (1), not only is it absent in the labor-managed firm, but the very organizational and controlling structure of the firm provides a perfect vehicle for— as well as invitation to—collusion among the members of the firm. As for (2), it is not entirely absent, but only partially so. For one thing, there is the income-distribution schedule which assigns each member of the working community a rigid coefficient of income participation. For that income share he ought to perform at the level of E_{max} (at least approximately) which was agreed on in the coalition; the range of variation in E which a member could fraudulently engage in is between E_{max} and E_{min}, the latter being generally well above the E_0 of a capitalist firm on grounds of the social constraint (imposed by fellow workers) previously referred to.

With a clear advantage of coalition among the members of a labor-managed enterprise, hindrance (1) entirely absent and hindrance (2) partly absent, we can be almost certain that the firm will approximately generate solutions such as e_1 in Figure 12.3.1, that is, solutions at or near the optimum satisfaction of each worker, constrained by a coalition-like (steep) transformation locus and not by an individualistic (flat) transformation locus. It also follows that provided that a capitalist firm and a labor-managed firm both impose the same minimum acceptable standards (such as E_0 in Figure 12.3.1), it could be only by the sheerest of accidents that both firms would operate equally efficiently — in an infinity of cases but one, the labor-managed firm would be likely to be more efficient in the sense of both producing more and making everyone better off (i.e., happier).

At least in theory, another situation should be considered. What if the labor-managed firm does not have any minimum acceptable standard of efficiency? Then, as a reader may easily verify from a construction such as that leading to e_4 in Figure 13.3.1, for a rather flat collective (i.e., coalition-type) transformation locus, the labor-managed firm might produce less than its capitalist equivalent. However, and this is very important, the real or enjoyment income (using Professor Fisher's terminology) of each participant in the labor-managed firm still would be superior to that of the workers in the capitalist firm. Note that the indifference at e_0 must be below that generating the solution at e_4.

Returning again to our analogy with the thousand-firm industry, perhaps the most important argument regarding it remains to be made. The two coalitions—among workers of a labor-managed firm and that among firms of an initially competitive industry—are analogous only when contemplated from the individualistic, or as we sometimes call it, private point of view. From the social point of view, the former is clearly optimal, the latter clearly undesirable. More exactly, it is a well-known fact that a monopolistic collusion among firms of an otherwise competitive industry leads, in a competitive world, to a general equilibrium solution which is inferior from the social point of view to the situation where all industries are competitive. On the other hand, the collusion among workers of a labor-managed firm leading to a solution away from the point of minimum acceptable effort (such as e_0 in the diagram) is always superior to the solution at e_0. As we have seen, in most instances this superiority of satisfaction (utility) carries with it a superiority of output in quality and/or quantity (recall here the three various dimensions of E).

12.6: A Reconciliation with the Analysis of Part I

Throughout the present chapter, the number of laborers L—or L_i, as the case may be—working in the labor-managed firm was treated as a constant and not as one of the variables under the control of the firm's management. On the other hand, throughout Part I—where we assumed an invariant quality of labor—the magnitude L was one of the key decision variables in the process of maximization of income per laborer. In the real world, clearly, L is a variable and so is (contrary to what we assumed in Part I for purposes of exposition) the quality or efficiency of labor. And consequently, if we want to present a realistic theory of behavior of a labor-managed firm, we must attempt to reconcile or, more precisely, to integrate the approaches of Part I and of the present chapter. Our presentation can be quite brief, however, because the integration does not lead to much that is new over and above what we know already from the two partial approaches.

First, it will be realized that if the director of the labor-managed firm knew exactly the degree of equilibrium effort E_e with which each of the workers would be applying himself in the final equilibrium of the firm, he could proceed to hire (or invite to participate in the enterprise) as many workers, each supplying the effort E_e, as to equalize the marginal value product of such workers to the firm's net income per laborer. Of course, this is an oversimplification. The director cannot generally take E_e as a constant. At least in theory, E_e must be determined jointly or simultaneously with the equilibrium employment L_e because the two variables are interrelated.

Perhaps most descriptively, this joint determination can be explained as a converging iterative process. Suppose that the managers of the firm first pick an employment level L_1, somewhere near where they think the final equilibrium employment should be, and let E settle, through the more or less autonomous collusive processes discussed earlier in this chapter, at an equilibrium level E_1. But now they find that with E_1 the marginal value product of L_1 is different from the income per laborer. Depending on whether this difference is positive or negative, they will now adjust employment to L_2 in one direction or another (according to the rules known to us from Part I). But for L_2, a new "collusive" equilibrium effort E_2, generally different from E_1, will be obtained, and so the process can continue until E_e and L_e are reached. Clearly, this will only happen on condition that simultaneously (1) the marginal value product of L_e at effort E_e be equal to the income per laborer, and (2) the *mutatis-mutandis* transformation locus (based on joint or collusive variation of E by all laborers), such as $e_0 e_1$ in Figure 12.3.1, be equal to the marginal rate of substitution between E and Y of the representative laborer—that is, to the slope of u.

It must be clear that the condition just stated is too refined and too complicated to be exactly attained in the real world. Rather, it will be attained only approximately, through what can be described as a two-stage process. The first stage is of a comparatively long-run nature and consists of employing a certain number of workers, fulfilling the optimum marginal conditions (i.e., $MVP_L = Y$) on the assumption of an expected most likely effort of these workers.[4] In the second stage then an exact level of E is determined through the previously described collusive process. Clearly, inherent in the second stage is a good deal greater flexibility than in the first, adjustment of E being feasible over very short periods of time; we can thus think of the second stage as one of a very short-run nature. The level of E actually obtained in the second stage will generally be somewhat different from the E contemplated when the specific number of workers was hired. But this, given the different time-characteristics of the first and second stages, is perfectly in order. One can only ascertain that a good or efficient management would make its decisions in such a way as to make approximately equal the average level of actual E computed for a period for which employment decisions are made (say, two years) to the expected E used in determining the equilibrium employment.

---

[4]In many situations the employment will be given by the full capacity operation corresponding to existing plant and equipment. In orders, the scale of operation of the firm—and thus also the level of employment—will be arbitrary on account of constant returns to scale.

The degree of inefficiency that could arise from imperfections of the realistic process just described should not be very important. Consider the equilibrium condition of the labor-managed firm's employment written slightly differently from the form we have used in Part I, namely

$$MVP_L = AVP_L - P_K K_0 / L$$

If a very short-run change in E takes place and affects the average value product of labor proportionately to the corresponding change in the marginal value product—a result which can be considered normal in the situation at hand—and if the cost of capital per laborer ($p_K K_p$) is comparatively small, the equality still will be approximately fulfilled after a change in E.

It is also interesting to consider briefly the impact of effort optimization in a labor-managed firm on the efficient size of the enterprise. Normally, one should expect that compared to a firm operating with fixed wages and thus, in the context of our analysis, with a minimum acceptable effort (see E_0 in Figure 12.3.1), the optimal size of the labor-managed firm will be less. The key ingredient of this deduction is that with increasing size and employment of the firm, for reasons discussed earlier in this chapter, the incentive to produce above the minimum acceptable effort (E_0) will normally be diminishing. Translated into customary analytical concepts we thus have a (single-input) production function of a non-labor-managed firm $X(L)_{n.l.m.}$ illustrated in Figure 12.6.1 and a production function $X(L)_{l.m.}$, the latter always being above the former, but the relative distance between the two diminish-

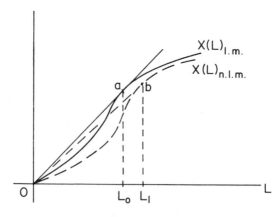

Figure 12.6.1

ing as L increases. From the diminishing relative distances, it immediately follows that the optimal scale of operation for the non-labor-managed firm, corresponding to b and L_1, must be greater than that of the labor-managed firm attained at the employment L_0. It is clear, however, that the optimum efficiency (i.e., average productivity of labor) for the labor-managed firm must exceed that of the other firm. Analogous results can be expected, as the reader will find easy to verify, for firms with any number of inputs. In other words, the locus of maximum physical efficiency derived in Part I can generally be expected to be nearer the origin for a labor-managed firm than it would be for any other firm using identical technology and a limit of minimum acceptable effort, but hiring workers at a fixed wage. The smaller efficient size, in turn, will guarantee a more competitive structure to an industry, *ceteris paribus*, in the labor-managed system. This only reinforces similar conclusions derived earlier in Part I.

To complete our attempt to integrate the analysis of the present chapter with that of Part I, there remains one important subject. We have to ask how variations in price will affect the supply of the product. As is indicated in Figure 12.6.2, the answer is not unambiguous. As-

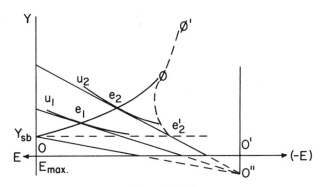

Figure 12.6.2

suming that there is some fixed cost of production, and assuming a product price p_2, we have the (collusive) transformation locus $0''e_2$. $0''$ is below the horizontal axis because with zero effort there would still be some fixed cost to pay in the absence of any production. The representative worker now maximizes his position at e_2, furnishing the corresponding amount of effort and earning the corresponding income. As price declines to p_1, the transformation locus shifts to $0''e_1$, the supply of effort goes up and Y declines. Finally, at a very low price p_0, we reach a maximum supply of effort E_{max} at a subsistence income Y_{sb}. We thus get a "backward-bending" supply of effort and, because effort varies with output, a backward-bending supply function of product X, based on the assumption of fixed employment. On grounds of arguments presented earlier in this section, we might want to refer to such a function as a "very-short-run supply."

The important finding regarding that function is that it by no means needs to be backward bending. One might argue on rather rigidly theoretical grounds that it would be such only in the vicinity of subsistence income, because one normally would prefer to supply maximum conceivable effort before starving. But even here, it is a well-known biological fact that near subsistence one is generally able to supply only very small effort, if any, and that with increasing income beyond subsistence one can, and one generally does, increase effort considerably. It is then only for very high levels of p and Y that further increases in these two variables are likely to (note that this is not a necessary outcome) lead to decreases in E and thus in supply of X.

We thus can conclude that with a fixed employment variations in product price can have either effect on product supply, that is, the supply function can be—on account of effort variation—either positively or negatively sloped. The fact that it can be positively sloped then counteracts, and actually negates, the conclusion of Part I to the effect that the short-run supply function of a labor-managed firm producing only one product will not be positively sloped.

This is as far as we can go in the integration of Part I with the present chapter. A few words to appraise the importance of the two types of analysis should be in order, even at the risk of repeating some of what was said in section 12.2. It is a definite impression of the present author that the extent of our analysis in Part I as compared to the extent of the present chapter by far overstates the relative importance of the traditional marginal analysis in comparison with that of the incentives problem studied here. Rather, the comparative size of the two segments of the present study should primarily be taken as reflecting the size of the body of doctrine dealing with the two subjects respectively. Anyone who has ever observed working habits and behavior in government or private firms, institutions, or workshops must be aware of the enormous range of possible variation of labor efficiency and/or quality (i.e., of our E). The minimum acceptable effort E_0 often may be of the order of 20 per cent of a reasonable effort, attainable without major strain or hardship only if a stimulus to do so is present. In some situations the preferences with respect to effort and income are not fully realized, and an initial inducement to move above the minimum acceptable effort to a reasonable level of E may lead to a realization that the "reasonable level" is preferable to the minimum level even without additional compensation.

In comparison, gains in productivity resulting from variation of factor proportions may be relatively unimportant. Thus, in the real world where information and the decision-making processes are not perfect, the managing board of a labor-managed firm may attach a far greater importance to, and spend a good deal more time on designing an environment best conducive to optimization of E along the lines discussed in this chapter, rather than to the more standard type of decisions of the type implicit in the analysis of Part I. Indeed, the latter may become a real issue only from time to time, especially in conjunction with new entry into an industry, or in conjunction with expansions of capacity or replacement of old equipment.

12.7: *A Postscript on Promotion Incentives*

Some may argue that our analysis of incentives in the labor-managed firms and especially our comparisons with other types of productive organizations was incomplete since it did not include consideration of incentives based on the possibility of promotion on the job. Undeniably, such incentives do exist, and can be of considerable importance. If we have not considered them thus far, and if we do not intend to devote to them much space, it is primarily because the phenomenon is well known and, more important, present in both labor-managed as well as other firms. The few remarks which follow are designed merely to point out some of the special aspects of promotion incentives as they apply to labor-managed firms.

One thing that we ought to realize is that incentives based on the expectation or hope of promotion are always inferior in quality, whether in a labor-managed or another productive establishment, to the incentives based on an effort-income transformation of the type discussed in this chapter. The promotion incentive in most situations involves a component of deception, and even of humiliation.

As for deception, it is a generally valid fact that the number of positions to which promotion can take place is far less than the number of those for whom such positions serve as a stimulus of effort. In consequence, the phenomenon is always bound to carry within itself a good deal of bitterness and dissatisfaction on the part of those whose expectations are not realized. Regarding the side effects of humiliation, on the other hand, the labor-managed form of productive organization has a definite edge over other forms. Whereas in the former someone whose expectations were frustrated has the right and possibility of appeal to the group to which he also belongs, in the other firms—the capitalist ones in particular—the final judgment is always with the "superior" employer and recourse elsewhere is generally impossible.

13. Further Specific Aspects of Labor-Managed Firms

13.1: *Introduction*

In the preceding two chapters, we have covered two among the most important specific problems of the theory of labor-managed systems: the problem of income distribution and the problem of incentives and productivity. Of equal importance is the specific set of problems raised by entry, exit (or liquidation), and major capacity expansion; to these we will devote Chapter 14. Besides these three main categories, however, there is a whole score of minor points, characteristics, or problems specific to the labor-managed system which ought not to be neglected if we want to acquire a rounded and comprehensive theoretical view of the subject matter. In many cases, such lesser points cannot be stated or proved in terms of formal and exact analysis. In many other instances there is actually nothing to be proved, a mere statement, or calling to the attention of the reader, of a given characteristic of the labor-managed system being sufficient. The purpose of the present chapter is precisely to assemble what we have just termed the "lesser points."

No clear-cut organization suggests itself for this chapter, most of the arguments which we want to make being on a similar plane—and generally not following one from the other. Nonetheless, most of them have one thing in common. They derive from—or are connected with—the relaxation of basic assumption (3), as stated in the introduction to the preceding chapter; that is, the fact that in a labor-managed firm, by definition, the labor force has other functions, rights, and obligations than those of a productive factor. Consequently, we consider it desirable to discuss first, in greater detail and with greater concreteness than has been done in Chapter 1, the very vehicle and expression of the new dimensions of the working community, that is, the process of labor management. Within that process many of the "lesser points" to be discussed in this chapter best come to light.

13.2: *The Process of Labor Management*

What we have termed labor management, that is, the activity of controlling and running the labor-managed firm, could also be referred to by such expressions as employee self-determination, industrial or producers' democracy, automanagement, and very likely by a number of others, some of which may even be better fitting and more descriptive than those we have been able to think of. But the terms are not essential. What is important is the substance behind them; it is this substance that we would like to develop here in some detail.

Our task is significantly helped by the fact that labor management is analogous to the process of democratic government in the political sphere. The process of labor management also must be based on distinct legislative, executive, and juridical (arbitration) activities, and as much as in a political democracy there must be a basic statute, or set of rules of the game, revised only rarely if ever, comparable to a political constitution. The one important difference, and very likely an important advantage of the labor-management instance is that the cooperation and consultation between the legislative and executive branches can be, thanks to the comparatively smaller size of production collectives, much more direct and immediate.

The comparatively smaller size of the production collectives also makes it possible to do away with permanent coalitions of the type of political parties, and thus to evaluate and act on issues with a good deal greater objectivity and flexibility.

The fundamental principle of labor management is that in any productive endeavor, although production is carried out by making use of capital assets, the supreme and superior factor is the human factor. Consequently, it is this human factor that ought to be given the control of the common endeavor. The best way is to do so by means of the democratic process of labor management. The power of control is not attached to productive contribution—indeed, if it were so, the capital owners might be given some 20 per cent of the vote—but rather derives from basic human dignity, equal with every member of the collective. Deriving from this is the principle of equal representation, that is that each member of the working collective, director or unskilled worker, should be given one vote.

The way in which the legislative function will be carried out in the labor-managed firm can vary from case to case and will depend, among other things, on the size of the firm. Especially because by far the most important portion of available time must be devoted to the productive activity of the firm,[1] the criterion of efficiency of that function is a very important one. Thus, the entire working collective may convene and be consulted only once a year, to evaluate, approve, or disapprove past performance of the firm, or participate in major decisions involving expansion, creation of new firms,[2] design or amendment of the basic statute, or the like. Most of the day-to-day function of control will generally be assumed by a small number of elected representatives of the working collective forming a board of control. In large undertakings, another body may be imposed between the base and the top of the legislative pyramid serving, among other things, as electoral college for the board of control, and also providing the board with an expression of the will of the whole collective.

The legislative—or controlling—branch and the executive branch, as usual, meet at the top, the board of control having frequent consultations with the director, or directors, of the firm. The exact modalities of selecting the top executive officer by the collective will vary from case to case and generally will be stated in the statute of the enterprise. In some instances, as is the case in Yugoslavia, the power of delegating a director may even be shared between the collective and some institution external to the enterprise.

Starting from the director, the executive functions proceed in a customary fashion as in any other enterprise, labor-managed or otherwise, through the commercial, technical, and other directors down to the department and workshop level. While consultations, inquiries and suggestions can exist short of the top of the two pyramids, the formal and binding relationships must be channeled through the top. Moreover, the executive branch must be guaranteed a sufficient degree of short-run autonomy to guarantee continuity of its functioning, and general endorsements or disapprovals by the working community can be put to vote only after periods of one year or preferably even less frequently.

For reasons some of which will become clear later in this chapter, equally important as efficiency of the (legislative) process of control is that the process facilitate and stimulate communication among different levels of the legislative pyramid and discussion among members of the enterprise at all levels. For example, attainment of

[1]This condition might change in the future with extreme automation.
[2]Some of these matters will be discussed in the following chapter.

what we have referred to in the preceding chapter as the collusive optimum effort solution will in a large measure depend on such discussion and communication.

13.3: *Intangible Incomes in a Labor-Managed Enterprise*

The disappearance of employee-employer conflict in a labor-managed enterprise renders the decision-making process in such an enterprise extremely flexible. Where in another organizational form a good deal of initiative and managerial energy either would be wasted, or never come to fruition on grounds of mistrust, bad will, or just a blind faith in the preservation of a *status quo*, the labor-managed structure can act and operate with far less friction and accommodate most broadly based suggestions, desires, or initiatives. In this context, perhaps the most important category of arrangements which the labor-managed enterprise is apt to provide is that of incomes other than those disbursed in kind on an individual basis. The two important categories of income that we have in mind here are intangible incomes, and incomes collectively received in the form of collective consumption. It is the first of these categories that will concern us here; the second will be our subject in section 13.7.

As the simplest example, take the case in which, in the context of our analysis of the preceding chapter, E reflects the hours of work per day per employee. The collective optimum (explained previously) may be at six hours, a large majority of the working community being in favor of such an arrangement. In a firm which has been operating initially with an eight-hour working day, the shortening of the working day by two hours can then be thought of as intangible income. It is another matter that this arrangement might lead to a less intensive utilization of scarce capital resoures if the number of shifts is preserved. But it is obvious that this need not be the case; on the contrary a two-shift operation with six-hour shifts will be far more acceptable and feasible than one with shifts lasting eight hours.

Along similar lines, and perhaps more important, the effort variable E of the preceding chapter may represent the number of working days in the year, and a reduction of E then again constitutes intangible income. The specific form of this intangible income may be the lengthening of annual leaves or of weekends. As before, such arrangements need not lead to underutilization of the firm's capital assets.

Especially in countries which have already reached a high standard of living, the flexibility of income derived from an intangible component may be quite important, and enhance over-all social welfare a good deal. Recall from Figure 12.6.2 that with increasing incomes (i.e., labor productivity) the optimum level of E—given by the locus Φ —will generally tend to decline when the equilibrium income is high. A historically established and stubbornly adhered to eight-hour working day, or ten-day annual leave, may then become a socially most undesirable solution beyond a certain point. Some writers argue that that point has been reached long ago in the United States and other western industrial economies. The flexibility offered by the labor-managed firm can in this context be an important factor of economic efficiency and social welfare.

Germane to the set of arguments just made are certain "new dimensions" of the labor-managed firm connected with the phenomena of technological change and automation. To most of these we will turn only later on in this chapter; one of them, however, belongs to the present discussion. The basic observation underlying our argument is that the quality, intensity, or even duration of work often is not so much controlled by the worker himself but rather by the equipment with which he has to operate. Certain types of equipment will require far greater efforts and often hardships than others. The worker may then prefer certain types of equipment rendering his task easier even at a loss of his tangible income. Moreover, the system of labor-management makes it possible to communicate such individual demands and initiatives to those who decide on capital-assets procurement and replacement. On the other hand, a collective contract between employer and union negotiated once in three years will hardly provide for accommodation of individual workers; usually, it is cumbersome enough to negotiate intangibilities concerning the whole labor force.

Also, on purely economic grounds of profitability, the labor-managed firm may adopt technical changes facilitating its members' tasks where the comparable capitalist firm would not do so. This is only an extension of the argument well known to us from Part I to the effect that, with generally higher returns per laborer, the labor-managed firm tends to employ more capital-intensive methods than its capitalist counterpart.

Still another instance of intangible incomes is that arising from retraining workers on the job, or during working hours outside the enterprise. But because this case has some other specific characteristics and ramifications, we will take it up separately in the following section. In the context of the present analysis, let it only be noted that through retraining and education important changes in the effort variable E and in the transformation functions—as defined in the preceding chapter—can arise for an individual, leading to increased satisfaction for both the man retrained and the working collective as a whole. Again, the labor-management regime constitutes an environment conducive to retraining and education, and thus to an over-all improvement in the quality of the labor force.

13.4: *Training and Education in and by the Labor-Managed Firm*

Many western economists like to think of training and education as an investment in human capital. While in many respects this transposition may not be quite adequate in describing the particular phenomenon, it provides us with a useful starting point for our present discussion. It must be clear that in some instances the labor-managed firm will find it desirable to give specialized education, training, or retraining to some of its members, and that the latter may be willing on their part to contribute to the costs of such investment in' human capital. It must be equally clear that the equilibrium behavior of a labor-managed firm with regard to investment in human capital will be quite different from that of a comparable capitalist or modern management-controlled firm.

In fact, we will show that normally the labor-managed firm not only will provide an environment highly conducive to training and education as a result of its behavioral laws, but also that, as a general rule, it will be considerably more successful in enhancing the professional qualification of the working population than other firms. Before we turn to a more careful and detailed analysis, two intuitive and somewhat crude arguments may be useful. First, let us recall from Part I that under normal conditions where a "capitalist twin" makes positive profits, the labor-managed twin—identical in all respects except for the management- and income-sharing regimes—will use more capital-intensive techniques of production. Extending the conclusion to human capital, we might conjecture that *ceteris paribus* the labor-managed firm would also tend to use better trained employees, that is, employees with a higher degree of human-capital investment. Consequently, to the extent that the labor-managed firm is in a position to affect the degree of qualification of its members through retraining and/or education, it will also push such a process further than would its "capitalist twin." Effectively, although the argument will be more involved than what is suggested in the explanation just offered, this is the conclusion that we will come to later in our discussion.

Our second commonsensical argument relies more on social psychology than on formal economics and involves a transposition from a situation encountered in modern western firms. In modern large American—but also other western—corporations, we often encounter a good deal of retraining and re-education (often lavishly endowed for the benefit of the trainee) at the very high echelon of the managerial hierarchy. In most cases the corporations engaging in such practice are of the modern management-controlled variety—and the training and education programs are conducted for those within the controlling group. If we now think for a moment of the labor-managed firm as of a management-controlled corporation where the management consists of the entire working community, it becomes apparent that training and education (i.e., investment in human capital within or by the firm) can be expected to occur more frequently. And, of course, income participation is still another dimension in the labor-managed system which can further stimulate the process in question. Clearly, the main thing that lies behind the argument just made is what we may call—using Galbraith's terminology—identification of the person retrained or re-educated with the firm. The higher the degree of identification, the less obstacle is there to investment in human capital. But all these things will become more apparent below.

The managers of the labor-managed or any other firm must, in deciding on whether to retrain or give education to a member of its labor force, consider the costs and benefits associated with such an action. If the benefits exceed the costs—both properly evaluated—the retraining should be undertaken because the excess of benefit over cost will increase the aggregate which the firm attempts to maximize: income per laborer in a labor-managed firm for all laborers, and profit in a capitalist firm.

Let us first consider the benefits. They will consist, first of all, of the increment in the value of output inputable to the improved qualification of the person retrained for the period of time—only an *expected* period at the time the decision to retrain is taken—in which the re-trainee will remain with the enterprise. In a labor-managed firm the period can be expected to be substantial, especially because the identification of the employee with his firm normally will lead to job stability. On this account then, the benefits in a labor-managed firm will tend to be higher than those in a western-type situation. But what may be more important are the often lifelong benefits accruing in an intangible form (as we have described them in the preceding section) to the object of retraining. By definition, these benefits are outside of the objective function of the capitalist firm (except, of course, for instances of paternalistic or humanistic inclinations on the part of the employer which, in any case, contain something socially unbalanced). By contrast, these benefits are very much an integral part of the objective function of the labor-managed firm which, as we know, attempts to maximize the returns per laborer. We only now are coming to a more realistic concept of return per laborer, including both tangible and intangible benefits. It ought to be noted that these benefits need not accrue to the man retrained only; to the extent that he will assume some of the cost of retraining through lesser tangible income, he, *ipso facto*, distributes some of his subjective benefits to his fellow workers.

Considerably less needs to be said about the costs of retraining and education. They are composed of (a) the possible reduction in productive contribution of the trainee during the training period, and (b) the actual education charges expended outside the enterprise. As for (b), the amounts involved can be expected, other things being equal, to be identical whatever the particular form of the enterprise. The costs falling under (a)—again, in comparable firms—may be somewhat higher in the labor-managed firm because, as we have shown in Part I, returns per laborer will generally exceed wages in a capitalist firm.

We have noted earlier in Chapter 11 that certain frictions and rigidities may arise in the allocation of labor resources throughout the labor-managed economy owing to the operation of the quasi-labor market, as opposed to the regular labor market in a capitalist economy. The possibility of retraining and education provides an important palliative against such inefficiencies. In particular, in cases of structural unemployment in some skill categories and excess demand for labor in others, a firm always has the possibility of hiring a new member, or taking someone in the enterprise already from among the former category, and retraining him for the latter category. This should lead to significant improvements in the general economic efficiency of the labor-managed system.

But the conduciveness of a labor-managed environment to training and education and its edge over other economic arrangements can also be seen and argued from another viewpoint. Not only have we found that the returns to *identical* labor categories will generally be higher in a labor-managed firm, but also we have concluded in the preceding chapter that the level of E at which a typical laborer in a labor-managed firm will be operating will generally be higher than that at which his peer will perform in a similar but capitalist firm.   Consequently, the income and the marginal productivity of a worker in a given category should be higher not on one, but on two accounts, in the labor-managed alternative. But retraining is nothing else than adding an additional laborer to a given labor category; and with a given cost of retraining, the comparatively higher benefits on the two accounts just mentioned should make retraining attractive for the labor-managed firm in many instances where the capitalist firm would decide against retraining. It is true that the cost component (a) stated above may be higher for the labor-managed firm, but this, in most cases, would not be a decisive factor. Also, and more important, it must be realized that if a firm wants to retrain, it generally does so because it cannot find a man of a particular qualification in the outside market. In these situations of "excess demand" in the labor market, the marginal productivity of labor generally will be above the real income actually received by workers in the particular category, and thus the inducement to retrain may be even stronger than what we have implied above on the assumption of equality of incomes to marginal value products.

One cannot conclude the present section without pointing out the very important—perhaps decisive—implications that the present analysis has for concrete problems of economic development of under-developed countries. A whole study would have to be written if we wanted to cover the subject adequately. Let it only be noted here that in many instances training and education is a real bottleneck—that is, a binding constraint—on economic development. And very often it may take a whole generation and enormous sums, unproductive in the short run, to reach a satisfactory level of education through a public effort. Training and learning while on the job may be the only short cut; and if there is a system of productive organization considerably better suited to the attainment of the results, it may be desirable, or even absolutely necessary, to adopt that system.

13.5: *Technical Change and Innovation in a Labor-Managed Firm*
In every man there is some inventive or innovative talent; it will range from the ability to produce major inventions for some to the ability of improving the way one ties one's shoe with others. While the

former type of major technological changes, if profitable, will generally find outlets into productive application whatever the economic system, the minor ones may or may not depending on the environment in which they are made. In this section, we will argue that the labor-managed form of productive organization is highly conducive to minor innovative activity within the firm. The question of major economic inventions and innovations will be taken up in conjunction with the problem of entry and major capital expansions in the subsequent chapter.

Probably the best way of distinguishing between what we have termed major and minor innovations is that the latter generally cannot be the subject of a full-time professional occupation. Rather, they will arise as an externality (external economy) of an activity whose primary purpose is something else than to innovate—generally to produce or contribute to the production of some good or service. More concretely, as in the above example of tying a shoe, a repeated act of production will stimulate reflection on how that act could be facilitated, or done more efficiently. As in the shoe-tying example, in some instances the minor innovation may not require any accommodation of the capital assets with which the worker is operating, but in most instances it will.

Clearly, along the lines of the argument developed in the preceding chapter, the situation most conducive to the application of minor innovations is one of an individual self-employed producer, provided that he is not constrained by financial limitations. As far as conduciveness —or the incentive—to innovate goes, the labor-managed firm is the second-best solution; and, regarding the problem of financial limitations, such a firm will generally be in a better position than the individual producer. Our argument of "second best" is based on several considerations. First of all, the self-management structure—as outlined in section 13.2—provides an excellent channel of communication, unparallelled in any other firm, between those who have innovative ideas, those who decide on and procure the capital implementation, and those who incorporate the innovation into the income-distribution scheme of the firm. Second, the innovator in the labor-managed firm need not worry that the capital owner will exploit the innovation and leave him with only a small part of the gain. It is true that he still may worry about not receiving what he considers a just share, but if he does, it will be much more preferable for him to know that those who benefit are his fellow workers and, what may be more important, as a member of the democratic working collective, he will be able to argue his case within that decision-making structure. In extreme cases, he can even recur to formal arbitration.

Still another consideration is that the labor-managed firm will be in a better position to accommodate and adjust to some negative effects which the innovation may have. For example, consider an innovation which substantially alters the capital-labor ratio at a certain stage of an integrated productive process. A sudden release of workers owing to such an alteration might produce serious hardships on the part of those affected. The labor-managed structure can adjust to such a situation by retraining, postponement of or phasing in the new techniques, temporary overemployment, or other means. All of these will be closer to a social optimum than the solution in other than labor-managed firms. In the latter, practices such as featherbedding often have to be employed in the situation at hand—practices which often involve extreme inefficiencies of resource allocation in the long run. In contrast to featherbedding, the labor-managed firm may tolerate overemployment in the short run while doing away with it in the long run through attrition, retraining, or in other ways. The general proposition which emerges here is that in a conflictless environment the social optimum most often is much closer to the private (or individual) optimum than in an environment containing a situation of conflict.

13.6: *Production-Mindedness and Identification in a Labor-Managed Firm*

We have spoken already about several types of intangibilities which either are inherent exclusively in the labor-managed form of organization, or appear to be more prominent in that form. But we have not covered, by any means, the whole range of such intangible effects. There are many others which are in some sense even more intangible and unmeasurable in terms of income or utility than those we have encountered thus far, but which are equally or more important for the labor-managed firm. We will devote the present section to a discussion of these effects.

At one occasion we have already alluded to the phenomenon of identification. It is well known to us from other than labor-managed environments. We encounter it under other terms, such as "team spirit." Galbraith sees in it the essential property of the leadership of the modern large corporation (see his *New Industrial State*). The phenomenon of identification, as the term suggests, implies the absence or disappearance of any conflict between the individuals within an organization and the organization itself. In Galbraith's theory of the large corporation, it applies to and is reserved for the "top five per cent" of the working population of the enterprise and presumably arises only in the largest productive establishments, those which are usually referred to as management controlled.

In the labor-managed firm, clearly, identification becomes the fabric of the entire one hundred per cent of the working community. By definition, the conflict between management and workers, or owner and workers, disappears in the labor-managed firm. Figuratively speaking, energies which otherwise would be expended on nourishing the "countervailing powers" and thus offsetting each other, now can be used in attaining the common goals of the organization and all of its members. It is almost like letting two horses pull side by side instead of at an angle of 150 degrees.

The social energies—if we may use such a term for lack of a better one—can be of two types. They may be intellectual, that is, of the type where a worker devotes his limited time resources to reflection on how to improve the performance of his enterprise instead of how to minimize his effort without it being noticed by his supervisors; or they may be emotive, that is, of the type where one member of the working community experiences affection toward all others, rather than indifference or even hatred toward the one on the other side of the employer-employee fence. While the former type of energies contributes to the enhancement of the efficiency and productivity of the labor-managed firm, and thereby indirectly to the well-being of the firm's members, the latter type does so directly and can be of overwhelming importance. If we realize how many men are led to leave or change jobs, even at substantial material losses on the sole grounds of personal incompatibility (though this may be less frequent in Anglo-Saxon cultures), the point just made becomes more clearly apparent.

Actually, even at the risk of being ridiculed, I cannot avoid expressing my conviction that the harmonization of the second type of energies, as opposed to their counteraction in instances where full identification is impossible, amounts to a question of life and death for the social groups involved. The objective of the firm now assumes two distinct elements, the two being of entirely different substance. The first type of energies (identified above) still contributes to some kind of material well-being. But the second type contributes to something that has nothing to do with material well-being, and yet is incommensurably more important and relevant for society and individuals than material well-being.

But let us now put our feet on the ground and consider some other matters not entirely distinct from the phenomenon of identification. Prominent among them is what we may refer to as production-mindedness on the part of the working community. In the same sense as the top five per cent in a large western corporation are production-minded—that is, follow and are concerned about the performance of their organization in the same way as one would be about that of a favorite football team or as a scientist would about the problem which he is working on—the entire working collective of the labor-managed firm will tend to be production-minded. Indeed, the fact that a worker in a firm not of the labor-managed variety exercises only the function of a factor or production, the faculties of organization, direction, and profit participation being denied to him, must split him into two distinct personalities: one a nine-to-five inhuman bundle of specific productive operations, and the other a human—as human as one can be after eight or more hours of hard work—at his worst living in a city slum and at his best with a drink and a backyard barbecue, with very little real besides his family to speak or think about. By the same token, once the other integral faculties of a man-producer are restored, the man acquires a far greater degree of internal unity, with what we have called production-mindedness as one of its attributes.

In explaining what we mean by identification in the labor-managed firm, we have found it expedient at several occasions to use as an illustration the attitudes and position of the "top five per cent" in a large western corporation. But it must be pointed out here, in order to better understand the labor-managed firm, that there is also an important difference between the two instances. The identification within the labor-managed firm is not only, quantitatively speaking, twenty times better than that among the top five per cent in a large western corporation because it involves one hundred per cent of the working population of the firm. There is a fundamental qualitative difference. It is only with a full participation within the labor-managed firm that identification can assume its true character, and lead to all the benefits which we have discussed above. Whether with five, or with fifty, or with eighty per cent participation in the controlling group, there will always remain those who rule and those who are ruled, and *ipso facto* often oppressed. This is not only a serious shortcoming for what those "on the outside" must suffer, but also, and perhaps primarily, for the unhealthy and unhappy state of mind of those who belong to the discriminating in-group.

Before concluding our discussion, the most primitive and straightforward effect of identification and conflict-disappearance ought to be mentioned. It is the disappearance of various tools of warfare between labor and management in general, and of strikes in particular. The comparative gains in economic efficiency that can be realized in this way by the labor-managed economy can be very important indeed, not to mention gains of other than purely material welfare.

13.7: *Collective Consumption in a Labor-Managed Firm*

Thus far, primarily in order to keep our analysis pure and neat, we have assumed that all net income of the enterprise is distributed among the members of the working community. It will be clear that in any real situation this would not be the case. Collective allocation of a part of income to investment, or reserve funds of all kinds, or to collective consumption will generally be found in an actual firm. While we will come to the former later in Parts III and IV, in the present section we want to discuss collective consumption in the labor-managed firm.

Before doing so, however, one very important point must be realized. The fact that a labor-managed firm engages in collective consumption is by no means in conflict with our basic principle of maximization of income per laborer. Whether the firm contributes to collective consumption or not, it still maximizes the income per laborer, the main objective of each of the workers still being to derive the highest possible income over a given production period; collective consumption merely means that the workers find it optimal to allocate a part of the maximum income to other than individual consumption. Actually, if we prefer, we may think of collective consumption as an entirely separate operation, based on a total distribution of net income among the members of the collective and a separate financing, from such incomes, of whatever the collective has agreed on to expend collectively.

Perhaps a few examples of typical instances of collective consumption should be given. One of the very important ones is housing; for instance, if the workers agree to build an apartment complex for their own use. Another would be special child-care services, nurseries, and the like. Still others would be recreational facilities of all kinds and special educational facilities which, among other services, could perform the training and retraining functions mentioned earlier in this chapter.

Why should the members of a labor-managed firm engage in collective consumption? And why should they do so differently or perhaps more frequently and extensively than members of any other firm? These questions must be given several answers, or answers on different levels. First, there are purely economic reasons. Most of what we have suggested above as examples of collective consumption are services subject to very important economies of scale. Out of a modest income an individual worker cannot provide an individual instructor for his children, a gymnasium, or even a private home. He can do so at a moderate cost, however, if all or most of his fellow workers want to join with him.

Of course, many of the services subject to collective consumption are services which otherwise would or should be provided by the local community, city, town, village, or district. But it is only too well known that even in countries as advanced as the United States, these services are highly deficient. And collective consumption on the public level will most often cater to the demand of the working community of the labor-managed firm far less adequately than collective consumption instituted within the firm. The proximity, quality, and other attributes of the collective consumption may well have to be "tailored" to the requirements of a particular community, and the members of the community are in the best position to do this tailoring.

We may now turn to some of the less economic factors. Collective consumption generally involves services consumed in common or at least in proximity (such as in apartment dwellings). It may be of positive value to the users of the services to associate with their colleagues and friends with whom they work, or their families, rather than with others. Clearly, there is no question of social class discriminations here, because those in the enterprise belong to all levels of income strata and there is no other yardstick of social stratification. At first sight, someone might object that the wife of the director might not want to associate with the wife of the factory janitor. While this objection is certainly applicable in the case of a capitalist firm, its fallacy as applied to labor-management is obvious: not only do the janitor and the director each have one vote in determining and controlling the affairs of the enterprise, but they are related by a bond of common interest for and in the operation of the firm.

This brings us to our second question, whether (and if so, why?) collective consumption should be a more frequent or differently based occurrence in the labor-managed system than in other systems. For one thing, and perhaps most important, one ought to observe that collective consumption—for dwelling, schooling, hospital services, and so on—does not cross social class boundaries very easily. If one designs a system with considerably reduced sources of stratification, one will *ipso facto* augment the occurrence of collective consumption. More concretely, the disappearance of a conflict relationship within a labormanaged firm, which we have stressed on several previous occasions, has its parallel on the outside of the enterprise in the disappearance of obstacles to the use of many services in common. One scarcely encounters the sharing of country clubs by workers and the management personnel in general; and even more rarely would such or similar facilities be established and promoted by a single firm in a capitalist environment. However, we do frequently find such facilities provided for and by the management personnel of a given firm. Again the phenomenon of identification comes to mind here: those who identify themselves with the firm will engage more readily in company-based collective consumption.

If, then, identification is extended to the hundred per cent of the working population of the firm, so also will be the occurrence of various kinds of collective consumption. One might argue that even in other than labor-managed firms, company-based collective consumption facilities can be provided for the workers separately; but even a child knows that this cannot succeed as long as the workers have any self-respect. An extreme, but true, analogy here is that of providing recreation camps for enemy prisoners-of-war.

13.8: *The Role of Labor-Managed Firms in the Community*

The role which the labor-managed enterprise can play in the community wherein it is located could hardly be overemphasized. That role is only what we may term an extroverted extension of the introverted faculties of labor management discussed in the preceding section. And the role of labor management which we want to discuss here is mostly quite specific to that form of management, largely not encountered in other systems.

Only in one sense are labor-managed and other firms concerned in the surrounding community in a comparable manner: both must rely, to a degree at least, on the community as a recruitment ground—and in that "professional" context they must maintain good relations and workable channels of communication.

The labor-managed enterprise, however, will generally go far beyond this, through its membership, in playing an active role in the economic and social life of the community. The basic principle, or fact, on which this contention is based is the following: contrary to any other economic situation, capitalist or centralized-socialist, in the case of a labor-managed firm those who hold and wield power also live face to face with the community at the level where serious problems in need of solution may generally exist. A worker's neighbor may be a poor man, comparable in all respects except that he does not have a job—or that he does not have the ability to give his child medical treatment equal to his more fortunate neighbor-friend.

Now compare to this the situation of a firm controlled by one million stockholders scattered around the country. The huge majority of them have never seen the environment of the firm and its workers "on twelfth street in Detroit"—and even if they had, most of them, being of another kind of environment, would hardly be much concerned. One generally must live very near a human problem before one decides to do something about it—and preferably one ought to feel and be equal to those to be helped. By contrast in the case of the so-called modern large management-controlled corporations, those who hold power will generally live in opulent surroundings, where one lives face-to-face, if with any problem, only with the problem of one's own emptiness and fundamental lack of purpose.

Even if this may mean a departure from the principles of maximization of income per laborer, narrowly defined, the scope which the labor-managed enterprise's community action can assume is truly enormous. For example, a group within the working population of the enterprise may find it unbearable to live on the same street with a few families who, while having heads of family as qualified as anyone else, are not employed. There is nothing simpler for them, as labor-managers, than to take steps leading to an offer of employment by their firm. The "intangible" satisfaction that they can realize in this way will far outweigh the slight material deviation from the "narrow" optimum marginal conditions established in Part I of this study.

In other instances, an enterprise can be of such importance in a given community that it will find it easier to provide collective consumption facilities of the type discussed in the preceding section for the whole community rather than for its members only. To the extent that collective consumption occurs more frequently in the labor-managed system—as we have argued earlier—so also will participation in community affairs.

13.9: *Labor Management and Industry Structure*

Inherent in the labor-managed system is a remarkably consistent tendency, or set of forces, working in the direction of a smaller optimum size of operation of firms and thus to a more competitive industry structure than in any other market economy. In this context we may recall five instances established earlier in our study. First, we have found that with the regular technologies of the first kind (leading to U-shaped cost curves for capitalist firms) the labor-managed firm will always produce less than a capitalist firm in a long-run equilibrium provided that the capitalist firm makes any profits. Second, we have found that with a (competitive) infinitely elastic demand curve and constant returns to scale there will be no impetus for the labor-managed firm to grow, while the profit-maximizing capitalist firm, *ceteris paribus*, would have to grow to infinite dimensions (this *reductio ad absurdum* only underscores the difficulty of preventing oligopolistic or monopolistic tendencies under capitalism). Third, we have found that with constant returns to scale—that is, with a technology of the second kind— monopoly or oligopoly power is impossible in equilibrium for any other firm but one employing only one man. In a realistic context this shows not only that strict constant returns to scale starting from zero output are a virtual absurdity, but also that in the very frequently occurring situation where we have increasing returns for a while followed by constant returns for a very wide range of outputs, the equilibrium must occur within the range of increasing returns whenever the firm has any market power. This means an optimum size of operation which may be only a small fraction of what it would be for a comparable capitalist firm and, in turn, a far more competitive structure for the labor-managed industry. Fourth, we have established unambiguously that a product-differentiating and sales-promoting firm will always be smaller and engage in less aggressive advertising under labor-management than under capitalist conditions as long as the capitalist makes positive profits. This again implies more competitive market structures under labor management.

Fifth and finally, we have shown earlier in Part III that the locus of maximum physical efficiency, which is also the locus of competitive equilibrium for the labor-managed firm in the long run, will normally be shifted toward the origin, that is, toward lower levels of output, owing to the diminishing power of incentive with increasing sizes of the firm, as compared to its position given (by the production function) for labor of invariant quality. As the reader will find easy to realize, the argument can also be extended for situations other than the competitive one, that is, for situations where the demand function has some finite elasticity.

In this section we are coming to a sixth, and possibly most powerful, force of the labor-managed system leading toward competition. Stated very briefly, the essence of the argument is that much more than in any other system, through what we may refer to as the operation of the subsidiarity principle, the natural enterprise (or firm) unit will generally be defined by its location—that is, in most cases, will coincide with the plant. An extreme example may illustrate the point. Consider a giant capitalist firm: let us say that it is composed of one hundred independent plants employing a thousand workers each. This is a perfectly normal occurrence in a capitalist economy, prompted by various forces, and generally associated with at least some degree of monopoly power. Having a hundred plants means having at least a hundred times higher total profits; hence those who control the firm, whether stockholders or management, are perfectly happy about the state of affairs. Not so in a labor-managed world. Those who have the power of control are scattered in a hundred different plants, with presumably different locations, and they certainly do not want to delegate representatives—in a most inefficient and cumbersome way—to some central governing body from which the executive direction would flow back to the individual plants. Nor with income sharing would they want to have their payrolls depend on the performance of ninety-nine other plants. Thus, all other things being equal, the single giant corporation in the capitalist environment would much more likely be a part of a labor-managed industry containing one hundred autonomous firms.

We certainly do not intend to suggest that this is the necessary outcome. Economies of scale combined with monopoly power are other forces which may work in the other direction, that is, toward integration. Consequently, we can say only that, compared to other systems, there is a strong and unique tendency toward full plant autonomy. But even if there are reasons for integration of the type just mentioned, two important things must be kept in mind. First, such tendencies always can be handled through public regulation and the resistence to breaking up will be far less strong in the labor-managed world on grounds of the centrifugal forces noted above. And second, except for marketing and advertising there is hardly any scope for economies of scale which could not be realized either on the plant level or by means of interplant (and thus, interfirm) market transactions.

In summing up our argument, we may elaborate a little on what is called the principle of subsidiarity which we have invoked at the outset. The principle states that in any dealings involving social groups, it is most efficient and desirable to find always the lowest number of men consistent with a given task or function. Using more technical language, what is involved here is a maximum decentralization of social affairs, but one *constrained* by the condition of reasonable feasibility. Our case of decentralization to the plant level is a very good example. It is a constrained maximum decentralization into independent and autonomous decision-making units; any further breaking up of the plant-firm into entirely independent and autonomous firms would clearly not be reasonably feasible in the same way as commercial policy of the United States could not be reasonably handled by the fifty independent states. On the other hand, it would be possible to have larger units, such as the hundred-plant entity of our above example—that entity, however, would not fulfill the condition of a maximum. Pushing the argument a step further, my conviction is that the single most important reason for the comparative inefficiency and lack of success of the centralist socialist economies is the gross neglect of the subsidiarity principle on the part of the managers of these economies.

13.10: *Labor Management and Externalities in the Real World*

In the context of a "dehumanized" labor-managed economy we have shown in Part I that external economies or diseconomies can be present, and have effects on the efficiency of resource allocation equally as undesirable as those of the same market distortions in a competitive capitalist economy. In the context of our analysis of the special dimensions developed here, it is a perfectly legitimate question to ask whether the new dimensions—that is, new functions, faculties, and responsibilities of labor—are to be expected to increase or moderate the losses in social efficiency imputable to external economies and diseconomies.

We need not reach too far for the answers to the question. In fact, several of the arguments presented in the earlier sections of this chapter contain the answers in particular cases—answers mostly favorable to labor management. Before we turn to a more specific explanation, a generalization may be attempted: by virtue of the fact that under labor management those who hold power and control also happen to be to a considerable degree those who suffer or benefit from external effects, there is a strong presumption that the processes leading to the correction of the effects of externalities will be more direct and more effective than they would be in other economic systems. It cannot be expected —except under special situations—that the entire loss of social efficiency will be eliminated under labor management; but, using the analytical framework of Chapter 7, one can be reasonably sure that the distance between the social optimum and the actual market solution, measured along the opportunity cost function, will be significantly less in a situation involving what we refer to as the special dimensions than in the "dehumanized world" of Part I.

Explanation through a set of examples is most convenient. Suppose, quite realistically, that in a given community there are a few large firms—an iron foundry, a steel mill, a chemical plant—strongly polluting air and/or a local stream. The marginal unit of output is worth significantly less to society than its price because its production also involves the external social disutility (of breathing dirty air or drinking dirty water) which has not entered as a real cost into the product's valuation.

Now under labor management those who suffer from the pollution, most of them likely to live in the immediate vicinity of their plants, are also the managers who can decide to take out part of their income in the form of clean air or water, and either spend some funds on purification or, conceivably, restrict production. Contrast this with the capitalist or Soviet-type centralist situation in which the owners who have control (shareholders or the state) are far away and in which the managers are likely to have their homes somewhere sheltered from or less exposed to the pollution.

If we change our example to include large numbers of firms—in order to conform to the customary theoretical framework of competitive conditions—the argument still holds. It is true that action taken separately by an individual labor-managed firm now will have little effect on remedying the situation. However, the entire working population of the town, in their capacity of managers and decision-makers of their respective factories, now can "collude" to clean their air or water. Such a concerted action by either the owners or managers of non-labor-managed firms again is far less likely, largely for the same reasons as in the small-numbers case.

It will be objected that one can cope with externalities through political action. This undoubtedly is true; but the argument holds equally for a labor-managed economy as for any other. What is more important, as manifested by some of the "greatest of democracies" of today, often a hundred years has not been enough for political action to move against social ills far worse than air pollution.

On the other side of the spectrum, turning now to external economies (rather than diseconomies), the line of reasoning is quite analogous. The externality of improving skills and the over-all quality of the labor force is a fitting illustration: the marginal unit of output of a firm having an important training side-effect is now worth more to the society than its price, part of the social contribution not having been cleared through the market. The labor managers can now undertake to increase or intensify production so as to reap additional external benefits where marginal private cost and benefit calculations would make a capitalist entrepreneur arrest expansion.

13.11: *Some Concluding Generalizations*

The entire discussion of Part II, and in particular that of the foregoing nine sections, all point in the same direction. The labor-managed firm, more than any other productive organization, tends to be—or at least to resemble—a living organism. First and foremost, this manifests itself in the unity of purpose of the entire working community— that is, attainment of the greatest satisfaction for everyone.

But as with a human being, the maximization of satisfaction cannot be reduced merely to the maximization of monetary income. As we have seen in so many instances, there are many dimensions to what we understand here by satisfaction—some of them even implying, or involving, a certain desirable relationship or a set of relationships with the social environment of the firm.

Another manifestation of the labor-managed firm's resemblance to a living organism can be seen by its adaptability and flexibility. For example, a firm operating on order, where each job is quite substantial but where the frequency of orders is not perfectly regular, can adjust much more easily than any other firm to such a situation by slowing down its activity at certain times and operating at a peak performance never attainable by other firms in times of high demand. A capitalist firm, in a similar situation, might have recourse to layoffs at times of slackening demand and barely increase its output in proportion to overtime—rigidly remunerated at a high rate—in periods of high demand.

Alternatively, say, in the case of developing countries, the problem of the so-called dual economy is far less likely to arise precisely because of the labor-managed firm's adaptability to local conditions—not to mention the perhaps even more important fact that in a labor-managed world an international transfer of physical assets could never be divorced from a transfer of control.

Not unrelated to what has just been said is the quality—or property—shared by most if not all labor-managed firms of having a home. This quality which can also be thought of in terms of belonging certainly is one of living organisms—and it has most significant, even if hardly describable, welfare implications, whether for a family or a labor-managed firm.

Perhaps the most immediate and easily grasped manifestation of the organic nature of the labor-managed enterprise is what we might term its internal hygiene. Like an individual with respect to his members, the firm will take great care to preserve the good health and safety of its participants as a matter of natural instinct, where similar care might constitute an irksome and often significant cost item in a firm of another type.

But we do not have to prolong the account of the properties giving the labor-managed firm its organic character. The unprejudiced reader will find it easy to do so if he so desires. Rather, as a final task of the present chapter, let us make an attempt to formalize what is essential in the arguments of this chapter and what all these arguments have in common. To do so we have only to expand the analytical apparatus of the foregoing chapter.

In fact, not only does the analysis of Parts I and II involve an oversimplification of the labor-managed system (as we have argued already), but so does—even if to a lesser degree—the analysis of the foregoing two chapters of Part III. The objective function of the labor-managed enterprise does not include only the income per laborer and the degree of effort (as defined in the preceding chapter), but it contains also a large number of other more or less quantifiable variables such as these reviewed in the various sections of this chapter.

All the variables of the objective function are connected by a feasibility frontier (or transformation locus) illustrated by the concave surface abc in Figure 13.11.1. Two dimensions, that reflecting income per laborer (Y) and that reflecting effort (E) are known to us from the earlier discussion and so is the transformation locus ab corresponding to these dimensions. But we have now introduced a new variable Z to represent the new variables—or dimensions. The latter category can be quite broadly interpreted, including not only the variables explicitly noted thus far, but also many others, even those that usually are

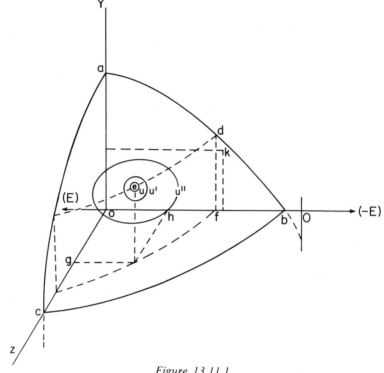

Figure 13.11.1

claimed to contradict the basic postulate of income maximization; for example, the rate of growth of the enterprise or the level of employment in the community surrounding it can alternatively be thought of as the variable Z.

As is indicated by the concentric equal-utility (indifference) lines drawn on the transformation surface, the collective maximum utility is attained at point e, corresponding to the level of effort measure by oh, to the level of income per laborer measured by fd and a (composite) dose of the other variables entering the satisfaction of the working collective measured by og. Clearly, the degree of satisfaction is unambiguously higher than that offered by a non-labor-managed enterprise, the feasibility frontier of the latter being represented by a rectangle such as that defined by points o and k. The facts that ab passes above k, that ab is a smooth (rather than rectangular) transformation locus, and that we have a third dimension Z all can be thought of as imputable to labor management.

It is true that both the E and the Z dimensions of the objective space of the labor-managed firm may contradict the postulate of maximization if income per laborer is narrowly defined as a monetary magnitude. Such a contradiction disappears, however, as soon as we define income as real income—or Fisherian enjoyment income; indeed, with such a redefinition, point e effectively is one of income maximization. And even if it was indispensable for analytical purposes to confine ourselves to narrower definitions of income in some parts of this study, the labor-managed firm should never, in the final analysis, be understood in any other context but that of our multivariate objective function.[3]

[3]Some may find it useful to conceptualize the approach of Parts I and II as one involving a fixed point on the E-axis and the absence of the Z dimension, whereas the more general analysis of the preceding chapter suffers only from the absence of the z-dimension, or more exactly from the absence of the many variables represented by Z.

14. Entry, Expansion, and Exit of Labor-Managed Firms

14.1: *Introduction*

In the preceding three chapters, we have discussed a large number of specific characteristics of the labor-managed firm and, in the chapter immediately preceding, we have come to the conclusion that many specific characteristics make the labor-managed productive organization resemble a living organism. What we have not discussed yet, some might say contrary to the natural order of things, is the problem of the birth and growth of such organisms—that is, in more conventional terminology, the problems of entry and capital expansion. Also, we have entirely omitted thus far the question of death, or exit, but this is a far less serious omission because such an occurrence is a pathological event rather than a necessity in the realm of organizations, especially of the productive type. The purpose of the present chapter is to study these and related questions.

The material which we want to cover falls into two distinct parts, descriptive and institutional on the one hand, and formally theoretical on the other. Even though we consider the two parts to be of equal importance, it may be more logical to take up the former first and then the latter. To each we devote four sections. In section 14.2 we first turn to the institutional aspects of entry and growth—that is, to the creation of new firms and their expansion, and the alternative forms which these can assume in a labor-managed system.

In the subsequent section we discuss the questions of exit or liquidation of labor-managed firms, together with the related problem of reduction of operations. A closely related problem, often raised by critics of the system presently discussed, is that of responsibility and risk-taking in labor-managed firms; we take it up also in section 14.3. The next institutional subject, treated in section 14.4, concerns the less developed countries. In fact, the problem of entry and creation of new firms in such countries is quite serious, and may constitute in some

280

instances the dominant limitation of economic development. The labor-managed mode of entry and firm operation has some special properties which can do away with such a limitation. In section 14.5, we study the problem of entry in relation to inventive activity and innovation.

Under the heading of formal analysis we must first handle the problem of the investment decision. We considered a part of it in Chapter 11 when we discussed some of the properties of the investment function in a labor-managed economy; we will complete our analysis in section 14.6. Section 14.7 is devoted to the problem of interfirm efficiency of allocation of scarce investment resources in a labor-managed economy, given the individual firms' investment criteria. In the next-to-last section, we comment and elaborate on some comparisons between investment decisions in a labor-managed firm and a comparable capitalist firm made by Benjamin Ward.[1]

Finally, in the last section we discuss the problem of mobilization of funds for entry and expansion, together with some theoretical implications of alternative forms of such mobilization. All of this discussion is conducted in the context of an individual firm. Some other, more aggregative and institutional aspects of financing will concern us in Part IV, especially in Chapters 15 and 18.

14.2: *The Entry and Expansion of Labor-Managed Firms*

The concept of, and motivation for, entry of new firms into an industry is not entirely new to us. In Part I we have dealt with them extensively, but we did so in terms of what we may call their "minimal" or "most primitive" form. We recall the postulate, used both in the context of industry and general equilibrium analysis, that in the long run entry will take place whenever the supply (or availability function) of labor is higher, at the going income per laborer, than the labor force actually employed in firms already in the industry, or the economy, as the case may be.

In the western-type theory of the capitalist system, the treatment of entry is not much more detailed than that which we have offered in Part I for the labor-managed system; but the oversimplification of the problem is perhaps less objectionable. It is usually postulated that the capitalist economy is endowed—more or less as a free good or service —with an unlimited number of entrepreneurs, or an unlimited amount

---

[1] *The Socialist Economy* (New York, 1967).

of entrepreneurial skill. And such entrepreneurs enter in whenever they observe a situation where profits can be made, establishing new firms and thereby reducing profits to zero—or to a "reasonable" level, depending on what exactly we understand by profit.[2]

Our concept of entry used in Part I is even more abstract. We do not even have an abstract person or "entrepreneur" on whom to pin the function which is needed for the analysis. What we have implied by our motivational rule for entry (recalled at the outset of this section) is that groups of workers who do not have employment or who can (presumably substantially) improve their income by leaving their current employment, organize in appropriate (equilibrium) numbers and enter industries offering highest returns. But it is clear that workers only rarely possess entrepreneurial and organizational faculties besides their principal qualification. Consequently, one must reflect a good deal more on the actual process or processes through which a new labor-managed firm comes into being.

Of course, the motivational rule for entry which we have used and developed in Part I should not be rejected; only its significance must be modified. Instead of taking it as a sufficient condition for entry, we redefine it as a necessary condition: obviously, it would be absurd to expect, as a rule, that workers would be forming new labor-managed enterprises under conditions less favorable to them than those which they are currently enjoying. And thus the void which our analysis of the present section should fill derives from, or is connected with, the sufficient conditions for entry. In other words, and more specifically, provided that the necessary condition of profitability (or advantage) to all potential members of a prospective labor-managed firm is fulfilled, what is the process, or what are the processes, which will actually bring about the creation, that is the entry, of that firm?

The truth of the matter is that there are four major sources of initiative leading to entry of labor-managed firms, and we should discuss them one by one. Two are "public" in nature—(1) local and (2) central government authorities; and two are social in nature (we are introducing here the term "social," symmetrically with the term "private" customary in western-type economics, to signify "other than public or official")—(3) groups of potential workers and/or employees organized for the purpose of entry, and finally (4) existing labor-managed firms.

---

[2]These postulates, more or less well borne out only in the United States, often are taken for granted more generally, even in situations involving developing countries.

Our discussion will be cast here in general terms, as far as possible with universal applicability. Some special aspects of entry in the less developed countries, entering mostly under headings (1) and (2) will be taken up in the section after next.

The labor-managed system offers a remarkable, and in the opinion of the present writer, remarkably efficient separation between creation (or procreation) of firms and the control of these firms. A local authority may be of the view that there ought to be an industry of a given kind in its district—probably half the local authorities in the world have such views, and perhaps most of them are justifiable on grounds of economic efficiency. In a western-type capitalist environment there will be very strong resistance to a new industry, or it may be impossible for the local authorities to do anything about it directly; at best, the authority will be in a position to design often cumbersome fiscal measures and hope that this will attract some industry, not necessarily the one which it would deem most desirable. On the other side of the spectrum, in a fully socialist environment, the authority will not only be in a position to create a firm which it wants to have, but it will also have to control it indefinitely, like a retarded child who never reaches independence—and the inefficiency of such situations, whether in the human or industrial realm, is obvious.

The labor-managed system combines the positive elements of the two extreme situations just considered: it permits the local authorities to act directly in establishing the enterprise, but once it is established, the authorities divest themselves of control, letting the labor-managed firm run its own affairs, and earn (outside of local taxes which can and generally will be levied) and distribute its net income. There will be only the transitional problem of selecting the management officers for the firm—that is, the executive branch—including a director of operations. The transitional period, however, can be very short, and even in the very first month a workers' assembly can be called on either to endorse the initial management team or to express a desire for its replacement in due course. The latter alternative, however, can be expected only rarely, as normally a rational basis for such action can arise only from an unsatisfactory actual performance.

In selecting the participants of a potential new labor-managed firm, the local authority will generally rely on its local human resources—indeed, in many situations, the availability of such resources must have given the initial stimulus to entry. Only for the highest echelons, in

smaller communities, would one expect the need of bringing in someone from the outside, an eventuality which can usually be solved by
advertising and competition.

The one weak point of entry originating with local authorities, as
compared to the three other alternatives, is that economic criteria of
efficiency may carry less weight than local, chauvinistic inclinations.
At least when larger projects are involved, there will normally be a need
for outside financing—that is, beyond the community or district—and
in such cases a more objective scrutiny of the viability of the project will
be necessary. In other situations, especially in lesser projects, some
degree of narrowly defined economic inefficiency, after all, should be
permissible, counting the contentment of the community at large as an
external economy.

Turning now from local to central government authorities, matters
do not change very much. One difference is that the central government will be likely to initiate entry of larger firms; in fact, for very large
ones of national interest the national or federal government, as the
case may be, is just about the only body which can assume the decision-
making capacity with regard to entry. Of course, this then fits very well
with the planning capacity of the central or regional authorities, if
planning belongs to the rules of the labor-managed economy. But we
will turn to this subject only in Part IV.

Another difference is that the central authorities will generally be in a
far better position to evaluate properly the feasibility and viability of
entering firms. For one thing, those making the decision will generally
be more detached physically—or locationally—from the projects, and
thus will put less, if any, emphasis on noneconomic criteria. For another, the central authorities quite certainly will be able to draw on
technical expertise superior to that available to the local authorities.
And finally, but not least importantly, the larger projects of entry
undertaken by the central authorities will involve considerably more
important investment resources and consequently also more important
development planning resources; and the latter, normally, ought to
guarantee a superior preliminary evaluation.

This completes our survey of the public sources of entry, and we can
now turn to the other two which we have identified as "social." The
first, entry initiated by groups of prospective members of a labor-
managed enterprise, comes closest to our abstract representation of
entry used in Part I. The process also is reminiscent of the formation
of western partnerships—but with the difference that once the firm is

created everyone working in it becomes a partner enjoying the same rights as anyone else. It will also be found that entry sponsored by prospective members usually—even if not necessarily—will generate smaller productive units. However, a social (or nonpublic) initiative often can be reinforced by public interest and involvement, and then lead, as a result of joint public-social action, to the formation of firms of any size. A significant advantage over public-sponsored entry is that the preliminary process of organization of the new enterprise normally will include—and often actually will be centered on—the formation and selection of the administrative organs of the enterprise, including the director. Thus the interregnum which we have identified as a necessity with the publicly sponsored entry of labor-managed firms will normally not arise.

The above comparison with western-type partnerships also suggests other similarities. Entry sponsored by groups of individuals is most likely to arise in fields of endeavor which require a high level of professional skill or qualification. It is in such strata that we most often find the professional skills combined with organizational faculties necessary for the formation of new firms. By contrast, an enterprise— if such an enterprise exists—requiring 99 per cent unskilled labor has a smaller chance to stem from the initiative of its prospective members. Also, to the extent that entry presupposes underwriting of a part of the investment bill, the more highly qualified individuals will generally be in a better position to fulfill the requirement. Of course, as we will argue in section 14.9 and in Part IV, self-financing of small social-based entries may not be the ideal thing. Concurrence or full funding by external sources may be preferable both from the narrow social viewpoint and from the viewpoint of the whole economy, because it normally will guarantee a minimum level of economic efficiency to the new entrant.

We come finally to the fourth, and in many respects most important, source of entry of new firms—namely, existing firms. A closely related subject, absent from the preceding three categories, is that of capacity expansion of existing firms, both as regards existing production lines and introduction of new products. The technical criteria of efficiency or desirability will be studied later in this chapter; for the moment we will concentrate on some general, nontechnical considerations.

Realistically, creation or procreation of new firms by existing firms is the most natural and organic mode. The matter can be argued on many different levels and from a number of different viewpoints. One consideration, but certainly not the most important one, is that an existing firm can serve as a source of financing for a new firm. As we have already said, questions of sources of financing will not concern us until later on. For now let it just be mentioned that the plowing back of incomes by labor-managed firms may not be the ideal procedure.

Far more important is that the existing firm is an ideal source and breeding ground for organizational and technical skills. Some of these have universal applicability; others pertain only to the specific type of trade or activity of the parent firm. But both are useful because normally the parent firm will first consider creation of firms with identical, similar, or related activities. This generation of skills has an objective or external value because it supplies the labor-managed economy with what is necessary for entry of new firms. But it also has an internal salutary effect because it allows a faster turnover of personnel within the parent firms and, in particular, promotion of larger numbers of capable men. Of course, there is an analogue to this in western-type firms, but only to the extent that expansion and creation of new productive units remains under the same roof of the same firm or corporation.

In the labor-managed world, on the other hand, the process of procreation may remain under the same roof, in which case it should be called expansion, but quite naturally it also can and very often will transgress the confines of the parent firm and become entirely independent. One argument underlying this contention has already been put forward in the preceding chapter. An expansion involving a new plant will normally lead to the creation of an autonomous self-management and income-sharing structure for that plant and thus, *de facto*, to the entry of a new firm. Second, and possibly more important, the resistance to the creation of competing firms, which is so natural to the capitalist system, is mitigated in the labor-managed environment by the fact that the "new competition," socially, is nothing but part of the old working collective. As between parents and children, resentment of competition may turn into the pride in good performance. In any case, if the market structure is perfectly competitive or anywhere near it, the parent firm need not be at all worried in the context just indicated.

This brings us to what we have referred to in Chapter 1 and Part I as the bee-swarm effect. Indeed, given the behavioral characteristics of a labor-managed firm, whether in the short run or in the long run, "good times" for the firm—that is, high prices and incomes per laborer—will generally be associated with a tendency to reduce the labor-capital ratio and, in some cases, this will also imply a tendency to reduce the number of participants in a given enterprise. As we have noted, this may cause, in the first instance, a dilemma for the working collective. Self-amputation is an unpleasant procedure in most instances, whether individual or social. It would appear especially difficult precisely because the times are good for the firm and incomes are high, and consequently better alternatives are hard to come by; attrition through retirement, proceeding at a comparatively slow pace, then is the only decent way for the working community to reduce its numbers outside of the generation of new productive units.

Entry is not only a very powerful tool in preserving the equilibrium conditions of the parent firm but also, as we have seen in so much detail in Part I, it is a highly desirable phenomenon from the point of view of efficiency of global resource allocation. For example, recall from Chapter 7 that after a change in relative prices it is precisely entry that makes the general equilibrium point move along the production frontier in the direction of a new efficient equilibrium. Without it, at best, no such movement would occur and, at worst, we might witness movement inside the production possibility arc, and in the opposite direction. Under some institutional arrangements with regard to financing, moreover, the good times and high incomes in the parent company may also provide the necessary wherewithal for the new entrant.

We may conclude this discussion of entry on the same note as that of the concluding section of the preceding chapter: The mechanics of labor-management in respect of entry and creation of new firms, as much as most other aspects of this organizational form, tends to resemble that of a living organism. Productive units are formed, expanded, contracted or liquidated much more in compliance with the needs and requirements of the human factor than in any other system. Where giant corporations or conglomerates are formed largely because of excessive availability of capital in a capitalist or neocapitalist environment, in the labor-managed situation the organization of a new firm or a new workshop may depend much more on the fact that if it were not created, some members of the working collective could not be efficiently employed. It will take the reader only a little additional reflection to verify the notion that these "organic" forces inherent in

labor-management are infinitely less likely to lead to inordinate con-
centrations of industrial power than the inorganic ones of modern
capitalism. A labor-managed industrial conglomerate is as likely an occurrence as the apocalyptic beast with seven heads and ten horns.

14.3: *Exit and Liquidation of Labor-Managed Firms and Some Related
Problems*

We may start our discussion of exit and liquidation by recalling
again the "minimal" treatment given to that subject matter in Part I.
In that part of the study, we simply postulated as sufficient for exit of a
labor-managed firm from an industry the condition that the labor-
availability function be entirely located above and/or to the left of the
(bell-shaped) income-per-laborer locus. In fact, as one would expect
in an abstract theoretical discussion, the condition is exactly the same
as that for a potential labor-managed firm not to enter an industry.
Clearly, such a postulate of symmetry is quite unrealistic.

In the same manner as in the preceding section with respect to entry,
we can treat the above condition as a necessary rather than a sufficient
condition. More specifically, we postulate that there is some "abstract
labor-availability function" defined in the absence of, or without regard to, the existence of the labor-managed firm, and that exit may but
need not take place as soon as the equilibrium income per laborer falls
below the level consistent with that function. Clearly, the availability
function that we have in mind here is that which served to provide a
necessary condition for entry, that is, the function prevailing prior to—
or, irrespective of—the formation of the working collective. But once
the firm is formed and has operated for some time, and a certain group
consciousness of the collective has formed, another function below, but
not entirely independent of, that just defined will become established
on which the actual act of exit or liquidation will depend. That function we can then think of as providing the sufficient condition for
liquidation. In some cases such a function can be influenced or rede-
fined by law or other act of public authorities.

There is nothing complicated in what we have just been saying,
even though our reference to our earlier theoretical concepts may give
the impression of complexity. All that is meant is that for a firm to
enter an industry the equilibrium income per laborer must be of a certain magnitude, and that for the same firm to leave the industry, the
critical lowest income generally will be less than the critical income

for entry; moreover, we have suggested that the minimum exit-income may be influenced or even defined by public authorities.

But let us now take a closer, more detailed and more realistic look at the phenomenon at hand. As we have suggested already, liquidation of a labor-managed firm will depend heavily on the incapacity of the firm to disburse, over a sustained period, a sufficiently high income. But the act of exit can assume several different forms. First, the firm may simply be forced to shut down because most or all of its workers, acting individually, have left it. Second, the workers' collective may take an *ad hoc* decision to liquidate. Third, the collective can write into its statute—or constitution (as we have explained it in the preceding chapter)—a provision halting operation when and if income per laborer declines below a certain level. Finally, the authorities may intervene on an individual or nationwide level and define—in the same spirit as some western governments define minimum wage rates—a minimum acceptable income, below which liquidation or other special proceedings must be engaged in.

Clearly, some very important definitional considerations come to mind at this point; how to treat depreciation charges on invested capital, and how to treat interest on and amortization of outstanding debt. For example, it would be irrational from everyone's point of view and socially inefficient to shut down when income per laborer declined below a given level, the latter being computed after all interest and amortization charges.

We can get rid of one potential complication for purposes of our analysis, which after all is a theoretical one, by assuming that all initial financing of the firm was done through sale of bonds (in the manner discussed in Chapter 9) and that depreciation charges on physical assets are disbursed, simultaneously, as retirement. Interest payments, on the other hand, are taken out of current gross income. All outside claims and liabilities of the firm are thus disposed of by the firm by the time its capital assets are fully amortized, and presumably the firm must engage at that time in a new and independent financing, retooling, and production period. In this way, the two major outlay categories that we have to be concerned about are interest charges, and amortization.

Both will normally be claimed by a single person or by a bank or other institution. At the time when the workers' community comes to the point of not being able to pay the minimum incomes—however defined—while still honoring its payments, the future of the firm will clearly have to be worked out in cooperation between the firm and the creditor. It would surpass the scope of this study to enumerate the alternative steps and modalities that could be recurred to in this context. Let it only be noted that once the working collective approaches the creditor with a specific set of alternatives, the creditor always can make a rational decision among these alternatives. Of course, bilateral-monopolistic gamesmanship, including bluffing, can be involved here, especially when there are no objective grounds for establishing the minimum acceptable income per man. It is at this point that clearly stated intentions in the enterprise statutes, or minimum incomes defined by public authorities, can play an important and salutary role.

Moving in the direction of a realistic situation, we should note that normally in enterprises which have been operating for some time under satisfactory conditions, the working collective will find it desirable to establish a reserve fund to cope with short- and even intermediate-run losses in gross income. Beyond depletion of such funds—or even prior to it—the firm also can recur to short-run borrowing and keep its income per laborer at the minimum required level in that way.

But perhaps the most important real palliative against exit and liquidation of labor-managed firms is the high degree of flexibility and adaptability of such firms, noted already in the preceding chapter. Even if the statutes of the enterprise contain provisions regarding the minimum acceptable income, such statutes—like state constitutions—can be revised in periods of emergency. Rather than shut down and possibly lose all income, the workers' collective may take the decision to work with substantially lower incomes, expecting return to better demand conditions or expecting modernization and substantial increases of productivity.

Especially when the general level of demand is low for an entire industry, or for an industry in a particular region, it is quite unlikely that those who would lose their jobs through liquidation would find alternative employment. Under such conditions the flexibility and adaptability of the labor-managed firms may be a question of life and death.

To give an illustration, the textile ghost towns of New England—embellished by collapsing brick walls of what used to be prosperous mills fifty or eighty years ago—would not have degenerated to their present state if the industry had enjoyed the degree of flexibility and adaptability spoken of here. And a far less painful transition or reorientation for the whole region could have been found. The notion behind these assertions is that the motivation of a capitalist entrepreneur is quite different from that of the labor managers running the firms that we are speaking about. While the former will make his decision to close or relocate his factory on a fairly cold-blooded profit-and-loss calculation—and thereby neglect the social factors that objectively ought to go into such a decision—the labor managers will be able to take into account all or most of the human hardships that liquidation would entail.

Perhaps this is an appropriate place to point out a common fallacy of western economic reasoning. It is often argued that the capitalist entrepreneur is entitled to extra profits—that is, profits over and above some normal cost of capital—because he carries the burden of the risk of liquidation. But in reality, the real burden of the risk is borne, far more than by anyone else, by the workers. Where the capitalist entrepreneur may lose a part of his bank balance or the value of his common stock, thousands of workers may be losing their livelihood for years. If, then, returns in excess of a normal return to capital—such normal returns being built into the labor-managed system—were justifiable as a premium for risk taking, the system discussed here would be vindicated.

Another and certainly more important argument belongs to the present section. We will conclude our discussion by developing it. In my experience, the most frequently heard and supposedly the most weighty argument used against the system based on labor-managed firms is what we may refer to as the "plundering effect." This argument says that the working community, which is given the management and the usufruct of the firm without having the actual full ownership of the productive assets, might "plunder" these assets, thereby transforming the limited form of ownership to a full ownership through the distribution of current incomes.

The fallacy of the argument can be argued on two levels, one behavioral, the other more institutional. In general terms, the behavioral argument is that one usually does not cut the branch on which one sits, or does not bite the hand that feeds one. Indeed, the plundering effect always implies transformation of productive assets into nonproductive assets, and thus implies short-run enrichment in exchange for long-run inability to provide livelihood. Of course, on the individual basis, one can invoke the argument of *après moi le deluge*—the individual worker after having plundered having the possibility of joining another enterprise—but the working collective, acting as a social group, cannot do the same. In its mind, first and foremost, must always be the survival of the enterprise. But even in the context of the individual worker, the argument is based on far less faith in the moral qualities of the worker than he deserves.

All this is said, and is valid, even in the absence of any control or enforcement on the part of public authorities and on the part of the financial lenders. In the real world, such control can always be guaranteed—if for no other reason, and through no other channels, but tax reporting and auditing for fiscal purposes. And thus we have a double safeguard against the plundering effect. This is not to say that it is entirely and absolutely excluded, but its incidence can be expected to be far less frequent than criminal acts and business practices in non-labor-managed situations.

14.4: *Formation and Entry of Labor-Managed Firms in Less Developed Countries*

More than savings or foreign exchange availability, lack of entrepreneurial technical and organizational talent constitutes in many less developed countries a real limitation on development, or what is sometimes referred to as development takeoff. Moreover, attempts by central authorities to alleviate such a limitation through conventional means can involve some other drawbacks which may render the application of such means very difficult, if not impossible. In this context, policies designed for the formation and entry of labor-managed firms, and labor management itself, can in many cases supply the solution of the problem.

Let us now be more specific and first spell out what the problem actually is in its conventional form. We will do so very briefly, through a highly stylized example. We are in a less developed country, which among other economic deficiencies experiences a complete lack of expertise and know-how in respect to the forming and running of industrial firms. The obvious necessity is to secure such know-how abroad or at home through training and education of some of the most talented young men in the country, respecting roughly at least some overall plan with respect to the future structure and composition of the industrial sector. Suppose that one thousand potential directors of specific productive firms are now available, together with supporting technical and other personnel, and the country goes ahead with the development of its industry. The country decides that the efficient form in which it wants to engage is one characterized by markets and decentralization. It has two alternatives: development of a capitalist or of a labor-managed industry. If it chooses the former, it gives (lends) each of the thousand men, say, a hundred thousand dollars and, in twenty years, there will be, if the program is successful, say, five hundred prosperous firms and five hundred millionaires. The takeoff objective will have been achieved, but at the cost of a comparative distributional inefficiency of having one industrial sector run by five hundred extremely rich men, whose outlooks and other psychological attributes may be far from ideal and who, moreover, by virtue of their money may be trying to run or influence public affairs to their own advantage. But what is most important, these five hundred men will have reached their exclusive positions for no merit of their own. Their education as well as the initial endowment will have come from national savings collected through taxation, inflation, or some other means which implies reduction in consumption by all, including the very poorest.

Thus the solution just described, currently aimed at by a substantial number of developing countries, while not bad, is at best a second-best solution. And this is not to mention the fact that the system thus developed will carry within itself all the general inefficiencies of conflict of the type shown or implied in this and the preceding three chapters.

On the other hand, retracing our schematic itinerary from the point at which the developing country has decided to engage in a decentralized and market-type industrialization program, but postulating that each of our thousand men and his supporting staff were entrusted with a hundred thousand dollars to form labor-managed firms, the results in twenty years will be different. There will be an industry without internal conflicts, allocationally as efficient or more so than the other, and entirely devoid of undeserved and unjustified distributional absurdities; more specifically, the five hundred millionaires will not be there. And actually, owing to the flexibility and adaptability of the labor-managed firms, so important especially in periods of takeoff, there may be seven and not five hundred firms surviving out of the initial thousand. And in addition, in each of the surviving firms, besides production, a very concrete and practical instruction in democratic processes will be going on—perhaps the most efficient way of reaching the much more difficult and abstract stage of full political democracy.

14.5: *Invention and Innovation in the Labor-Managed Economy*

Next to the argument of "plundering" discussed two sections back, perhaps the most important criticism of the labor-managed system is that it fails to provide, or provides inadequately, the stimulus for major inventive and innovating activity. By "major" we mean activity involving normally a full-time occupation and dedication, and we distinguish it from "minor" innovating activity, generally arising as a by-product or external economy of other primarily productive occupations; we recall that the latter type of innovating activity was discussed in the last chapter, where we found that the labor-managed system actually favors it to a considerable extent.

The purpose of the present section is to discuss in general the problem of invention and innovation in the labor-managed system and, while doing so, also to answer the above criticism. Defining invention as the development of new productive processes or new products, and innovation as the introduction of inventions made in the past leading to increased economic efficiency of one kind or another, our first question is: How well is a labor-managed system likely to perform by way of stimulating invention?

The central point of the critical argument referred to above is that in a labor-managed economy a potential inventor will not be able to introduce his invention in a firm of his own and thus derive the scarcity rent associated with the invention. While the first part of the argument obviously is true—except of course in situations where the inventor can handle the production individually—there are many other ways in which the inventor can derive the benefits from his invention. Actually, even in systems where direct exploitation by the inventor is possible, this alternative is becoming less and less frequent, and other methods are becoming prevalent—methods which can be used equally well in the labor-managed economy.

The first method is for the inventor to dispose of his invention by selling the patent to an established or a potential labor-managed firm. He may do this in one of a number of ways, ranging from forming a partnership (i.e., small labor-managed firm) with a few of his friends, with a provision for gradual disbursement of the cost of the patent, to auctioning off the patent in a competition among a number of labor-managed firms and possibly an official institution. Alternatively, inventors who want to minimize risks, or who need to work in a team of other men with similar qualifications, or who cannot subsist while working on an invention, can be engaged by a research department of a (presumably large) labor-managed firm or can work in a labor-managed firm whose primary purpose is invention. Still another alternative is for the official authorities themselves to provide all of these and other outlets for inventive activity.

Actually, more than anything else, the answer to the initial criticism, and to the whole problem of incentive for major invention, will depend heavily on the institutional arrangements of a particular labor-managed economy. It is certain that the authorities together with the productive sector of the economy can produce an environment at least as conducive to major inventive activity as any other economic system. On the other hand, it is also true that in a purely "liberalistic" labor-managed system relying exclusively on market forces in all of its economic performance, the inventor's activity might be hampered to a degree, but certainly not made impossible, by his incapacity to engage in direct exploitation.

When it comes to innovation, the labor-managed system *in general* is likely to be equally as, or somewhat more efficient than, other decentralized market systems. In the *specific*—and realistically most likely—case of a socialist labor-managed economy, however, the system appears to have a significant (perhaps a formidable) edge over other decentralized market systems. The "slight" advantage of the labor-managed system *in general* in the sphere of innovation derives from the absence of conflict between labor and management in that system and thus avoidance of such lasting anomalous resistances to innovation as featherbedding and the overscrupulous matching of tasks with official qualification (such as having special men in movie production for moving flower pots).

The considerable edge of a socialist labor-managed economy resides—to state it in the most summary manner—in the very fact that productive capital is owned by the entire society, which can demand that capital be embodied in the most productive conceivable physical and other assets. In other words, the socialist ownership, almost by definition, precludes the existence of monopolistic advantages based exclusively on withholding of technological information by some firms from the others.

The institutional forms through which the spreading of technological knowledge, and thus the universalization of innovation, in a socialist labor-managed economy can take place are varied. Organizations and associations of individual industries, officially or autonomously organized, are among the most logical and probably most efficient alternatives. Universalization of innovation within the labor-managed sector, through similar associations, may also prove desirable in a mixed economy including both private and labor-managed sectors. The benefits derived in this way for the labor-managed sector can serve as an infant-industry protection of the sector in the early years of its existence.

14.6: *The Investment Decision in the Labor-Managed System*

The subject which we want to discuss in this section is not entirely new to us. In Chapter 8 we have already discussed, with regard to a national aggregate investment function, the variation in physical investment as related to variations in the rate of interest. Of course, such a discussion had to be based on a theory of investment. Also, in a somewhat different, more streamlined and more abstract setting we have examined in Part I the relation between the cost of capital assets, or of the use of capital assets on the one hand and utilization of capital on the other.

The purpose of this and the subsequent two sections is to study the investment decision as realistically as possible—that is, leaving out any theoretical streamlining—at the same time putting emphasis on the individual investment decision for an individual firm, rather than studying the effects of many such decisions on aggregate investment. Although any one firm can consider simultaneously several investment projects or one project at varying levels of size or intensity, we find it preferable to speak, to begin with, about a single well-defined project which is invariant in size. The problem then is whether and why such an investment project will be constructed (undertaken) in a given labor-managed setting. It will be noted that at this stage of our discussion the distinction between projects for expansion of existing firms and for development of new firms becomes nonessential. More will be said about this matter below.

The critical magnitude—or ingredient—entering the investment decision is also known to us already from Chapter 8. We only have to present it here somewhat more carefully in more general terms than we did in that chapter. We may refer to the magnitude as the net multiperiod income per laborer, and use for it the notation A. For simplicity, we assume that there is only one type of labor, but the reader should find it easy to alter the analysis to include alternative assumptions. The more or less philosophical problem arising from the fact that in the future over which the discounting operation is performed different individuals may be employed at different times we dispose of, as before, by postulating that all members of the labor-managed firm are equals, whether in time or in space. We will refer to the number of those employed in period (year) j as L_j. The initial cost, if any, of a project we again will call C_0, and the net returns—that is, net income of the enterprise—in period j we will refer to as R_j; it must be emphasized that R_j *always* pertains to the total or integral operation of the firm and *not* to some particular returns imputable to a particular project.

Moreover, we can realistically assume that the working collective of an existing enterprise or the founders of a prospective enterprise, even at the time of the investment decision, envisage a certain rate of increase in the incomes per laborer, reflected by a function $f(j)$ with $f(0) = 1$. With all these assumptions and the additional one that there is a perfectly competitive capital (i.e., loanable funds) market with a single rate for all maturities and for both borrowing and lending,[3] we can now spell out the definition of A as

$$A = \frac{\sum_j R_j(1 + i)^{-j} - C_0}{\sum_j L_j(1 + i)^{-j} f(j)} \tag{1}$$

$$j = 1, 2, \ldots, n$$

where n can be thought of as the "reasonable" time horizon, or planning period of the existing or newly entering firm.

Perhaps an example may illustrate this somewhat uncommon concept of multiperiod income per laborer. Suppose that it is computed, for a given firm after it undertakes a specific project, to be $1,000. On the assumption that all the evaluations entering the computation are correct, this means that 1,000 times $f(j)$ dollars will be generated for each and every man currently employed in all periods $1, 2, \ldots, n$. Of course, if the time horizon n is finite, it must be made sure that after the n periods there are just enough realizable assets left to pay off all outstanding debt at that time.

For an existing firm contemplating a discrete investment project, two magnitudes A can be computed: one with the project undertaken, call it A_1, and the other in the absence of such a project, A_0. In the latter

---

[3]Admittedly, these assumptions are unrealistic; but it will be realized that they are customary in the present context, and also that they can be altered without fundamental difficulty, but also without adding anything basically new to the analysis.

case C_0 in relation (1) becomes equal to zero. The obvious criterion for undertaking the project then becomes

$$A_1 > A_0 \qquad\qquad (2)$$

When the investment decision involves the entry of a new firm, clearly, only the magnitude A_1 makes any sense, A_0 strictly speaking being equal to zero. But this does not mean that all projects yielding a positive net multiperiod income should be undertaken. A concept of opportunity income—or alternative income—of those who would work in the prospective enterprise must be introduced. In practice, an a priori amount, which may be referred to as A_0, must be determined by the founders or the official authorities, or by consulting the potential members of the firm, and that amount is then introduced into the decision criterion, that is relation (2).

It ought to be realized that what we have referred to here as a discrete project may involve any number of physically different projects —for example, construction of a new plant, repair of the old, and development of a mechanized transportation facility within the undertaking. What makes such a collection a single discrete project is that it is considered as an invariant package. If variation in the composition and size of the package is permitted, obviously, A_1 should be computed in the way indicated above for all such packages (recall that in all cases the calculation involves the inclusion of the existing firm, if any) and the one package with the highest A_1 should be selected.

If, alternatively, a limitation of investable funds is present—that is, if C_0 cannot exceed a prescribed maximum—the investment decision still remains simple and based on relation (1). Only in this particular case, all the packages involving C_0 in excess of the limit must be eliminated. The (now constrained) maximum A_1 still is the objective.

14.7: Capitalist and Labor-Managed Investment Decisions Compared

In the context of an existing firm, the investment decision in a labor-managed economy as presented in the last section can be assimilated to that of a capitalist firm. Supposing that prior to the project being undertaken the multiperiod income per laborer A_0 is the same as the contractual wage-remuneration of a fully comparable capitalist firm— that is, supposing that the capitalist "analogue-firm" makes zero profits measured at present discounted value over the entire planning period— then for a given project the capitalist firm will make exactly the same investment decision as the otherwise identical labor-managed firm.

More specifically, the capitalist firm will, for the same market rate of interest, reject the project which the labor-managed firm would have rejected, and vice versa. This conclusion should be easily understood, because if what was taken as income per laborer in the labor-managed situation without the project, A_0, is taken as contractual labor remuneration in the situation without the project in the capitalist firm, the preproject profits of the latter firm must by definition be zero; and if the labor-managed firm accepts a specific project, A_1 must exceed A_0, and thus if each laborer kept receiving A_0—as is the case in the capitalist alternative—a positive residual of $(A_1 - A_0)$ times the number of labor units involved could be extracted, which is nothing else but the increment in (and also the totality of) the profit of the capitalist entrepreneur. But such an increment is exactly what the capitalist looks for in order to engage in the investment project.

We can thus conclude and summarize what has been shown thus far by saying that if the capitalistic equivalent makes no profits, then investment decisions in the two systems will be identical. In fact, this is only another version, in a new context, of a conclusion already obtained for long-run equilibria of the firm in Part I.

The logical corollary of this is that the decision-maker considering a single new project in the labor-managed system can put himself into the shoes of a capitalist investor who initially makes zero profits—and then just follow the precepts of capitalist behavior.

The logical next question is how the investment decisions within the two systems compare when initially the capitalist makes positive profits—that is, pays his workers wages falling short of the income per laborer in the other system. Retaining the postulate of *ceteris paribus* for the two types of potential investor, the answers are not too difficult to obtain, provided that we are willing to be less than absolutely rigorous.

Using L_0 for some average measure of number of labor units involved prior to the project and L_1 for a similar measure pertaining after the project, it is clear that the change in profit on the part of the capitalist $(P_1 - P_0)$ can be approximated by

$$P_1 - P_0 = (L_1 - L_0)(A_0 - W) + L_0(A_1 - A_0) \qquad (3)$$

where W is the fixed wage paid by the capitalist before and after the project.

It is clear that if labor employment increases or is not changed too much by the project (with by definition $A_0 - W$ positive, $A_1 - A_0$ positive

—that is, acceptance of the project by the labor-managed firm), this must lead to the acceptance by the capitalist because the left-hand side of (3) then also must be positive. On the other hand, if the project is highly labor saving, that is $L_1 - L_0$ is negative and large in absolute value, the first product on the right-hand side of (3) will become negative and large and thus can more than offset the second term, thereby rendering $P_1 - P_0$ negative, and thus leading to rejection by the capitalist firm.

A far less relevant mirror image of these two conclusions is that if initially the capitalist is losing money, that is $A_0 < W$, a strongly labor-saving project can be accepted by the capitalist even though it would be rejected by the labor-managed firm and that a project having other than strong negative effect on employment may be rejected by the capitalist even though it is accepted by the labor-managed firm. The reader will find it easy to verify these two conclusions from relation (3). Using that equation, he will also be able to establish other significant results bearing on the relation between investment decisions under the two systems.

The results derivable from relation (3) are not entirely new. Some of them were obtained in a different manner by Ward.[4] Ward further concludes, also consistently with (3), that the labor-managed firm will tend to invest in more capital-intensive projects. This is illustrated by the fact that if $L_1 - L_0$ is negative and large in absolute value, the labor-managed firm may invest where the capitalist would not; of course, this presupposes something that Ward only implies, namely that the capitalist initially makes positive profits, that is $A_0 - W > 0$.

The tendency toward higher capital intensity of investment projects is further considered by Ward as a factor affecting the comparative efficiency of resource allocation; to that subject we shall now turn.

14.8: *The Investment Decision and Efficient Resource Allocation in the Labor-Managed Economy*

In this section we want to ask how well the rules of the game of investment perform in allocating scarce investment resources throughout the labor-managed economy. We will not be able to answer the question completely, nor is it possible or useful to treat it rigorously. Rather, we will attempt to explain some of the main tendencies of

[4] Benjamin N. Ward, *The Socialist Economy*, pp. 210, 211. Unfortunately, Ward's diagrammatic representation is somewhat unclear.

general investment allocation inherent in the investment criteria of section 6 of this chapter.

Throughout the present discussion, we will assume perfect knowledge of future investment returns on the part of actual and potential investors. Especially because of the interdependences which must exist among projects—for example, investment by one group in a shoe factory will have entirely different returns if another factory is also constructed by another group—the assumption is absurd for a realistic fully decentralized economy. We make it nonetheless, because we will be able to postulate imperfect knowledge only in conjunction with the economic planning discussed in Part IV. Here let it only be noted that one of the most significant contributions of planning, in any otherwise decentralized system, is precisely the avoidance of inefficiencies stemming from gross imperfections of knowledge and foresight on the part of the individual investing units. It also ought to be noted that the assumption of perfect knowledge is probably the most frequent in all discussions of the problem at hand, whether in connection with a labor-managed or any other economic system.

As we have already suggested in Part II, the investment criteria of section 6 have one important good effect. They tend to equalize incomes per laborer among firms and other potential investors; and as we know from Part I, this is desirable not only on grounds of equity, but also and for some perhaps primarily, on grounds of a higher degree of Pareto-type efficiency. The argument underlying this conclusion is simple, and we have stated it already in its crudest form with reference to entry of new firms and unemployment. It will be noted that for potential entrants who are unemployed, the critical index of opportunity-income $\bar{A}_0$ will generally be the lowest of all A_0's in the economy, and thus the impetus to undertake a given project will be the strongest for these entrants. And this in turn will generally be translated into the allocation of investment funds to the group with the lowest $\bar{A}_0$ and hence into an increase in the lowest income; but the same must hold also in an economy without unemployment. With about equal access to information about potential projects for all, the richest firms—that is, those with highest A_0's—will find it most difficult to find viable projects where $A_1 > A_0$, and even if they find some, the marginal gain $(A_1 - A_0)$ may be so small that they may not find the project really worth the effort.

The tendency toward equalization just explained will be even stronger, and be realized more rapidly, in a realistic context (found even in the richest countries) of loanable funds rationing. The margin $A_1 - A_0$—a random estimate anyway—will then become an important index of the viability of a particular project and hence of the desirability to make the corresponding loan. For any institution charged with plan implementation, the margin can serve as an equally important indicator—but this brings us again into Part IV.

The tendency toward equalization of incomes per laborer throughout the labor-managed economy has another very important and, fortunately, desirable effect. Suppose that each project is variable in size and is pushed by each actual investor to the point where, given the market rate of interest, the last dollar spent on it keeps the corresponding income per laborer unchanged (i.e., we have reached the maximum income per laborer). If now the incomes per laborer are equalized—or approximately equalized in a realistic context[5]—a reallocation of a marginal, say, thousand dollars from one project to another can only reduce total national income and product, income per laborer having declined in both. On the other hand, if incomes per laborer are not equalized, then funds reallocations among projects—even though projects are carried to optimality given a single competitive rate of interest—may be desirable because they lead to a higher national product.

We can thus conclude that the investment mechanism of the labor-managed economy will produce a tendency or convergence toward Pareto-optimality, as much as an equally idealized capitalist system.[6] This conclusion seems to be at odds with Ward, who argues that Pareto-inefficient investment decisions can be taken in the labor-managed economy because in some instances, identified in the preceding section, a labor-managed firm may invest even when the profit of a capitalist would decline. Provided that equalization of incomes per laborer is attained, Ward's argument appears to me as fallacious. The criterion which he uses as indication of Pareto-inefficiency, that is, a decline in capitalist profits, is irrelevant. What counts is the equalization of factor returns. In the general equilibrium setting— which must be used if we want to speak about Pareto-efficiency—the

---

[5]In the context of our discussion in Chapter 12, it also ought to be specified that the equalization or approximate equalization pertains to incomes corresponding to identical intensities or efforts of labor.

[6]We are using the qualification "idealized" primarily to recall the central assumption of perfect foresight which is the ingredient necessary for optimality in both situations.

decline in profits (note that the profits here and in Ward's writing[7] are a residual over and above the interest cost of borrowed capital) may have resulted from a movement either away from or toward, or even along the locus of, Pareto-optimality.

14.9: *Mobilization of Investment Resources by the Labor-Managed Firm, and Some Related Problems*

In considering an individual labor-managed firm thus far we have been focusing on the demand for, and the utilization and allocation of, investment resources. With respect to the mobilization of such resources very little specific has been said—or assumed—beyond the postulate of a perfectly competitive loanable-funds market where the labor-managed firm could borrow (and in fact at times lend) at a given rate of interest. Indeed, if it could be expected that in most instances such a loanable-funds market condition would prevail, not much more would have to be said in the context of an individual firm. Unfortunately, such is not the case, and thus we have to push our analysis somewhat further.

Two sets of considerations—not entirely unrelated—must concern us. First, the market faced by an individual labor-managed firm may not be a perfect one; the firm's borrowing and lending rates may differ, and especially the former rate may be related to the volume and other modalities of the loan. Second, the labor-managed firm may want to, or more exactly be brought to, engage in self-financing.

The first thing to realize is that in the case of a perfectly competitive market ruled by a single rate of interest there would be no scope for self-financing. Whenever the criterion of section 14.6 were satisfied at the going rate, the necessary funds could be borrowed and an increase in the income per laborer generated without any recourse to collective savings on the part of the firm. Of course, this does not preclude the possibility that individually—or even collectively—the members of the enterprise can save, using the same credit market and thus contributing indirectly to the financing of their own project. But this can be considered an entirely separate operation, not having anything to do with the investment project.

Another important fact is that even if the firm desires to engage in self-financing for one reason or another, this normally will not conflict with or vitiate its fundamental operating principle of maximization of

[7] *The Socialist Economy*, p. 212.

income per laborer. The firm's interest still will be to maximize the income per laborer, and then, using any number of conceivable criteria, it may allocate from the maximum amount (per laborer) a certain fraction to self-financing, that is, to the generation of future income. But as indicated by our criterion of section 14.6, the future income entering the objective function again must be the income per laborer; if it were otherwise and, for example, maximization of growth or of *total* income were pursued for the future, this might imply a reduction of income of each individual member of the enterprise. Of course, it is conceivable that the labor-managed firm would see in its bigness a positive value irrespective of what this does to the incomes of its individual members. But such "megalomaniac" firms and corresponding economic systems, as inefficient from the social point of view as they are from that of the individual workers, are not our concern.

Let us now turn to the various departures from a "perfect" loanable-funds market. For example, it can be required by the lender (bank, official lending authority, or other) that a certain proportion of each investment project be currently financed by the firm. This requirement may, as in Yugoslavia, be supplemented by the requirement of full repayment from current income of the firm at a later date; in this case the labor-managed firms become fully self-financed in the long run. Alternatively, the borrowing and lending (i.e., deposit) rates may be different, and/or the lending rates may be different for individual households and firms acting collectively. Moreover, liquidity of savings undertaken through an external intermediary will normally be quite different from that of reinvestments.

In all these instances, the transformation of present into future income—that is, saving—by the members of the enterprise will be permitted to assume alternative and nonequivalent forms, depending on whether it is performed individually or collectively (through actions taken by the firm), and depending on whether intrafirm or extrafirm channels are employed. And accordingly, it will be perfectly rational under some conditions to choose the intrafirm collective transfer, that is, ploughing back of earned income.

The point is clearly brought out by Pejevic,[8] who considers an extreme situation: suppose that the labor-managed firm cannot borrow at all collectively, and suppose that—as required by our definitions of Chapter 1—it is impossible to convert assets of the labor-managed

[8] See his paper presented to the Meetings of the Southern Economic Association, November 1968.

enterprise into income. The workers of the labor-managed enterprise have now two alternative ways of saving, that is, of converting present into future income: (1) to save through investment in their firm, and realize future income in the form of current returns (the principal embodied in the assets of the firm being irrecuperable), and (2) to save through some external intermediary (bank or other) where a contractual rate of return as well as the principal are recuperable. Clearly, it will take a far higher current rate of return before the first way of saving is chosen.

If the assumption of no borrowing for the firm is replaced by a less stringent and more realistic one, permitting of partial external financing of projects—coupled possibly with future repayment from current income—the rate of return need no longer be far in excess of the market rate of interest (on private savings) to induce ploughing back of current income. It must be realized that whether partial or full self-financing is required, no expansions of plant and equipment could ever take place without such financing; and it would be hard to conceive of a situation where no labor-managed firms could be found for whom it would pay to expand their capacity using retained earnings. Especially in the context of real situations where technology and product designs are changing over time, modernization and corresponding investments may be imperative at virtually any cost.

That there is no scope for self-financing of labor-managed firms under certain capital market conditions should not detract from the fact that the arrangement can be quite inefficient and hence quite undesirable for the labor-managed economy as a whole. Accordingly, it ought to be recurred to only in situations where the increments in national savings secured through self-financing could not be obtained in any other way. In other words, self-financing would seem to be justifiable only in the early stages of economic development, when the national savings availability constitutes a binding constraint. But even in early stages of development, as we will show in Chapter 18, a mere ploughing back of the competitive income share of capital—the share which must be paid by the labor-managed firms to the owners of capital assets, society or otherwise—will normally be sufficient to generate a significant rate of economic growth.

The inefficiency which we have just alluded to resides primarily in the fact that the subjective costs of capital to labor-managed firms will be bound to vary considerably, and this in turn will tend to produce an allocation of investments throughout the economy falling far short of the optimum. Suppose for example that no basic charge is levied on the assets of the enterprise, and thus that the cost of capital to the firm consists exclusively of the interest charges and repayment of principal on the financial loans.[9] Such costs may be very high in the first one or two decades after investment, and thus call for a low capital-labor ratio. But once all or most of the cost disappears in older firms which do not expand further, there will be a strong tendency—via amortization and replacement—to adopt the most capital-intensive techniques. On the limit—and admittedly this is a *reductio ad absurdum*—if the technology (production function) were entirely subject to diminishing returns to labor, the "old" firm could not reach its equilibrium short of employing only one man. What has just been said for one firm holds also among firms: with self-financing the young and growing firms will tend to have high costs of investment funds and correspondingly high marginal productivities of (internal returns on) capital, while old firms will have low ones. The Pareto-inefficiency of resource allocation in such a situation is obvious. And even if a basic charge is levied on all assets of the enterprises, whether corresponding loans were repaid or not, the inefficiency just noted can at best be only reduced, but not eliminated.

A corollary of what has just been said is that major differentials as between firms in incomes per laborer actually earned need not be an indication of the efficiency and viability of the firms. Indeed, the apparent viability of the old firms, or a near failure of the new ones, may not be much more than an optical illusion.

Two more possible drawbacks of self-financing and the lack of a well-functioning capital market must be noted here. First, on the macroeconomic level, the comparatively low subjective (opportunity) costs of capital just noted can, especially in more developed labor-managed economies, lead to unemployment of labor. There simply may not be enough capital in the self-financed firms to employ all available labor, given the subjective capital costs and the implied marginal labor productivity. The second difficulty arises in connection with entry and creation of new firms, so important for an efficient operation of the labor-managed economy. We have noted earlier in this chapter the important role that labor-managed firms can play in generating entry of new firms. It will be obvious that if the financing of such firms is to be secured from incomes of the parent firms the process will be seriously impeded compared to the situation in which financing can be secured from the outside.

[9]Amortization funds are not permitted here to be used for repayment.

Even if it is necessary to supplement the supply of investment funds over and above funds that would be available otherwise, it would be preferable to separate the fund-mobilizing function from funds allocation. For example, in a socialist situation, a producers' income tax can be levied (on top of current income of capital) whose proceeds are added to the supply side of a competitive national loanable-funds market. In this way not only will all funds be made available competitively to the most efficient users, but also, and perhaps more important, an outside observer representing the legal owner, society, will be able to pass judgment on the soundness of proposed investment projects. Also, such an observer may need the opportunity to influence the flow of national investment resources in accordance with a social development plan.

A careful reader may object that in the above discussion of inefficiency stemming from the age—or proportion of paid-off capital—of the labor-managed firms we have neglected the possibility that labor-managed firms may lend at a market rate of interest, and thus that we should have considered for the old firms the opportunity cost of the use of investment funds. One answer to this objection is that in a labor-managed system where self-financing—and thus first- and second-class assets—exist, retirement of real assets and depositing at interest the corresponding funds may not be permissible. The other answer is that if such retirement-cum-lending is possible, the absurdity alluded to above does not disappear, but is only altered. For example, with one hundred per cent repaid funds, an old firm can proceed gradually to retire all its real assets and all its laborers (participants) but one, with the last man (now director of a financial institution) earning the market rate of interest times the initial net worth of the enterprise. Contrast this with a situation of a perfect capital market with no self-financing, where retirement of real assets coupled with depositing of the corresponding funds at the market rate of interest merely indicates an orderly and efficient curtailment of the operations of a labor-managed firm.

We can conclude by saying that especially for the labor-managed economy, an investment-funds market as perfect as possible is imperative. Practices of self-financing inspired by or borrowed from the behavior of large western corporations are not only inefficient for a labor-managed economy but are literally against the very nature of labor-management. Indeed, labor-management is a way of separating man from the evils of, while retaining the positive aspects of, ownership, and self-financing with its implications is only a retrogression to an inferior state. Of course, we are not arguing here that self-financing should be prohibited and external financing made mandatory; the labor-managed firms should always be free to invest from their own income if they so desire. Rather what we do argue is that such capital market conditions should be secured as to make self-financing unnecessary in most, if not in all cases. The allocation of income (after taxes) to alternative uses, including investment, must be a fundamental right of the labor-managed enterprise.

PART IV
ECONOMIC POLICY
AND PLANNING

15. Basic Institutional and Legal Forms of the Labor-Managed Economy and its Implementation

15.1: *Preliminary Considerations*

In the preceding three parts of the study we have developed the theory of the labor-managed system as it pertains to the behavior of autonomous decision-making units—firms and households. We sometimes refer to that portion of economic theory as "pure theory." On the other hand, in Part IV we will take up subjects deriving from activities of the public sector—that is, the government—directed toward the labor-managed economy for purposes of direction and regulation. The material is organized under three major headings: (1) the institutional and legal setting and the implementation of the labor-managed economy; (2) problems of economic policy (microeconomic and macroeconomic); and (3) problems of economic planning and plan implementation. Subjects (2) and (3) will occupy our attention in the subsequent three chapters; the present chapter is devoted to (1).

The subject of the present chapter is a very important one. Not only does it fill an important and thus far empty space in our general theory of the labor-managed economy, but it may be among the most helpful in permitting the reader to visualize the various concrete forms that a labor-managed economy might assume. Indeed, the abstractions of economic theory developed in the preceding fourteen chapters may not always be the best guide to the practical reader's imagination.

Judging from the many conversations that the present writer has had with applied economists and policy-makers, there are scores of concrete problems to be answered. The question perhaps most frequently raised is whether the Yugoslav-type socialist version of the economy is to be considered the only possible one. A related question, cast in a more dynamic context, is how one can make the transition to—or implant—a labor-managed system, whatever its final "equilibrium" form. Another question, or in fact a whole spectrum of questions, is directed toward such problems as the legal form of ownership, actual guarantees to the lender, and imputation of losses in bankruptcy. Finally, there is the problem of what institutions, if any, are required for a smooth and efficient functioning of the labor-managed economy.

Any country that might contemplate the formation of a labor-managed economy, or merely of a labor-management sector, would have to be concerned with the concrete problems of the type just outlined as much as with the more theoretical and abstract questions of the efficiency of the system treated in the earlier parts of the study. It is not my intention—nor is it within my capacity—to develop a cookbook recipe for labor management, but we ought at least to make a serious first step in the direction of a *rapprochement* between abstract theory and actual implementation of the system; we ought to do so precisely for the benefit of those who might consider labor management as a real alternative.

These introductory considerations lead us logically to the outline of this chapter. We will begin in the subsequent section with the consideration of possible alternative forms of a labor-managed economy, as related to over-all national economic strategy. In section 3 we will discuss some important problems of transition to a labor-managed system, while in the concluding section 4 we turn to institutional questions. In particular, section 4 is devoted to what we refer to (perhaps for lack of better terminology) as the national labor-management agency, an institution—or a set of more or less independent institutions—designed to fill the needs of a labor-managed economy beyond those that can be taken care of efficiently by the labor-managed firms on their own.

15.2: *Alternative Forms of Labor-Managed Systems*

It must be clear that the basic characteristics of labor management expounded in the first chapter permit of diversification of the system, depending on other characteristics which were not explicitly included in the definition. The purpose of the present section is to identify and discuss briefly what we consider the most important among such varieties of the labor-managed economy.

The most convenient way is to use as a backbone of our exposition a general schema which will permit us to make the several distinctions. The schema is shown in Figure 15.2.1. Using two-ended arrows to indicate correspondence, we first make the distinction between the general categories of labor-managed systems on the one hand and western capitalism and Soviet-type systems on the other. While in the former

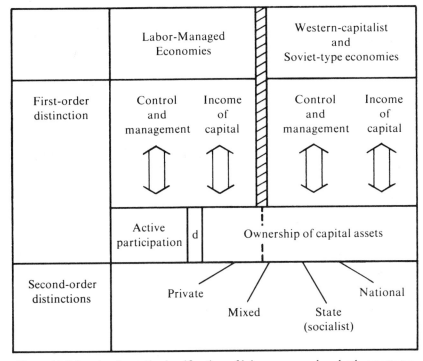

Figure 15.2.1. A schematic classification of labor-managed and other systems

income corresponds to, or goes with, ownership and control, and management corresponds to active participation in the enterprise, in the latter both functions—income and control—correspond to capital ownership. These are the basic characteristics which underly what we wish to refer to as the first-order distinction, which can be thought of as between humane and "dehumanized" systems. The distinction of the two "pure" systems permits us now to define a hybrid or mixed economy in which the two coexist—that is, in which a labor-managed sector is in operation side by side with another sector, which may be private and capitalist or state-owned and state-operated.[1]

[1]To avoid confusion with some other hybrid forms, we may refer to this one as the *first-order hybrid,* or first-order mixed system. Of course, some might argue—and probably correctly—that the first-order hybrid forms could never survive indefinitely. But this is not our concern at this stage of the argument where we are primarily interested in a comprehensive *taxonomic* survey. The matter is discussed, however, in my forthcoming study, *The Participatory Economy: An Evolutionary Hypothesis and a Development Strategy.*

Although this is not exactly on the main path of our exposition, it will be quite useful to point out that the first-order distinction just outlined lends itself to further categorizations. For example, a traditional producers' cooperative, or what is just about the same as the form referred to by some as "syndicalism," can be obtained from the definition of labor management in Figure 15.2.1 by deleting the dividing line marked d and substituting for it the word "and"; in other words, the system is one in which participation in ownership and in activity coincide. Alternatively, in partnerships of the American type we recognize a situation such as that just identified, but with an additional type of active participation by those—often very numerous—who have no share in control and management. Still another form is that of the many modern large corporations that are referred to as management-controlled; in these the dividing line marked d remains, but what is marked "active participation" in the diagram is a very small fraction of total participation, composed of the inner circle of higher executives.

Let us now return to the main path of the argument. Next to the first-order distinction which has just been considered there is a set of second-order distinctions. They are the far less important, even if the more traditional and better known ones; they pertain equally to the labor-managed and the non-labor-managed systems, and derive from the nature of tenure of capital assets. As indicated in the diagram, we can think of at least four important forms, depending on whether capital ownership is private, of the state—that is, socialist—mixed of one form or another, or, finally, national. The fourth alternative, just mentioned, is rather specific to our discussion of labor-managed systems, and we will enlarge on it several times in this chapter.

While in the non-labor-managed systems the distinctions just made are as a general rule important—in fact, most of the sociopolitical stratification in the twentieth century has been based on them—this is far less the case for the labor-managed economies where management of economic activity of productive organizations is not linked to ownership. Nonetheless, within the context of a labor-managed sector or economy it is possible to visualize a situation where all capital accumulation would be assumed by private savers, the corresponding funds then being loaned out in a suitable manner to labor-managed enterprises. It is another matter that the corresponding funds might be quite insufficient in many instances to finance a satisfactory rate of development, and it is also another matter that such a situation might entail existence of an inactive rentier class which might be deemed undesirable by the society.

Alternatively, capital formation might be entirely left to the state, financed from budgetary surpluses based on current taxation incomes and the returns on previously accumulated capital. It immediately follows that a hybrid, or mixed, situation is conceivable—and in fact quite likely in real situations—where there is tenure by both private individuals and the public sector. This can be identified as a hybrid or mixed system of the second order because it rests on the distinction of the second order.[2]

We finally come to our concept of *national ownership*. Since it is closely interwoven with the *national labor-management agency* to which we devote all of section 15.4, the reader will become best acquainted with the concept at that stage of the argument. However, we may attempt here a brief explanation, or definition. We understand by *national* ownership of capital a situation in which, after an initial funding by the state or private individuals in the form of irrevocable transfers, further additions to the capital stock are made through additions of the entirety of income of capital (paid, by definition, by the labor-managed firms using the nationally owned capital). From this definition of national ownership it follows that (1) no withdrawals from the earnings of capital can ever be made by anyone for purposes of consumption; (2) that the capital stock must grow as long as income of capital—that is, marginal productivity of capital, under competitive pricing—is positive[3]; and (3) that national ownership in fact is no ownership whatsoever in the traditional sense because it gives neither power of control nor a right to consumption to anyone; it only serves the nation (or a given society) adopting it as a vehicle for indefinite growth and expansion. The beneficiary of national ownership thus is everyone and no one at the same time. The social advantages of this form must be obvious.

Scores of further—we might call them third-order—distinctions could be made, depending on further specifics of the labor-managed economy. We will not go into these in anything approaching a systematic manner, nor will we supplement our schema to introduce them. Rather let us merely point out a few which seem to be of importance.

---

[2]Cf. the hybrid system of the first order defined on p. 313.

[3]In Chapter 18 we use a simple theory of growth in analyzing the development potential of an economy whose capital stock is wholly nationally owned.

Perhaps the most important set of distinctions turns around the question of self-financing by the labor-managed firms. We have discussed the matter at the end of the preceding chapter and concluded that self-financing may not be the most desirable way, even if it can raise national savings; we will also return to this subject in the context of transition strategy in the next section, and in the context of institutional solutions in the last. Here let it only be noted that labor-managed firms may be called on to generate part or all of their capital, even if they, as legal persons, are not owners of such capital. Thus we can think of fully externally financed firms, fully self-financed firms, and of mixed situations combining both modes of financing. In addition, it is possible to distinguish a fully or partly self-financed firm where the saver is not directly the working collective—that is, the enterprise—but rather a grouping of some or all its participants (such as a credit cooperative formed by the members, designed primarily to extend credit to the parent firm), legally separate from the enterprise, lending to the enterprise at a commercial rate, and borrowing from its depositors as individuals (rather than as a collective). In fact, many of the shortcomings of self-financing pointed out in section 14.9 can be avoided in this manner.

Another set of distinctions, related to those just made, concerns the nature of guarantees given to the lender by the labor-managed firms. There is a whole spectrum of solutions, including insurance schemes administered by independent insurance agencies (similar to small savings protection in the United States), reflection of the risk in a differential lending rate, and covering of risks on an actuarial basis, with uniform lending rates, by the lending agency. Again, more will be said in this context in section 15.4.

15.3: *Questions of Transition and Implementation*

For an individual, government, political party, or any other group that might be convinced of the wisdom of having a labor-managed system, a question perhaps more important than that of which form of the economy to adopt would be the question of how to perform the transition from an existing system to the labor-managed system. Obviously, nothing too specific can be said here because the answer to such a question would depend heavily on the particular social, political and economic conditions of the country where the implantation was contemplated. Nonetheless, some general observations can be made, and that is the purpose of this section.

In principle, and in the vast majority of cases, the transition is from what we have identified in our schema of the preceding section as the non-labor-managed system to the labor-managed system. More exactly, recalling the two major systems belonging to the former category, we can speak of a transition from western-type capitalism and from a Soviet-type command system. Perhaps more descriptively, we can speak of transitions *from the right* and *from the left.*

We may first speak of the former, which historically has never been attempted in a conscious and rapid manner, although in several western countries we may be witnessing a slow, more or less autonomous, and unconscious transformation. Further categorization may be desirable. The transition *from the right* can be (1) assisted, or (2) autonomous or spontaneous. Within the first category we may further want to draw lines between global and partial approaches on the one hand, and publicly assisted and privately assisted ones on the other.

Let us consider the *autonomous* alternative. We will argue that this alternative in fact does not offer much real possibility by pointing out the most important resistances, or obstacles, likely to arise in a liberal capitalist environment. Besides its main purpose, this discussion will also make it easier for us to identify the most important reason for what we have termed the *assisted* transition, and also the forms and scope of the assistance.

The pragmatic argument against the spontaneous transition is quite simple; it resembles the argument against spontaneous liberal capitalism as a vehicle of economic development. In both instances the approaches simply did not work historically in the majority of countries. But let us now try to identify some of the reasons why the autonomous approach did not work.

Probably the single most important obstacle to the spontaneous development of a labor-managed system within a capitalist environment is what we may call "the dilemma of the collateral." In a nutshell, this dilemma is the reluctance of banks and other potential leaders to lend without collateral—that is, without a share of "own" funds of the labor-managed enterprise—coupled with the tendency toward degeneration of labor-managed firms into partnerships, or other forms of second-class employment situations, where self-financing and collateral are present.

Indeed, especially for a small or newly entering firm, it is almost unthinkable in a western economy to receive full external funding—that is, funding which carries only income and repayment obligations, without participation in control by the lender and without participation by the borrower in financing. On the other hand, with collective self-financing by the members of the labor-managed firm (here we might more appropriately speak of a producers' cooperative) those who have contributed their savings will very often be reluctant to hire new workers on a basis of equality, and will make instead the implicit or explicit reservation that the newcomers are not entitled to the same benefits as the "founders." Even if this may not be apparent at first sight, a similar situation might be found in some farm cooperatives emerging from a land reform[4] where the "founding" families who were given the ownership of the land would be extremely reluctant to take in new members on a basis of equality; rather, and especially, if they were perfectly free to act, they would tend to hire additional help, if needed, as ordinary laborers at a fixed wage. It may be useful to note here that if the land were leased to the farm cooperative, an optimum adjustment of employment to the size of the holding without any status discrimination would be far more feasible. In addition, there would be the possibility of linking the leasing contract to the conditions of equality for all participants.

But what we have identified as the dilemma of the collateral is not the only obstacle to the spontaneous transition. Even if the large majority would be likely to benefit from labor management in the short run, and just about everybody in the long run, the majority of those who hold power, whether in capitalist industry, modern large corporations, or in labor unions will see in labor management a threat to their positions. For bankers, in a perfectly liberal environment, it is possible to discriminate in extending credit; for suppliers it is possible to withhold supplies; for intermediate-goods buyers it is possible to discriminate in the selection of sources of supply. Factual examples of all this certainly are not lacking. Nor can it be contested that social pressure can be exercised by, say, the business community on men possessing advanced managerial or technical talent not to join a labor-managed firm. It is unnecessary to prolong this discussion: the reader, if he wants, will find it easy to find many other obstacles to a spontaneous transition.

The obvious conclusion is that the transition from the right can hardly be accomplished unless it is assisted. There are several major objectives that any such assistance must aim at. First, there is a certain necessity for attaining a critical mass for the labor-managed sector.

[4]E.g., the *asentamientos* in Chile, operated collectively by a large number of families.

Indeed, the survival of an isolated specimen in a basically hostile and distrustful environment of another species is most unlikely. The second criterion is that of equal treatment. By this we mean fulfillment of the condition of equality of opportunity in all respects, guaranteed by law and enforced, if necessary, by appropriate sanctions. A third objective is to give a clear legal form and definition, for purposes of taxation, making of contracts, and so on, to the labor-managed enterprise. Finally, and perhaps most important, there is a need for an institution, public, semiofficial, or private, to serve the many and diverse needs of the labor-managed sector as a whole.

We have alluded to this institution already as the national labor-management agency and we devote to it most of the following section. Since we will return to the subject in much more detail, only a few general points are needed here. First of all, the agency, hereafter referred to as NLMA, would serve as the principal vehicle of full external financing of the labor-managed firm, and thus prevent what we have called above the dilemma of the collateral. Moreover, the NLMA could fulfill directly, or be instrumental in the fulfillment of, the other three above-mentioned objectives. Thus, a legal department would be charged with the realization of the objective of equal treatment, the investment and lending strategy would pursue the objective of a critical mass (or size), and other departments would handle the relations between the NLMA and the public authorities.

As we have already argued in the preceding section, in the case of *national* ownership of capital of the labor-managed sector, the NLMA would be the repository and administrator of that ownership. In fact, the national-ownership alternative would be the most desirable one for the transition from the right, because it would guarantee, subsequent to the initial funding, the independence of the labor-managed sector from the traditional sector of the economy. The initial funding, in turn, could be either public—provided that there was political support for it[5]—or private, or it could combine the two sources of funds. Of course, independence and exclusive adherence to the initial statutes of the agency would be imperative, whichever the form of initial funding

[5]In some instances special conditions rather than an over-all realization of the desirability of labor management might provide such a political will. For instance, in the United States, the problem of the inner city and the problem of racial minorities could be tackled through a special NLMA and labor management in the relevant areas. Not only would such an approach be economically more effective, but also it would have significant advantages on the humane plane as compared with the "black capitalism" or other solutions preached by the Nixon administration.

(in the case of national ownership) and whatever the form of ownership.

Finally, let us recall our initial distinction between the global and partial approaches from the right. The former implies a transformation of the entire economy into a labor-managed one at one time, while the second implies a transformation of only a part, perhaps a minor part, but large enough to attain a sufficient critical mass. In the very long run, of course, the partial transition is very likely to turn into a global one, but it need not; but this is not our concern here. On the whole, the global transition from the right is not only highly unlikely from the point of view of political feasibility—it is virtually unthinkable in a setting of political democracy—but it also appears as quite undesirable from the economic point of view. No a priori theory in social science can be as convincing as an empirical (experimental) test; this is especially so when those who must form an opinion are not just scientists but the entire population. Moreover, the partial approach in the period would be ideal not only to allow the people to exercise free choice and change their minds, but also to give everybody the possibility of comparing the two sectors. Of course, given all this, the conditions of equal treatment, critical mass, and an appropriate legal form for the new labor-managed sector would have to be scrupulously fulfilled. On the political plane, on the other hand, the strength of the partial approach is that it is highly democratic in spirit, not advocating the system for everyone but only for those who by free choice—political as well as economic—want to have it.

So much for the transition from the right; let us now turn to what we have called the transition from the left, that is, transition from the Soviet-type command system. There are some similarities and some differences between the two types of transition. In both, a significant gain in output and efficiency of resource allocation can be expected from the transition; the gains may be most impressive in the instances of transition from the left at a fairly advanced stage of economic development.

From the point of view of institutions, the transition from the left appears easier because it normally would involve a dramatic simplification of the institutional apparatus (along with decentralization and introduction of markets), whereas the transition from the right almost unavoidably calls for the formation of new institutions. Similarly, the transition from the left has a comparative advantage in the context of what we have referred to as the dilemma of the collateral. Indeed, investments in the labor-managed sector in this instance would have to be financed by some type of official NLMA, and the latter would have to follow given instructions in its policies; at the same time, degeneration into other than labor-managed forms of productive organizations could be prohibited as a matter of political decision.

From the doctrinal point of view, matters seem to be the other way round. As so many episodes drawn from the recent history of the Soviet-type systems tend to indicate, there is an enormous ideological ballast in these systems which makes any transformation in the direction of labor management extremely difficult. In the smaller countries of the block, in addition, the problem is compounded by the resistance of the dominant member; so much so that a full-scale movement toward a labor-managed form of economic organization in all the economies of east Europe may have to wait for endorsement and acceptance by the Soviet leadership. The transition from the right could be expected to be considerably less hampered by "official doctrines"; if there is a resistance in this context, it is one based on individual prejudices, conservatism, and the confusion of labor management with "socialism," rather than on a conflict of labor management with some well worked out and coherent doctrine of western capitalism.

Returning now to the question of institutions, it can be said that by and large even in the case of an approach from the left, there would be a role—perhaps not as decisive a one—to be played by an institution such as the NLMA. In this sense the discussion of the next section is also relevant for the transition from the left, even though in some details appropriate adjustments or qualifications would have to be made. For example, to have the NLMA financed primarily or exclusively from private (individual) sources would be highly unlikely in a country starting from a socialist Soviet-type situation. Similarly, there would be less scope, if any, for a legal division of the agency looking after cases of discrimination. And finally, the planning and research functions of the NLMA could be assumed by existing institutions devoted to these activities. At the same time, transformation of socialist—or government—ownership of capital into a national one, administered by a NLMA, independent in its current operations from the government,[6] would be most desirable.

Very likely the most serious problem that any economy approaching from the left would have to overcome would be that of a transition to a

[6]A status comparable to that of the United States Federal Reserve System may serve as an illustration of what is meant here.

"rational" price structure. By definition, the labor-managed economy is a market economy while the Soviet-type socialist economies are non-market economies with prices in many instances quite different from those that would result from market forces—or, for that matter, from a correct shadow-price calculation. Clearly, the imperative would be not to attempt any transition from one price structure to a new one, to prevail in a labor-managed equilibrium, too rapidly; this could be extremely damaging. Not only could serious misallocations result from an overly fast transition, but the chaos and inefficiency of such a transition might incorrectly be taken for an inherent characteristic of the labor-managed system.

Without going into any details, it seems that the best method of coping with the difficulties just noted would be to adhere to what may be called a "strategy of viscous prices." This strategy simply is one where each firm or industry is permitted to adjust its prices by at most some small percentage per unit of time—say one per cent per month—starting from the official prices of the pretransition period. (Of course, such a rule would have to be changed in case of rapid over-all price inflation.) At the same time, under the system of "viscous prices" all positive or negative social preferences for certain products would be embodied in a system of taxes, subsidies, and tariffs, these also being adjusted only gradually from their actual or implied pretransition levels to the desired levels. In this way, it would take some five or seven years before the final rational price structure were reached. Of course, in instances where monopoly or strong oligopolistic tendencies were unavoidable, price controls still would be necessary (see Chapter 16 in this context), also proceeding gradually from the initial price levels. But these situations could be quite rare, especially if over the adjustment period (of five years or so) an equilibrium rate of exchange and a free foreign exchange market also were sought—also through the method of viscous prices. Clearly, the advantage of the viscous-price strategy is that it gets the economy to the desired position eventually, but at the same time gives time to the decision-making units—especially firms—to perform a smooth transition, without drastic and sudden alterations in incomes, employment, factor proportions, and so on.

15.4: *The National Labor-Management Agency*

As we have indicated on several occasions in the foregoing sections, our purpose here is to discuss in greater detail the national labor-management agency.

The first point to be made is that the schema presented here should not be taken as an exact blueprint of the form that any such agency must assume. Rather, we want to indicate through the concrete case of the NLMA the principal functions of an organization—or set of organizations—fulfilling the needs of the labor-managed sector of the economy other than those that can easily and naturally be taken care of by the individual labor-managed firms themselves. Another important point is that what we present here is what we might call the "maximal version" of the NLMA, tailored primarily to the conditions of a

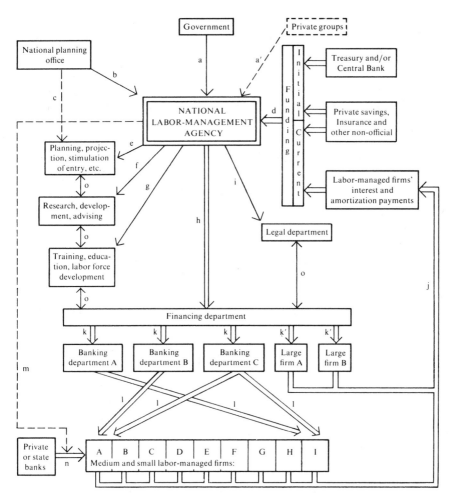

Figure 15.4.1. Schematic representation of the national labor-management agency

developing country, the approach from the right, and a mixed (partial) situation. But this should not bother the reader, since the agency in other situations could merely drop one or more of its functions or departments. For example, in the case of a global approach, there would be only little scope for a legal department, prosecutions of discriminatory practices against the labor-managed sector, by definition, being ruled out; but there still might remain the necessity to settle disputes among the labor-managed firms. Alternatively, the planning department of the NLMA in a socialist economy (approaching from the left) could be a part of, or identical with, the national planning office.

The schema of Figure 15.4.1 in its *broad outlines* is self-explanatory. The arrows connecting two or more elements of the schema indicate various types of functional relationship or interdependence. We have used double lines where flows of funds, whether capital funding or cur-. rent income of capital, are involved, single solid lines to indicate other major links, and broken lines for what we may call secondary (less important) links. Each of the connecting lines is marked by a letter of the alphabet, running from *a* to *o*. It is according to these functional links —and corresponding letters—that we can best organize our more detailed discussion of a national labor-management agency. In the rest of the section we devote a paragraph to each letter, or related group of letters.

a and *a'*: By administrative decision and/or act of the legislature the government establishes the NLMA, providing it with an appropriate juridical status, definition, and supporting set of rules or legislation which guarantees the agency an equal treatment with, and protection against, other sectors of the economy (if any). Initial funding will be discussed below under *d*. Alternatively (*a'*), the NLMA can be established by a private group or individual; but in that case certain legal questions (definition, protection, etc.) must be cleared by the government.[7] In addition, the founder, whether the government or other, would lay down a basic statute concerning the purpose, over-all rules of operation, selection of the director or the board of directors of the

---

[7]As an example of a private founder of an NLMA and of the labor-managed sector, the Ford Foundation could become the NLMA by being given all the assets of the Ford Company, without power to control but with an agreed income-earning power per unit of capital, while the control and management of the company itself were assumed democratically by the employees of the company. Beyond that point, of course, the principal funding operations of the NLMA (i.e., the Foundation) out of current income would have to be directed toward the further development of a labor-managed sector of the economy.

NLMA, and so on. The board of directors could be jointly appointed by the founder, the government (if the founder is private), and by the membership of the NLMA, that is, the labor-managed firms.

d: This represents the first step of the funding circuit. As illustrated, we have what might be thought of as the most likely real situation, where national ownership is combined with private lending to the NLMA; of course, either of the two could be the rule without existence of the other. First, we have the initial funding from official resources (in the form of direct transfers from the treasury, or through central bank funding using newly printed money), establishing the basis of national ownership, as discussed in section 15.2. Private funding, on the other hand, could either be in a form similar to that from official sources, that is, initial unilateral transfers, or as current deposits with, or loans to, the NLMA. Finally, we have current funding from the remuneration of capital by the labor-managed firms and their depreciation allowances. After many years of operation, the current funding of this type would be by far the most important, and keep the labor-managed sector expanding at a rapid rate.[8] In case of exclusively national ownership, this would be the only source of current funding.

h: The capital funds thus collected would be channeled to the financing department of the NLMA, which would further allocate the funds according to the basic statute of the NLMA, and in consultation with the other departments of the agency (see under *e, f, g, i*).

k and *k':* Two types of major users would compete for funds available for any given period: individual and independent banking units (*banking departments* in the diagram) of the NLMA and large firms in need of important funds. A minimum amount negotiable at this stage could be specified. There could be one or two dozens of the independent banking departments; assuming about the same number of large firms competing at any time for the funds available to the NLMA, the capital market at the stage *k* and *k'* would be quite competitive.

l: The smaller capital transactions—that is, all borrowing by medium and small firms and smaller sums borrowed by large firms—would be carried out through the intermediary of the independent banking departments. These departments, motivated by a maximizing objective and regulated by the NLMA, would compete among themselves in extending their credit services. The large number of the departments, in

[8]In this context, see the growth model in Chapter 18; note also that there we count only on current income of capital and not on depreciation funds.

turn, would guarantee to each individual borrower a treatment as objective and nondiscriminatory as possible. Indeed, if one department rejected a firm's loan application, the firm could still seek credit from any or all of the others.

m and n: In any of the mixed situations in which the labor-managed section is only one of the sectors of the economy, of course, each labor-managed firm could seek credit from the regular credit market. In particular, private or state banks could extend credit to the labor-managed firms. In fact—as indicated by *m*—the NLMA could serve here as an underwriter or guarantor of such loan transactions, thus rendering this possibility more attractive to the outside banks, and securing easy credit terms for the member firms.

j: Except for possible minor income (profit) margins by the intermediating banking departments, the income from loans extended would flow to the NLMA. The labor-managed firms would also normally be required to deposit their depreciation funds with the NLMA. Of course, some provision would have to be made that such funds would always be immediately available for replacement purchases.

b, c, and *e:* Of paramount importance to the labor-managed sector would be the planning department of the NLMA. Its principal responsibility would be to study trends within the entire economy in order to facilitate optimal entry and production decisions by the member firms. The department would provide the same information to the banking departments to improve the quality of their credit operations. In the mixed situation, in which there is a non-labor-managed sector, the planning sector of the NLMA would cooperate with the national planning office (and/or other comparable agencies) in carrying out the objectives of the national development plan. On the other hand, in an entirely labor-managed economy, the national and agency planning offices could become one and the same. Especially in mixed situations in which labor management is approached from the right (see the preceding section), the NLMA could play an extremely significant role in the carrying out of national development plans; indeed, in the absence of a labor-managed sector and an NLMA, the possibilities of action in western-type economies are rather limited.

f: As we have already argued elsewhere, besides the research and development activities of the labor-managed firms themselves, there would be a good deal of scope for such activities by the NLMA. In addition to actual research, the department would be concerned with efficient proliferation of new technologies, whether original or borrowed, acquisition of patents, and technical and administrative consulting.

g: In conjunction with the results and/or objectives of the planning department and the technical research department, long-range strategy in the sphere of labor-force and skill development would have to be pursued by a special department of the agency. In particular, the department would be charged with the elaboration of plans for training and education, especially on the level of advanced skill categories, and carrying out of such plans through scholarships, training and retraining centers, and so on. The department could also serve as a clearinghouse for information about job vacancies and labor force availability, and perform other related tasks.

i: The activities of the legal department would be directed both within and outside of the labor-managed sector. On the outside, its principal responsibility would be to defend the member firms against discrimination from the outside of the economy, and at the same time to serve as a legal adviser of firms in cases of conflict with nonmember firms. Similarly, the department would handle legal questions involving the labor-managed sector and the government. On the inside, besides dealing with interfirm relations, legal questions of debt liability by the members to the NLMA would be handled by the legal department. More specifically, we can mention in the latter context settlement of cases of bankruptcy, definition of liability by the concerned parties, writing of contracts and credit agreements, leases (in cases of land tenure), and so on.

16. Microeconomic Policy

16.1: *Introduction and Outline*

As far as economic analysis goes, we have already covered all major subjects except one: namely, the subject of the national (or global) direction of the labor-managed economy—that is, more specifically, the problems of economic policy and economic planning. We will devote the last three chapters of Part IV to it. The present chapter and the next discuss microeconomic and macroeconomic policies respectively. The emphasis in these two chapters is primarily on the mechanics of policy-making, such as, for example, answering the question of how a specific tax will affect such and such an economic variable; or alternatively, of how a specific inefficiency (e.g., a monopoly) can be controlled or prevented through policy within a labor-managed economic environment. In Chapter 18, on the other hand, we turn to the subject of economic planning, study the objectives and targets of the labor-managed economy, and—in part utilizing the "mechanical" results of Chapters 16 and 17—attempt to identify and understand the approaches through which the objectives can be attained.

Our specific task for the present chapter falls under six distinct headings, and we will utilize these headings for the subsequent six sections. In section 2, we examine, basically in the context of the theory presented in Part I, the effects of various instruments of economic policy on the main variables reflecting the operation of a labor-managed firm. It will be realized that what is meant here by "context of Part I" is a set of simplifying assumptions regarding the nature of the labor-variable, as it enters the productive processes of the firm; homogeneity, uniformity, invariant quality, and an over-all passivity in matters of management are the principal assumptions.

In section 3 we again study the reactions of the labor-managed firm to various policy instruments, but this time we do it within the context of the analysis of Part III, where at least some of the simplifying assumptions just mentioned are relaxed. We also attempt to present a balanced synthesis of the two types of effects within the labor-managed firm. In both sections 2 and 3, we study a perfectly competitive situation. The monopolistic case is examined in section 4, including (1) the problem of monopoly control aimed at eliminating monopoly inefficiencies, and (2) the effects of various policy instruments on a monopolistic labor-managed firm. Section 5 is devoted to the study of a competitive industry. Clearly, whenever the industry is composed of a fixed number of firms, the policy problem is extremely simple once the desired answers are found for an individual firm within the industry. However, the analysis becomes somewhat less straightforward when freedom of entry and the possibility of exit from the industry is envisaged.

The remaining two sections of the chapter contain analyses cast within a general equilibrium framework: both are directed toward the identification of various "frictional" inefficiencies which may arise in the labor-managed system, and to the corresponding policy-remedies of such inefficiencies. While in section 6 we are primarily concerned with the efficiency of resource allocation within a single industry, section 7 deals with similar problems in the context of a full general equilibrium analysis.

As the reader will realize—especially the reader who has read the first three parts of the study carefully—we can proceed very rapidly by building on, or referring to, the theoretical results obtained earlier. Only in rare instances will we have to use new diagrammatic or mathematical formulations; in most cases, our analysis in Part IV is nothing else, in the technical sense, than a straightforward extension or elaboration of what we have done before.

16.2: *Economic Policy and the Competitive Labor-Managed Firm (I)*

Let us first consider the effects of various policy instruments on the short-run equilibrium of a competitive firm producing a single product. To that effect, we recall the basic equilibrium (marginal) condition of equality between the value of marginal physical product of labor and the income per laborer, namely, using our old notations:

$$p(1 - T)X_L = [p(1 - T)X - p_K K_0]/L \qquad (1)$$

The only new thing now appearing in the relation is the term $(1 - T)$ where T is a constant sales-tax rate, so that both of the value products (marginal and average) are reckoned in terms of the net return per unit of sales to the firm after taxes; of course, p remains the market price, including tax if any, at which X is sold. Dividing both sides of relation (1) by $p(1 - T)$, we obtain

$$X_L = [X - p_K K_0 / p(1 - T)]/L \tag{2}$$

an expression which best lends itself to a diagrammatic representation of the equilibrium of the labor-managed firm. Such a representation is given in Figure 16.2.1. It is known to us from our earlier analysis, and

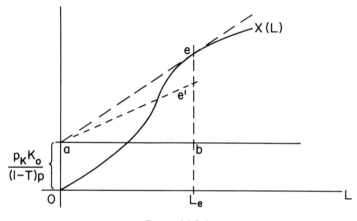

Figure 16.2.1.

thus we have only to recall that the equilibrium (maximum) income per laborer (as measured in terms of X) is given by the slope of ae (recall also that the segment be is nothing but the numerator appearing on the right-hand side of relation (2)). All the possible policy parameters are contained in the term $p_K K_0 / p(1 - T)$, and accordingly the effects of policy changes will be immediately obtained by translating such changes into the corresponding shifts of point a in the diagram. The imposition, or increase, of a sales tax will shift—*ceteris paribus*—point a upward. This in turn will make the line ae "roll" along the production function $X(L)$ to the right and upward, and the slope of ae will decline. Consequently, such a policy action will reduce the income per laborer, increase employment and output, and, of course, reduce the marginal productivity of labor. In other words, the backward-bending short-run supply curve of the labor-managed firm will shift to the right, owing to the imposition or increase of a proportional sales tax.

Exactly the same effects will be the result if the authorities, as a matter of policy, increase the cost of capital to the firm, p_K, through taxation or otherwise. Note that the increase in p_K will also shift point a in Figure 16.2.1 upward.

Recall that we make the same assumptions in this section as we did in Part I of the study; in particular, we assume a homogenous labor force of constant and exogenously given quality. Therefore, we can now consider the effects of an income tax levied as a proportion (not necessarily invariant with the amount of income actually earned) of income per laborer. The slope of the line ae' in the diagram indicates the income after taxes received by each member of the firm and is known once that of ae is given. Obviously, it will be at a maximum when the corresponding slope of ae—that is, the income per laborer before taxes—is at a maximum. Consequently, the income tax just considered will have no effect on the equilibrium of the firm except that it reduces the take-home pay of the members of the enterprise. But, of course, this presupposes that the take-home pay never falls below the level given by the labor-availability (supply) function; if it did, of course, the firm normally would have to shut down, or—along the lines of our analysis of Chapter 4—reduce output to take into account a positively sloped availability curve.

In the case of joint production in the short run, the results are analogous to those just obtained for income taxes and capital taxes (i.e., taxes altering p_K), and for sales taxes imposed simultaneously on all products; of course, in addition to the effects previously identified, we will also witness a substitution effect (in production) in favor of the product or products not taxed.

All that has been said thus far pertains to both technologies of the first and of the second kind (i.e., subject to increasing-diminishing and constant returns to scale). Turning to the long-run equilibrium, we have only the former technology in mind. The long-run effect of policy on a labor-managed firm producing under constant returns to scale, as we know, can have determinate effects on the output-factor ratios only, the corresponding absolute magnitudes remaining indeterminate.

Let us now invert the order of our discussion, and start with the tax easiest to understand, the income tax. On the same assumptions as before of constant quality, homogeneity, and sufficient labor-availability, it must be clear that the income tax will have no other effects on the operation of the labor-managed firm in the long run except the reduction in take-home pay. Indeed, the income per laborer after taxes is maximized when that before taxes is; and thus the original optimum conditions remain undisturbed by the tax.

The capital tax also need not detain us very long, as the long-run effects of variation in capital cost have already been studied in Part I. A policy-induced increase in p_K will shift, *ceteris paribus*, the factor-input allocation point along the locus of maximum physical efficiency in the direction of an increased labor-capital ratio; normally—but not necessarily—this implies an increase in the employment of labor and a reduction in the employment of capital. Total output may increase or decline, the former alternative, as we have argued in Chapter 3, being a somewhat more likely one. Finally, the income per laborer is bound to decline, and so is, correspondingly, the marginal product of labor.

A sales tax, obviously, also can but shift the factor-allocation point along the locus of maximum physical efficiency. To find out in what direction, we recall that in addition to relation (1), the long-run equilibrium of the labor-managed firm is defined by the condition of equality between the marginal value of capital and the price (cost) of capital, that is

$$p(1 - T)X_K = p_K \tag{3}$$

where $p(1 - T)$ again represents the amount actually received by the labor-managed firm per unit of output sold. With constant p_K and p, obviously, X_K must increase if T increases, and hence the movement along the locus of maximum physical efficiency resulting from an imposition or increase in the sales tax must be in the direction of less capital and relatively more labor employment. As before, this may imply either direction of change as regards output, but a decline is somewhat more likely. The income per laborer must decline.

16.3: *Economic Policy and the Competitive Labor-Managed Firm (II)*

In the present section, we want to use the framework of Chapter 12 to study the effects of various fiscal instruments on the behavior of the firm. It will be recalled that in Chapter 12 we relaxed the assumption of a labor force of invariant quality, used exclusively in its role of a factor of production; instead, we postulated that the effort supplied by a representative worker can and will vary with the returns associated with that effort, and that the arrangement of self-management will serve as the key vehicle of productivity and welfare optimization.

Specifically, let us take three taxes, the income tax, the capital tax (i.e., a tax altering p_K for the enterprise), and a sales tax, and ask how the performance of individual workers and thus the performance of the firm will be affected by their imposition, or alteration. The marginal adjustments of the conventional variety which have been studied in the preceding section are disregarded for the moment. In Figure 16.3.1, we

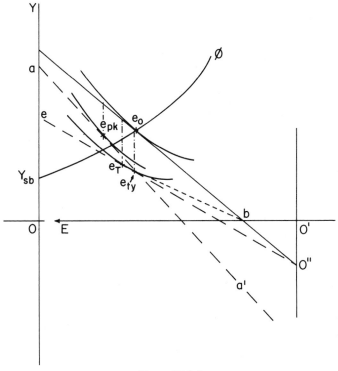

Figure 16.3.1

find the diagrammatic representation underlying the analysis; it is basically the same as that known to us from Chapter 12, so we do not have to elaborate on it.

Prior to the imposition of (or increase in) a tax, the collective (or coalition-type as we have termed it in Chapter 12) transformation locus faced by the workers of the labor-managed enterprise is $0''\,be_0$; it is drawn as a straight line, not because it would have to be, but because we have no special reason to postulate convexity of one kind or another and also because the results which we are after are basically independent of the convexity. Given that slope, we have derived the Engel's or income-consumption line Φ. Its over-all pattern indicates that—as one would expect—neither (real) income nor negative effort (i.e., ease) are inferior goods, and that the workers will supply the maximum conceivable degree of effort (prior to starvation) at the subsistence income Y_{sb}.

Suppose now that an income tax of some 45 per cent is imposed. Clearly, at zero income, none will be paid so that point b in the diagram still obtains as a feasible-opportunity situation faced by the representative worker. As income increases, however—that is, as we move (in respect to before-tax situations) along be_0 in the northwest direction—the 45 per cent income tax must be paid, so that the representative worker's feasible options are those given by be_{ty} ("ty" here indicates "tax on income"). The maximum satisfaction and hence the equilibrium solution will be reached at e_{ty}; the effort supplied and hence the output of the firm have not changed appreciably from the initial situation given by e_0, but the income of the representative worker has dropped by some 45 per cent, the corresponding amount now constituting government (or the taxing agency's) revenue.

The case of a sales tax is similar, only the pivoting of the collective opportunity-cost locus now is not around b, but around $0''$. The situation is comparable to that studied in Chapter 12 in respect to the supply curve of the labor-managed firm, and the fact that $0''$ is common to all the opportunity-cost loci simply reflects that with zero effort (and hence zero output) the cost (negative income) $0'0''$ cannot be affected by any tax imposed per unit of output or sales. As is shown in the diagram, we have chosen such a sales tax as would keep the typical worker as well off as the previously studied 45 per cent income tax. Clearly, the sales tax is of a lesser rate (some 30 per cent) than the income tax, and thus we find the equilibrium solution at e_T. With the same level of satisfaction (real income) on the part of the workers, the tax produces a slightly higher tax revenue and appreciably higher effort and output, and consequently it can be considered as superior to the income tax. This superiority will always be present, whether the new equilibrium point e_T actually corresponds to an increase or a decline in E from e_0. But it must be recalled that normally both points e_T and e_{yt} will be to the left of e_0; this is so because all the price-consumption lines should normally pass through Y_{sb} (except in the very long run as was the case with Φ' in Figure 12.6.2) on the Y axis, because "wiggling irregularities" of such lines are highly unlikely, and because with extremely high slopes of the transformation loci one would normally expect an asymptotic approach to the vertical axis originating at $0'$.

Our last tax, that imposed on capital or nonlabor inputs in general, appears as the most efficient. The corresponding transformation locus now is that illustrated by aa'. It leads to an equilibrium at e_{pk} ("pk" recalling that the effect which we have primarily in mind is that on p_K) which clearly, other things being equal, stimulates effort and thus output most. The output will be that generating income (before tax) given by the point on be_0 directly above e_{pk} (as shown by the broken vertical segment). Clearly, the favorable situation results from the very steep slope of the transformation locus aa'. It is so steep, actually more so than even the original transformation be_0, because with increasing effort and hence value of output and (more or less) constant costs of nonlabor inputs, the tax per dollar of sales should diminish. But even in the limiting situation, in which the nonlabor inputs would increase *pari passu* with E and the value of output, the transformation locus with tax would be parallel to be_0 and thus our new equilibrium would be on Φ; we would still be facing a situation superior to those equivalent in terms of real income (utility) but generated by the other two taxes.

The reader will realize that the aggregate effect of any of the taxes considered on the performance of a labor-managed firm will be the summation of the two sets of effects discussed in the preceding section and the present one. Actually, the summation strictly speaking is quite an intricate one because the parameters entering the decision-making process in one section are, or at least may be, variables in the other. As a first approximation, however, this may not be a very serious hindrance for reasons already expounded in Chapter 12. Let it only be recalled that we have concluded that variations in E normally should not affect too much the equilibrium condition of equality between the marginal value product and income per laborer; indeed, both sides of the equality will be affected in the same direction, and often by a comparable amount, if the effort of labor application changes.

It may be useful also to recall the main thrust of our conclusions. If we term as "unorthodox" the results such as the increase in supply and output from a tax, then what we have concluded in the present section tends to be even more unorthodox than the results of the preceding section. While all three taxes tend to increase output (or at least its economic value) under the heading of incentives-analysis, we recall that an income tax was neutral in the context of traditional analysis of behavior of the labor-managed firm, and the other two taxes lead to unorthodox results unambiguous only in the short run and on the assumption of no joint production.

16.4: *The Monopolistic Labor-Managed Firm and Control of Monopoly*

Given the work which we have done in Part I and III and in the foregoing two sections, we can take an important shortcut at this stage of our argument. Provided that we substitute for the concept of value of marginal product the concept of marginal revenue product in the analysis of section 16.2, all the rest of the analysis remains largely unaffected so that the conclusions obtained for the competitive firm—perhaps with minor alterations—also pertain to the case of a monopolistic labor-managed firm. For example, a sales tax will increase the volume of output of a monopolistic firm in the short run, as it was bound to do for a competitive firm in the single-product case. The long-run effects of various taxes, on the other hand, can be approximated for a monopolistic labor-managed firm by postulating a demand function of (finite) constant elasticity, and then substituting for the concept of the locus of maximum physical efficiency (used in the analysis of section 16.2 for the competitive firm) the locus on the production function of the firm defined by the constant-demand elasticity, as explained in Chapter 6. As an example, then, we immediately can obtain the result that a tax on capital (altering p_K) will generally increase the labor-capital ratio while increasing or lowering total output of the monopoly—there being some presumption that the latter outcome would be more likely.

The transposition from a competitive to a monopolistic firm is even more straightforward when it comes to the incentives-analysis of the type presented in the preceding section. We have only to recall that we have really never explicitly specified the nature of our firm in section 16.3. If the diagrammatic presentation used there pertained to a competitive firm, then with a less than infinitely elastic demand function of a monopolist, all that would have to change is that the slopes of the various (collective-type) transformation loci would become flatter. But otherwise all the rest would still hold; and because we have never dwelt on the absolute levels of the slopes in the preceding section, but only on the comparative changes of these slopes resulting from various policy actions, all the conclusions of the preceding section hold also for a monopoly. For example, if we have shown that a capital tax is the most efficient one for a competitive firm, the same conclusion also obtains for a labor-managed monopoly.

There is another and more novel subject to be taken up in this section. It is unnecessary to elaborate on the various inefficiencies which may result from a monopolistic situation, whether in a labor-managed or a capitalist environment. This we mostly take for granted. The problem with which we want to deal here is that of control of monopoly by public authorities with a view toward eliminating some or all of the inefficiencies inherent in monopoly power.

In the labor-managed monopolistic situation we can distinguish two major sources of inefficiency: the first is technological, and results from the operation at less physical efficiency than the maximum consistent with technology and factor supplies; the second is of a market or allocational variety, and results from the fact that generally the marginal value products of labor will be different from those in other industries. As is well known, the inefficiency of the latter condition derives from the fact that with different marginal value products reallocations of labor would lead to an increase in real national product.

We now turn to a more rigorous analysis of the problem of monopoly control. We do so first in the context of a short-run equilibrium; later on we will indicate the comparatively simple alterations leading to the solution for a long-run equilibrium. In Figure 16.4.1-a, we find the total revenue function (curve) of a monopolistic labor-managed firm,

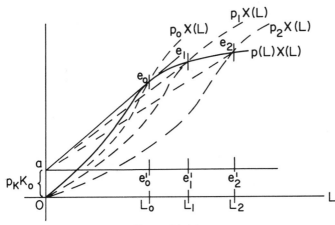

Figure 16.4.1-a.

$p(L)X(L)$, plotted against employment L as an independent variable. The demand function, $p(L)$, plotted against the same independent variable is shown in Figure 16.4.1-b below. With a fixed cost $p_K K_0$,

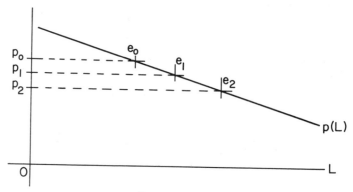

Figure 16.4.1-b

the equilibrium of the monopoly is found at e_0, at which point the income per laborer is maximized at the level indicated by the slope of ae_0 (reflecting both the income per laborer and the marginal revenue product of the firm).

Consulting Figure 16.4.1-b, we find that the equilibrium price at monopoly equilibrium is p_0. With that price we now construct a value-product curve $p_0 X(L)$ in the upper (a) diagram. Obviously, it passes through e_0 and must have a steeper slope at that point than the monopolistic $p(L)X(L)$. From the steeper slope we immediately see that the income per laborer is less than labor's marginal value product. Supposing that the income per laborer is at least as high as in other, assumed competitive, industries in the labor-managed economy—for otherwise the monopoly could hardly exist—the value of marginal product at e_0 will certainly be above the values of marginal product in the competitive sector where, as we know, labor incomes effectively equal the value of marginal product.

In consequence, it will be economically more efficient to control the monopoly price through a maximum price at a level below p_0. Consider, for example, p_1 in Figure 16.4.1-b leading to the total value-product locus $p_1 X(L)$. This is the locus of possible alternatives for the monopoly to the left and below e_1; to the right of e_1, it is the old revenue-product locus $p(L)X(L)$. Given the kink at e_1, it is clear that at least for a small reduction of price imposed by the authorities (such as from p_0 to p_1) the new equilibrium will arise at e_1 where the income per laborer again is maximized. The market is again cleared at this point, and with a reduction in both p and the marginal product (note that this must have happened with an increased employment given the law of diminishing returns) the marginal value product also must have been reduced. Hence, with the price control and resulting increase in output, sales, and demand, we have also moved closer to the social optimum because the marginal value products in the monopoly and the competitive sector have come closer together.

The authorities now can take the income and marginal value product of the competitive sector, call it Y_0, and adjust the monopoly price in such a way as to make the monopoly's marginal value product equal to Y_0. Suppose that this happens for the maximum price p_2. Given the corresponding equilibrium point e_2 in Figure 16.4.1-a, as we know, the economy as a whole would have reached its social optimum, in the sense that the relative price ratio now equals the marginal rate of transformation between the monopoly product and the competitive product—that is, the highest social indifference curve is now tangential to the production-possibility curve.

Even at e_2, however, the slope of $p_2X(L)$ (i.e., the marginal value product of labor) still is higher than the income per laborer in the monopolistic firm—given by the slope of ae_2—and consequently it would be difficult to induce production by the monopoly at the level of employment L_2 because the workers would be earning less than Y_0. In consequence, the authorities who want to achieve a social optimum must engage in another policy. One possibility is a capital subsidy, reducing p_K, and thus shifting point a in Figure 16.4.1-a downward and increasing the slope of ae_2. Another possibility is a negative income tax—that is, an income subsidy given to each laborer. In either case, the subsidy would have to produce at least an equality between incomes in the monopolistic firm and in the rest of the economy.

But an entirely different result from price control is conceivable. To produce the desired equality of Y_0 and the value of marginal product along $p(L)X(L)$, one may have to depress the price charged by the monopoly so much as to make the marginal value product of labor less than the income per laborer. In that situation, as the reader will easily verify, the firm would want to establish an equilibrium (comparable to a competitive equilibrium) at a level of employment below that indicated by $p(L)X(L)$, thereby producing a situation of excess demand for

X at the maximum price imposed. The obvious remedy for this situation is the reverse of the secondary control indicated above. Instead of subsidizing the cost of capital, the authorities now can charge a tax on capital, thereby shifting point a in Figure 16.4.1-a upward, lowering the slope of the line tangential to the value-product contour, and consequently moving to the right—all the way to $p(L)X(L)$—the. equilibrium point.

To sum up, perhaps in somewhat different terms, let it be said that the authorities of the labor-managed economy always have the possibility of rendering a monopolistic firm perfectly efficient in the short run in all respects—that is, in respect to national income maximization and distributional efficiency. But they have to do it by supplementing the customary procedure of maximum price (or outright price control) by another policy instrument. Such a secondary instrument which will always work is a capital tax (positive or negative—i.e., a subsidy). Another is a fixed charge or subsidy, unrelated to any of the performance variables of the firm; it will be noted that such measures also will affect fixed costs and thus shift point a up or down.

Turning now to the long-run situation (of course with technology of the first kind, which is the only one permitting of monopoly in the long run), it will first be observed that a price control will produce the desirable effect of moving the monopoly from a point of less than maximum physical efficiency toward the locus of maximum physical efficiency. The problem is which price exactly should be chosen in order to attain a social optimum.

We know that market forces and the maximizing behavior of the firm will produce an efficient allocation of capital (i.e., interindustry equilization of marginal products of capital). In that case, what about setting the maximum price at the level for which the marginal value product of labor (along the locus of maximum physical efficiency) equals the incomes and marginal value products in the rest of the economy? If that price leads exactly to clearing of the market, we have the solution of long-run control of a labor-managed monopoly. If there is a small excess demand or supply, the market can be adjusted through a sales tax or a subsidy. If there is a large excess demand at such a price, most realistically, the authorities should initiate entry of a new firm— or new firms—into the same industry while preserving the appropriate price control (unless of course the number of new entrants is large).

The last observation brings us to the question of oligopoly. And the answers are quite analogous to those obtained here for a monopolistic labor-managed firm. There will always be a maximum price, possibly coupled with some tax or a subsidy, which will produce, whether in the short run or in the long run, a socially optimal, or at least near-optimal, solution in a labor-managed economy. In the long run, of course, it may also be necessary to induce entry of new firms into the oligopolistic market structure—but this was the case even in the monopolistic situation.

16.5: *Economic Policy and Equilibrium of the Competitive Industry*

Our task in the present section is very simple. We have only to put together some of the analytical building blocks obtained earlier and derive the desired conclusions. First, from section 16.2, it will be recalled that in the short run or the long run both the capital and the sales tax merely shift the supply function of each competitive firm upward—of course, on the assumption that no limitation arises because of a limited labor availability; such limitations will be studied below. And thus, postulating no entry or exit, recalling that the supply function of a competitive industry is a (horizontal) summation of the supply curves of its individual member-firms, and assuming a downward-sloping demand function, the following can be concluded if the incentive effects (of the type studied in Part III and section 16.3) are disregarded.

In the short run, and with only a single product produced, the price will decline and sales increase in an industry where either a sales or a capital tax is applied. Of course, we postulate here stability of the market equilibrium. Otherwise our study of the impact of taxes would be meaningless in the context of a free and competitive market. The results become ambiguous when joint production is postulated in the short run and a sales tax is imposed on only one product, and in the long run for either single- or joint-product industries; prices and sales now can either decline or increase, a reduction in sales and an increase in price again being a somewhat more likely outcome of either a sales or a capital tax levy in the long run. If the incentive effects on the quality and intensity of labor are built into the analysis, all the tax impacts just derived ought to be corrected in the positive direction; for example, a sales tax is likely to produce an even greater increase in sales in the short run. In addition, the income tax is no longer neutral; rather, on account of the incentive effect, it also will tend to stimulate production.

We may now look briefly at what happens with a long-run equilibrium with free entry into and exit from the industry. We now must postulate, as we did in Part I, a labor-availability function. For simplicity, let us assume that it is horizontal, presumably at the level of some national minimum acceptable labor-income. We recall that, under conditions of free entry and in the long run, the case under study is just about the same as it would be in a capitalist situation. Either using this notion or referring to our analysis of Chapter 5, it becomes immediately apparent that an increase in or imposition of the three taxes (income, sales, or a capital tax) will shift the long-run supply function of the industry upward, the corresponding adjustments in sales being performed primarily by entry and exit of firms. Of course, with a declining demand schedule, the price will be increased and the output and sales reduced.

Considering the extent of work that we have done previously, related to the problem of the present section, we consider ourselves justified in stopping our analysis at this point and suggesting to the reader —to the extent that he is interested—that he work out the more exact answers to specific questions on his own. For example, questions of the exact quantitative impact of various taxes, of the impact of taxes on intermediate products, and of a value-added tax might be considered.

16.6: *Toward an Efficient Resource Allocation in a Labor- Managed Industry with Different Technologies*

In the last section of Chapter 5, it will be recalled, we showed the possibility of a less than optimally efficient utilization of productive resources in a competitive labor-managed industry where different technologies are used by (or available to) different firms. The essence of the argument is very simple: with different technologies, the equilibrium incomes per laborer in different firms will not be identical, and consequently the equilibrium marginal productivities of labor also will not be identical. Consequently, there will exist reallocations of productive resources, and of labor in particular, which will improve the output of the industry from given productive resources. The reader may refresh his memory at this point by returning to Figure 5.6.1 and the accompanying analysis.

The obvious problem of economic policy which then arises is how the authorities of the labor-managed economy can produce the most efficient allocation of resources through policy action. Clearly, in the context of long-run analysis where the marginal productivities of capital are equalized among firms through operation of a competitive capital market, the aim of the policy-maker is to also bring the marginal products of labor to equality, thereby producing a solution for the industry such as that illustrated by point e_3 in Figure 5.6.1. Obviously, this is not a simple—or at least not a conventional—task, because, as the reader will realize, it implies a long-run dislocation of the equilibrium of the more efficient firms (we again assume only two segments of the industry as in section 5.6) from the locus of maximum physical efficiency to a point somewhere beyond that locus into the range of diminishing returns (of the production function of the first kind).

Before turning to such an optimal policy, let it be noted that the policy-maker generally will have a simple policy at hand—of the second-best variety—which will produce part, but not all, of the improvement in resource allocation. It is a capital tax levied in the more efficient segment of the industry making the marginal rates of substitution in the two segments equal, even though the absolute levels of the marginal productivities in the two industries remain different (i.e., higher in the more efficient segment) and even though firms in both segments still operate at their respective loci of maximum physical efficiency. In terms of our diagram in section 5.6, this means moving from e_1 to e_2, a point on the contract curve.

But let us now turn to the "first-best" policy, leading to a point such as e_3. In brief—as we will show presently—such a policy consists of a combination of a second-best policy just outlined, that is, a capital tax, and a proportional sales subsidy applicable for sales in the more efficient segment of the industry beyond the locus of maximum physical efficiency. The subsidy is designed to move the firms belonging to the more efficient segment into the region of diminishing returns of their respective technologies. As we are about to show, the exact rates of the capital tax and sales subsidy are readily obtainable from the data defining the problem.

Using the general setting of section 5.6, let us postulate for simplicity that the price of the product of the industry in question is a given constant $\bar{p}$ (given by, say, the world market price), and so is the competitive price of capital, $\bar{p}_K$. Given the technology of the first kind applicable to the less efficient segment of the industry, this determines exactly the factor proportions (not the level of output) and, consequently, the marginal (physical) product of capital and labor in that sector, call them $\bar{k}$ and $\bar{l}$ respectively. Calling t_K the capital tax rate, and s_x the sales subsidy rate for outputs X beyond the maximum physical efficiency point X_0, we postulate for the most efficient pattern of resource allocation in the economy the following to hold for each and every firm of the more efficient segment of the industry:

$$(\partial X/\partial L)(dR/dX) = (1/L)(\bar{p}X + s_x[X - X_0] - K[\bar{p}_K(1 + t_K)]) \qquad (1)$$

$$(\partial X/\partial K)(dR/dX) = \bar{p}_K(1 + t_K) \qquad (2)$$

$$(\partial X/\partial L) = \bar{1} \qquad (3)$$

$$(\partial X/\partial K) = \bar{k} \qquad (4)$$

$$R = \bar{p}X + s_x(X - X_0) \qquad (5)$$

With the production function specified, (i.e., $X = X(K,L)$), this is a system of five equations in five unknowns, K, L, R, s_x, and t_k, which are readily computable from the data. Actually, given the nature of the system, there normally should be only one solution. With these results for each of the firms in the more efficient segment of the industry, and the exogenously prescribed number of these firms, we immediately get the total resources to be used by that segment (i.e., the coordinates, measured from 0_1, of point e_3 in Figure 5.6.1).[1] And given the total capital resources to be used by the industry (i.e., the vertical dimension of the box diagram in Figure 5.6.1) we immediately obtain, from the factor proportions which must prevail in the less efficient segment, the number of firms, level of output, and the labor employment in the less efficient segment. Note here that we could not have specified both dimensions of the box diagram as data, once we had postulated given product and capital prices. Such a specification was possible in Chapter 5 where p and p_K were not specified.

We can thus conclude that if more than one technology is used in a single industry, the inefficiency inherent in such a situation in a labor-managed world can be eliminated through a combination of a capital tax and a sales subsidy for outputs beyond the point of maximum physical efficiency; the exact rates of such fiscal instruments can be computed through a procedure such as that shown in equations (1) through (5), above.

It must be emphasized, however, that the situation discussed here and in section 5.6 is quite special, and depends heavily on the existence of firms with technologies which are not accessible to other firms. Especially in the socialist version of a labor-managed economy, this may

[1] See p. 94.

be a highly unlikely situation as, indeed, the society may, through action of the government, impose on all firms the sharing of the most efficient technology of the period. Also it ought to be recalled that the entire analysis of the present section and section 5.6 is based on the assumption of the technology of the first kind. The case with technology of the second kind (constant returns) is only a degenerate instance of what we have just shown. Even microscopic doses of the two instruments (s_x and t_K) will eliminate all of the inefficient segment of the industry, and only the efficient segment with a single technology will be retained.

In concluding, it should also be noted that the same corrective effects as those discussed in this section can be secured through a lump sum tax (i.e., a fixed tax unrelated to performance) levied on the firms of the more efficient segment of the industry. The magnitude of the tax should be such that the marginal value products of labor (and hence incomes per laborer) are equalized in the more efficient and the less efficient segments of the industry. With (long-run) technologies of the second kind, any lump-sum tax on the more efficient firms will suffice to have the superior technology employed by the entire industry.

16.7: Correcting Imperfections of a Competitive General Equilibrium Solution

In Part I we were able to identify some imperfections which may arise under special conditions in the general equilibrium solution of the labor-managed economy. We are also aware of certain imperfections which can arise in any market economy, whether labor-managed or capitalist. The purpose of the present section is to recall or to identify the most important among these imperfections and suggest and explain policy remedies for them.

The first imperfection which we want to study resembles that discussed in the preceding section except that it arises between competitive industries rather than within one industry. As before, its principal cause is the absence—or impossibility, for one reason or another —of unlimited free entry into an industry; free entry in the long run is assumed in all other industries. Supposing that X_1 is the output of the industry with limited entry, while X_2 represents the output of the other industry (where such a limitation is not present), the long-run general equilibrium of the labor-managed economy on the assumed conditions is illustrated by e_2 in Figure 16.7.1. It is located below the maximal

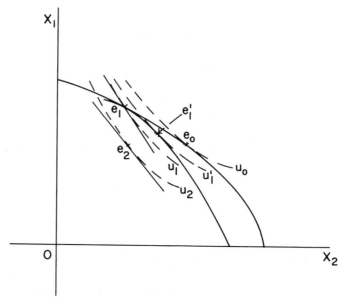

Figure 16.7.1

production-possibility locus (the solid line passing through e_1 and e_0 corresponding to free entry in all industries), and the relative prices of the two products at that point are those indicated by the slope of the indifference contour u_2. With limited entry in the first industry, the income per laborer in that industry is expected to be high, higher than in the other industry and, with incomes per laborer equal in equilibrium to the values of marginal products of labor and the values of marginal product of capital equalized through competition in the capital market, the economy cannot be operating at the contract curve (as explained and constructed in Chapter 7) in its production box-diagram. In other words, the allocation of capital and labor in the economy is not Pareto-optimal.

The policy-makers of the labor-managed economy can now engage in remedial action in two different steps. The first is to bring the allocation of productive resources to the contract curve in the box diagram, and therefore to the maximal production possibility locus. This they can do by imposing a capital tax in the industry with limited entry so as to equalize the marginal rates of substitution (between capital and labor) in the two industries. In this way, they attain the maximal production-possibility locus at a point such as e_1. But as is indicated by the slope of u_1, relative prices now do not reflect the marginal rate of (technological) transformation at e_1; this is so because the values of marginal product of both capital and labor in the first industry are higher, by a common percentage margin, than in the second industry.

The absolute maximum solution for the economy is at e_0 in Figure 16.7.1. But we know that it is attainable only with perfectly free entry in all industries, and consequently (on the assumed conditions of limited entry in the first industry), there is no conceivable further policy action that would lead from e_1 to e_0. However, there is a policy action which can lead to an improvement starting from e_1. As with the second-stage policy of the preceding section, it is possible to give a subsidy to each of the limited number of firms in the first industry for outputs beyond the locus of maximum physical efficiency (preserving the capital tax which leads to the contract-curve allocation of productive resources) to the point where the values of marginal products (of both capital and labor) become identical in the two industries. This will then lead to the equilibrium, with marginal rates of substitution and transformation equalized, at e_1' in Figure 16.7.1. The inferiority of e_1' to the optimal solution at e_0—as indicated by u_0 and u_1'—is of course imputable to the limitation of entry and the consequent operation of the first industry at a less than maximal level of physical efficiency. The production-possibility locus has exactly the same definition as that passing through e_1 and e_0, except for the assumption of free entry into the first industry.

The second imperfection which we want to discuss has been well known for some time in the context of western-type analysis of economic development, with X_1 representing the output of industry and X_2 the output of agriculture. Even with perfectly free entry in both of these industries, it is argued that a positive differential between incomes per laborer (wage rates in the capitalist case and actual residual incomes per laborer in the labor-managed case) is necessary between industry and agriculture in order to induce the transfer of labor resources from agriculture into industry. If such is the case, and all the equilibrium marginal conditions hold in both industries—including the equalization of marginal products of capital throughout the economy —the labor-managed economy cannot be at the locus of maximum production possibilities in the long run; rather, it will again be at a point such as e_2. The policy-maker's course of action in this particular situation is quite straightforward: subsidize labor incomes in industry, possibly securing the necessary tax revenue by taxing labor incomes in agriculture. This subsidy or subsidy-tax rate should be computed in such a way as to eliminate—in conjunction with entry, exit, and flow of resources from one industry into the other—the differential between marginal value products in the two industries. When such an equalization is obtained, the economy will have moved from e_2 directly to the optimal point e_0 in Figure 16.7.1.

Next, as the third imperfection, consider the case of short-run adjustment to changes in demand conditions. As we have shown in Chapter 7 in a good deal of detail, an uncontrolled short-run adjustment of the conventional (not social) type can produce a considerable inefficiency in the general equilibrium solution of the labor-managed economy, especially if the industry in question produces only one product and there are possibilities of capital-labor substitution. As we will argue in Chapter 18, forecasting, indicative planning, and appropriate stimulation of entry are the true and lasting remedies in such a situation. However, if the policy-makers are caught unaware, so to speak, by a sudden change in demand—reflected in our general equilibrium representation by a substantial change in the relative price ratio—fiscal policy can prevent most of the inefficiency.

To show this, suppose that initially we are in a long-run optimal situation at e_0 in Figure 16.7.1. An unforeseen improvement in the price of X_2 relative to that of X_1 now takes place. We know that in the long run and with free entry and exit the new general equilibrium solution should be found somewhere southeast of e_0, also on the maximum production locus passing through e_0 (such a point is not in the diagram). However, without free entry and, in the short run, with immobile capital resources, a short-run equilibrium can arise at—or at least there may be a tendency toward—a point such as e_1'. Recalling now that in both industries the equilibrium marginal condition is of the form

$$pMPP_L = (pX - p_K K)/L$$

it becomes obvious that if the authorities adjust p_K through a capital tax (subsidy) in the second (first) industry in proportion with the respective changes in product prices, the marginal condition remains undisturbed and hence the economy remains at e_0 instead of moving in the short run toward e_1'. Of course, one inefficiency remains in the fact that we are now at e_0 with a relative price ratio more favorable to X_2 than is indicated by the marginal rate of transformation at e_0. This inefficiency can be eliminated only through movement of resources and exit and entry of firms.

One important point must be stressed however. The policy just suggested in order to remain at e_0 does not eliminate the forces of long-run adjustment which eventually should lead to the long-run optimum. Note that keeping p_K proportional to product price in both industries does not eliminate the fact that the second industry experiences a higher income per laborer—that is, does not eliminate the basic impetus for exit and entry in the desired direction.

The last imperfection that we want to speak about is perhaps the most notorious one—at least most notorious in the context of western-type competitive theories of general equilibrium. It derives from the phenomenon of economies (or diseconomies) external to individual firms of an industry, but internal to the industry. Typically, if such externalities are present—of course, assuming now perfect competition and free entry throughout—we will find ourselves at a maximum producible point, such as e_1, but the relative prices (indicated by the slope of u_1 at e_1) will now be different from the social transformation rate (indicated by the marginal rate of transformation or the slope of the transformation locus). As illustrated in Figure 16.7.1, we are facing a situation of external economies in the second industry or external diseconomies in the first industry (or both). More specifically, it costs the society less to increase output of X_2 by a small amount, in terms of X_1, than it costs in the free competitive markets. The obvious recommendation then is to stimulate production of the second at the expense of the first industry, while remaining at the locus of maximal production possibilities. As is well known, this can be done by imposing a sales tax on X, and subsidizing the sales of X_2 to the point where the relative difference between the marginal rates of substitution and transformation is exactly equal to the rate of tax or of subsidy if a single policy tool is used, or to the sum of the two rates if both tools are used. When this equality is attained and, of course, the economy is given time to find its long-run equilibrium with free entry and exit, the labor-managed economy will reach its optimum solution at e_0 in Figure 16.7.1.

17. Macroeconomic Policy

17.1: *Outline*

By macroeconomic policy in a labor-managed economy, we understand measures designed to influence the aggregate general equilibrium solution developed in Part II. The purpose of the present chapter is to study various aspects of such a policy. Thanks to Part II—to which the reader may want to return at this point to refresh his memory—our task is a comparatively simple one.

First, in the subsequent section, we establish the basic multipliers underlying any design of economic policy. These multipliers tell what effects can be expected from a unit dose of various economic policies. In section 3, some key policy combinations are then considered, leading to alternative specific short-run targets.

From Part II, it will be remembered that danger of instability in the labor-managed economy arises, if at all, in respect to short-run macroeconomic equilibrium. Section 4 is devoted to this particular problem and especially to the derivation of policy measures guaranteeing stability of the aggregate general equilibrium.

In section 5 we discuss a macroeconomic system designed by Ward for the labor-managed economy.[1]

In the concluding section, finally, we make an attempt to appraise the general scope of macroeconomic policy in the labor-managed economy, using the results of Part II and those of the earlier section of the present chapter. We feel that such an over-all appraisal is necessary, especially because the problem of macroeconomic policy in the economy concerning us here is qualitatively quite different—even if this may not be apparent at first sight—from the problem as it arises conventionally in the capitalist economy.

[1] Benjamin Ward: *The Socialist Economy* (New York, 1967), pp. 228–236.

17.2: *The Effects of Major Macroeconomic Policies*

In Part II, we have studied extensively the effects of various autonomous changes in the major markets—such as shifts in aggregate demand for goods, for money, for bonds, or a change in the capital stock—on the aggregate general equilibrium solution for the labor-managed economy. At the present stage of our discussion, we want to study similar effects, but this time caused by deliberate policy actions rather than by autonomous structural changes. While the causes of changes in the general equilibrium are quite different in nature, the formal analysis leading to the results sought is almost the same as that developed in Part II.

It only need be noted that at the level of aggregation of the macroeconomic analysis, the effect of a one-million-dollar increase in government spending—considered here as a policy-induced action—on the endogenous variables of our aggregate general equilibrium is exactly the same as that of an autonomous increase in consumers' demand by the same amount. With fiscal policy, the transition is only slightly less straightforward as, indeed, a one-million-dollar increase in taxation will have an initial impact on effective demand of one million times one minus the marginal propensity to save. Turning now to other markets, it should be clear that the effect of a change in the price of capital P_K on the general equilibrium will be the same whether the change is policy-induced or not.

Similarly, an increase in the autonomous demand for bonds will have the same effect as an increase stemming from government open-market operations; only the latter alternative is somewhat simpler than the former because open-market operations normally are conducted in terms of money so that a policy-induced increase in demand for bonds can be thought of as equivalent to a policy-induced reduction in the supply of money (and vice versa). The former alternative, on the other hand, can be accompanied by a matching reduction in demand for either money, or goods, or even productive services.

The remarks just made on behalf of the policy-induced changes in the bond market are of paramount importance for our discussion of economic policy. In fact, from now on we can consider an expansionary monetary policy as equivalent—in our general equilibrium structure of Part II, including the bond market and excluding, by

Walras' law, the money market—to an increase in excess demand for bonds.

With these remarks in mind, we can directly take over the results obtained in Chapter 10, and summarize them for the present purpose. The summary is diagrammatically expressed in Figure 17.2.1. The

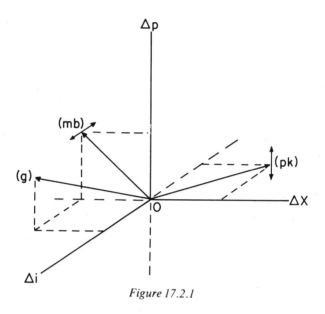

Figure 17.2.1

vector marked (g)—standing for government spending or tax reduction—indicates the impact of a one-million-dollar increase in government spending, or in nongovernment spending stimulated by a corresponding income tax reduction, on changes in the three key macroeconomic variables, Δp, ΔX, and Δi. Using the broken segments of the three coordinate axes for negative, and the solid-line segments for positive, values of the changes, we immediately read off what we have inferred from the analysis of Chapter 10, that the policy (g) will reduce national product and increase the general price level and the rate of interest.

On the other hand, as indicated by the vector marked (pk)—referring to alterations in the price of capital p_K—a unitary increase in p_K will definitely (of course assuming stability throughout) increase national product and reduce the rate of interest; the impact on prices is ambiguous, as is indicated by the up-and-down arrow at the end of the policy vector. Finally, monetary expansion—or a government-induced increase in demand for bonds—marked by (mb), will reduce, on its own, the level of national product (and employment) and at the same time be price-inflationary. That same policy's impact on the rate of interest is ambiguous, this again being indicated by the double arrow.

The three (or four, if fiscal policy is counted separately) individual policies just summarized are the principal tools in the hands of the short-run policy makers of the labor-managed economy. The three will generally be sufficient to attain any prescribed target in the space defined by the three axes of Figure 17.2.1. But a more detailed exposition of this is our subject for the subsequent section.

17.3: *Attaining the Macroeconomic Targets*

A brief examination of the three basic policy vectors in Figure 17.2.1 leads to the conclusion that these vectors are mutually independent, that is, are neither colinear nor placed all three in one plane. This means, as is well known from the general theory of economic policy, that any point in the space of Figure 17.2.1—that is, any specified policy target—is attainable through an appropriate combination of the three basic policies. The exact design of an appropriate "policy diet," or policy prescription, it will be recalled, is done by addition of fractions of the three policy vectors, the fractions themselves (larger or smaller than unity) being determined as the solution of the policy problem. The reader may find it interesting to plot several hypothetical targets into the space of Figure 17.2.1, and study the corresponding policy diets leading to such targets.

On our part, we will discuss four typical targets and the policies required to attain them. They are illustrated in Figure 17.3.1 by points T_1 through T_3'. T_1 is perhaps the most significant because it indicates

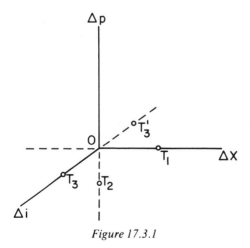

Figure 17.3.1

on the part of the policy-makers the desire to preserve price—as well as interest-rate—stability, but to increase national product and thus, by implication, national employment. For the purpose of our analysis we will treat ambiguous directions of the basic policy vectors as zero directions, so that the vector (pk) is as drawn, embedded in the Δi-ΔX plane and the (mb) vector in the Δp-ΔX plane. It should be apparent by simple inspection of Figure 17.2.1 that there will be a vector-combination of a negative dose of (mb) and a positive dose of (g)—that is, monetary restriction coupled with budgetary expansion—yielding a vector embedded in the same coordinate plane as (pk). And some combination of positive doses of (pk) and the new combined vector— call it $(g-mb)$—should lead to T_1. More explicitly, it can be concluded that in order to attain T_1, one would generally have to increase the cost of capital to the productive sector together with monetary restraint and budgetary expansion—of course, the exact doses of the three policies being determinable only from an exact set of data defining the situation.

Before we turn to the other targets, let it also be noted that in some real situations either the rate of interest or the price level, or both, may be considered irrelevant by the policy-maker. If such is the case, one policy instrument (basic vector) can be dropped for each irrelevant variable. For example, it must be clear that, if only an increase in output and employment constituted the target, any one of the three basic vectors could be used in isolation to attain it.

Consider now target T_2; it can be described as a purely price-deflationary target, with interest rate and employment stability. Using a construction analogous to that undertaken in respect to T_1, it will first be noted that negative doses of (pk) and (g) should combine into a vector embedded into the Δp-ΔX plane and this vector, combined with a negative dose of (pk), should reach the desired target. More explicitly, a pure price deflation in a labor-managed economy will generally require budgetary restriction, tight money, and a reduced cost of capital.

Finally, as our last example, let us consider the case in which the authorities desire to increase or reduce the rate of interest, without affecting the other two target variables. The two targets T_3 and T_3' reflect such policies and, clearly, either will be reached by applying the same combination of policy instruments as the other except for the signs—or directions—of these instruments. We thus have to consider only one of the two targets, say, T_3. As the reader may want to verify, using a construction similar to the previous ones, that target—that is, a pure increase in the rate of interest—will normally be attainable through budgetary expansion (i.e., $+(g)$), monetary restraint ($-(mb)$) and a reduction in p_K ($-(pk)$).

17.4: *Macroeconomic Stability and Policies Supporting It*

One of the important findings of Chapter 10 regarding the aggregate general equilibrium of the labor-managed economy was that one could not exclude on a priori grounds—judging from the signs of underlying structural parameters—the possibility that such an equilibrium would be unstable. Of course, in the context of a real situation, one may argue that this need not concern the policy-maker becausᵉ an unstable equilibrium could never last for any extended period and a stable equilibrium would have to be reached through the operation of free competitive markets once the slightest disturbance of the unstable equilibrium occurred. While in part this argument is valid, the possibility of occurrence of unstable equilibrium should be entirely dismissed as a real issue. For one thing, even if the economy is operating at a stable equilibrium, structural parameters can change over time—as a result of economic policy or otherwise—and transform a stable into an unstable situation leading to major disturbances and variation in prices, employment, and interest rates.

For another thing, and perhaps more important, the theoretical possibility of instability can always be taken as a warning that even if a real equilibrium is stable, the variations in the variables of the general equilibrium system may be significant when the equilibrium is disturbed (in a simple Marshallean market this would correspond to a situation in which, with stability, the elasticities of the supply and the demand schedules are almost identical).

In either case, if there is a policy which would lead to the elimination of the possibility of unstable equilibria, such a policy should definitely be employed by the authorities of the labor-managed economy; not only would this guarantee the absence of extreme disturbance in employment, inflation, or other areas, but also such a policy would be bound to make the whole system operate more smoothly.

As a matter of fact, the policy does exist. Furthermore, it is both extremely simple and easy to implement because it calls for a once-for-all instruction instead of repeated discretionary action. The once-for-all instruction is to keep the cost of capital assets to the labor-managed firms proportional to the general price level—that is, let $p_K = \bar{p}_K p$, where $\bar{p}_K$ is a real cost of use of capital assets, a constant in the short run. There are several practical ways in which this requirement can be fulfilled; but in essence all that is meant here is that when the general price level fluctuates, so also should the cost of capital to its users. Besides the policy objective which we are concerned with here, this has the commonsensical merit of not letting the producers benefit from lower real prices of capital resulting from general price inflation.

To substantiate the argument, let us rewrite our equilibrium condition for national employment, using our new policy instruction; it becomes

$$pMPP_L = p(X - \bar{p}_K K_0) \qquad (1)$$

The general price level p now cancels out from both sides of the equation, and we are left with a single equation in a single variable L (recalling that $X = X(L)$), which generally has a single solution $L = L_0$, and thus leads to a single equilibrium level of output $X = X_0$.

Supposing for simplicity that the government pegs the rate of interest (i) at a constant level—through open market operations in the bond market—the effects of the policy instruction just suggested can easily be shown using the analytical apparatus of Part II, and in particular of Chapter 10. With i a constant, the two endogenous variables to be considered now are p and X, measured along the vertical and horizontal axes in Figure 17.4.1, respectively. The vertical line Φ at the level of national product X_0 is the diagrammatic representation of the equilibrium condition (1), while $X = \bar{X}$ is the locus of equilibrium combinations of p and X, well known to us from Part II. On the other hand, Φ' represents the equilibrium locus for the (quasi) labor market— necessarily downward sloping—as it may have been prior to our policy instruction regarding pricing of capital. As indicated by the arrow (pointing in the northeast direction), the policy instruction has, so to speak, rotated Φ to a vertical position.

The equilibrium loci $X = \bar{X}$ and Φ yield an equilibrium solution for the economy at e, and—again using the analysis carefully developed and explained in Part II—that equilibrium is necessarily a stable one, as indicated by the directional arrows representing the dynamic forces of adjustment for points away from equilibrium. Two typical adjustment paths have been shown by arrows originating from points a and b.

It will be noted that these two paths are nonoscillatory. Actually, this is a necessary result because Φ, as we know, can be crossed by an adjustment path only vertically, and Φ itself is vertical. Our policy of

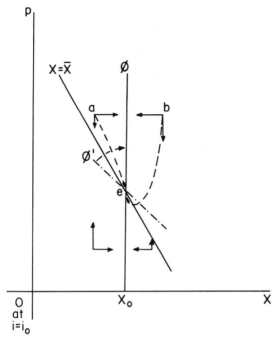

Figure 17.4.1

stabilization therefore has a secondary stabilizing effect. It not only renders the equilibrium necessarily stable, it also eliminates any possibility of oscillatory (cyclical) adjustment to equilibrium once that equilibrium is disturbed.

As the reader may verify using the analytical tools of Part II, the equilibrium with Φ' would have been unstable. Moreover, as we have argued earlier in this section, a Φ' which would have been more steep than $X = \bar{X}$ would have led to wider variations in equilibrium p and X than a Φ resulting from given shifts (structural alterations) in the two markets considered. The reader may also find it interesting to verify that with our policy instruction ($p_K = \bar{p}_K p$), all the Routhean mathematical conditions for dynamic stability are now satisfied. For example, note that in the first condition the one determinant with the undesirable sign now vanishes because the differential of the equilibrium labor condition with respect to p vanishes.

17.5: *Comments on Ward's Macro-theory and Macro-policy*

In his *The Socialist Economy*, Ward covers part of the ground which we have gone through in the foregoing sections, using a simplified macroeconomic general equilibrium system. His results, especially with respect to economic policy, are significantly different from ours and consequently we consider it desirable to explain these differences.

Ward's aggregate general equilibrium system is a reduced one, containing only two markets: (1) the labor market (or what we have in this study referred to as the quasi labor market), and (2) the money market. Ward's equilibrium condition in the first market is the same as that used here, namely, that the value of marginal product of labor be equal to the income per laborer; in terms of mathematics

$$p(\partial X/\partial L) = (1/L)(pX - p_K K_0) \qquad (1)$$

As equilibrium in the money market, Ward uses the well-known quantity equation[2]

$$M_0 V_0 = pX \qquad (2)$$

The subscripts "0" are ours, and indicate that the corresponding variables are taken as constants. Recalling that in the short run X is a function of only the labor force employed in the economy, L, equations (1) and (2) are relations between the general price level, p, and the national employment, L. The labor-market equation is represented in Figure 17.5.1 by the backward-bending employment function reminis-

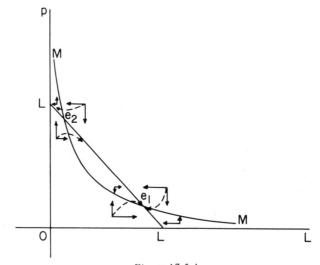

Figure 17.5.1

[2]We omit here a discussion of whether the quantity equation actually can or should be used; for a thorough discussion of these problems the reader is referred to Patinkin's *Money, Interest, and Prices* (2nd ed., New York, 1965).

cent of the supply function of X from Part II, while the money equation resembles the well-known rectangular hyperbola. We have marked the two contours LL and MM, respectively.

The dynamics of the situation is represented by the arrows in the various "quadrants." From Part II we know that the horizontal arrows must all point toward the LL line; for example, a disequilibrium point to the right of LL is one where the marginal value product of labor will be less than the income per laborer, and thus employment must be reduced. On the other hand, it will be noted that whenever we are above (below) the MM line, the money market must be in excess demand (supply) and thus the price of money $(1/p)$ must be increasing (declining)—that is, p must be declining (increasing). This is reflected by the vertical arrows.

A brief examination of the resulting patterns of dynamic adjustment —recalling also that the LL line can be crossed by an adjustment path only vertically and the MM line only horizontally—immediately leads to the conclusion that e_1 is a stable equilibrium while e_2 is an unstable one. The danger of instability of the aggregate general equilibrium is again apparent. However, whether Ward's system or our more complete one is taken for representation of the operation of the labor-managed economy, it is equally apparent that in a realistic situation a free competitive equilibrium at e_2 could never persist; and thus for purposes of comparative statics and economic policy analysis the only equilibrium that should be considered is e_1.

Recalling that monetary expansion shifts the MM line in Figure 17.5.1 in the northeast direction, and that an increase in capital charges (increase in p_K) shifts the LL line to the right, we immediately find that the former policy action raises the price level and reduces employment (and output) while the latter lowers prices and increases employment (and output). These results, conforming to the more general ones of our own analysis, are diametrically opposed to those obtained by Ward,[3] who conducts most of his analysis assuming the equilibrium e_2, apparently not realizing that the equilibrium is an unstable one.

At least for the more theoretically minded reader, it may be interesting to note that even if by the sheerest of coincidences an equilibrium such as e_2 existed for a time, the results of policy action still would be

[3] See in particular p. 243 of *The Socialist Economy*, where Ward concludes, among other things, that "the anomalous microeconomic behavior with respect to output response is converted to anomalous price response at the macroeconomic level." The truth of the matter is, of course, that no such conversion occurs, the macro and micro results remaining mutually consistent.

in the same direction as indicated in respect to the equilibrium at e_1. Suppose for example that we are at e_2, and monetary contraction shifts the MM line to the left. Point e_2 now finds itself on LL below the new point e_2, and our dynamic analysis tells us that from such a point prices must decline and income increase. These directional changes are precisely those obtained with respect to e_1. The simple rationale of this argument is that when an unstable equilibrium is disturbed (here by policy action), the new solution cannot be expected to be again at the unstable equilibrium in a free-market situation.

17.6: A General Evaluation of Short-Run Macroeconomic Policy in a Labor-Managed System

Having gone through the formal analysis of short-run macroeconomic policy, it is time to evaluate that policy in the context of the actual conditions of a labor-managed economy. As we have pointed out in section 17.1, this evaluation is especially desirable because the situation at hand is, in a number of respects, quite different from that of a capitalist economy for which traditional (Keynesian) analysis was originally designed.

The first thing to observe—or to recall from what has been said previously—is that there is no rigidity of wages in the labor-managed system, whereas in the conventional Keynesian analysis of national income determination such a rigidity is the very cornerstone—as well as the very stumbling block—of the general equilibrium system. By and large, less than full employment equilibria in western economies derive from that rigidity. In the labor-managed economy they cannot arise from the same causes, but they can, as we have seen, arise from the special conditions of what we have termed the quasi labor market.

This difference is a fundamental differentiating factor between the two situations. Wage-rate rigidity in the Keynesian situation renders the short-run supply elasticity of national product high, and this in turn renders alterations of effective demand, and economic policy action in general, a powerful factor of national employment (or unemployment) adjustment. On the other hand, the supply elasticity of national product in the labor-managed economy can generally be expected to be very low (even if the stabilizing instruction explained in section 17.4 is not adhered to) and, moreover, is negative. That it will be very low in the short run is quite certain because, starting from any actual equilibrium, in the upward direction firms will be reluctant to release workers when conditions are getting better and, going in either direction, rapidly diminishing marginal factor productivities can be expected on account of quasi-fixed coefficients that tend to prevail in the short run. Moreover, at full employment the elasticity must by definition be zero for declining price levels.

Consequently, short-run economic policy should primarily be considered in the labor-managed economy as a policy to manage and influence the general price level, which, indeed, can be highly sensitive to such policy, and possibly as a tool to alter the rate of interest. This is not to say that short-run economic policy should not be used at all in coping with unemployment, but rather that it should be used in this context only as a second-echelon device. The primary responsibility for full employment should be given to long-range forces and long-range economic policy, about which more will be said in the following chapter.

To be only a little more specific at this stage of the argument, let it be said, as an example, that alterations in the cost of capital to the producers certainly should play an important role in determining how much of the national labor force will be employed. But that factor should not be used in the short run—that is, played with every three months or so—but rather be the subject of a well-planned long-range strategy revised every five years or so.

If that strategy is a correct one, then the very inelasticity which rendered short-run policy toward full employment ineffectual will guarantee to the managers that the sudden changes in effective demand will not affect national employment a good deal. What they will have to be concerned about under changing economic conditions are price variations, but these they will be able to cope with effectively through monetary policy—provided, of course, that they have mastered that subtle instrument of economic policy, and provided that the appropriate freely operating institutions are in existence.

Also, it should be noted that even in the absence of long-run economic planning and policy there will be natural long-run forces which will tend to work in the direction of the full-employment target if at a point in time such an employment level does not exist. As we have noted already in Part II, these forces are embodied in the natural process of entry of new labor-managed firms. We also recall that in this particular respect the labor-managed economy is basically different from the capitalist one. Speaking more figuratively, there are far greater penalties attached to the short-run policy makers going to sleep in the capitalist system of present-day western type than there are in a labor-managed economy. This is so because if there is a lack of effective demand and unemployment in the capitalist world, the very forces which produce the situation also serve as a barrier to new entry and corresponding increases in employment. On the other hand the forces which lead to unemployment in the labor-managed world are also the forces which stimulate the entry of new firms and the employment in such firms.

To conclude, we may restate something that has been said earlier in this section in different words and in a slightly different context. Business cycles as we know them in the western economies (or at least have known them through the end of the 1950's)—that is, cycles in real output and employment—are far less of a threat in the labor-managed economy. If there is a danger of a short-run cyclical nature, it is a wide variation in prices. But even this danger, noting that speeds of adjustment in values generally are far higher than in respect to outputs, can be deemed less serious.

18. Economic Planning and Growth in a Labor-Managed Economy

18.1: *The General Problem of Long-Range Planning and Control*

Before we turn to the most important specific aspects of the subject, it is imperative—more so than at any other stage of the present study—to discuss the problem of long-range planning in a labor-managed economy in general terms. We must ask and attempt to answer the key questions of the scope and of the purpose of economic planning in a labor-managed market economy. This is the first and main purpose of the present section. A second purpose is closely related: to identify and outline the main specific headings—or categories—under which the subject matter at hand should be discussed in the subsequent sections of the chapter.

The most important fact has been stated already on at least two different occasions earlier in the study: economic planning—or a plan—is not a *conditio sine qua non* of the labor-managed economy. It is only because we are used to thinking of labor-managed economies as "socialist," and of socialist economies as "planned," that we are sometimes led to identify the labor-managed system with economic planning.

To use a metaphor, the function of the plan in a labor-managed market situation on the one hand and in a Soviet-type economy on the other can be explained in the following manner. Take a raft floating down a stream as illustrative of the long-range growth and development of an economy. The plan in the Soviet alternative is the very water of the stream, without which the raft would necessarily be stranded; not only all growth, but most of economic life itself would be bound to disappear without it. In the labor-managed alternative, by contrast, the water is in the stream whether there is economic planning or not. Actually, the water is provided in this instance by the markets and the related rational action in these markets by various economic units—firms, households, and possibly others.

The purpose of economic planning—broadly defined—in the labor-managed economy now can be easily explained with reference to our metaphor. Actually, four purposes or roles, and correspondingly four types of planning activity, can be distinguished. The first purpose is avoidance of friction. The stream is quite shallow, and if left unattended, the raft frequently would touch the bottom and thereby be either slowed down or temporarily sent in a wrong direction. All measures, whether of short- or of long-run nature, designed to avoid such friction are a part of economic planning.

Second, there is the steering of the raft. The river is winding. Were it not for the steersman, now and then the raft would come to one of the banks and temporarily get caught or slowed down. Third, there is propulsion. If left entirely to itself—that is to the motion of the water —the progress of the raft might be quite slow. Also, without propulsion, it might be more difficult to fulfill the second purpose of the plan, steering. Fourth, and finally, with so much activity going on in respect to the three preceding tasks, those involved—that is, the whole population—are bound to become economy and growth conscious, and this in itself—most would agree—is a positive factor of economic development. We state here the fourth point primarily for the sake of completeness, and we will not devote much attention to it in our detailed discussion.

Still by way of a general discussion, it ought only to be noted that the above four roles of planning could just as well have been suggested in respect to planning in any other market economy, in particular, in one of the capitalist western type. For example, France's present-day indicative planning, except perhaps for the role of propulsion, could be explained and understood under the same four headings. However, there is one fundamental difference between the labor-managed and other market situations. It is apparent from the theory presented in this study—and we will try to make it even clearer in this chapter— that the benefits to be reaped from the four types of planning activity in a labor-managed economy will generally be more important than those that can be derived in other market systems.

We can now outline the material which we want to cover using as headings the first three aspects of planning in the above schema. The first is the avoidance of friction, and we will devote to it the subsequent section. Although the subject is quite broad, we need not spend too much time with it because a number of individual topics which belong to it have previously been discussed. Among these are monopoly control, coping with differences in technology, and others.

The second heading is "steering." Actually, we must distinguish two types of steering which will be analyzed in sections 3 and 4, respectively. The first type is steering based on foresight—that is, the steersman sees a bend far ahead on the river and steers the raft into the middle of the stream so as not to hit the bank. The second type is steering based not on foresight, but on the belief that the free working of markets (i.e., the free flow of water) does not yield the optimal course of the raft over time. Again, we have encountered some instances of this variety earlier in the study.

We come now to the third heading, "propulsion"; we will devote the concluding section of the chapter to it. Clearly, in economic practice it corresponds to the problem of mobilization of investment resources for development, over and above what would be forthcoming from a free competitive capital market.[1] The important thing here is to match certain specific modes of resource mobilization with the growth potential of the labor-managed economy. To a degree, then, we must also take up some aspects of the growth theory for that economy.

In concluding this introductory section, two more things ought to be noticed. First, by and large, the three general headings of "friction-avoidance," "steering," and "propulsion" correspond to activities which are independent (although propulsion may assist steering). Therefore, the labor-managed economy may select various degrees, or various levels of planning, by adopting any one, any two, or all three categories of planning activity. In the subsequent sections we will not be concerned with this possibility of "partitioning" the planning problem; however, the reader ought to be aware of it, and may want to consider on his own some of the partial planning situations.

Second, the reader should be made aware of something implicit in our conception of planning (or planning activity). As we use it, the term is inclusive of all deliberate activities of the government (central or local) designed to influence the course of the economy in the direction of greater efficiency, whether allocational, or distributional, or of growth (i.e., developmental). Especially in respect to the first category —avoidance of friction—some might prefer the term *economic policy*, or *policy-making;* however, we feel that even here the terms *planning* or *planning activity* are appropriate as a broader category including, among other things, economic policy-making and implementation.

[1] For young developing economies an equally important problem often is that of mobilization of foreign exchange resources; but we will not be concerned with it primarily because in respect to the economies studied here there is not much new over and above the general formulation of the problem.

18.2: *Avoiding Frictions in Growth*

As we have noted already, a number of subjects belonging to the present section were discussed in part or in full at various earlier stages of the study. Control and regulation of monopolies, avoiding instability of macroeconomic equilibria in the labor-managed economy, or coping with technological differences within an industry are only a few such subjects—and we will return to them and elaborate on them whenever necessary later in the section. For the moment, however, let us speak about two other spheres of friction prevention which, though we are acquainted with them by implication from earlier parts of the study, have not yet been tackled in the context of planning and plan implementation. They may well represent the two most important aspects of the policy-maker's task in the economy with which we are concerned.

The first category we may refer to—perhaps not most elegantly—as *the shortening of the long run and acceleration of entry.* In Chapter 7 we have shown quite conclusively how adjustments of a general equilibrium to changing demand conditions can lead to Pareto-suboptimal solutions, and how the efficient (optimal) adjustment will be secured in the long run with free entry. If then the long run can be shortened—so to speak—and appropriate entry and exit can be accelerated through action of the authorities, this will enhance the efficiency of operation of the system. Recalling also that it is precisely the long run and entry that increases substantially the supply elasticities in the labor-managed system, it should also be apparent that the avoiding of friction just outlined will also have a positive effect—sometimes decisively so—on the stability of the general equilibrium solution.

Before turning to some of the main courses of remedial action that can be envisaged, a few realistic comments should be made regarding the actual dimensions, or extent, of the particular friction that we are considering. We may say that, as stated in Chapter 7, the case in fact is painted in the darkest colors, the short-run supply elasticities implied both being negative. As we are well aware, this will be the case only if the products in question are produced by single-product industries. In the case of joint (or multiple-product) production the elasticities will be much higher, most often positive, and thus losses to efficiency from short-run adjustment will be a good deal less. Moreover, when the technologies involved are of the second kind (i.e., linear homogeneous) for each firm, the firms may, with changing product-price relationships, skip the short run, realizing that all scales of operation are efficient in the long run, and thus avoid changes in their labor participation (employment). Finally, the industry which tends to gain in the relative price adjustment may simply reject short-run reductions of output and employment—which they should engage in on grounds of strict maximizing behavior—on grounds of internal labor solidarity, that is, on grounds of what we have termed in Part I social behavior.

Nonetheless, all of these arguments which soften the impact of short-run structural adjustment cannot do away with the implied inefficiency altogether. Nothing short of entry, exit, or possibly adjustment in output by firms operating under constant returns to scale can produce a Pareto-optimal solution. The accelerating and prompting action of the authorities must step in at this point as one of the possible remedies; another remedy will be found under the heading of steering activity and as such will be examined in the subsequent section.

In a labor-managed economy where entry can originate from different sources (as discussed in Chapter 14), the government and local authorities must be ready, as one line of approach, to rapidly initiate and process entry of new firms wherever there is opportunity to do so. Alternatively, various measures may be brought to bear on existing firms to diversify or, to the extent that they operate under constant returns to scale, to expand. Analogously, in industries whose relative prices are declining, exit of firms—or more realistically, reorientation into other fields of activity—should be promoted if conditions warrant such an adjustment. Of course, in a growing economy it may be only very rarely that an outright exit and liquidation of an existing firm would be necessary as a result of structural changes in national demand; with a general expansion all that may be needed is that the numbers of firms in the adversely affected industries temporarily remain constant.

Turning now to entry initiated by existing firms and by groups of individuals, the authorities should first see to it that official action related to such entry (or exit) be conducted promptly. Perhaps more important, the authorities should provide and disseminate to the economic community at large information on which sectors are currently doing well, which are slackening, and in what degree this is so. This information will be useful to potential entrants or firms which want to reorient their production or just to diversify.

Assuming that the capital market—in one or the other of its specific forms consistent with labor management—takes care at least approximately of the equalization of capital productivities on the margin, the objective of the authorities in pursuing their adjustment-prompting action should be to produce, as closely as possible, an equality of incomes per laborer (of course, in the realistic context, we think here of equality of incomes of comparable skills and qualities of labor) as between industries. Actually, this objective can be thought of as the golden rule of static efficiency of resource allocation in the labor-managed economy. Indeed, if that objective is attained at all times (at least approximately), and assuming rational income-per-laborer-maximizing behavior of all firms, we can be sure that the economy is close to the (Pareto-) optimum; of course, this also presupposes the conventional assumption of competition throughout.

The second policy, or planning activity, which we want to discuss may be as important as that just examined. Like the preceding policy, it also has its parallel or counterpart in the sphere of planning through steering to which we will turn in the following section. The friction-avoiding aspect which we want to discuss here consists of the *provision and proliferation of information regarding current investment, investment projects, and plans* of firms and potential entrants throughout the economy. We have suggested in Chapter 14 that the assumption of independence of investment projects is absurd; it will matter a good deal for one project, over its lifetime of say twenty years, whether another similar or related project is undertaken or not. But if this is so, each potential investor should know as well as possible what others in his field are doing. Actually, he might want to do better than just knowing; he might want to be able to sit down in a conference with his colleagues from other firms and work out joint investment plans for the industry so as to prevent major waste of resources or efficiency which might arise from overinvestment or underinvestment respectively. Of course, the steering activity (to which we want to turn in the next section) in respect to investment projects may do part or most of this for him.

The *facilitating of entry* discussed above in relation to reducing the frictions of structural adjustment is also a potent factor of full-employment policy. Perhaps a small example—or case—can illustrate the point. Suppose that in a growing labor-managed economy a sudden increase in demand leads to a reduction in employment (together with increased incomes). Alternatively, unemployment may increase merely from an increase in population and the labor force. Those unemployed or voluntarily leaving their original employment now are in an excellent position to compete for national investment funds—whether in a fully competitive capital market or in an authorities-controlled investment process—and establish new productive units.   Additional impetus to do so and facilitating and prompting of entry of this type in general will necessarily promote full employment.   Of course, this can be only a second line of approach, next to a sound interest rate and capital cost structure; for example, with capital costs (p_K) way below their equilibrium level, important unemployment can arise which cannot be stemmed through new entry—at least not entirely—unless the now scarce investment funds are rationed exclusively to new firms. But in either case, with unrealistic capital costs, resources are bound to be allocated inefficiently.

In the preceding chapter we analyzed in some detail the methods and effects of *monopoly regulation*. Such regulation, clearly, is one of the friction-avoiding or friction-reducing devices at the disposal of the labor-managed economy. At this stage, where we are more concerned with real situations, let it further be noted that what has been said previously about the *control of monopolies* holds by and large also with respect to *oligopolies* of small numbers of firms, each of which exercises some degree of market power over its product. Here again a combination of a price control with a capital tax can produce an efficient solution in the short run. More generally, and more importantly, a price control (rendering of the demand elasticity infinite for each oligopolist) will bring the firms concerned to the locus of maximum physical efficiency in the long run. If the particular price selected yields a solution for which income per laborer equals incomes in other, presumably competitive, industries together with equilibrium in the particular oligopolistic market, then we can be sure of a long-run (Pareto-) optimal solution. If only the income-equalization condition is fulfilled at the price chosen while market disequilibria are present in the oligopolistic market, a sales tax or a sales subsidy will equilibrate the market and we will again be at the locus of production possibilities for the economy as a whole. However, the situation will not be optimal because the marginal rate of transformation will not equal relative prices (of oligopolistic and other products). However, elimination of firms from, or addition of firms to, the oligopolistic industry will then be sufficient to produce a fully optimal situation.

The analysis just carried out is quite important because oligopolies, especially in manufacturing, occur frequently in the real world. It is particularly relevant for young economies—in early stages of development—which at the same time do not have large internal markets for many manufactured products, and cannot rely on the regulating effects of foreign competition[2] because of imperfections (of many kinds) that tend to beset the foreign exchange market. Under such conditions the authorities of the labor-managed economy—and for that matter of any economy—may find it expedient on grounds of efficiency to regulate prices. This will permit them to let the oligopolistic industry operate more efficiently, even if sometimes with fewer firms. Of course, the first and simplest instance is where the first manufacturing firm of a given kind is established in a less developed country. A price control will bring it to the technologically most efficient production point and to a level of output higher (and of price lower) than it would otherwise have been operating at. Unless the resulting income per laborer in the monopoly equals incomes in other industries, the solution again will not be the best, but it will be a second best, generally superior by far to what would have come with complete *laissez faire*.

The term "friction prevention" is perhaps best descriptive of another activity that the authorities of the labor-managed economy should engage in: that is, the *prevention of factor immobility* among regions and among industries. Because the problem contains very little new in respect to a labor-managed situation, over and above its conventional statement in the context of western-type market economies, we do not have to dwell on it at length. Let it only be noted that any factor immobility will generally tend to yield suboptimal general equilibrium solutions under changing structural conditions. Enhancement of mobility, by any of a wide variety of means, will then be bound to lead to a more efficient resource allocation.

Beyond this point, the policies for improved efficiency or stability, as discussed in Chapters 16 and 17, fit into the present section—under the heading of avoiding of friction—without alteration. Let us just recall that coping with external economies and diseconomies, coping with the Hagen-Manoilescu problem of differential factor returns in "old" and "new" industries, the resolution of the problem of different technologies, and the stabilization of the macroeconomic equilibria are likely to be the most important of these policies.

18.3: *Steering the Labor-Managed Economy on Grounds of Foresight*

Even if the avoidance of friction in respect of structural adjustment were maximally effective, there would still remain important inef-

[2]Note that ideally, with free imports at a given exchange rate, foreign trade can supply the high, or infinite, demand elasticity for import-competing industries which otherwise —in our analysis above—must come from internal price regulation.

ficiencies in the operation of the labor-managed economy. The simple reason for this is that even once the friction-elimination action is taken, it may take one, two, or three years or longer before the adjustment is fully effected. For example, realization of high incomes in a certain branch of the economy may lead several new firms to enter, but it will take three years before they start operating and producing the desired reduction in corresponding prices. In terms of the parable of the introductory section, the simple point being made is that if remedial action is taken only once the raft starts to run aground, this will always imply a certain degree of inefficiency, however apt and however prompt the action may be.

Clearly, the only way in which the residual friction—or inefficiency —can be avoided is through planned intervention of one kind or another, based on prediction of future structural changes. A precondition for this is a correct analysis of trends and prediction of sectoral final demands in the future, as much as an accurate structural-flow description of the economy which permits checks of consistency between final demands on the one hand, and current input and investment requirements on the other; we will return to some aspects of this subject later on in this section.

But assuming that all the necessary data, including correct predictions, are available, let it first be noted that the steering based on prediction is related to—or is to be conducted with respect to—both major sources of friction (or imperfection) discussed at the outset of the preceding section: delays involved in long-run adjustment and entry of firms on the one hand, and imperfect knowledge and uncertainty in respect to investment projects deriving from project interdependence on the other. It must be clear that, once target or expected levels of output and demand are known for the next five or ten years, both sources of friction can be mitigated through appropriate action—that is, the raft can be steered into the proper position in the stream.

The steering then can be conducted on two different levels—with widely differing degrees of thoroughness. The less thorough approach is something close to what in France is called "indicative planning." Well elaborated predictions, targets, and/or projections are publicized as much as possible, so that the members of various industries can use such data as inputs into their individual production and expansion plans, or possibly organize conferences and engage in some sort of division of labor in designing the investment and production plans for the industry. The authorities also can engage in some indirect stimulating or punitive action to channel, so to speak, the industry into a path more closely resembling that postulated by the plan.

The second and more thorough level is based on a direct participation of the authorities in the national capital market. It is here that the socialist economy, or one adhering to what we have termed the national ownership, has a definite advantage, because—as we have argued in Chapter 15 and elsewhere, and as will be further illustrated in section 18.5—the authorities must in the name of the society keep their eye on and most often conduct the allocation of national investment resources. Especially in early stages of economic development, the government budget may be the most important part of the total supply of loanable funds. Even if it is not, some government agency still ought to serve as an intermediary between the lenders and ultimate borrowers for investment into capital assets which, by definition, are owned by society. At least the role of underwriter for purposes of protection of social capital, as suggested in our purely theoretical discussion of Part II, should be retained by the government.

In practice, and more concretely, the aim of the steering activity in respect to future investments and development of new firms should be the same as that of the friction-preventing activity discussed in the preceding section: to keep incomes per laborer in comparable skill categories about equal at all times—that is, to prevent major income maladjustments resulting from structural changes. The reason for this is clear: income equalization will guarantee, by and large, the equalization of marginal value products; and with a competitive capital market—as we have seen in Part I in the context of Pareto analysis, and in Part III in the context of the theory of investment—the investment criteria of the labor-managed economy will then guarantee operation of the economy at an optimal level.

It would be beyond the scope of the present study to go into the details of actual planning and projection techniques for the labor-managed economy. For one thing, they are not much different from those customarily used, whether in centrally planned economies or in planned western-type economies. The two important and relevant criteria here are projection of demand and consistency of interindustry current and capital flows with such projections. A possible set of methods for the Yugoslav economy was examined by Sirotkovic[3] and elaborated on by the present author.[4] Only some general remarks need be made here.

---

[3]Jakov Sirotkovic, *Problemi Privrednog Planiranja u Jugoslaviji* (Zagreb, 1961).

[4]J. Vanek, "Economic Planning in Jugoslavia," in Max F. Millikan, ed., *Economic Planning* (National Bureau of Economic Research, 1967).

Perhaps the most important and interesting one is that the input-output and activity-type analysis customarily employed in dealing with the problem at hand is extraordinarily well suited for planning in a labor-managed economy. One could almost say that these methods and labor management were predestined for each other. My rationale for saying this is as follows: it is commonplace among economists that in national planning the greatest value of input-output and activity analysis does not lie in million-equation schemes registering every minute category of output, but rather in a more or less detailed sectoral representation of the economy, including anything between two and, say, two hundred individual sectors. It is equally clear that long-range planning and checking of consistency is needed most where (natural) adjustment elasticities are lowest. In the labor-managed economy, it is precisely the intersectoral adjustment elasticities that can—as we know from all of our analysis—be expected to be low, while the intrasectoral elasticities, ruling the sphere of economic life left more to the market forces, can generally be expected to be a good deal higher, even in the short run, on grounds of joint production. To be more concrete, the crux of our argument is that, for example, the price elasticities and cross-elasticities within a sector, such as iron foundries, will be considerably higher than similar elasticities for the total of iron-foundry products and, say, footwear because a single firm can be expected to produce all or most iron-foundry products (and hence will be capable of substituting internally), while there is hardly a firm in the world which produces both shoes and iron manufactures. If, through various methods of steering based on foresight, the appropriate sectoral productive capacities can be guaranteed over time by interaction of both market forces and planning, market forces alone can be relied on to elaborate the detailed product mix within each sector.

18.4: *Steering the Labor-Managed Economy on Grounds of Differences between Social and Individual Valuations*

As we have noted already, avoiding disruptive adjustments to changing structural conditions in the future is not the only object of steering the labor-managed economy. Even if the stream on which our raft is floating is perfectly straight and there is no possibility of friction, the natural course—that is, the course determined by the operation of markets, in the context of the economic situation studied—may be deemed not desirable by the society acting as a single decision-making unit. It is such instances that we want to study in the present section. Again, we do not have to be overly thorough in our discussion because

most of the problems arise in all economic situations and are not specific to a labor-managed economy; only the planning (or policy) instruments by means of which they are tackled may be different and specific.

Significant examples of what we want to discuss are the economies
and diseconomies external to firms, but internal to specific competitive
industries, which we have both explained and shown solutions for at
the close of Chapter 16. We recall that in that instance the authorities
of the labor-managed economy were to steer the economy to an optimal solution—that is, a solution with marginal rates of transformation
and substitution equal—through a sales tax and/or subsidy appropriately applied. Perhaps the best known other case in point is that of
an infant industry tariff, also justifiable on grounds of an imperfect
operation of the market mechanism—though the imperfection now is
of a somewhat different type.

Another category, quite different from that delineated by the presence of externalities, includes cases in which society, acting as a whole
through political channels rather than through the market mechanism,
takes a different—one might say, a more responsible—view of the
economic universe than what markets would yield and imposes its will
through appropriate policy action. Perhaps the most significant case
in point is that in which the society, acting through its government,
takes a longer view than individuals would take, and for the sake of a
considerably higher future consumption curtails present consumption
while increasing accumulation of capital assets; this may be the most
important aspect of planning and policy-making in a labor-managed
economy, especially if it occurs in an early stage of development, and
we will devote to it all of the next section.

But there are similar cases in which a different social time preference
takes precedence over individuals' desires as expressed through the
markets. Conservation of natural resources is one. Another, perhaps
more important—again for a developing economy—may be discriminatory prevention of nonessential imports in favor of developmental
capital goods or raw materials or fuels. In all these cases, the only
thing that the authorities must look out for is to perform the steering
of the economy while preserving market equilibria. The labor-managed
economy is a market economy, and thus market forces must be re-
spected, as otherwise a good deal of distributional inefficiency and confusion are bound to arise.

Basically, if in social (collective) judgment, use of some products—
whether intermediate or final—is to be discouraged, this should be

done through sales taxes rather than through discretionary limitations of supply; the latter can only produce artificial scarcity incomes (or rents) on the part of the producers. Also let it be noted that in the context of the general equilibrium analysis of resource allocations, sales taxes are consistent with production on the production-possibility frontier (provided that factor incomes in various industries still are equalized), while a quantitative restriction, which as a general rule can be expected to raise incomes per laborer over the national average level, will be inefficient because it will lead to output below that frontier.

There is no precise or unique definition of what economists mean by regional economics and regional economic planning. But we can be sure of one thing: a good portion of those subjects really involves what we have termed steering on grounds of differences between social and individual valuations.[5] The argument is very simple. External diseconomies, transportation difficulties, low skill levels, and lack of technological know-how in certain backward regions of a country can be such that if strictly market forces were left to allocate resources and productive capacity throughout the country, these regions would never develop. Society as a whole may act to disregard the criteria of optimal investment allocation and foster the development of the backward regions. Of course, sooner or later the diseconomies mentioned above are bound to be reduced and eventually disappear altogether, and at that point the regional problem outlined here disappears. Actually, the situation—or more precisely, its rationale—is analogous to the situation of an infant-industry tariff.

The only point we want to make here in respect to the subject of regional steering is that again, as in all other instances, there will be more and less efficient instruments in attaining given objectives. While it would be too difficult to go into all the conceivable instances of regional plan implementation, let it only be noted that the various policy instruments discussed in this and the foregoing two chapters, possibly transformed somewhat for the regional task, will normally suffice.

18.5: *Planning, Propulsion, and Growth in a Labor-Managed Economy*

In this concluding section we are coming to what we have identified earlier as the "propulsion" of the labor-managed economy. We have

---

[5]Actually, what remains of the discipline after steering based on valuation differences is taken out is something comparable to what we have termed steering based on foresight except, of course, that emphasis here is given to a "smoothly flowing" regional and spatial economic allocation over time.

also indicated in the preceding section that in fact the phenomenon of propulsion is one significant instance of steering—or more precisely, altering the speed—on grounds of differences between social and individual values. In simple language, the central factors of propulsion in an economy are capital formation and efficient allocation of resources, including capital; efficient allocation was our concern through a number of previous chapters and thus we can concentrate here primarily on the first factor.

This brings us into the sphere of growth theory—more specifically, into the sphere of aggregate growth theory, because as we have indicated, structural efficiency should not concern us here. As a description or characterization of western economic organization, growth theory has attained, of late especially, a fairly advanced and sophisticated level. To my knowledge, no formal growth theory has been cast specifically for the labor-managed economy. This should not bother us very much, however, because once the degree of abstraction and simplification inherent in the existing growth theories developed in the western context is accepted, these theories are equally applicable to, or relevant for, the labor-managed situation.

Actually, one might even argue that most of the aggregate theories of economic growth, and in particular those referred to as neoclassical, are better suited for the labor-managed world than they are for the western-type capitalist situation. This is so, for one thing, because there are (as we have seen) at all times natural and automatic forces in the labor-managed economy to produce full employment of resources in the long run, a condition which need not exist in the western economies. Moreover—and this is not a proposition entirely distinct from that just made—price flexibility is far more likely to be present in the labor-managed economy.

Thus, in examining some of the key problems of propulsion of the labor-managed economy, we are at least as justified to use existing growth theory as are those who use it in studying western economies. This greatly simplifies our task. We do not have to worry about the formal development of growth theory, but instead we can draw on existing models and put them to work in studying the growth potential of the labor-managed economy (i.e., in studying our problem of "propulsion"). In some respects we will be able in this process to "capture," or incorporate into the growth model certain specifics of the labor-managed economy.

A comprehensive aggregate theory of economic growth has been developed by T. Bertrand and myself.[6] It not only permits consideration of many different kinds of technological change, but can be used to handle situations of increasing and diminishing returns (of the national technology), or to consider alternative savings functions. Moreover such a theory may include as special cases most of the standing simpler growth theories, such as the Harrod-Domar theory, the Solow-Swan neoclassical theory, and a number of others.

Basically, it is postulated that national output is produced from capital and labor, the latter growing over time at a prescribed constant rate of growth, while the former grows through accumulation of net savings. A given fraction of capital stock, c, must be replaced every year, and savings are derived from two individual savings functions, one depending on the income share of capital, Φ, the other on the income share of labor. Moreover, constant rates of factor-augmenting technological change a and b are postulated for labor and capital respectively,[7] and the national production function is homogeneous of order h ($\gtreqless 1$).

The basic characteristics of the growth process resulting from these postulates are summarized in the following five equations extracted from the article referred to in note 6:

$$\bar{k} = \frac{(a + m)h - (a + m - b)T}{1 - T} \tag{1}$$

$$T = \Phi + E(h - \Phi)(\Sigma - 1)/\Sigma h \tag{2}$$

$$E = (ds/d\Phi)/(s/\Phi) \tag{3}$$

$$y = (a + n)h + \Phi(\bar{k} + b - a - n) \tag{4}$$

$$y = k + (\dot{k}/k)Q - E\dot{\Phi}/\Phi \tag{5}$$

where n, k, and y are the rates of growth of labor, capital, and gross national product respectively, Σ is the elasticity of factor substitution for the national production function, Q is the ratio of gross to net savings (i.e., gross to net investment), s represents the average gross saving rates, d indicates differentiation, and a "dot" above a variable is a differential with respect to time (so that k/k simply is the rate of acceleration of capital, and $\dot{\Phi}/\Phi$ represents the growth rate of the factor income share of capital). Furthermore, $\bar{k}$ is the so-called asymptotic

---

[6]See Trent J. Bertrand and J. Vanek, "A Theory of Growth with Technological Change, Variable Returns to Scale, and a General Savings Function," *Rivista Internazionale di Scienze Economiche e Commerciale*, 1 (January 1969).

[7]In simple language, this implies that efficiency of each unit of the two factors is increasing over time at a constant rate.

rate of growth of capital toward which the actual rate k will converge over time, and when it attains it, k must be stationary.

In what follows, we will first use the above equations in describing the first twenty years of growth and development of an economy using some simple "central" or "average" assumptions reflecting some characteristics of the labor-managed economy as well as some reasonable values of parameters as they are likely to arise in the real world. Following that, we will use the "central case" as a point of departure and a standard of comparison in analyzing some other pertinent situations of growth propulsion. Clearly, we cannot be exhaustive in this endeavor; an independent and more extensive theoretical study of the growth potential of the labor-managed economy would be necessary, possibly including two sectors, one modern and industrial and one traditional and primary, but this is beyond the scope of the present work.

Our central case is extremely simple. We assume an indefinitely durable capital stock (i.e., $c = 0$ and $Q = 1$), Hicks-neutral technological change (i.e. $a = b$), unitary elasticity of substitution (i.e., $\Sigma = 1$), and constant returns to scale (i.e., $h = 1$). As for the initial conditions, the other "realistic" numerical parameters, they are as follows.

We start observing the economy at a rather early stage of economic development. The level of gross national product is postulated to be as high as the entire capital stock of the economy. On the assumptions made earlier (actually the assumption of a Cobb-Douglas production function, implied in $Q = 1$), we know that the competitive income share of capital is constant, and we will assume throughout that it is equal to 0.3.

Suppose now that the savings-investment generating scheme, as discussed in Chapter 15 is one based on national ownership; the national labor-management agency decides to take the earnings of capital entirely out of personal disposable income and plough back the entire competitive share of capital (i.e., what capital would earn if it were paid its marginal value product at all times) into national investment. This constitutes what we refer to as case 2. Case 1 is only slightly different; we postulate that one-third of the share of capital Φ is used for current government consumption, while the remaining two-thirds is invested every year. Since Φ does not change over time, we are actually constructing results for an economy with constant average savings rates of 0.2 and 0.3 in cases 1 and 2 respectively. As a set of realistic rates of growth of the labor force and of technology, we take $n = 0.02$, and $b = 0.03$. While the first rate corresponds to a real figure approximately observable in many countries, the latter estimate is based on the postulates that in countries on the frontier of technical advance technology improves at somewhere near two per cent per annum and that a less developed country (which we attempt to illustrate here) can do better than that in the long run by narrowing the technological gap through imitation. Since savings are generated solely from the earnings of capital, E takes the value 1 in this example.

Assuming that in period zero the capital stock and national product both were at the level of 100, the rates of growth of income y_1 and y_2 for cases 1 and 2 together with corresponding rates of growth of capital, were computed for twenty years in Table 18.5.1. For case 2—that is, the situation in which all of the competitive income share of capital is reinvested, we have also computed the actual levels of national product,

Table 18.5.1: Numerical illustrations of growth in a labor-managed economy*

Time period	y_1	y_2	k_1	k_2	Y_2	K_2	r_2
0	—	—	—	—	100	100	—
1	10.4	13.4	20.0	30.0	113	130	2.24
2	9.9	11.9	18.1	25.0	127	163	—
3	9.4	10.9	16.7	21.7	141	198	—
4	9.1	10.2	15.6	19.3	155	237	—
5	8.8	9.7	14.6	17.5	170	279	2.80
6	8.6	9.2	13.8	16.1	185	324	—
7	8.4	8.9	13.0	15.0	201	374	—
8	8.2	8.6	12.3	14.1	219	429	—
9	8.1	8.4	11.8	13.3	237	486	—
10	7.9	8.2	11.4	12.6	256	545	3.15
11	7.8	8.0	11.0	12.0	276	610	—
12	7.7	7.9	10.6	11.5	298	680	—
13	7.6	7.7	10.3	11.1	320	754	—
14	7.5	7.6	10.0	10.7	344	832	—
15	7.4	7.5	9.7	10.3	320	914	3.25
16	7.4	7.4	9.5	10.0	397	1002	—
17	7.3	7.3	9.3	9.7	425	1097	—
18	7.2	7.2	9.1	9.5	455	1197	—
19	7.1	7.2	8.9	9.3	488	1303	—
20	7.0	7.1	8.7	9.1	523	1420	3.30
∞	6.3	6.3	6.3	6.3	∞	∞	—

*For underlying theory and assumptions, see text of section 18.5.

Y_2, and capital stock, K_2, attained, and the implied *incremental* (not total) capital-output ratio r_2.

As is apparent from the table, our hypothetical economy does very well over the twenty-year period. Especially when it invests all of its competitive capital income, it starts out with a rate of growth of national product of over 13 per cent, that rate declining to about 10, 8, and 7 per cent in five, ten, and twenty years respectively. The asymptotic—or natural—rate of growth corresponding to the situation, as given by equation (1), is 6.3 per cent. All these growth rates are not only quite satisfactory, but they are illustrative of patterns realized by some of the very successful economies of the real world. Even with the 20 per cent savings rate, the growth rates are substantial, starting at over 10 per cent in the twentieth year (note that $\bar{k}$ is independent of the savings rate, equal to 6.3 per cent for both cases).

In absolute terms, the corresponding performance may be even more illustrative. Starting at the level of 100, national product increases in case 2 by over 150 in the first ten years, and more than quintuples in twenty years. Because of several offsetting forces, the variations in the incremental capital-output ratio are less pronounced; nonetheless, an increase, also tending to diminish in intensity, is observable in that magnitude over time. This is also a pattern frequently observable in the early stages of development in the real world.

It should be clear that if our labor-managed economy pursued—as does Yugoslavia—a more vigorous savings-investment policy, tapping not only the competitive income share of capital, but also asking the labor-managed firms (besides paying for the use of social capital) to repay investment loans provided from the central funds, or to finance part of their projects immediately, the growth picture would be even more satisfactory. Such a set of policies might add another 10 or 15 per cent of national product to capital formation every year, and thus bring the product in twenty years in case 2 to some sevenfold of the initial level.

All this, of course, is said on the assumption that nothing is saved from the income of labor—that is, income earned by households whether via tax and budgetary surplus or via direct household savings. If such savings are forthcoming, they can be added on top of those generated by the competitive earnings of capital.

On the other hand, the picture can be made somewhat less bright, especially where there are only limited natural resources. In that case the national production function is likely to become less than unit homogeneous (i.e., $h < 1$), and the growth rates will be correspondingly less. On the other hand, in economies experiencing labor surpluses in the early stages of development, the parameter Φ (even if not entirely disbursed as income of capital) can be equal to one.[8] This then pushes the asymptotic rate of growth of capital $\bar{k}$ to infinity, and the actual rates of growth of capital and income (k and y) then must grow continuously. Of course, this holds only within the theoretical model. In the real world, with capital growing at an accelerating rate, sooner or later (but rather sooner) full employment of labor must eventually be reached, even if at first labor resources from the traditional sectors are tapped and transferred. Thus diminishing returns will set in which will nullify the absurd (theoretical) result that $\bar{k}$ would be infinite.

[8]Note that implicit in the Harrod-Domar theory with only capital a scarce factor, Φ is equal to one.

19. Summary and Conclusions

19.1: *Principal Findings of Part I*

Partly to conform to an accepted practice and distinction among western economists, partly in order to be able to handle a very complex theoretical problem, in Part I we treated the labor-managed economy in what we may term its "dehumanized" form. Specifically, we neglected most of the human aspects and implications of labor management and merely developed a comprehensive microeconomic theory of a system in which income per laborer (rather than profit as in the capitalist system) is maximized as the most fundamental objective of the labor-managed productive unit. The principal findings about the behavior of such a system are as follows.

The static equilibrium of a labor-managed firm is defined in very much the same way as that of a capitalist firm; that is all variable factors of production, including labor, and including capital in the long run, must in equilibrium earn their respective marginal revenue products. It will be recalled here that by "marginal revenue product" is understood the increment in revenue of a firm, whether competitive or monopolistic, attributable to the employment of the last unit of a particular factor. Of course, this statement of the equilibrium precludes monopsony in factor markets; but introduction of such market structures is straightforward and follows the conventional lines.

While the definition is seemingly conventional, the equilibria thus obtained for a labor-managed firm are quite different. Some of the most important static results, on the assumption that the firm finds all the labor it needs for equilibrium operation,[1] are as follows. In the long run (i.e., with all factor inputs variable) a fully competitive labor-managed firm must operate always at a point of maximum physical efficiency (i.e., where for given factor proportions the factor productivity is at a maximum). In the short run—with plant and equipment (i.e.,

---

[1]We will speak below about the situation in which this condition is not fulfilled.

382

capital stock) fixed—the equilibrium can be either below or above the optimum operation. But considering that in practice a firm is growing by successive additions to capital stock, one can conclude that most firms in a growing economy, especially where there is a tendency for capital-labor ratios to increase, would operate at less than optimal capacity. Compared to an otherwise identical capitalist firm, the labor-managed firms will always have a smaller size and a higher capital-labor ratio, whenever the capitalist "equivalent" operates with positive profits (i.e., in the majority of cases). The opposite conclusions hold when the "equivalent" firm loses money—a situation applicable only in the short run.

From what has just been said, it follows that the long-run equilibrium of the labor-managed firm under perfect competition is indeterminate whenever the technology is subject to constant returns to scale. This situation is approximated beyond a certain level of operation in many, if not most manufacturing firms.[2] In practice, this indeterminacy then can give the labor-managed firm the opportunity to follow other objectives (our principal concern in Part III) such as maximization of local employment. While the scale of operation under the conditions just described is indeterminate, of course, the factor proportions and capital-output ratio are uniquely given.

Turning now to the case of monopoly, oligopoly, and monopolistic competition—still confining ourselves to static equilibria—the most important conclusion is that whenever the labor-managed firm has any monopoly power, its equilibrium must be in the range of the production function where it is subject to increasing returns to scale, that is, with conventional production functions, falling short of the optimal scale of operation. It further follows that constant returns to scale over the whole range of conceivable operations and monopoly power are mutually inconsistent. In practice, the important implication is that in general oligopolistic market structures will be more competitive under labor management than under capitalism, and thus the degree of monopolistic price-cost distortion will be less. An implication of the same forces is that there will be far less tendency toward oligopolistic warfare in the labor-managed situation. At the same time, in a purely monopolistic situation—where for one reason or another the number of firms is limited to one—our earlier conclusions regarding compara-

---

[2]It will be recalled that the long-run equilibrium of a fully competitive capitalist firm operating under constant returns to scale is determinate, zero, or infinite output, depending on whether the unit costs cannot or can be covered by price.

tive scales of operation stated for the competitive firm obtain: for
example, a capitalist monopoly realizing positive profits (most monopolies are of that kind) will be less restrictive, and employ more labor
per unit of capital than its labor-managed "equivalent."

The comparative tendency of market structures to be more competitive under labor management is strengthened considerably in the
highly realistic cases of product differentiation and sales promotion.
While there is scope for differentiation and advertising under labor
management these activities will never be as strong in this particular
case as they are in a capitalist situation. More specifically, if we can
ascertain that a capitalist firm producing a differentiated product and
engaging in advertising makes positive profit, then we can be sure that
it produces a higher volume of output and makes a greater effort in
advertising than a comparable labor-managed firm. This has very important implications for a number of reasons. First, given the size of
the market, we can be sure that fewer firms will operate in a capitalist
market structure than would be operating under similar conditions in
a labor-managed structure. Second, and perhaps more important, with
a lesser degree of advertising by the labor-managed firm, we can be sure
that the more extreme forms of advertising such as high pressure promotion, exhortational advertising, and other similar types will be foregone by the labor-managed firm whereas they will be engaged in by the
capitalist equivalent. The comparative advantage for the labor-
managed economy can be enormous. Not only can resources be di-
verted from advertising to other more productive and more construc-
tive activities, but also some of the external diseconomies usually
associated with high pressure advertising will be avoided.

Remaining within the realm of static equilibria, let us summarize
some of the key findings regarding the supply of and demand for labor.
It must be clear that the labor-managed system, even in its "dehumanized" form as studied in Part I, does not contain a conventional labor
market. While it is still possible to think of a supply of labor, or "availability function" of labor, confronting an individual firm, a conventional demand function emanating from the equilibrium operations of
the firm is not defined. Instead, the firm has a single demand point—
that is, a unique configuration of income per laborer and amount of
labor (number of laborers) required. If that point is consistent with the
labor availability facing the firm, as we have assumed thus far in this
section, the equilibrium of the firm will be that consistent with the
demand point. If the potential demand point is not consistent with the

availability function and the latter is infinitely elastic, then the firm cannot operate at all. If the availability function is less than infinitely elastic, then there will be a more or less extensive range of possible operation of the firm even if the demand point is not consistent with the availability function; the size of the range will vary, among other things, with the degree of inelasticity of the availability function.

More could be said by way of a summary about equilibria of competitive and oligopolistic market structures, but we will do so only below in the context of comparative statics; to that subject we now turn. Perhaps most unconventional are the results concerning the short-run behavior of a labor-managed firm producing a single product. The short-run supply elasticity of such a firm (i.e., a firm maximizing income per laborer) will generally be negative or zero. With a fixed capital stock a labor-managed firm will reduce or keep unchanged its output—and correspondingly inputs of all variable factors of production, including labor—when the price of its single output increases, and vice versa. The zero-elastic situation will obtain whenever the input coefficients are fixed; this situation is very likely in the short run.

Of course, in the vast majority of cases, we have firms producing more than one product. In such situations the tendency toward a negative supply elasticity will generally be more than offset by the tendency to substitute in production a more expensive product for one which is relatively cheaper, and thus the short-run elasticities of supply of a single product normally will be positive. However, when prices of all (or most) products of a firm increase simultaneously, the negative- or zero-elastic situation still can be expected in the short run, on the assumptions underlying Part I. Of course, in any real situation, involving all the dimensions of labor, reductions in output with higher prices should be considered most unlikely, as, indeed, this would imply that the working collective would be engaging in self-mutilation in a period when everybody's income is increasing, in order to secure further increases (often only very small or hardly perceptible ones). Nonetheless the general conclusion must be retained that the labor-managed firm is one characterized by short-run supply elasticities lower than those that would be associated with a comparable capitalist firm.

As usual, relaxation of the assumption of the short run—that is, the postulate that capital stock can also be optimally adjusted—will augment (in algebraic value) the supply elasticities and have a corresponding impact on the demand for productive factors of an individual firm. However, the above stated general expectation regarding lower elasticities in the short run still is to be retained for firms with technologies subject to increasing and then diminishing returns in the long run. When constant returns to scale are present, of course, we know that the scale of operation of the firm is indeterminate in the long run, and thus the supply elasticity also remains indeterminate. However, this indeterminacy permits the labor-managed firm to pursue other objectives —in particular to avoid in the long run the reductions in employment which might have been called for on grounds of short-run optimum adjustment.

The derivation of industry supply functions and demands for productive factors other than labor presents no difficulty: these schedules are nothing but an aggregation of corresponding schedules of individual firms within the industry. If the number of firms is fixed, postulating a restricted entry into the industry, the over-all properties of the supply schedules for the industry will be similar to those established for an individual labor-managed firm, and the schedules will be defined within a range consistent with the labor supply function. The latter function now plays the same role as the minimum cost point in the capitalist theory in fixing the bottom of the industry supply curve (with restricted entry).

If we alter the assumptions and postulate free entry (and exit) in a competitive industry, matters change a good deal. The basic rule for entry into the industry is that all of the labor availability not be utilized by the industry, given the conditions of the product market. If such "available" labor exists, it can compete in the national markets for capital resources and form new firms which enter the industry. The conditions for exit are analogous, in reverse—that is, availability must fall short of the requirements of labor at given product-market conditions. To any prescribed income per laborer now corresponds a specific number of firms and a specific equilibrium position of each firm; in other words, the competitive industry now again has a demand function for labor, and, by the same token, a full-employment supply curve of its product (or products). If the conventional assumption of identical technologies within the industry is made—still postulating the dehumanized environment—the product supply function will be the same as that of a comparable capitalist industry facing the same supply of labor. In particular with a horizontal supply of labor (i.e., infinitely elastic) and identical technologies, the supply of product also will be infinitely elastic, adjustments in the size of the market taking place exclusively through adjustments in the number of firms. As a general rule, the comparative inelasticity of market schedules disappears in the labor-managed environment, once freedom of entry and exit are permitted.

Obviously, once the supply of the competitive industry is determined, the formation of price in the product market is conventional, price being determined at the point of equilibrium of supply and demand. In the ideal case of free entry, horizontal supply of labor, and identical technologies, as in the capitalist situation, the equilibrium price will exactly exhaust factor costs—that is, will be identical with the average cost—provided that the income per laborer is reckoned as an element of cost. But contrary to the capitalist situation, this price-cost relationship will obtain even in less than ideal market situations. In the ideal case, all incomes per laborer throughout the industry will be equal, and thus, with competitive markets assumed for all other productive factors, the industry will be utilizing productive resources Pareto-optimally. If technologies are different, the allocation within the industry will tend to be suboptimal, the more productive firms generally underproducing and the less productive ones overproducing. But a simple set of policy tools is available to overcome such a misallocation. Of course, all these efficiency considerations are based on a strict assumption of identical quality of labor. If incomes in different industries vary because of different labor efficiencies, obviously, with technologies otherwise identical, optimum efficiency of resource allocation still will be preserved.

The factor-market schedules of labor-managed firms and industries with respect to resources other than labor are much more conventional than the situation encountered for labor. Of the many results that were obtained only a few of the most important need be mentioned: other things remaining unchanged, the over-all capital-labor ratio of a labor-managed firm will vary inversely with the price (cost) of capital. But the demand function for capital will again, on the whole, have a low elasticity (in absolute value), lower than that of a capitalist firm. In general, all factor-demand elasticities will tend to be less, because any increase in a price of a factor other than labor will tend not only to increase the marginal product of that factor and thus to reduce its employment, but also to reduce the income and marginal productivity of labor, and thus raise employment and output higher than they would be with marginal product of labor unchanged.

We have also studied other than perfectly competitive market structures. The principal results on monopoly we have stated already—

and we cannot overemphasize here the implicit conclusion to the effect that given market conditions, market structures in a labor-managed economy will tend in general to be more competitive, *ceteris paribus*, and to reveal far less tendency toward oligopolistic market warfare than capitalist market structures.

Turning now to more formal statements and theories of monopolistic or imperfect competition, and of oligopoly, it can be said that most if not all of the conventional theories have their analogue in the labor-managed world. In particular, we have studied in greater detail the transposition of Chamberlin's theory of monopolistic competition, and found that in the "pure" case characterized by identical technologies and identical (or better, symmetrical) demand conditions, the industry solutions are the same, provided that free entry (again, in the labor-managed world, governed by the excess of income over the position of the labor supply function) is guaranteed. The more general Chamberlinean solutions, and the Cournot, Bertrand, and Stackleberg solutions of duopoly or oligopoly have also been studied, but we will not enter here into the details of the corresponding findings.

The concluding chapter of Part I, dealing with the general equilibrium of the labor-managed economy, is perhaps the most important of that part of the study; it is definitely the most significant for the analysis of economic efficiency of resource allocation and social welfare. Since we will return to the subject in a more synthetic manner later on in this chapter (section 6) only a few words need be said here. On the conventional "ideal" assumptions of perfect competition, perfect mobility and variability of all productive factors, identical technologies within each industry, and free entry, the labor-managed economy will automatically (1) operate with a full employment of all of its productive resources, and (2) allocate these resources Pareto-optimally. In other words, the perfectly competitive labor-managed economy (in its dehumanized version, it should be recalled) will operate in the long run at its maximum production-possibility frontier. If any of the "ideal" conditions are relaxed, including most importantly the assumptions of the long run and of freedom of entry, the economy will—as is always the case—depart from the optimum, and often will do so to a greater extent than an equivalent (otherwise equally ideal) capitalist economy. This departure is the direct result of the low short- and long-run elasticities established in the chapters dealing with partial equilibria and its extent will vary with the degree of these inelasticities. If, for example, most of the adjustment to changing economic conditions (i.e., changing underlying parameters of the general equilibrium system) is of the intrafirm variety, and thus elasticities remain high, both the departure from the optimal frontier, and the comparative disadvantage of the labor-managed economy, may be very small—vice versa for adjustments which are primarily interfirm or intersectoral.

One fundamental conclusion from the general equilibrium analysis is the paramount importance of free and speedy entry in the labor-managed economy. More is said about the subject in Part IV dealing with economic policy and planning, and correspondingly more will be said about it in section 4 of the present chapter. Another significant conclusion is that what might appear as a drawback from the narrow and rigid point of view of an individual firm maximizing income per laborer—for example, failure to reduce output and employment in the short run with increasing prices—turns into a significant virtue from the social (or national) point of view, because the departure from optimum will be less important.[3] Still another, and perhaps more important fact, is that in the case of constant returns to scale of individual firms, with changing market conditions, the firms whose equilibrium is indeterminate in the long run may simply desire to adjust their capital stocks, and thus also reveal the desirable supply elasticities and reduce considerably the inefficiencies of general equilibrium adjustment.

19.2: *Principal Findings of Part II*

While Part I was devoted to the study of microeconomic behavior of the labor-managed economy, Part II covers the subject conventionally identified as macroeconomic theory, or the theory of national-income determination. The general framework of the analysis still retains some of the simplifying characteristics introduced in Part I—characteristics which we have described as dehumanizing the labor-managed system. Specifically, we still assume that there is only one type of labor in the economy, of constant and uniform quality, acting solely as a factor of production, the only reflection of labor management and income sharing being the objective of maximizing income per laborer.

As is well known, the principal objective of macroeconomic theory is the explanation of how, in the short run, the level of national income (product), the general price level, the level of aggregate labor employment, and the rate of interest are determined. Following recent prac-

---

[3]Of course, in the realistic context of a nondehumanized system, even from the point of view of an individual labor-managed firm it will normally be preferable not to reduce employment.

tice, the answers are obtained from a general equilibrium system consisting of four distinct markets—markets of goods (and services), bonds (securities or loanable funds), money, and labor. Of course, the labor market, for reasons explained in Part I, is a different species from all other markets in the labor-managed economy, and thus can be thought of as a "quasi market." However, from the point of view of formal analysis the quasi market contains the same type of information as all other markets, that is, a restriction on the permissible values of the endogenous variables of the general equilibrium system.

While it is recognized that labor management can have an impact on the specific parameters defining each of the four markets, there is no reason to believe that the fundamental nature of the money and securities markets should be different in the labor-managed economy from what they are customarily postulated to be in western-type (or Keynesian) macroeconomic theory. However, the product market and what we have called the quasi labor market are changed fundamentally for two reasons. First, and most important, we have the principle of maximization of income per laborer, which yields, as we have seen in Part I, a new set of product-supply and labor-demand conditions. Second, one component of aggregate national demand (effective demand), namely the investment function, also changes its basic nature because of the different principles underlying the investment decision in the labor-managed firm. This qualitative change, however, does not lead to very significant changes of the conventional investment function; specifically, the latter still remains negatively sloped with respect to changes in the rate of interest.

A significant parametric characteristic—and one of the strong points of the labor-managed economy—is the absence of any wage-price rigidity.[4] It derives naturally from the absence of conflict and countervailing union power in the labor-managed enterprises and the residual nature of labor remuneration.

This price-wage (or more exactly, price-labor-income) flexibility prevents states of unemployment of the Keynesian type in the labor-managed economies. This does not, however, preclude unemployment or less than full capacity utilization altogether, because of the special short-run nature of the quasi labor market. In the absence of prompt

---

[4]It will be recalled that this rigidity is the most important cause of unemployment and less than capacity output in capitalist economies, as well as a cause of inflation in these economies.

entry of new firms, and with capital costs to the producers too low in real terms, short-run labor unemployment is a possibility in the labor-managed economy. This unemployment, however, will generally not be too serious because even in a period of "depressed" conditions, the long-run forces of entry and even expansion of existing firms will not disappear. Thus even if there is temporary unemployment, there will be a simultaneous natural tendency to correct such a state of disequilibrium in the longer run. It may again be recalled that such natural forces are not present in western-type capitalist economies.

Because we will return to the problems of macroeconomic policy—which are, in effect, problems in comparative statics—we may go only very briefly over our findings regarding the adjustment of the macroeconomic general equilibrium to changing economic conditions. Probably the most important general notion is that the low supply elasticities established in the context of macroeconomic theory in Part I do not disappear when we come to deal with the aggregates. On the contrary, because the salutary effect of substitution in production disappears when we consider variations in the general price level, the low elasticities become much more of a real issue in the macro-world than they were in the micro-world.

Strongly backward-bending supply functions of national product need not be feared in any realistic situation. On the grounds that fixed coefficients are likely to prevail in the short run and that with increasing incomes the working collectives are most unlikely to engage in short-run self-mutilation, very low and for practical purposes zero short-run elasticities can be expected. This has both advantages and disadvantages. The main disadvantage is that the product market may undergo fairly strong variations in price as a result of changes in total national demand. The corresponding advantage is that such changes in demand will generally have little effect—if any—on national employment and the level of national output. Another significant fact is that the labor-managed economy will be far less susceptible to long-range inflationary pressures.

Beyond the natural forces, the safeguards for full employment and a high level of economic activity in the labor-managed economy are thus to be sought in the long-range economic policy and planning. Short-run policy instruments are most suitable for controlling the price level and possibly the short-run rate of interest; but this brings us to the subject matter of Part IV which will be reviewed only in section 4. In that section we also will take up the multipliers linking the endogenous variables, such as the level of national product and employment, the price level, and the rate of interest, to prescribed changes in the various markets defining the general equilibrium, whether stemming from alterations of policy instruments or imputable to autonomous causes.

19.3: *The Analysis and Principal Findings of Part III*

The principal simplifying assumptions of Parts I and II—assumptions which led us to speak of the analysis of the two parts as "dehumanized"—were (1) a single type of labor skill, (2) invariant quality and intensity of labor, independent of remuneration and of the productive environment, and (3) exclusive capacity of labor as a factor of production—that is, a complete neglect of the managerial function assumed by labor in the labor-managed economy. In Part III the three assumptions, or sets of assumptions, are gradually relaxed, chapter by chapter.

In Chapter 11, the first of Part III, we treat of the situation in which there are many different skills, or categories of labor, but the assumptions of constant quality and exclusive productive function are retained. The analysis is carried out both in respect to the behavior of an individual labor-managed firm, and in respect to the industry and general equilibrium. Under the new conditions, the working collective must agree on a specific distribution schedule, allocating a distribution coefficient to each labor category. Once this is done, the equilibrium condition for labor employment remains the same as in the uniform-labor case; namely, in equilibrium (i.e., when the firm maximizes its income per laborer) each labor category must be receiving its marginal revenue product. The comparative statics of the new situation, if not conventional, is also quite straightforward and consistent with common sense. Thus, for example, an increase in the price of a product will generally reduce the employment of all types of labor, and an increase in a distribution coefficient will reduce the employment of the corresponding labor category. All these results are summarized in Table 11.2.1.

Conceived in a broader industry or general equilibrium setting, the formation of incomes of different labor categories will be somewhat different from that attained by conventional labor markets in situations where labor is merely a factor of production. In pure theory, there is a process of complete convergence of labor remunerations among firms and industries in the labor-managed economy, based on competition and entry. More realistically, however, income-distribution schedules and corresponding incomes will tend to be the outcome of an inter-action between the will of the working collective and external influences of the more conventional market variety. The latter will guarantee the absence of major interfirm income differentials, while the former—that is, internal decision-making—will give the possibility of preserving a certain degree of individuality and independence to the labor-managed enterprise in matters of remuneration. In particular, the collective will can be expected to produce more equal income distribution within the firm than what would be dictated by market forces. With marginal equilibrium pricing in each firm, of course, this can lead to slight departures from "narrow" physical Pareto-optimality for the industry and the whole economy. The question remains, however, whether this conclusion is not only an illusion stemming from too narrow an interpretation of optimality. Indeed, the preservation of an income-distribution schedule—to a degree at least—as the working collective wants to have it, will generally be worth a small marginal departure from the physical maximum producible by the economy.

Relaxing the second simplifying assumption—that is, the assumption of an invariant quality and intensity of labor—reveals perhaps the greatest strength of labor-managed enterprise. Stated very briefly, the conclusion is that the labor-managed productive organization comes the closest to, and may even surpass, a self-employed individual with respect to the attainment of an optimal balance between income on the one hand and effort (i.e., duration, quality, or intensity of work) on the other. Stated in more conventional terminology, it can be said that the labor-managed enterprise appears to be the best form of productive organization (of more than one individual) from the point of view of the incentive it gives to its members.

If we postulate that any firm—whether capitalist, Soviet-type, or labor-managed—must operate with a certain limit of minimum acceptable effort, then normally the labor-managed firm will perform by far the most efficiently—that is, will produce the highest output in quality and volume. Moreover, if such a limit were abolished, it would be only the labor-managed firm that could remain in operation. The capitalist and Soviet-type firms (adhering to a fixed-wage scheme) would be bound to go out of business.

Although there is now a certain asymmetry between effects of changes in (nonlabor) factor costs and product price, the behavior of the labor-managed firm with variable and endogenously determined quality of labor retains some of the characteristics established in Part I. In particular, a low or even a negative supply elasticity of the product, imputable exclusively to adjustments in labor effort to changing incentives, is still the most likely outcome.[5] And it must be noted that while in the "dehumanized" context of Part I a negative supply elasticity was —or could be—in a sense a result of an "inhuman" management decision—which might have been foregone in a labor-managed firm—in the present context a low or negative supply elasticity is the result of optimal behavior not involving any basic human conflicts.

Considering that adjustments in work intensity and effort to changing economic conditions can take place—so to speak—overnight, while other basic business reactions (of the type studied in Part I), even those referred to as "short run," are taken for periods of at least a year or so, the question arises whether or to what extent the former adjustments can distort the firm's and thus the social optimum operation, based on longer-range decisions. The answer is that such distortions can arise, but the technical nature of the underlying decision-making criteria indicates that there will be a good deal of what we may call "internal offsetting" at work which will guarantee that such distortions, if any, will remain small. Especially in view of the considerable gains that the labor-managed firm can expect from its inherent qualities of incentive creation, the possible (not necessary) losses to social efficiency should be considered as negligible.

A highly relevant consideration is that the range of "reasonable variation" in the real value of output on account of incentives and changing effort can reach into hundreds of per cent. For example, if the three attributes of effort—duration of work, intensity and quality—can each "reasonably" vary between 100 and 200 per cent, the total "reasonable" variation in effort is between 100 and 800 per cent. By contrast, in the sphere of the Paretoan (or marginalist) comparison, the relevant ranges are normally of the order of one hundred times smaller, say between 100 and 110 per cent.[6]

---

[5] In the case of very poor countries the elasticity of supply with respect to price can be quite high, however, because of the improvement in nutrition, health and strength that increased earnings will entail. These same factors can also make the labor-managed alternative far more desirable for the developing nations than any other economic organization.

[6] For example, empirical studies of the *gross* "marginalist" gains from the European Common Market for the union, conducted under the supervision of this author, indicate that these gains were not higher than 0.5 per cent of national product.

Finally we relax the third simplifying assumption of Parts I and II, that is, the assumption that labor acts exclusively as a factor of production. In other words, we now turn to some of the aspects of operation of the labor-managed firm stemming from, or related to, labor's managerial function. In fact, to be exact, the third assumption was already partially relaxed in our above discussion of incentives and effort variation. Clearly, the field opened by this alteration of the general framework of our analysis is enormous, and we could not hope to be exhaustive in covering it, especially because the field spreads well beyond the confines of economics.

What we were able to cover we organized into two parts, Chapters 13 and 14. In the first of the two we deal with a comparatively large number of subjects, not necessarily integrated or deriving from each other, bearing on the principal aspects of a labor-managed firm deriving from the new capacity of laborers as managers. Subjects such as the actual process and forms of labor management, training, and education in the firm, intangible and nonmonetary incomes, labor-originating technical change and innovation, and several others are studied. We will not go here into the substance of this analysis, because the task would be too extensive and repetitive; the reader may turn to Chapter 13 itself. Only two general remarks seem to be in order at this point. First, the analysis in Chapter 13, almost without exception, leads to the conclusion that the opening up of the faculties and range of operation of the members of an enterprise constitutes a positive factor in the over-all performance and operation of the firm—even though we made no special effort to consider only subjects which would yield conclusions favorable to labor management. The second general notion emerging from Chapter 13 is that labor management tends to transform an enterprise into something resembling a living organism—much more so than any other form of productive organization—one of its main virtues being the high degree of adaptability to, and integratability with, its immediate environment.

Chapter 14, the last of Part III, has much greater unity than Chapter 13. We deal in it with the problems of entry (i.e., formation or creation), expansion, and exit of firms in the labor-managed economy. Clearly, all these phenomena are heavily influenced not only by labor management but also by the specific legal and institutional forms assumed by a labor-managed economy. The subject matter of Chapter 14 falls into two distinct parts. The first concerns the legal and institutional aspects of entry and related problems, while in the second we deal with the more technical and formal questions of the investment decision in the labor-managed firm.

At least four different originators of entry of firms are distinguished: central authorities, local authorities, existing firms, and groups of (private) individuals. Besides creation of independent new productive units, another important modality of entry emanating from existing firms is—from the point of view of its impact on markets and the economic structure—adoption of new lines of production by these firms. A special section is devoted to the formation and entry of firms in the developing countries; it is shown that the labor-managed form is ideal in a number of respects, and can play a decisive role in situations where a lack of entrepreneurship constitutes a barrier to development.

Central to the second part of Chapter 14—dealing with the investment decision—is the objective (or decision) function to be used in deciding whether a specific project, a new firm or an expansion, should be undertaken or not. By contrast to the present discounted value or internal return criteria normally used by capitalist firms or potential entrants, in the labor-managed system the objective will be (in a way and with qualifications detailed in Chapter 14) the maximization of the discounted income per laborer. Under perfect market conditions (including the capital market), the criterion again, as in the conventional capitalist case, can be formulated in two versions, one with reference to discounted values, the other with reference to the internal rate of return.

Of key importance is the question whether the investment criteria of the labor-managed system produce an optimal allocation of capital resources in the economy. The answer is that provided that other markets operate perfectly, a perfect capital market will lead to a social optimum. If the condition of perfect competition in other markets—in particular in the labor market (or quasi labor market)—is not fulfilled, then social optimum cannot be attained; but neither can it be attained by a freely operating capitalist economy.

19.4: *Summary and Conclusions of Part IV*

In Part IV we studied the principal problems of general and specific policy confronting an economy based on labor management. With regard to the general problems our principal purpose was merely to point out to the reader that a labor-managed economy need not be a socialist economy. Indeed, the actual form of ownership of physical or financial capital is not the basis of distinction relevant here; what makes an economy or a sector of it labor-managed is the manner and the right of controlling a common activity of a collective of producers. And thus we can have labor-managed economies which are socialist, and those which are not. Moreover, either economy—but especially the non-socialist one—can be mixed in the sense that two sectors, one labor-managed and the other more traditional, may coexist in it. The only important stipulation is that in a mixed economy the two sectors must be placed on a plane of legal, institutional, and political equality. This in turn will normally call for the formation of a national labor-management agency.

In fact, the distinction between labor-managed and non-labor-managed is far more significant than the distinction between socialist and nonsocialist. While the former involves a whole way of life bearing on every hour of a man's active day, the latter, from an individual's point of view, may not mean much more than a different distribution of wealth and income.

By far the major part of Part IV is devoted to specific problems of economic policy and economic planning. The customary distinction between micro-economic policy, macro-economic policy, and questions of long-range planning is adhered to. Under the first category, the basic effects of principal policy instruments first are established using the theoretical structure developed in Parts I and III. Thus, for example, it is established that a proportional income tax will not have any effects—will be neutral—with regard to the behavior of the labor-managed firm if labor is of constant quality, but will be effective in the context of the analysis of Part III, that is, it will modify the incentive to work; the modification is likely to—but need not—lead to an increased output. As another example, it can be established, also in the more realistic framework of Part III, that a capital tax will have a considerably more stimulating effect on the effort supplied and output of the labor-managed firm than a proportional income tax. For other results of this type the reader must return to Chapter 16.

Another approach in that chapter is less academic. The question can be asked how certain imperfections which may arise in the labor-managed economy can be coped with through fiscal or other policy instruments. One of the most important cases in point is that of monopoly—and by implication, the case of oligopoly. It is shown that an optimal course of action in coping with such market imperfections (i.e., in coping with reduced social efficiency caused by monopoly) will generally involve two instruments: price control and a fixed tax or subsidy.

Other policies are designed to cope with structural inefficiencies resulting from differences in technology or other imperfections within an
industry or within the economy as a whole.

The next major subject of Part IV is the short-run macroeconomic
policy. The discussion is based on the analysis of Part II, and as we
have pointed out above, involves basically the study of changes in the
aggregative general equilibrium resulting from changes in structural
parameters. Because we have not been concerned with an open economy, we can distinguish two major traditional macro-economic policies, monetary and budgetary—the latter including both fiscal and
government-spending policies. In addition, we have a third policy instrument, the variation in the cost of physical capital, which can be
interpreted either as a tax on productive capital assets, or, with capital
stock fixed in the short run, as a constant tax on each undertaking. The
directional results (or multipliers), to which we will turn presently, also
reflect analogous results corresponding to autonomous changes in the
aggregate equilibrium structure. Thus, for example, an autonomous
increase in consumption demand is equivalent in its effects to increased
government spending or reduced taxation, and an autonomous increase
in demand for money has the same effect on the economy as a restrictive monetary policy.

The key results for each of the three policies are as follows. An increase in the cost of capital will generally increase output and employment, reduce the rate of interest, and have a neutral or ambiguous effect
on the price level. Monetary expansion, on the other hand, will nonconventionally tend to reduce output and inflate the price level—the
effect on the rate of interest being ambiguous or nil. Expansionary
budgetary policy, finally, will, also nonconventionally, tend to reduce
output, increase the general price level, and increase the rate of interest.
The nonconventional—or unorthodox—effects on the level of employment are the direct result of the negative short-run elasticities established in Part I, and should be understood as such. The first observation is that on the whole, these elasticities will, even if negative, be
extremely low for reasons given previously, and, therefore, the price
effects can be expected to be quite high. The conclusion thus is that
macroeconomic policy in the labor-managed economy is much more
an instrument to control the general price level than one to influence
employment and general activity. Control and management of the
latter must be primarily a task of long-range steering of the economy—
or economic planning—relying on the equilibrium adjustment of all

factors of production, including capital (a factor which is assumed constant in the context of short-run macro-policy). Entry, broadly defined and including also diversification of existing firms and adoption of new products by such firms, not only serves as an important vehicle of lasting prosperity for the labor-managed economies, but also, even in periods of unemployment, it should operate as a long-run force in the direction of restoration of a full-employment equilibrium. If such a long-run effect is superimposed on the short-run effect established above, then, of course, some of the unorthodox short-run results can be partly corrected. In no event, however, can it be postulated that short-run supply elasticities should be high or even infinite, as is often done in the context of western Keynesian analysis; the latter, it will be recalled, is based on the assumption of rigid money wages, an assumption which cannot have its correspondence in the labor-managed environment. In conclusion, it must be said most emphatically that everything considered, the short-run low elasticities of supply of national product should not be counted a disadvantage of the labor-managed economy. If they render short-run national-income policies comparatively ineffectual, by the same token they guarantee that short-run disequilibrating or cyclical forces (of the type we know from western market-economies) will be by and large ineffectual in producing short-run cyclical variations. Indeed, it is better to be immune to measles than to have superior remedies against measles.

We finally come to our last—but certainly not least important—subject of long-range planning or steering of the economy. I have throughout preferred the term *steering* to indicate the true nature of government interference ideal for the labor-managed economies, and to distinguish it from the more conventional concept of planning in the so-called centrally planned economies, where the plan is the very soul and body of the economy. In the remainder of the present section I will concentrate on some fundamental general observations, leaving it to the reader to turn to the preceding chapter for the details.

The most general notion is that the labor-managed economy, while viable without any planned policy intervention, will benefit a good deal from such intervention if the latter is sufficiently well founded on fact and solid economic analysis, is as simple as possible (i.e., using the minimal number of instruments), and can proceed smoothly (i.e., is not subject to major leaps from year to year or from planning period to planning period).

More than in any other market economy, benefits to be derived from some kind of minimal indicative planning are enormous. Especially because of the crucial relevance of entry (most broadly defined, not necessarily involving formation of new firms) for an efficient operation of the economy, the authorities of the labor-managed economy will assist the productive sector by facilitating the flow of economic information of all kinds throughout the economy, by correctly forecasting future sectoral demands, indicating the intersectoral requirements, and even steering investments in a broad and general manner according to such forecasts. And of course, especially in the less developed economies, the authorities will have to assume at least some of the task of mobilization of capital resources. A capital market as perfect and as smoothly operating as possible, at least partly assisted by central intervention or an advisory role of the government, is also highly desirable. Specifically, the cost of capital must be consistent with efficient resource allocation and full employment.

In fact, the minimal—and most likely optimal—tool of long-range steering in the labor-managed economy, once the proportion of national resources for investment is agreed on, is the allocation of such resources by major sectors of economic activity. Of course, this presupposes that there is a reliable set of final-demand consistent and intersectorally consistent targets (or forecasts) for major sectors, or branches of the economy. The all-important target as well as indicator of efficiency of such a policy is the approximate equalization of incomes for identical skill-categories. (Of course, important and fully justifiable exceptions can arise on grounds of interregional factor immobility, especially in developing countries.) If major differences of comparable skills occur as a result of major sectoral supply scarcities, they not only indicate an inefficient income distribution, but—and above all—they also indicate that the economy is operating below its potential. Of course, the extreme inefficiency of this type is the case of actual unemployment, where earned income differentials are at a maximum. And these also, as we have argued earlier, must be avoided as a matter of long-run rather than short-run economic strategy and policy.

19.5: *A Summary Appraisal of the Labor-Managed System*

Clearly, an appraisal of the labor-managed economy can be made either against an absolute standard of abstract optimality, or against other economic systems. Broadly speaking, the two other systems that we have in mind here are the western-type market economies on the one hand, and the Soviet-type centrally planned and basically non-market variety on the other.

Because we have done very little along these lines, we will speak only briefly about the direct comparison between the labor-managed and Soviet-type economies. One empirical comparison of growth efficiency in Russia and Yugoslavia was attempted by the present author, and it came out strongly in the latter country's favor.[7] Such a statistical exercise cannot, however, be considered fully conclusive with respect to the two systems. Of greater importance is the comparative work bearing on the western-type and Russian-type systems; in this context Bergson, for example, also gives the Russian type an inferior rating.[8] Especially with respect to more advanced economic structures—primarily because of the technical difficulties of substituting at frequent intervals "millions of equations" for the invisible hand—the conclusion is highly plausible. In any event, it would be hard to refute the proposition that the western-type economy with its present-day ability to avoid major cycles and unemployment is at least as efficient in utilizing its productive resources as the Soviet-type command system; and this is all that need interest us here.

Indeed, we do not need to be concerned with more than the proposition just stated because the labor-managed market system, if properly steered, appears as definitely more efficient than the western-type market system, and consequently, it also appears as definitely more efficient than the Soviet-type economy. It is to this key comparison with capitalist market economies, containing within itself also the other appraisal against an absolute standard, that we now turn.

The subdivision of the present study into Parts I through IV provides us with a convenient organization of the material. In Part I we found that the ideal long-run general equilibrium solution is as (Pareto-) optimal as an ideal capitalist market economy. Short-run adjustment is bound to produce less than optimal operation in both systems, but the labor-managed economy is probably somewhat inferior if prices are fully flexible in both systems. Since in a realistic capitalist situation price-wage flexibility and intersectoral wage equalization are impeded a good deal, more so than in the labor-managed economy, the comparative disadvantage of the labor-managed economy stemming from

[7]J. Vanek, "Yugoslav Economic Growth and its Conditions," *American Economic Review*, 53 (May 1963).

[8]A. Bergson, *The Economics of Soviet Planning* (New Haven, 1964), p. 341.

imperfections of short-run adjustment can on balance, as a first approximation, be considered eliminated. The fact that market structures will tend to be comparatively more competitive—other things being equal—in the labor-managed economy also is a factor to be considered. And thus, especially if the imperfections of short-run adjustment are minimized through appropriate indicative steering of the economy, within the analytical framework of Part I—that is, a Walrasian general equilibrium with full employment of resources and a "dehumanized" homogeneous labor force of equal quality for both systems—the labor-managed system can safely be considered at least as efficient in respect to resource allocation as the capitalist economy.

As we proceed and move in the direction of more and more realistic frameworks in Part II (macroanalysis) and especially in Part III (special dimensions of the labor-managed system), the labor-managed economy tends to gain ground considerably. In the short-run sphere of macro-analysis we have noted already (1) the lesser susceptibility of the labor-managed economy to depressions stemming from short-run demand variations, (2) the continuing and inherent long-run tendency to correct states of unemployment in the economy, and (3) the reduced danger of long-range inflationary pressures. But the most fundamental advantage of the labor-managed system emerges in a score of special dimensions, or special attributes and characteristics, not at all present in other economies, whether capitalist or of the Soviet variety. Thus the relaxation of the assumption of a unique type of labor leads, in the labor-managed economy, to a solution through a democratically agreed upon income distribution, partly affected by market forces and partly by the desires and requirements of the working collective. If we add to it the fact that controlling ownership of capital is entirely excluded in the labor-managed economy, and that normally the labor-managed economy will be either of a socialist type or based on national ownership (as discussed in Chapter 15), we immediately see that the distributional efficiency of that economy will better approximate the social optimum than that of other existing systems.

The greatest advantage of the labor-managed firm—and thereby of the system based on such firms—is its capability to produce optimal incentives in governing the level of effort and quality of labor of its members; we have spoken about this already in section 3 of this chapter. The corresponding gains may reach into hundreds of per cent of national product. Finally, we have a whole group of more or less important specific characteristics of labor management which with very few exceptions render the system preferable from the social point of view. We have also noted these in a summary manner earlier in this chapter.

Our general conclusion then is that the labor-managed economy is not only highly efficient in absolute terms, but also more efficient than other existing economic systems. This holds from the point of view of both allocational and distributional efficiency. The evaluation is based entirely on economic criteria. It remains to broaden our framework of reference to spheres other than the economic—for instance, the sociological, psychological, political, and philosophical—and to reassess the comparative rating in this broader scope. But such considerations are our subject for another volume.

Index

405